Ottoman and Turkish Jewry

Community and Leadership

Edited by
Aron Rodrigue

Indiana University Turkish Studies 12

Bloomington

General Editor for the Turkish Studies Series is İlhan Başgöz.
Editorial Board:
Gustav Bayerle, Yuri Bregel, Talat S. Halman,
Halil İnalcık, Larry Clark, Aron Rodrigue,
Nazif Shahrani

Indiana University Turkish Studies 12, *Ottoman and Turkish Jewry: Community and Leadership,* was designed and composed
by CompuType, Bloomington, Indiana.
Cover Art by Janis Kearney
(after the motifs of a Prayer Shawl, Ottoman, 1898, private collection;
and the *Tuğra* of Mehmed III)

Copyright © 1992 by Indiana University Turkish Studies
All rights reserved

No part of this book may be reproduced or utilized in any form or by any means, electronic or mechanical, including photocopying and recording, or by an information storage and retrieval system, without permission in writing from Indiana University Turkish Studies.

The publication of Indiana University Turkish Studies 12, *Ottoman and Turkish Jewry: Community and Leadership,* was made possible by a grant from the Institute of Turkish Studies, Inc., Washington, D.C. Grateful acknowledgment is made to the Institute for its continuing support for this as well as for other volumes in the Series.

For a full listing of all volumes published to date, write for the Series brochure to: General Editor, Turkish Studies Series, 143 Goodbody Hall, Indiana University, Bloomington, IN 47405.
FAX: 812-855-7500

Library of Congress Catalog Card Number: 91-77684
ISBN: 1-878318-03-9
Printed in the United States of America

CONTENTS

PREFACE — vii

ARON RODRIGUE
   Introduction — ix

JOSEPH HACKER
   The *Sürgün* System and Jewish Society in the Ottoman Empire during the Fifteenth to the Seventeenth Centuries — 1

JEAN-CHRISTOPHE ATTIAS
   Intellectual Leadership: Rabbanite-Karaite Relations in Constantinople as Seen through the Works and Activity of Mordekhai Comtino in the Fifteenth Century — 67

LEAH BORNSTEIN-MAKOVETSKY
   Jewish Lay Leadership and Ottoman Authorities during the Sixteenth and Seventeenth Centuries — 87

MINNA ROZEN
   Strangers in a Strange Land: The Extraterritorial Status of Jews in Italy and the Ottoman Empire in the Sixteenth to the Eighteenth Centuries — 123

JACOB BARNAI
   Messianism and Leadership: The Sabbatean Movement and the Leadership of the Jewish Communities in the Ottoman Empire — 167

AVNER LEVI
   Shavat Aniim: Social Cleavage, Class War and Leadership in the Sephardi Community – The Case of Izmir 1847 — 183

ISRAEL BARTAL
   From "*Kollel*" to "Neighborhood": Revisiting the Pre-Zionist Ashkenazi Community in Nineteenth-Century Palestine — 203

ESTHER BENBASSA
   Zionism and the Politics of Coalitions in the Ottoman Jewish Communities in the Early Twentieth Century — 225

RIVA KASTORYANO
   From *Millet* to Community: The Jews of Istanbul — 253

PREFACE

The idea to bring together a series of articles on Ottoman and Turkish Jewry in the form of a book crystallized during the panel on this subject at the Second International Conference of Turkish Studies held at Bloomington, Indiana, in May 1987. I would like to thank Professor İlhan Başgöz for encouraging me in this task.

Much of the scholarship on Ottoman and Turkish Jewry is in languages other than English. One of the purposes of the present collection of articles is to make this scholarship more widely available in the English-speaking world.

All diacriticial marks from the Hebrew transliteration have been omitted. Otherwise, the transliteration system is based on a simplified version of the *Encyclopedia Judaica* usage. Turkish words, with the exception of those that have widely accepted English versions, have been spelt according to the rules of modern Turkish.

I would like to thank the Institute of Turkish Studies at Washington, D.C., for helping financially in the publication of this book.

My thanks also go to Melissa Deckard for typing the entire manuscript, and for cheerfully entering and re-entering all the changes made during the editorial process. Last, but not least, I would like to thank Joan Clinefelter, my research assistant, whose input and work is represented in every page of the final product.

Aron Rodrigue
Stanford University

INTRODUCTION

One of the most fascinating features of Jewish life in the Balkans and the Eastern Mediterranean during the centuries of Ottoman rule is its great diversity. Not only were the communities of different backgrounds and origins, but they were also internally diverse, with issues of class, status, and place in the religious hierarchy all acting as centrifugal factors. The Jewish communities were an integral part of the mosaic that comprised the Ottoman Levant, but they themselves reflected the very heterogeneity suggested by the image of the mosaic itself. In this respect, they were quintessentially Ottoman. In a setting very different from the idealized mono-cultural societies attempted to be created by the successor nation-states that followed the demise of the Empire, with little pressure from the state to conform to centralizing models, Ottoman Jewish communities evolved, in large part, according to internal and external dynamics structured by largely local factors.

However, in spite of the paramount significance of the local context, there were frequent occasions in the history of Ottoman Jewries when the action by the state and the ruler had, as can be expected, a decisive impact. The period of the entry of Jewish communities under Ottoman rule was, in this respect, particularly eventful. As the article by Joseph Hacker demonstrates, the local Byzantine Jewish communities, or the Romaniotes as they were known, were affected profoundly by the Ottoman policy of *sürgün*, the compulsory resettlement of populations not as a punitive measure, but because of primarily economic and political considerations. The very image of the economic utility of the Jews and their perceived importance in economic development made them likely targets of this policy well into the sixteenth century. Whole communities were transferred from the provinces and brought to populate the newly conquered Istanbul. One of the reasons why there were no Jews in Salonica at the time of the arrival of the Iberian exiles after 1492 was precisely because the autochthonous Jewish community had been moved to the capital. Later on, the Sephardim of Salonica also became objects in the same policy, with 150 Jewish families being moved from the city in 1523 to the island of Rhodes.

The re-structuration of communities in their new surroundings went hand in hand with the practice of creating congregations according to place of origin. Hacker argues quite persuasively that this development which has been associated with the exiles from the Iberian peninsula was already a well-established characteristic among the *sürgün* Romaniote communities, most notably in Istanbul, but also elsewhere in the provinces. It is hence important to note that the lack of unified communal stuctures that was to be an important feature of Ottoman Jewish life until the modern period was already in evidence at the very genesis of Ottoman Jewry itself.

The Karaite communities were also subject to the same policy of resettlement, and congregated overwhelmingly in Istanbul. This sect which had split from normative rabbinical Judaism in the eighth century over the question of the acceptance of the oral law, had a long history of acrimonious and tense relations with the Jewish community. However, as the article by Jean-Christophe Attias makes clear, there were also periods of rapprochement between the two groups, both in daily relations and in the study and discussions of religious issues. In the circumstances that prevailed around the time of the conquest of Istanbul, the noted Jewish scholar Mordekhai Komtino was the teacher of both Rabbanites and Karaites. This does not mean that the two groups accepted each other. As Attias demonstrates, Komtino's writings on the Pentateuch had as a sub-text the age-old confrontation with the Karaites over the literal and traditional interpretation of the scriptures. But the very *engagement* with the Karaites in Komtino's life and writings points to the new intra-communal Jewish context of Istanbul at the time of the conquest.

The arrival of the exiles from the Iberian peninsula at the end of the fifteenth and throughout the sixteenth centuries altered considerably the demographics of Ottoman Jewry. The new arrivals through their sheer numbers eventually swamped the local Romaniote communities. Even though distinctions between the two groups lasted until the seventeenth century, most notably in Istanbul, the stronghold of the Romaniotes, eventually the latter assimilated into Sephardi Jewry with the exception of a few isolated locales in Greece such as Yanina. Small numbers of Ashkenazi Jews who had been migrating from Europe to Ottoman lands since the fourteenth century also often underwent the same process of assimilation. The names Tadjer (from Deutscher) in Bulgaria and the ubiquitious Eskenazi (from Ashkenazi) found in most Sephardi communities down to our own days are markers of this development. Nevertheless, in time, as the numbers of arriving Ashkenazim increased to sustain separate communities, their public existence reverted to the old pattern of established, distinctive congregations in the large centers.

The lack of an Empire-wide Jewish communal body and a centralized hierarchical authority (which has no religious basis in rabbinical Judaism) meant that each local Jewish community had to deal separately with the government in Istanbul and with its representatives in the locality. As Leah Bornstein-Makovetsky shows, the communities had, especially in the sixteenth century, government appointed functionaries known as the *kâhya* among their own members who acted as intermediaries and who were responsible for the ensuring of the implementation by Jews of the government's decrees and regulations in all matters, but especially in the collection of taxes. Depending on the time and place, lay communal leaders, the *parnasim*, also fulfilled the same tasks. Recognition by the center gave a great deal of power to these individuals, which buttressed their status within the community. But their position was not fixed and they were subject to internal social control by both religious and other lay leaders.

City-wide communal structures that transcended the synagogue/congregation had to come into being because of the unified and rationalized action that issues such as tax-collecting, and communal charity and welfare required. Even in the most divided centers such as Salonica, such city wide bodies had been created by the seventeenth century. The Jewish community always tried to present a unified front towards the outside world, and was reluctant to accept arbitration from outside its own institutions. Nevertheless, the ultimate sanctioning power of the state meant that individual Jews could and did have recourse to Muslim law courts. The appeal to a stronger power outside could not be prevented, in spite of the opprobium that such action elicited within the larger body of Jews.

A complex set of fluid relations characterized the relationship between the communities and the center. Most Jews had to deal with local officials. Local factors, such as the uprightness and honesty of the local governor, were crucial in matters related to security and proper tax-collection. If these became problematic the Jews could either attempt to influence the officials in question or appeal to Istanbul. It is in the latter scenario that the significance of certain important Jews in the capital emerges. In a society where personal intervention based on webs of client-patronage relationships ran parallel to established bureaucratic relations, wealthy Jews in Istanbul were in a position to help fellow-Jews from elsewhere by intervening with the appropriate authorities. Hence, like in most other Jewish communites in the world, leadership did not have to be formal or official, and could be exercised by influential members of the community through unofficial channels. In this respect, even though Istanbul Jewry had no formally recognized privileged place among the communities of the Empire until the nineteenth century, it was in fact, *de facto*, the most significant one as far as Ottoman Jews' relations with the center were concerned.

However, one group of Jews managed, by and large, to escape many of the constraints of the control of the community and of the government. These were the *Francos*, the so-called "foreign" Jews under the protection of European powers. The genesis of this development is explored in Minna Rozen's article on the phenomenon of extra-territorial legal status. The very success of the Iberian exiles and their descendants in the economic relations between Italy and the Ottoman East made them highly desired elements in Italian cities. "Levantine" Jews under Ottoman protection managed to circumvent many of the restrictions put on other Jews precisely because of their Ottoman connections, and because of their perceived importance for the lucrative trade with the East. The process of amelioration in the status of the Jews in Italy and in Western Europe in general began with the granting of special rights and privileges to these Ottoman Jews.

But the changes in economic fortunes, and the ascendancy of European economic and political power from the seventeenth century onwards meant that the same set of factors could be reversed. Utilizing the capitulation treaties, many European states such as France used some non-Muslim merchants, among them Jews, as their *protégés* in the Ottoman trade. These Jews and their families, known as *Francos*, came to occupy privileged positions within the communities of the Ottoman Empire, and sidestepped most communal regulations as well as Ottoman taxation and restrictions. They formed distinctive groups in places like Istanbul, Izmir, Salonica, and Aleppo well into the 19th century, and played a vanguard role in the westernization process undergone by Sephardi Jewry in the modern period.

Religious, social, and ideological frictions arose with great acuity at different periods in the history of the Jews of the Ottoman Empire, and affected all aspects of communal life. The most important crisis was the one engendered by the Sabbatean movement in the middle of the seventeenth century. The social and religious consequences of the great outburst of mass enthusiasm for the false messiah, Sabbetai Sevi, and the sense of tremendous letdown that followed his conversion to Islam, had reverberations for many decades. As Jacob Barnai argues, while a small group of followers followed the false messiah into Islam and formed the *dönme* sect, many others remained within the Jewish fold, but continued to maintain belief in Sabbetai Sevi. Some very important rabbinical figures in the Ottoman Empire and elsewhere remained as secret Sabbateans within the Jewish communities. The ideological cleavages that such a development brought in its wake proved difficult to heal immediately. The secret believers were faced by an overly zealous traditionalist rabbinical orthodoxy that was now determined to stamp out at its inception any similar messianic movement. The rabbinical leadership became rigid and set in its ways, unwilling to grapple with new ideas and intitiatives, while the remaining Sabbateans continued to exercise a somewhat corrosive influence well past the seventeenth century.

Communal institutions and leadership were not well equipped to deal with social conflict. Frictions between the rich and the poor affected Ottoman Jewry like all other segments of the Ottoman population. Occasionally, the conflicts broke out with great ferocity and brought communal life to a standstill. The situation analysed by Avner Levi in Izmir in the middle of the nineteenth century is a case in point. Indirect internal taxation such as the *gabela*, the tax on kosher meat, had for a long time been the mainstay of communal finances. This essentially regressive tax weighed disproportionately upon the poor, and the rich oligarchy who ran communal affairs refused systematically to increase their payment of direct taxes, with most of the rabbinical elite dependent upon the rich for their living siding with them publicly. In spite of the protestations and threats by the representatives of the poor, it seems quite clear that the rich prevailed in the end, as was the case in most similar occurrences. Izmir was particularly rife with such social conflicts, issues over taxation and the election of the Chief Rabbi giving rise to major crises that paralysed communal affairs several times in the nineteenth century. Until the onset of westernization, the lay oligarchic elites and the religious leadership dominated most Jewish communities, and ruled through formal and informal means. While there were frequent challenges from below, none proved effective in the long term.

Ideological conflicts that began to affect the Ashkenazi world from the time of the Jewish Enlightenment (*haskalah*) in the eighteenth century over issues of the opening of the community and of individual Jews to the outside world and to its influences, and over the new place of the Jew in modern society, eventually came to have an impact on the Jews of the Ottoman Empire. It is important to focus on Ottoman Palestine as a profoundly significant area where many of the major issues that affected the larger Jewish world were refracted and made their way to the rest of Ottoman Jewry. The Jewish communities of Ottoman Palestine constituted, in many ways, a microcosm of the various Jewries of the Empire. Arab-speaking Jews and Sephardi Jews of Iberian origin had been present in the area for centuries and were the formally recognized communities by the state. Ashkenazi Jews began to arrive in significant numbers from the eighteenth century onwards. As Israel Bartal maintains, in the nineteenth century the Ashkenazi communities of the pre-Zionist era became outposts of European Jewish orthodoxy, coalescing around the issue of the rejection of modernity. Living side by side with the Sephardim, the Ashkenazim nevertheless formed distinct communal entities, the most notable of which was the *kolel*, a sub-community of scholars engaged in full-time study. These unique institutions were supported by the orthodox of Eastern Europe, and came to create, in a distilled form, an idealized alternative to the traditional community that was in the process of disintegration in Europe under the twin impact of the Jewish Enlightenment and the centralizing policies of the modern state.

While the *kolels* were a late development, it is interesting to note that in many ways, they fitted the age-old pattern of decentralized sub-groupings that remained characteristic of Ottoman Jewish life till the end. However, they also reflected the deep ideological fracturing of the Jewish world in the modern world.

The new developments, the profound transformations that the Jewish communities began to undergo in the nineteenth and twentieth centuries together with the rest of the Ottoman Empire, all led to new forms of communal politics and leadership. This was most significant in Istanbul. The Young Turk revolution of 1908 opened the way to the rise of new forces within the community. Esther Benbassa demonstrates the extraordinary incursion of mass politics in the internal life of Istanbul Jewry. The westernized notables associated with the French Jewish organization, the Alliance Israélite Universelle, attained power after the revolution with the election of Haim Nahum to the Chief Rabbinate. However, the latter's design to centralize the communal structuring of Ottoman Jewry, and the rule of his "Alliancist" power base were challenged by the rise of Zionism within the community. The old cleavages between the rich and the poor, the Ashkenazim and the Sephardim, the traditionalists and the modernizers, all re-emerged, and were cleverly utilized by the Zionists using the methods of modern mass politics in the struggle for power. The ensuing stalemate in communal affairs lasted until the end of the Empire.

The new Turkish Republic that arose out of the ashes of the Ottoman Empire affected profoundly the life of the Jewish communities that remained within its new borders. The Jews became more integrated into their surroundings and underwent a process of rapid Turkicization in the second half of the twentieth century. However, as Riva Kastoryano argues, integration did not lead to the weakening of a distinctive ethnic identity. Communal structures remained fluid in direct continuity with Ottoman times. But, the fact that after the emigration of the poorer elements in the middle of the century, most of Turkish Jews are now congregated in Istanbul, live as a fairly compact group, and have all more or less undergone the same process of upward social and geographical mobility, has meant that the community as a whole forms a distinct cohesive unit, more so than any other period in its history. While an integral part of the Turkish bourgeoisie, the Jewish community at the same time manifests a new re-articulated sense of ethnicity that has come to incorporate the diverse components of the Jewish and Turkish contexts.

Throughout their history, the Jewish communities in the Ottoman Empire have shown remarkable powers of adaptation and resilience. As all the articles in this book confirm, communal structures and forms of leadership remained in a state of perpetual flux, deeply affected by rivalries based on issues of ethnic origin, class, and ideology. However, the underlying realities of the Ottoman Levant which emphasized the distinctiveness of each group, as well as the cohesive bonds of Jewish religious identity which in the final analysis transcended other differences, all contributed together to the making of a multi-faceted Jewry that was an integral part of the Ottoman fabric. The tearing of this fabric with the collapse of the Empire was to introduce a new set of complex, trying, and ultimately dangerous factors to the Middle East and the Balkans that were to prove to be less kind and infinitely more problematic to the Jewish communities of the area in the twentieth century.

Aron Rodrigue

Joseph Hacker
The Hebrew University of Jerusalem

The *Sürgün* System and Jewish Society in the Ottoman Empire During the Fifteenth to the Seventeenth Centuries

The following is an attempt to examine a central feature of the policies adopted by the Ottoman Empire and its rulers towards their subjects, and the effects of these policies upon a certain ethnic-religious group, the Jews.[1] The Ottoman *sürgün* system seems at first glance unrelated to the Jews specifically, and even less so to the organizational and social processes which were taking place within this society. It will, however, be shown that this system had considerable influence upon the shaping of the character of Jewish society and its internal organization, as well as upon both the community in general and the individual in particular.

Major issues in the history of Ottoman Empire Jewry have not as yet been adequately clarified, and the question before us is one of these. Our topic is vital to the comprehension of the growth of Jewish society in the Empire and the appreciation of its division into sub-groups. It is extremely significant not only in connection with the legal status of the Jews, but also with regard to the shaping of their social character and relations with Muslim government and society.

A number of factors have contributed to the fact that topics of this kind have remained inadequately clarified, or have not even been considered for study, though we shall neither spell them out nor analyze them here. Common stereotypes, on the one hand, and insufficient interrelationships between the study of the history and institutions of the Ottoman Empire and the study of Jewish history, on the other, are undoubtedly at fault. A culprit no less to blame is, however, the paucity of material (dating from the fifteenth century), its diffusion, its incidental character and the errors which accompanied its transmission from one generation to the next.

A. THE OTTOMAN *SÜRGÜN* SYSTEM

The apparent meaning, for our purposes, of *sürgün* is "exiling" or "resettling,"[2] for the meaning of the root "sur" and the suffix "gun" is indeed exiling, persecution and expulsion, excommunication or simply a person in exile.[3] The *sürgün* policy towards the subjects of the Ottoman Empire was not necessarily a punitive policy. The policy had, in fact, two different aspects: on the one hand, it was implemented as a punishment affecting individuals or groups who were punished by being exiled far from their previous dwelling place, it being forbidden to leave the place of exile without the permission of the central authorities. On the other hand, it was implemented as a method of transferring populations from one place to another for the colonization and resettlement of areas conquered by the Empire. While sections of the conquered populace were exiled far from the area where they had previously lived, other populations were transferred there from various parts of the Empire so as to populate the place and develop it right after its conquest.

As a punitive policy enacted with regard to the individual, the *sürgün* system was applied at two levels:

1. As a punishment for various crimes, economic or moral, with the guilty partly exiled to a settlement within the borders of the Empire and forbidden to leave his place of exile without official permission. It is self-evident that such a person was forbidden absolutely to live in his former town of residence. Such a *sürgün* may well have been punished in additional ways in his place of exile—by means of various limitations placed on his activities or by compulsory labor and so on.[4]

2. A second type of *sürgün*, done on an individual rather than a collective basis, relates to statesmen, relatives of the ruler or people close to him, bureaucrats and others who were no longer in favor or who had lost power. Such people's power in official circles had weakened to such an extent that they no longer exercised any influence there, or perhaps the courtier upon whom they were dependent had lost his position and they had come down in the world along with him. They were on occasion forced into exile, where they received the status of *sürgün*; yet, as far as they were concerned, this exile was not accompanied by additional punitive measures, and the place of exile was less uncomfortable. Such people were sometimes appointed to various positions in their places of exile. The main aspect of their punish-

ment was their being banished, along with the heavy economic losses such exile and extended residence in exile causes[5]. Though, as already noted, Jews, too, like other subjects, suffered occasionally from this kind of punishment, it did nothing to shape Jewish society in any particular direction. Consequently, this discussion will not be a thorough consideration of the punitive measures adopted by Ottoman society or its influence on Jewish society or Jewish social norms or even its exploitation of these for its own purposes.[6]

This discussion will concern itself with that *sürgün* which made up an integral part of the Ottoman policies of expansion where, as result of the rapid conquests and territorial expansion, an intricate policy of resettlement was implemented, involving massive population transfers from one region to another—all in accordance with local and contemporary requirements. This policy incorporated the development and stabilization of the new territories and guaranteed both their loyalty to the authorities and the exploitation of their human resources for the development of the settled areas and their economies. It was implemented over an extended period of time; the policy was already established in the fifteenth century, and continued thereafter in the sixteenth and seventeenth centuries as well.[7]

In actual fact, the execution of this policy involved the implementation of a population transfer in the territory of the Ottoman Empire. While part of the local conquered population was transferred to previously conquered territories, population from long time Ottoman territories was transferred to the new areas. These operations involved the entire population of the Ottoman Empire: Muslims, Christians, Jews and others. Thus, it may not be concluded that the aim of this exiling operation was mere Islamization, though this aim was undoubtedly present in some cases, especially in the areas of European Turkey.[8] Nevertheless, as already noted, this population exiling operation had other aims as well. At times it was intended to subdue rebellious elements in a region already under Ottoman control; on other occasions it was used to settle and develop a region badly ravaged by battle and pillage, or to undermine local authorities and aristocratic cliques in recently conquered areas. On occasion such steps had more than one aim at the same time. Their common denominator was the transformation of towns and districts important for the security and economy of the Empire from unreliable cities and outposts into controlled regions of economic utility. This Ottoman policy was already in place centuries earlier, even before the Ottoman entity became an empire, and its roots are anchored in operations which were common under Byzantium and the Seljuks; in another form and on a more limited scale, it could be found even in the policies of Venice and its colonies.[9]

This article focuses on this topic and on its influence on the consolidation and development of Ottoman Jewry, and though there were other forms of compulsion which were implemented with regard to either individuals or population strata to accomplish various special tasks and needs vital to the authorities and to the public welfare, this paper does not deal with them.[10]

This policy assumed decisive proportions from the time of Mehmet II's conquest of Constantinople. The circumstances of this conquest and the importance of the city to its new rulers were what brought about the implementation of this policy to an extent previously unknown under Ottoman rule. Thus, it calls to mind features of earlier historical periods, when ancient kingdoms—such as Assyria and Babylonia—exiled entire peoples and large populations.

B. THE RESETTLEMENT OF CONSTANTINOPLE, THE *SÜRGÜN* AND THE JEWS

The task of resettling the city after conquering it in 1453, pillaging it and taking its population captive, and the flight of many of its inhabitants, became a major enterprise of Mehmet II.[11] Mehmet II's desire to make the city his capital and the center of his kingdom made the task that much more difficult. Thus, shortly after the conquest, Mehmet took initial steps to settle the city by releasing his quota of captives who had been taken by the army and were the Sultan's portion of the spoils, by attracting fleeing inhabitants, by adopting a policy of tax exemption, and by giving settlers homes or land to build on, and so on. This policy was implemented with regards to the entire population. At the same time, Mehmet II issued decrees of population transfer from various regions of his kingdom to the city. These decrees were repeated time and again. Some were not carried out as the ruler desired, and on occasion he himself went out to ensure that productive elements with economic expertise, as well as craftsmen, settle in the city. As early as 1453, he had residents transferred to the city, a step which became increasingly common throughout 1454-1459 and thereafter. On occasion many residents of a given locality were exiled; on other occasions, it was economic population strata or people of a given profession that were exiled; and, sometimes, one out of every ten residents of an area. In 1459, Mehmet appealed to escapees and to released captives to come and settle in the city, and he promised them special consideration (tax exemptions, housing, etc.). Furthermore, Mehmet II and his successor, Bayezid II, continued to exile many residents to the city from the areas conquered after 1453.[12] Mehmet II implemented a policy of accelerated development, a policy which required speedy populatory measures and a channeling of resources; the creation of lenient taxation parameters and relatively free economic activity; and comprehensive rehabilitation and reconstruction activities.

This policy of accelerated development, with its weighty aims, led to Mehmet II's relatively comfortable policies towards religious minorities. These were transferred *en masse* to the city, were given buildings according to their needs, and enjoyed various benefits. This policy of attracting people to the city also led to a voluntary migration of elements from outside the Empire.[13] Either way, the city was settled by a considerable percentage of Christians and believers of other faiths who prospered in their labors and their trade, though the authorities were careful to continue with their process of Islamization and de-Christianization of the city itself. Despite this religious trend, the Sultan allowed churches to exist within the city, and even appointed and recognized the Patriarch as the representative of the Greek community.

From descriptions of the events which affected the inhabitants of cities conquered by the Ottomans, and from a description of Muslims' and others' repeated attempts to free themselves of the obligatory transfer to Istanbul after the conquest of Constantinople, it is completely evident that setting out and settling in the ruined city were considered a severe decree. A study of the status and obligations of a person exiled by decree shows that from the time the person was exiled to a certain region, he was forbidden to leave it without permission of the *subaşı* (the chief of police) or some other representative of the authorities. Not only was he himself forbidden to leave the area, but his children were likewise forbidden to leave; he was sometimes forbidden to marry a person from anywhere else, and could not at times marry a person who was not, like himself, an exile. Furthermore, he was obliged to engage in a certain occupation if it was for this occupation that he had been exiled, and was not permitted to change his occupation. Though he enjoyed a partial tax exemption for a given period of time and in most cases a place to live as well, the property (real estate) he had owned in his previous domicile was on occasion taken from him by the authorities— without compensation, and sometimes divided up among the military. These limitations on his freedom would continue indefinitely. In fact, a person becoming a *sürgün* would assume a special appropriate legal status which clearly differentiated him from the other residents of the region: in his personal status, in his freedom of movement and sometimes in his occupation as well. In Istanbul, for example, all new arrivals were first organized in special neighborhoods and in predetermined areas according to their origin, and they were not permitted to move to other parts of the city to reside.[14] It seems that the populating of Istanbul, which took about a hundred years, from the period of Mehmet II to that of Süleyman the Magnificent, at the very least, was a central focus of the implementation of the policy of exiling and resettlement. In fact, it would seem that most of the city's inhabitants took up residence there at first as exiles and not of their own free will. How did the Jews fit in with these processes?

1. Eliyah Kapsali and Jewish Historiography (a)

The main Jewish source to cast light on the encounter of the Jews with the Ottomans and the steps taken at the time of the conquest of Constantinople, upon which scientific study has relied upon until now, is Eliyah Kapsali's book, *Seder Eliahu Zuta*, which was compiled in Crete in 1523.[15] This book is known to have been left in manuscript form until the second half of the nineteenth century. As a result of the circumstances under which it was published and the way the book *Divrei Yosef* by R. Yosef Sambari was printed, confusion set in and scholarly literature gave the impression that Sambari's gleanings were Kapsali's writings.[16] In the meantime, the study of the Jewry of the Empire at its onset was strongly influenced by the descriptions of both the conquest of Constantinople and of the policies implemented by Mehmet II shortly thereafter. The following is Kapsali's wording:[17]

> In the first year of Sultan Mehmet, King of Turkey . . . the Lord aroused the king, Sultan Mehmet, King of Turkey, who then proclaimed throughout his kingdom, and in writing, too, saying:[18] Thus spoke Mehmet, King of Turkey: the Lord, God of Heaven granted me of the kingdoms of earth and commanded me to attend to His people, the seed of Abraham His servant, the sons of Jacob, His chosen ones, to provide them with a livelihood in the land and to grant them a safe haven; whoever of you, of His entire people, may his God be with him and may he go up to Constantinople, the seat of my kingdom, in the best part of the land where each man sits under his grapevine and under his fig tree, with silver and gold and property and livestock—settle in the land, trade with it, and take hold of it.
>
> The Jews gathered together from all the cities of Turkey, both far and near, each person coming from his own place, and the community gathered in Constantinople in its thousands and its tens of thousands.[19] The heavens

helped them, too, and the king provided them perfect estates and houses filled with all kinds of goodness. The Jews resided there with their families and their clans; they were fruitful and swarmed and multiplied, and the land was full of them. From that day on, whenever the king conquered a place where there were Jews, he would immediately shake them up and drive them from there - and dispatch them to Constantinople, the seat of his kingdom, and he would pick them up and cuddle them for ever. Now, since the Jews feared the Lord, he provided them with houses filled with all kinds of goodness in a place where formerly, at the time of the King of Byzantium, there were only two or three congregations, the Jews increased in numbers, becoming a people with more than [40] communities, for the land could not support them altogether—for their property was overwhelming.

Mehmet II is here depicted as a sort of second Cyrus saving Israel and inviting the Jews to the chosen land, Istanbul, his capital city. Here we have an explicit royal proclamation aimed at the Jews, the content and message of which—despite its wording based on the words of Ezra and verses from the Pentateuch—are unambiguous. Mehmet, the divinely ordained ruler, desires to favor the Jews. He *invites* them to Istanbul, provides them with refuge and favorable living and economic conditions. The response of the Jews is both positive and enthusiastic, and they come of their own free will from all the cities of his kingdom. The king provides them with property and housing, and the Jewish community flourishes. There is no similarity whatever between this and the *sürgün* with all its accompanying features.

Yet in the idyllic picture we find a sentence with a different atmosphere enveloping it: "From that day on, whenever the king conquered a place where there were Jews, *he would immediately shake them up and drive them from there—and dispatch them to Constantinople* (emphasis mine). . . . "[20] Yet this sentence, which bears unimpeachable witness to the fact that Eliyah Kapsali was familiar with various aspects of Mehmet II's resettlement policy, including the forced exiles to Istanbul, remains in glorious solitude and is swallowed up by his effusive praise. Moreover, it, too, can be construed as a word of praise, in that it indicates that Mehmet viewed the Jews as a positive, constructive element, and thus desired to resettle them in his capital city.

Accordingly, the recorders of Jewish history from the days of H. Graetz on, described in idyllic colors the evolution of relations and links between the Jews and the Ottomans,[21] and even the conquest of Constantinople and the fate of the Jews of the city were not depicted authentically. These approaches affected the understanding of the scholars of the Ottoman Empire who relied on students of Jewish history and upon "their sources."

Thus, they tended to contintue to minimize and swallow up all tensions in those relations and links, and to describe them as idyllic only.[22]

What is the significance of this description and what is its cause? What is known of this subject from Turkish and Christian sources, on the one hand, and from Jewish ones, on the other?

2. The Muslim and Christian Sources

It should be emphasized that Mehmet II implemented his *sürgün* policy to repopulate the city immediately subsequent to its conquest and after he had departed. Testimony to this effect can be found in the writings of both Christian and Ottoman historians and chroniclers. Mehmet II's policy after the conquest of the city is dealt with in detail.[23] Eye witnesses, close friends of the ruler or of his ministers, Ottoman administrators and others, describe the sequence of events. According to these descriptions Mehmet II adopted two main methods of populating his capital city. On the one hand, he released his quota of captives out of the total number of those taken captive, to enable them to engage in the rebuilding and development of the city. On the other hand, he called upon the escapees to return, promising to restore their property to them if they returned by a given date. He also appealed to foreign elements, such as the Venetians, to send back those who had fled to the Venetian colonies to Istanbul.[24] These "escapees" included Jews. Many seem to have fled to Chios. At the same time the forced mass exile into the city got under way. According to one source, the Sultan succeeded in transferring to Istanbul in a short period of time (by 6 August 1453—within about two months!) some thirty thousand people by sea, including exiles and other migrants.[25] Another source tells of the transfer of five thousand families in the month of September from Anatolia and from Rumelia. These families had to arrive in Istanbul during September—otherwise, they would be put to death.[26] Yet other sources provide a description of the tremendous effort made to repopulate and rehabilitate the city. Thus, for instance, Tursun Beg writes at length on this topic,[27] while in many sources we find complaints of the bitter fate of the conquered population in general, and of those exiled to Istanbul in particular.[28]

In two of the reliable sources, which scholars consider basic for a description of the events, we are told that the Jews were among those exiled to Istanbul from cities of the Empire in general, and from Rumelia (the European portion) in particular. The first of these is M. Kritovuolos who had comprehensive knowledge of the repopulation of Istanbul. He relates that when Mehmet conquered Constantinople, his first objective was to repopulate the city. Mehmet issued a decree to all parts of his kingdom, to the effect that as many inhabitants as possible be transferred to the city. These residents included "not only Christians but also his own people and many Jews."[29] The second source is F. M. Angiolello, who relates that since the Jews were so few in number, relative to so great a city, Mehmet ordered all the Jews of his kingdom, in Anatolia as well as in Rumelia, to move with their wives and children to Istanbul. He states that they were resettled in groups according to their origin, and their new places of residence were named after their places of origin.[30] Both thus stress not only the arrival of the Jews in Istanbul as *sürgün*, but also the especially large number of Jews, relative to their portion of the entire population. Thus, as already determined by U. Heyd, as late as the seventeenth century the list of the Jewish communities of Istanbul split into two groups: the one—part of the *sürgün*, including mainly Jews of Byzantium and subjects of the Empire—and the other—those who "came voluntarily", *kendi gelen*, who were mainly of Spanish and Portuguese descent.[31] Though Heyd had no intention of making broad inferences from these facts, he did note that this was a list of the communities exiled forcibly to the city after its conquest by Mehmet II, a list of considerable importance for those interested in the Jews of Byzantium in the fourteenth and fifteenth centuries.[32]

The result of the examination of the list of communities is that of the 24 *sürgün* communities listed by Heyd and the three additional ones noted by H. Gerber, six originated in Anatolia and five in Istanbul and its vicinity. The location of two is doubtful, while fourteen communities were exiled from European Turkey. How many exiles were there in these communities and what do we know about them? From the list it is not clear when these communities were exiled to the city. Some may possibly have been exiled to Istanbul at a later period (like the community of Egribo [Negroponte], which went into exile after the conquest of the island by Mehmet in 1470), and there is, of course, no certainty that this list of exiled communities is complete. As for the number of exiles and the manner of their resettlement in Istanbul, conclusions may be drawn and statistics gleaned from the listings of an as yet unpublished partial census of Istanbul dating from 1455.[33] Data concerning the names and number of communities may similarly be deduced from lists of public endowments dating from the sixteenth century in Istanbul.[34]

From the data already gleaned it would seem that among the Jewish exiles from European Turkey there were 42 families from Izdin (Lamia), 38 families from Philipopoli, while other families arrived from Edirne, Trikala, Nicopol and other places.³⁵ Furthermore, these Jews who were transferred from the Balkans seem to have arrived at a relatively late date, around 1455, and settled in deserted and neglected areas, replacing *sürgün* Muslims who had been brought there earlier but fled *en masse* from the city. From lists of communities whose taxes were made over to Mehmet II's public endowments as late as the sixteenth century, it appears that the number of places from which Jews were exiled to Istanbul was even greater than the number of *sürgün* communities listed in seventeenth-century censuses. These lists included fifty groups of Jews based on their origin, yet it is difficult to decide whether these were all *sürgün* or whether some of them had been appended to the public endowments at a later period, or even if they were appended to the lists although they had arrived of their own free will and not forcibly. Whichever is true, it may be stated that the phenomenon of *sürgün* encompassed most of the Jews of the Ottoman Empire in the fifteenth century, and the testimony of the Greek historians and authors who noted that most, if not all, of the Jews of the Empire were exiled to Istanbul at some stage of the repopulation of the city is probably accurate.

It is thus surprising that so decisive a phenomenon in the history of this Romaniot Jewry went apparently unnoted in their writings and left no traces for subsequent generations.

3. The transfer of population in Jewish contemporary writings

A careful examination of the writings of a number of contemporary Byzantine Jews and a study of the writings of various persons living in the Latin colonies in the Levant show that these events did indeed make their impression on the people of that generation. Before we make a study of a few of their writings, however, it should be noted that appropriate attention has also not been paid to those comments of the fifteenth-century Karaite inhabitants of the Ottoman Empire which have appeared in print. A study of their works reveals that the exile of the Karaites to Istanbul was comprehensive, and left an indelible impression upon them. The Karaite Kaleb Afendopolo relates in his book, *Patshegen Ketav Ha-Dat*, the changes which took place in the Karaite community's Torah-reading customs:

> Now, this was customary until the great King, Sultan Mehmet, son of Murad Beg of the house of Osman, captured the city of Constantinople in the year 5213 (1453). And in the year 5215 (1455) he expelled all the Jews in his kingdom and resettled them in Constantinople, from the city of Adrianople

The Sürgün System and Jewish Society in the Ottoman Empire / 11

> and afterwards Pravato and others. This was customary, viz., for the beginning of the Torah to be in Nissan, for four or five years after they came to Constantinople until the ruling of the sage, R. Menahem ben Yosef, the grandfather of my teacher, R. Eliyah Bashyachi ben Moshe, who was gifted with sharp intelligence with which he defeated his enemies, who desired to restore the matter to its original state, for the disagreement was already rife . . . until the arrival of a wise man named Eliyah Shubashi, who was a leader of the Jews . . . and on the Sabbath following the day of *Shemini Atzeret* in the month of *Tishri*, when the Torah portion was the *Aharei Mot* portion according to their custom, the aforesaid R. Eliyah rose up and began the Torah anew, reading the Bereshit portion. Now because of his influence in the kingdom and the advice of the sages amongst the congregation and the heavenly assistance from the Creator of all, those who desired to implement the Torah reading order as written in the Torah of Moses and the customs of our sainted forefathers, the entire community kept silent and did not protest, for in this way the proper custom was restored to its pristine glory. . . .[36]

This passage contains several interesting points. For one, the author claims this was an expulsion of "all the Jews" of the kingdom, and even if we assume that he was referring only to the Karaites, this remains an exile of all the Karaites. The leaders of the Karaite community took advantage of this opportunity to implement far-ranging reforms among the Karaites concentrated in Istanbul, reforms not acceptable to everyone. Although these reforms were the consequence of a pact between the educated and the monied classes, the sages of the community and those elements recognized by the authorities, it would seem that the main factor facilitating the mutual attraction of the Romaniot Jews and Karaites was their encounter as exiles in the capital city of the Empire, undergoing reconstruction and repopulation. Each of these groups was more open to external influences and to mutual attraction after having been uprooted from stable, organized lives and reduced to the status of exiles from various towns having to shape their lives anew and rebuild their administrative and economic bases. Their common plight undoubtedly contributed to this as well.[37] However, just as in the rabbinic camp there were those who opposed this tendency to draw closer, so there were in the Karaite camp.[38] One of these, Shabbetai ben Eliyah of Pravato, also had an explanation of the developments which affected the Karaites in his day:

> We, the Karaite community, have dwindled, and our books, which used to enlighten us, have vanished. We have begun to learn from the Rabbinic Jews. Moreover, as we join with them in exile in Constantinople, we have become accustomed to their books, as we always hear their commentaries from them . . . and the hearts of our spiritual leaders have almost come to believe in them,

some having already agreed with them completely and hesitate, saying that the truth is with them.... And when I, Shabbetai, the youngest of my family and least important of my clan, the son of Eliyah of the exiles of Pravato transferred to Constantinople, understood this I was filled with zealotry....[39]

According to this objector, adopting Rabbinic Jewish customs—both Karaite and Rabbinic groups being in exile in Istanbul—is the root of all evil. Adopting Rabbinic customs is the cause of the innovators' reforms, and so the objector speaks out bluntly against this adoption and mutual attraction which took place in times of crisis.[40]

These sources show that the extent of Karaite exile was not only great, but it also had decisively influential consequences with regard to the shaping of their religious and social character.[41] The extent of their exile can be deduced from the fact that the entire Karaite leadership known from before 1453 in Edirne was moved to Istanbul. From this point on, the Karaites in Istanbul came to be known as the Edirne or Adrianople community in both internal and official sources,[42] while the Edirne Karaite community itself suffered a severe eclipse.

It is not only in Karaite sources that traces remain of the events of the fall of Constantinople and of the resettlement policy implemented in its wake. R. Ephraim ben R. Gershon of Veroia (Karaferia) was a doctor and a preacher who lived in a number of Levantine towns in the middle of the fifteenth century and whose autobiographical writings, which have been preserved in manuscript form, have been described in detail.[43] In the manuscript,[44] which is a compilation of homilies and commentaries, mention is made of the following dates: the years 5210[45] and 5215[46] (1450 and 1455). He relates that he was exiled "from my homeland and I came to the town of Egribo."[47] From his description it is evident that he came there "from the Ottoman Empire,"[48] and it would seem that Ephraim ben Gershon arrived from Veroia to Negroponte via Zeitun (Lamia), located next to the island. He lived in Negroponte for a number of years, and from there he travelled to Zeitun and thence to Istanbul.[49] In the year 5229 (1469) he was living and preaching in public in Istanbul.[50]

From his manuscript it would seem that he was an eyewitness to the events of the transfer to Istanbul, which even had their effect on his own life. He often mentions the exile, calling himself "Ephraim ben Gershon the exile."[51] He states that "the exile does not permit me to sleep, and I have come to look like a pitchfork";[52] elsewhere he writes: "I have come to be like the nipples of a virgin, and have been transferred from one community to another."[53] In fact, the sequence of his wanderings is puzzling. From Veroia he moved to Negroponte in the middle of the fifteenth century,[54] and in his homilies delivered there he gave expression to the troubles of his personal exile and the deterioration of his economic situation. In one of his homilies he even paints a picture of a reality in which everyone was destined to be deported:

> Those who remained tranquil and were not forced into exile did not feel that this could be a repetitive phenomenon—that even if he were not exiled, his son would be; and if not his son—then his grandson would . . . spreading lies saying that exile was not destined but merely the desire of the individual, and not thinking that one fate could encompass everyone, whether a good person, a sinner, a righteous man or an evil one. . . .[55]

After spending some time in Negroponte, he prepared to set out for Istanbul; while in Negroponte he apparently composed a homily and noted at its onset: "This I shall deliver in Constantinople if I go there."[56] This is a short homily, of peculiar form and interpretation, and is fully intended for those being exiled to Istanbul, in their honor and for their comfort. The following is the wording of the homily:

> Who is this, coming up out of the desert like pillars of smoke, more perfumed with myrrh and frankincense than all the powders of a merchant.[57] This verse is to be interpreted with regard to you and your lands and the fields around your cities[58] and the properties of your forefather,[59] and your fields and your vineyards, and your vines and your fig trees and your homeland and the honor and glory of your lives. Why did this come about in your days?[60]—now lend me your ears and listen, so that your spirits may be revived.[61] "Who is this", and where will one find such a community as this excellent one which came up from exile? This is the meaning of who is this, coming up out of the desert, in other words: you have come up here as the result of *dibbur*, the word, the utterance, of the great prince. This is the meaning of "from the *midbar*, the desert." "Like pillars of smoke"—when you were traveling from your place on your way here, you all became bitter sects,[62] in other words: each and every sect was weeping great sorrow and distress. This is the meaning of "like pillars of smoke." "More perfumed with myrrh and frankincense"[63]— each and every one was bitter because he was scattering his *levanim*[64] (money), for the gematria of *mor levona* (myrrh and frankincense) equals that of *mefazzer* (scattering).[65] This is the meaning of "more perfumed with myrrh and frankincense than all the powders of a merchant." Its purpose is to indicate the fact that when the hedonists and wealthy elders were on their way, the dust rising before them used to harm them. This is the significance of "than all the powders of a merchant."

Ephraim ben Gershon was planning to deliver this sermon before exiles to Istanbul from the towns of Rumelia (European Turkey); it is reasonable to assume he intended to do so in the future before people he was familiar with. Jews had been exiled to Istanbul from Veroia and from Lamia (Zeitun) as well, as is apparent from the census listings of 1455, and from the lists of *sürgün* communities.[66] In contrast, he was clearly not aiming at the Negroponte community, for they went into exile after the island was conquered in 1470, and he arrived in Istanbul earlier.[67] These exiles abandoned their property and their "homeland"[68] in accordance with the decree of the "great prince"—either the Sultan or whoever he had put in charge of the implementation of the decree. The move to Istanbul involved not only a loss of property and the abandonment of places to which they were emotionally attached, but also suffering, great expense and damage to one's health.[69] In his sermon he stressed their financial and emotional links with their previous homes, and he tries to comfort them by describing their virtues and their strength in overcoming suffering. The end of the description provides us with an indication of the nature of their journey, whether on foot or by carriage; it was, at any rate, not a maritime journey. The dust was that of the convoy making its way from the Lamia region to Istanbul.[70]

It would thus seem that Ephraim ben Gershon had escaped from Veroia (an Ottoman territory) to Negroponte (under Venetian control), apparently as a result of the expulsion decrees issued in Veroia after the conquest of Constantinople. However, he felt cut off from his previous environment, and was not enamored with the attitude of his neighbors towards him, though he seems to have been accepted by them. He desired to be reunited with is original community, which had in the meantime gone into exile to Istanbul, and so he, too, set out in their wake to the city. This would seem to be a concrete example of a Jew escaping from the Ottoman sphere of influence (apparently from Veroia via Lamia), just after the conquest of Constantinople, and Mehmet II's appeal to Venice to return the escapees to Istanbul was aimed at people such as he. David Jacoby has already noted that a flight of Jews may have taken place between 1453 and 1457, estimating that they were residents of Lamia who fled to Negroponte,[71] an assumption which is confirmed by the words and the personal history of Ephraim ben Gershon. Also his supposition there, that residents of Negroponte began to migrate to Istanbul because they preferred to be Ottoman subjects rather than Venetian ones as a result of the conditions which had developed there, might be supported by Ephraim ben Gershon's voluntary trip. It is thus not surprising that things changed completely, and in 1459 the Senate in Venice ordered steps to be taken to return them to Negroponte.[72] Furthermore, from a document from the year 5218 (July 1458) it may be inferred that there already was a Negroponte community in Istanbul which engaged R. Moshe

Kapsali[73] and so it can be assumed that the number of people leaving Negroponte was increasing.

From this description of events it becomes clear that despite the suffering and the losses sustained by the exiles because they moved to Istanbul (and could not have left the city even had they wished to do so), people such as R. Ephraim, who had previously escaped the exile itself, gathered there too. At the same time, he did not avoid speaking out critically and did not view the Jews' living in Istanbul in only a positive light. In a sermon he delivered in the year 5229 (1469) he says:

> All this stems from our enslavement and the sorrow we cause ourselves in our pursuit of a livelihood; we call upon God and He will hear our voices, He will take pity and have mercy on us and redeem us. . . .[74]

R. Ephraim views the Ottoman Empire as the prophet Daniel's fourth kingdom from which Israel shall be redeemed when it collapses, and the Jews return to their homeland.

Ephraim ben Gershon's words are relatively moderate, and were not written under great emotional stress. We encounter more severe descriptions of the fate of the Romaniots in a group of letters copied by Michael Balbo of Crete. Michael Balbo was a well known personality, and one of his Hebrew manuscripts—ms. Vatican 105—has been closely perused in scientific literature.[75] The manuscript is a kind of literary anthology compiled by Michael Balbo (born in Nissan [Spring] 5171 (1411) and still alive in December 1480),[76] in which he included writings of his own as well as those of others. Among all these, he copied over letters received by the community of Candia, during the period when he served that community in official positions and at other times. In the main, recognizable features were left out of these letters, but such details were at times overlooked in the documents, most of which date from the second and third quarters of the fifteenth century.[77] The importance of several of these letters for the history of the Jews and the Empire during the third quarter of the century[78]—including some which refer to the Ottoman conquests and the events which accompanied them—is very great.

One of these letters, which sports a very intricate and complex opening chapter,[79] customary in the Jewish society of Byzantium and the Levant, and which was apparently sent from the community of Corfu[80] in order to be of assistance to a wealthy Jew who had lost most of his property in the political upheavals and in his own captivity, contains a passage which describes contemporary events incidentally:

> The Sons of the Lady are wandering from place to place, under the pressure of the slaves, whereas the Sons of the Maidservant[81] are quiet, controlling every plan. They send the Sons of the Lady down to the pit,[82] while the taskmasters pressure us steadily. At this time the King maker enthroned a king of the Archers[83] over each town and district; he decreed that the poor, wandering nation go into exile, and went to gather them up to the daughter of Edom,[84] Constantinople, and the Almighty enabled him to succeed.[85] Everyone lamented. The robbery[86] and the disaster, the famine and the sword and the forced conversion of children at this time defy comforting. All are affected and desolated by the oppressor,[87] and there is no tranquility. . . . [88]

This letter paints a picture of Jews severely harmed by the Ottoman wars and conquests in the days of Mehmet II. The description indicates that the Jews of Corfu were well aware of the processes of the Ottoman conquest. The conquest was accompanied by the appointment of governors over the occupied territories by the "Kingmaker," ie., the Sultan.[89] These Muslim governors were responsible for the stabilization and the development of the conquered region. At the same time, this letter describes the colonizing activities and the transfer of the Jewish population to Istanbul. Whether the letter is describing the conquest of an area previously under Byzantine or Latin control, subsequent to the conquest of Constantinople, or an event during the conquest of Constantinople itself and its consequences, the process is similar. The people view their exile as a catastrophe, and the conquest as manslaughter and loss of property. The picture is one of crisis and distress. This letter also hints at the phenomenon of converting Jewish children to Islam. In fact, this would seem to be the first evidence of the fact that in the heat of the conquest, the fate of Jewish children was the same as that of Christian children: conversion, in order to absorb them into the Janissary army. The induction of Christian children into the Janissary army, known as *devşirme*,[90] was one of the harsher decrees imposed upon the conquered populace, and various towns that surrendered to the Ottomans without resistance requested, and sometimes received by virtue of this, an exemption from the *sürgün* and from the *devşirme*.[91] The evidence before us is somewhat vague. Were the conquerors incapable, in the heat of battle, of distinguishing between Christian inhabitants and non-Christians? Or perhaps they had not yet formulated the policy familiar to us from later periods, in accordance with which they exempted the Jews from *devşirme* and even forbade them from being drafted into the Janissary army.[92]

From the letter, furthermore, it becomes clear that the person for whom it was compiled had gone into exile to Istanbul, and lost whatever he had owned. When he tried to return and engage in trade, he was taken captive, and now people succeeded in redeeming him from captivity and in rehabilitating him and his family.[93] Another source also discusses the fate of Jews in this unstable period and their captivity at the hands of the Ottomans.[94] In this source, the Ottomans are termed "men of wickedness and deceit, Riphath and Togarmah" (referring to Genesis 10.3), and fear is expressed, lest the captives "be assimilated" into their captors. The personal histories of two of the intellectuals of the period show, too, that they were captives, and it would seem that they were referring to their captivity at the hands of the Ottomans. R. Mordekhai Comtino tells of his imprisonment in the town of Edirne,[95] whereas R. Shalom Anabi of Istanbul—who was in contact with R. Michael Balbo who copied many of his writings—wrote of himself: "Ensnared in the net of captivity," or "who surrounded us so that we were ensnared in the net of captivity."[96]

The picture painted by the writings of these Romaniots in the Ottoman Empire and in the Latin colonies on its outskirts during the third quarter of the fifteenth century, is one of people who underwent heavy suffering as a result of the processes of conquest and population transfers to Istanbul. Though these actions were not aimed at them, they had an effect on most of the Jewish residents of the Empire in the days of Mehmet II. It is no wonder that the Romaniot Jews living on the islands of the Mediterranean Sea under Latin rule, who heard of the events taking place in their immediate vicinity, regarded the Ottomans with reserve and hostility, as conquerors and as rulers. R. Ephraim ben Gershon, *after having settled in Istanbul*, delivered a sermon about the Ottomans in the year 5229 (1469) without distinguishing at all between them and the other authorities and exiles:

> By "Ciryat Arba" he indicates Constantinople where four kingdoms held sway and were hinted at in the word "Ciryat": How? The letter "C"—Constantine who built the city; "r"—Romans—Constantinople is the daughter of wicked Rome; "y"—Yevanim, Greeks; "t"—Turks. And from the hands of the Turks we are to be redeemed at the end of the fourth kingdom, this being the redemption yet to be visited upon us, may it be speedily and in our days. I still have to provide you with a tangible explanation of how we are to be redeemed from Turkish hands. . . .[97]

He even viewed them as the Ishmaelites mentioned in *Pirkei d'Rabbi Eliezer*, and foresaw the redemption as a catastrophic process. From Istanbul and the transfer of population to that city there would develop the transfer to Eretz-Israel (Palestine):

> . . . it is Hebron. This is to say that Constantinople links us with our Father in Heaven, and brings us nearer to our return to the land of Canaan—and this as

> the result of our burdensome enslavement and pain we cause ourselves to run after our livelihood. We call to God and He will hear our voice, and will ... take pity and have mercy upon us, and ... God ... will redeem us by upsetting the guardian angel of evil Rome,[98] for no nation falls below unless its angel falls on high. ...[99]

His desire to comfort his audience is evident, since the sermon was delivered during a period of crisis in the city. This sermon also contains criticism of Jews seeking power, though at the same time it is clear that after his arrival in Istanbul no change took place in Ephraim ben Gershon's basic approach to the Ottomans. As a Jew living (and who apparently was also born) under Ottoman rule, he perceived no difference between this regime and a Christian one, with regard to the function and status of these kingdoms in universal history and with regard to their place in the redemption of the Jews from among the Gentiles. At first he preferred to move to a Venetian area; later he returned to the Ottoman sphere of influence and rejoined his brethren in Istanbul, where he spoke in public, hinting at his reservations regarding the regime and the kingdom. Under this Ishmaelite government, just as under other authorities, there prevailed circumstances where the individual would be well advised when "in exile amongst the seven tribes and *asked to pay taxes or to convert* (emphasis mine), hand over a portion of your capital, in order to be saved. This is the meaning of 'Give a portion to seven,' i.e., to the seven tribes."[100]

It may thus be assumed that in the first two decades after the conquest, a period when the harmful effects of both the conquest itself and the policy of exile were still very tangible, the conquered and exiled Jews and their contemporaries recalled very clearly what had happened to them, and these memories certainly influenced their attitudes towards the Empire and its ruler. Even though this approach may not have been completely uniform, and there may have already developed varying points of view, the available sources show that these viewpoints were those of the Romaniot Jews whose writings have survived.[101]

4. Eliyah Kapsali and Jewish Historiography (b)

Eliyah Kapsali of Crete's historic composition which he wrote there in 1453 shows no signs of those aspects already noted in the writings of the Romaniot Jews during the third quarter of the fifteenth century. Kapsali, who describes at great length and in picturesque terms the fall of Constantinople in 1453, devoted an extremely literary description to the fall of the city.¹⁰² The central motif of his composition is the joy at the fall of Byzantium, the result of the latter's evil actions against the Jews. Throughout this description, no indication whatever is made of the fate of the Jews during the conquest and immediately thereafter; nor is there any mention of the existence of a Jewish community in Constantinople or anywhere else. The Ottomans are described as a powerful and cruel, strange and foreign, fierce people and their king as "the king of kings" (*rex regis*), with enormous power, devoted to his goals and very great talent. He expounds freely and deals with various aspects of the conquest and its consequences: "Because of the evil [done] to Israel this trouble has befallen her, for all of His ways are just." He is happy that in this city "there remained not a single live person and its roads were desolate," that "God brought about a massacre in Botzra," "that they are all trapped, sold into slavery,"

> "that they collect up their war casualties in heaps and the land stank . . . the Greeks have been thoroughly annihilated," Divine fire fell from the skies, burned among the Greeks and consumed them why did God do so to this land . . . to astound the remains of this people and even to astound me, the writer . . . how the ruling kingdom of Greece fell . . . for they did not come to the help of God's heroes, to be merciful to the Jews . . . for all Jews are well aware that the evil kingdom of Greece destroyed the holy people, they stunned them, they tortured them, they hated them, and we should not be puzzled as to why this evil decree befell them—*for all His ways and His paths are mercy and truth, and God is zealous for His land and He takes pity of His people* (emphasis mine) . . . for they rejected the laws of the Jews, they abrogated their Sabbath, and so their kingdom ceased to be. . . .

He renders a verdict on the kingdom of Byzantium and on its rulers, and at the beginning of his description he announces: "And since the Greeks acted evilly toward My people and My nation, I have handed (the kingdom) to a violent person." One notes here the Messianic hope and expectation that the Final Redemption would come in the wake of the fulfillment of the prophecy referring to "the daughter of Edom."¹⁰³ Throughout the description of the catastrophe which befell Byzantium and Constantinople—the slaughter, the fire, the looting and the captivity—the author justifies these deeds against "the Greeks"; he does not criticize the conquerors in any way whatever but rather expresses his admiration of their power, and makes not the slightest mention of any Jews being involved in the event. In contrast, in Michael Balbo's aforementioned notebook there is a dirge to the fall of Constantinople into Ottoman hands,¹⁰⁴ which was probably written shortly after news of the event had been received. This dirge calls the conquerors "a violent people." "The embroidered great eagle, Riphath and Togarmah" is here depicted as one who destroys, who ruins, who robs and kills Jews. This is a dirge in which R. Michael Balbo mourns the fate of the Jewish community of Constantinople, and according to his description, this event was a terrible disaster for the Jews, who were robbed and killed by the conquering force, as were the other inhabitants of the city. Any attempt at comparing this dirge with Eliyah Kapsali's description must immediately perceive the difference between the contemporary writer, writing just after the event itself,[105] and the later writer who clearly reveals his support for the Ottomans and his hatred for Byzantium.

Eliyah Kapsali's approach is one in which the new conqueror, God's rod of wrath, did well in all his deeds, including his cruelty, and God Himself fulfilled the expectations of His children: "God is zealous for His land and took pity of His people" and "All he did was good and timely."[106] What brought about this change in viewpoints from the first generation to the second and third generations?

It would seem that one can reply with a fair degree of certainty to this question, at least with regard to Eliyah Kapsali. Throughout his work, which was compiled between the fourteenth of Sivan and the twenty-fifth of Elul of 5283 (June to September 1523) under the impression of the conquest of Rhodes by the armies of Süleyman the Magnificent, he stresses the fact that it was God who brought the Ottomans to the level of a world power, and it was on a divine mission that the Ottomans were defeating the Christian world. Already in the introduction to his work he proclaimed:

> Pass through the gateways of this book, turn to the way of God, study its tales, read and see that God, in His wisdom and understanding, rendered this Turkish nation great... The Turk is the rod of His wrath, the staff of His anger, and by means of him He takes His vengeance of the gentle nations and tongues and states whose time has come....[107]

He repeats this again and again throughout the book.[108] Part of their success is even to be attributed to the assistance given them by the Jews.[109] It would seem, however, that the main reason for his approach is supplied by the events of the Spanish expulsion and its aftermath. The Spanish and Portuguese expulsions were the main events of his day, and served as the main motif of his writing.[110] Throughout his narrative, he emphasizes the fact that the Ottomans viewed the Jews as a positive element and a desirable population. The Jews "were invited" by Mehmet II to his capital city, "to the best part of the land"; they accepted and came, and were even brought from other places—yet all this is viewed as a positive step, for they were not being exiled to some desert land, but rather "to Constantinople, the seat of the Kingdom."[111] Contrary to this approach which views the Jews as a desirable, constructive population, Eliyah Kapsali compares the approach of the Christian kings who drove the Jews out of their homes at the close of the fifteenth century:

> Some of the Gentile Kings were led astray by their evil hearts ... and they expelled us from our shelters in their territory and shouted after us, "Male!" (Jer. 12.6) Yet the soul of this king (Mehmet II) was steeped in goodness: not only didn't he drive the Jews out from before him, he even gathered them together from the distant towns and brought them to the capital city of the Kingdom, and said to the Jews: You shall dwell with me and do business with the country.[112]

In light of the differentiation between this expulsion, driving the Jews out of the land, and the Ottoman "expulsion", leading the Jews to the center of the state in order to develop it, it is possible to comprehend the revolution which took place in attitudes. Istanbul had been transformed from a desolate city to a prosperous one, and the initial problems were all forgotten. The prosperous Jewish community itself was the clearest indication of the intentions of the Ottoman rulers.

In dealing with the period of Bayezid II, Kapsali overtly links events with the Spanish expulsion, as follows:

> Just as Sultan Mehmet gathered the Jews living in other communities and *brought them to live with him in Constantinople* (emphasis mine) and said: Come and shelter in my shade as we have written, similarly his son, this Sultan Bayezid treated the seed of Abraham, servants of God, well ... and did not cast them out from before him as some of the Gentile Kings did to us, crying out "male" (Jer. 12.6) after us wherever we went. Were it not for this, the remnant of Judah and traces of Israel, exiled from Spain and Aragon and Portugal and Sicily by the unsheathed sword of the wicked King of Spain would have been lost. . . .[113]

Bayezid II, who continued Mehmet II's policy with regard to the Jews, according to this extract,[114] not only settled the Jews and did not drive them out, he also absorbed the exiles from the Iberian peninsula and saved them from annihilation. Bayezid was the savior and redeemer of "the pleasant and scattered Jews of Spain."[115] Kapsali hosted them, and compiled at great length from their tales the history of the Jews of Spain and their "great and terrible" Expulsion. It is thus no wonder that the Christians were grasped as persecutors, and the Muslims as saviors. Of these latter, the Ottoman Sultans were the those who determined the policies, and they saved the Jewish people:

> For our brethren, the children of Esau, drove us out and did away with us and destroyed us. . . . Spain from before us, and Portugal behind . . . they enforced every evil decree upon the Jews—those by the sword, by the sword . . . and those by famine, by famine . . . and it was horrible . . . were it not for the Lord of Hosts who preserved our remnants and made us find favor in the eyes of Sultan Bayezid, King of Turkey, who received the Jews in his kingdom cordially . . . we would be as in Sodom and Gomorrah, without strength as without God, and the memory of Judah and the scattered people of Israel would be lost. . . . Just as God deliberately brought evil upon the King of Spain, so He brought good upon Sultan Bayezid - for he received the Jews cordially, with love and brotherhood and great affection. And God blessed the Turks because of the Jews—because they said to the Jews: Build yourselves cities for your children and corrals for your livestock, settle wherever you like, and no one will cause you shame . . . while we thought the expulsion (from Spain) was evil, God planned it for the good . . . and the salvation began in 5252 (1492), according to the promise: "when the morning stars sing (*BeRon*: numerically 1492) together" . . . for He who gathers together the scattered ones of Israel gathered us together so that we would be ready for the ingathering of the exiles. . . . [116]

According to Kapsali's grasp of events, the decisive historic event in the lives of the Jews during his lifetime was the process of the expulsion of the Jewish from the Christian lands, which reached its peak with their expulsion from the Iberian peninsula. This expulsion endangered the survival of the Jewish nation. The Ottoman Empire, headed by Bayezid II, saved the people from annihilation. Thus, the figures of Mehmet II, who had devised the policy with regard to the Jews, and Bayezid, who continued it, were spotless in every way. Critical descriptions of the Sultans' figures, their personalities and their other characteristics, which appear in Christian writings, become positive with Kapsali, and the critical negative ones vanish completely.[117] This is true, too, of the description of their attitude toward the Jews, including the subject under discussion—the *sürgün* system. Kapsali conceals all criticism and tries to cover up and obliterate inconvenient facts. He strives to evaluate their activities on the basis of the final result, and ignores the means by which they were achieved. This is also apparently the reason for his complete neglect of the Romaniot Jews and their fate at the time of the conquest of Constantinople, and the suffering of the others exiled there after the conquest. Of what significance is this suffering of a small number of Jews who recovered just a few years after the suffering and the troubles, as compared with the saving of the emigrés from Spain and Portugal from the annihilation or forced conversion planned from them by the Christian nations?[118] Eliyah Kapsali, resident of the Levant, was deeply influenced by contemporary attitudes and by the approach of the Spanish emigrés after their expulsion, who viewed the Sultans as merciful kings and as saviors; so influenced was he that he completely suppressed the fifteenth-century history of Romaniot Jewry.[119] Furthermore, though he was well aware of the fact that Bayezid II's policies towards the Jews were very different from those of Mehmet II, and that in his day attempts were made to pressure the Jews to adopt Islam and strict decrees were promulgated against the existence of synagogues erected after the Ottoman conquest,[120] he was still careful to describe Bayezid II as the perfect Jew lover and protector. The truth is revealed with his description of Selim, Bayezid's heir. Here he saw fit to praise Selim as follows:

> Now on the third day of the reign of Sultan Selim, the Sultan gave an order and permitted the Jews to reopen the synagogues his father, Sultan Bayezid, had closed ... for he was pious ... and he even restored to Judaism many Jews whom the Turks had forced to convert contrary to their own wishes. ...[121]

And so not only did he conceal the fate of *sürgün* Jews and disguise them as voluntary migrants who came to settle in the royal capital at the invitation of the King; not only did he obscure the bitter fate of the Jews of conquered Constantinople; he also attempted to cover up as much as possible the zealous policies of Bayezid II against religious minorities—including the Jews—after the expulsion. And all this to avoid harming the image of the Sultan and his major work: throwing open the gates of the kingdom before the expelled Jews of Spain and Portugal, guaranteeing their physical security and preparing the conditions for their free economic activity. There is thus in his book not a single hint or even trace of criticism of the Sultans of his generation: Mehmet II, Bayezid II and Selim I.

It is this description by Eliyah Kapsali and the embellishment of it by Yosef Sambari that became the version accepted by modern historiography of the history of the Jews in the Ottoman Empire.[122] The *sürgün* phenomenon and all its attendant features have not been considered at all. If the *sürgün* was mentioned at all in the writings of the scholars of the Empire, it was held to be an insignificant, indecisive episode in the history of the Jews. The relations between Jews and Ottomans were thus felt to be both idyllic and monotonous from their very inception, with no distinction made either between kinds of Jewish population or between one period and another throughout the fifteenth and sixteenth centuries.

C. JEWISH GROUP TRANSFERS IN THE SIXTEENTH CENTURY

The *sürgün* policy applied in full to Istanbul over a lengthy period of time was not unknown in other areas. From time to time, with the conquest of new territories, this policy was reinstated and the lives of the local populace—including local Jews—were affected by it. The policy was applied not only by Mehmet II, but also by Bayezid II, who fought few battles or wars, and rather than engage in the expansion of his realm applied himself to stabilizing and strengthening it. Thus, in the areas where he did wage war and conquer, he behaved similarly to his predecessors.[123] He also exiled to Istanbul one part of the conquered populace, whereas others he transferred to other regions while simultaneously bringing inhabitants from the Empire to the conquered territory.[124] It is not known if the Jews were involved, as a population group, in these population transfers.

However, in the days of Selim II and Süleyman the Magnificent we hear of a number of cases where Jews were among those exiled and transferred from one region to another. We shall thus review these events and their consequences.

1. Exiling Jews from Egypt to Istanbul

Selim II conquered Syria and Egypt from the Mameluks in 1516-1517. Contemporary authors described at length his war, his victory and the stabilization of the Ottoman regime in that region, events which were thus well documented. Ibn-Iyas,[125] in his chronicle, also describes at length and in detail the exiling of Egyptians to Istanbul after the conquest. According to his account, over a thousand families went into exile. Besides the upper stratum of Cairo's Muslim society, many merchants were exiled—Muslims, Christians and Jews—as well as a good number of craftsmen with various skills.[126] The impression gained from his descriptions is that this population transfer sufficed to disrupt normal business activity in Egypt, for among those exiled were merchants and the trading officials of many companies engaged in international trade. There is no information available on the number of Jews transferred to Istanbul, nor on the effect of the exodus of the Jewish communities of Cairo and other places upon Egypt itself.

Eliyah Kapsali devoted only scanty attention to this topic, though the event took place during his lifetime and he considered it one of the major events of the period. In his narrative, which spreads over scores of pages,[127] he dealt with details of the conquest and with subsequent events. He devoted long descriptions to the fate of the Mameluks, commented on the fate of the Jews during and after the war,[128] and even discussed the booty which was brought to Istanbul.[129] All he tells of the transfer of people from Egypt to Istanbul relates to the fate of the notables of Mameluk society, and he makes no mention whatever of Jews. The following is his description:

> At that time five large boats set out from Alexandria in Egypt, full of gold and silver and other treasures of Egypt, on their way to Constantinople. together with a *çavuş* of the master (the Sultan); the boats also held many notable men, of the great ones of Egypt and of her judges of the first line. The King had commanded them to appear before him in Constantinople, as he had done with all the great ones of Egypt: he did not leave them there in Egypt, but rather led them to Constantinople and transferred them to the towns. . . . [130]

The reliability of the information on Egyptian Jews related by Ibn-Iyas would seem to be doubtful, for Eliyah Kapsali stresses that he enjoyed firsthand information of the events in Egypt, and on occasion he notes his sources. One of the main sources for his description of the events in Egypt was a well known gentleman who was an eyewitness to them:

> For the stories of Egypt, I relied on the word of many, notable friends who were there then, especially a courageous and trustworthy friend who was there during the war, from the beginning of the affair until its end—R. Yitzhak El-Hakim. He related the stories to me and I put them down in ink in a book. . . . [131]

This person is known to have been learned, whether he was a doctor or not, and his family is known to have moved from Egypt to Istanbul. Could he not have told of the exiling of Jews among the other exiles? Did this event not leave an impression of Jewish society in Egypt and elsewhere during that period?

In fact, even the chance sources available today do provide echoes of this event. Thus, for example, R. Levi ben Habib tells of a case in Jerusalem which was brought before him. The Jerusalem community pawned some property which had been left in the city without heirs to inherit it, and so had become a community endowment. R. Levi relates that the community had never dared pawn this property until one of the heirs, who had been living in Egypt, was exiled to Istanbul in 1517 or in 1518. This is the original wording:

> He further testified before me in evidence, saying that when the aforementioned R. Moshe Vitalis died, his daughters were not present, for they had already married husbands a long time before, and ever since then they had not

returned to Jerusalem. As long as R. Abraham de Hereira was in Egypt the community was unable to touch the aforesaid courtyard, neither to pawn it nor to sell it, for he, being a relative of the heiresses—the daughters of the aforesaid R. Moshe, would have objected. *Only after they exiled R. Abraham de Hereira to Istanbul* (emphasis mine) did the community pawn that courtyard to R. Yaakov di Vaena. . . . [132]

Elsewhere he relates:

> When I came to these lands and passed through Constantinople, I heard there had been an old man there, a Sicilian, who maintained he was a scholar who had been brought as a *sürgün* from Egypt, and used to relate. . . . [133]

R. David Ibn Zimra was asked about the inheritance of a property belonging to a family which had gone into exile in Istanbul. The wording of the question shows that the family had attempted, even before they left, to ensure the possibility of their return to their home when the time became ripe. They had their home rented out, and some members of the family did indeed manage to free themselves from their place of exile in Istanbul[134] and to return home—to Egypt, it would seem. All the sources indicate that the effects of that exile remained deeply felt, both in Egypt and elsewhere.

A substantial change took place here, in contrast with the previous exiles of Jews to Istanbul. It is clear that the Jews exiled in this case were not of the autochthonous Jewish population, but rather emigrés from Spain and Sicily who had wandered into Egypt at some unknown date, before the expulsion from Spain or perhaps after it, their name and origin testifying clearly to this.

Yet another source, a letter found in the Cairo *geniza* dealing with business matters, is concerned with the affairs of a number of persons who were *sürgün*. The letter is vague and in need of detailed analysis, but an initial study suffices to show that its writer, Meir Saragos of Egypt, had sent it to Yaakov mar-Hayyim, in Egypt, in the first half of the sixteenth century:

> for we hear from you . . . now that they do not want to let any *sürgün* go. I have already written to you of how I spoke to be rid [. . .] to the *kadı* about the court of Tripoli. And he said: if he is a *sürgün*, no. In the case of Moshe Menir, too, they said that since he is *sürgün* it is not possible. As I wrote to you, when you wrote your name in the *Hukum*, the *defshiah* [sic] asked about [or: in charge of] the home of *sürgün*, asked me where that translator is from and if he wasn't a *sürgün*. For I wasn't present, and I am the one who has to inform them that you are a *sürgün* lest we have trouble later on . . . wait until these *sürgünish* come from there, until we see what happens to them and if they are allowed to go. . . . You, too, will go, and if they go . . . go with them to lessen the cost. . . . [135]

The Sürgün System and Jewish Society in the Ottoman Empire / 27

This may be a description relating to a number of Jews in Egypt who fell victim to the *sürgün* of 1517. The description tells of the limitations and the supervision to which they were subjected and which prevented them from moving from their location and accepting appointments to the positions they desired. The limitations of a *sürgün* are very prominent here. Similarly, it is clear that the phenomenon of *sürgün* was common and many were ensnared in its coils. People were responsible for dealing with the affairs of those who became *sürgün*, while the latter attempted to free themselves by attaching themselves to some position—either to avoid going into exile or to leave one place of exile for another, steps which were forbidden to any *sürgün*.

2. Exiling Jews of Salonica to Rhodes

In contrast to the paucity of information concerning Jews transferred from Egypt to Istanbul shortly after its conquest by Selim II, there is more information available concerning the transfer of Jews to Rhodes in order to settle and develop it, just after its conquest in 1522 by Süleyman the Magnificent. The significant information available is found in the personal writings of Yitzhak Ibn Farash, who was exiled from Spain to Portugal and later left for Salonica, where he settled in 1508.[136] Yitzhak Ibn Farash wrote:

> From Salonica, Monday, the 13th of Av 5283 (1523) there went to Rhodes against their will[137] a hundred and fifty of the richest and most respected landlords[138] in the country, men, women and children, at the command of the king, His Exalted Majesty, Sultan Süleyman, an official coming and taking them off by boat.[139]

This passage alone makes it clear that we are dealing with the transfer of 150 Jewish families from Salonica to Rhodes about half a year after its capture in December 1522, in order to resettle it and develop it. The number of people moved was high, for an average community at the time did not include so large a number of Jews. Only in a few big cities and towns was the number of Jews greater than this.[140] According to the table compiled by Barkan, of the seventeen cities of the Empire selected as a sample, there were more than 150 Jewish families in only four cities during this period: Istanbul, Salonica, Edirne and Trikala. In such cities as Bursa, Serres, Ankara and so on, the number of Jews was far smaller or completely non-existent, according to the census. At later dates as well, the number of Jews in the Balkan cities was not significant, again according to the data gleaned from the censuses.[141] On the other hand, in Salonica itself the number of

Jews had already swelled during this period, reaching some 3,143 families and 930 single people in the year 1519.[142] It is thus understandable why the Jews were taken specifically from Salonica and why the forced exiling of 150 families, as painful as it may have been, had no serious effects upon Jewish community life: they made up less than 5% of the Jewish population. It will be recalled, however, that the families exiled made up a productive and capable stratum of society, so that it is possible that their exile did have some ill effect upon the economic activity and social structure of the community, and that its impact was considerable. Selecting people "of the richest and most respected . . . in the land" was deliberate; its aim was the creation of an economic infrastructure and an attempt to develop the place, in this case Rhodes, by transferring an economic infrastructure and experienced people to increase the economic and social activity there. Just who determined the identity of the exiles in this case is unknown. It may have been the central or local Ottoman authorities or, perhaps the leadership of Salonica's Jewish community. Drawing an analogy from what is known about Safed (see below) the community leadership did have some influence in determining the identity of the exiles, even if the authorities determined their category.

The impact of this exile is indeed noticeable in the internal, legalistic, sources of sixteenth-century Ottoman Empire Jewry. The hasty and rapid process of exiling the *sürgün* led to various familial, social, economic and legal complications. For example, there is the story of a father-in-law who did not have time to pay his son-in-law the dowry due him after his daughter became engaged to him: "And after the engagement they led off Reuben as *sürgün* to Rhodes in haste, and while going to Rhodes Shimon [the son-in-law] was nowhere to be found: he left his house there, leaving orders with the community to sell the shop he owned in Sofia and to pay Shimon what he owned him so that he would marry his daughter."[143] In another case, a rich woman who left Salonica as a divorcee, did not take her writ of divorcement with her or perhaps lost it. When she wanted to remarry five or six years later, she ran into difficulties.[144] Salonica's communities wanted to reduce to a minimum the economic harm caused to those leaving, and so ruled that anyone leaving the city without having sold or rented out his property would not lose it, since he was forced to leave hastily. This was in contradiction to the rules and customs, whereby a person leaving town without completing arrangements for his property would lose his claim to the possession of the property. R. Samuel de Medina, in dealing with this problem, relates:

> And for this reason, when the *sürgün* went to Rhodes, they set up their property, so that it would not be said that anyone moving lost his rights of possession, unless a person went out of his own accord and might give away or sell it before he left. But those who left involuntarily did not lose. My opinion is that this is similar to the ruling that when a person leaves voluntarily his relative is not sent to take over his property, for though he had time to make his will known, he did not do so—thus raising the question, perhaps he did not want his relative to be sent to take over his property.... Thus we rule that if a person leaves voluntarily without giving away or selling his property, it becomes as if he had relinquished title to it, but if he leaves involuntarily it is not fitting that he lose his rights without recompense.... [145]

Nevertheless, mention is made of those who managed to sell their real estate before leaving. The following is such an account:

> Before R. Yosef Elbagli left for Rhodes with the others, he sold his title to the courtyard and transferred it to the community, but not before stipulating with them that they collect only a certain rent from the house and from a shop.... [146]

When objections were raised to the community's occupation of the courtyard, it turned out that the community "had built other shops in the courtyard over and above those that were there after the *sürgün* had gone...."

The factor common to all these sources is that the people being discussed were well-to-do and even rich. The aformentioned father-in-law owned a house in Salonica and a shop in Sofia, and had promised a sizeable dowry (8000 *akçes*) for his daughter's marriage. He owned a large courtyard in which there were butchershops and craftsmen's workshops and which provided a comfortable income. The woman whose writ of divorce got lost was reputed to be "a rich woman who had left Salonica... and arrived in Rhodes, and the Jews who came together with her, who were aware of her divorce,... tried to solve her problem." Some "five or six years" later witnesses to the divorce were not to be found, for "... they had gone abroad," while the scholar responding could write: "... how could so great and rich a woman leave her husband to go to another town.... Were her husband alive, would he not ask about her and about the great sum of money she has—over two thousand gold florins...." And so, there could be no alternative: she was certainly a divorcee.[147]

In Rhodes itself a distinction was made between those who had come from Salonica as *sürgün* and the local inhabitants, whether of ancient origin or later arrivals, as indicated by the regulation adopted on the island and reflected in a question put to R. David Ibn Zimra:

Question: the community of Rhodes agreed to take upon themselves with exceptional strictness, that no Jew, *sürgün* or otherwise, could be a *kehaya* over the community or over any part of it.[148]

These exiles would seem to have been forced to remain in Rhodes, and were unable to leave,[149] but the sources adduced make it evident that people did succeed in escaping from the island even though they were forbidden to do so. In this way, those witnesses who could have testified to the divorce of the rich divorcee vanished. Similarly, we are told that of the two sons of the father-in-law who inherited his property in Rhodes, "the elder went to Bruse, and he sent some money from there to one of his relatives here in Constantinople and died shortly thereafter."[150] In contrast to the *sürgün* story from Egypt, which is missing from the writings of the Jewish historians of the period, the exodus of the Jews from Salonica to Rhodes is mentioned briefly by Yosef Hacohen: "At that time Süleyman the Turk sent many Jews to settle in Rhodes, where they still live securely to this very day."[151]

3. The Exiling of the Jews of Buda, Hungary, to Towns of the Kingdom

In the year 1526, after the battle of Mohács, Süleyman the Magnificent took Buda, the ancient capital of Hungary, and garrisoned it. Because of the state of his kingdom and the unrest in its Asiatic provinces, he was forced to leave with his army a short time after the conquest. The sources relate that despite the fact that the Jews were among the few who had remained and had delivered the keys to the city into his hands, and he entered it without a battle, he still took them with him,[152] leading them off in boats as *sürgün*.[153] This account is based on contemporary Christian testimony, on Ferridun Ahmed Beg, and additional eyewitnesses. Their testimony shows that the Jews were dispatched as *sürgün*, in the category of craftsmen and tradesmen, just like their brethren in Egypt after its conquest.[154]

In later censuses carried out in the Ottoman Empire, the Jews of Buda appear as a separate community in a number of places. This is true of Istanbul in the lists of the communities of the city from 1603 and 1688,[155] where the community of Buda is listed among those communities which came voluntarily (*kendi gelen*) and are not *sürgün*, and of Edirne (Adrianopol) where a community of emigrés from Buda appears both in the censuses of 1568-9 and 1603-1617, and in other sources as well,[156] and here, as *sürgün*, specifically. It is difficult to decide just when and why these communities were founded, as it is to understand how it is that the Buda community of

Istanbul is not considered part of the category of *sürgün*.[157] It is at any rate clear that many of the Jews of Buda, and perhaps almost all of them, were transferred to the cities of the Empire, as is attested by the Ottoman and Christian sources, and as shown by Hebrew sources as well. Thus, for instance, there are extant a number of testimonies to the fact that there were *sürgün* communities originating in Buda and in Hungary in general, in the towns of Sofia,[158] Kavalla,[159] and, according to one source, in Salonica as well.[160] Though here, too, it is unclear just when these Jews were brought to Sofia and Kavalla from Hungary, whether after 1526 or after 1541 (the final conquest of Buda and its environs), it would seem to have been after the initial conquest. At any rate, we are dealing with a widespread phenomenon of population transfer which led to the establishment of communities of emigrés from Buda and from Hungary (in the case of Sofia, 60 families, which made up over half the Jews of the town), in the Balkan cities, in Edirne and in Istanbul, and perhaps even in Safed.[161]

4. *Sürgün* Decrees Later Canceled

After the conquest of Cyprus by the Ottomans in 1571, the authorities initiated widespread activities aimed at resettling the island and developing it. These efforts also included widespread population transfers, including the dispatch of one out of every ten Muslim families from certain areas in Anatolia.[162] These activities included several attempts to transfer Jews from the towns of Safed to Cyprus. In October 1576, a decree was issued expelling a thousand families, and in August 1577, a decree was issued to expel five hundred families.[163] It would seem, however, that these decrees were never enforced because of the appeals made by the Jews to the authorities and the intervention of the *kadı* of Safed on their behalf, on the grounds that the execution of the decree would lead to the destruction of the infrastructure, the economic activity and the revenue of the Ottoman treasury in Safed.[164] This intervention undoubtedly stemmed from the considerable dimensions of the expulsion, which would certainly have led to the complete collapse of the Jewish community of Safed. The expulsion was indeed averted and, despite the pressures applied by the governor of the island, the reprieve of the Jews was confirmed in January 1579.[165] However, at the same time, that same governor succeeded in delaying a boat with 100 Jews on board who had been on their way from Salonica to Safed, and in getting permission to resettle them in Cyprus, despite their desire to go on to Palestine.[166] The attempts to expel the Jews from Safed left an impression upon the Jews of the town. R. Yosef de Trani writes of the year 1577: "There was the problem of the *sürgün* decree, for the island of Cyprus was captured, but the decree was abrogated",[167] while the *kadı* of Safed relates that as a result of the decree, the traders ceased trading or other economic activity. And no wonder, for if the decree had materialized and a thousand families had been removed from the town, only about 500 Jewish families would have remained, according to the available statistics.[168] That is, about two-thirds of the Jews of Safed, a majority of the town's population, were about to become *sürgün*. And, as the *kadı* put it, their real estate—houses, lots and so on—would have lost their value completely, and the financial damage done to them and to the authorities from the loss of tax monies might have been heavy. It is thus no wonder that this decree was abrogated.

It would seem that the tale told by Yosef Mataron, a disciple of R. Moshe Alsheikh, about the *sürgün* decree imposed upon him and his family and his attempts to have it abrogated are connected with this event.[169] His description also makes clear just how severe the Jews considered this decree to be and how far they were willing to go in order to have it cancelled. Even if we assume that this document relates to a later event which took place in Safed, we can date it no later than 5455/1595.

During this period various members of the Jewish communities in Salonica, Safed and elsewhere, whose status was questioned, who lost favor with the authorities, or were caught engaging in economic and criminal offenses, were exiled to Cyprus.[170]

The information concerning the attempt to move a group of Jews from Lepanto as *sürgün* in the 1570's may possibly be connected with an attempt to settle them in Cyprus. This attempt did not materialize for the very same reasons that the expulsion from Safed never took place. The local population, and especially the Ottoman administration, did not view the transfer of the Jews to other regions positively because of the damage they expected to their economic activity and to the revenue flowing from this activity to their own purses.[171]

From the various facts exhibited here, it may be deduced that the *sürgün* system remained in force throughout the sixteenth and the beginning of the seventeenth century, and affected to a very considerable degree the lives of the Jews of the Empire. These facts, which certainly do not reflect every event which actually took place, show that whenever a significant conquest occurred—under Selim I, Süleyman the Magnificent or Selim II— Jews were moved from their homes and, as they were considered a productive element of the population, it was considered good to exploit them for purposes of regional development. Whenever the Jews were living in territory recently conquered, they would be exiled to Istanbul or some other urban area, while on other occasions they were moved from their homes in the Empire in order to resettle and develop new territories.

D. THE INFLUENCE OF THE *SÜRGÜN* UPON THE CHARACTER OF JEWISH SOCIETY IN THE EMPIRE

The facts already referred to concerning the broad application of the *sürgün* policy on the one hand, and the extended period of time this policy was implemented on the other, also indicate the role played by this phenomenon in the shaping of the lives of the Jews of the Ottoman Empire from the middle or late fifteenth century on.

1. The *sürgün* system shaped the fate of the Jews more than other population groups, because the authorities selected the Jews for the purpose of colonization. This selection stemmed from their economic qualifications, their occupations, and from their public weakness. For contrary to the Muslims, for example, the Jews found it difficult to oppose such a decree and to resist it. In the days of Mehmet II, scores of Jewish communities moved to Istanbul in the wake of the king. The Jewish population was comprised of two major groups as it is told of Mehmet's Jewish doctor: "and he dwelt amongst the Jewish people who were in the city when it was captured *and whom the King transferred from the towns he had inherited from his ancestors.*"[172] In the days of Selim and Süleyman the Magnificent, these transfers were carried out firmly and determinedly, whereas from the 1570's on, the Jews managed to have such decrees cancelled by various means. Furthermore from the 1570's on, we learn that activities on the part of the community and the exiles, such as lobbying the authorities, along with ransom and bribery payments, abrogated the royal decree.[173]

2. Another reason for the significant influence of the exile upon the Jews for purposes of colonization was the relatively small number of Jews. The transfer of Jewish population groups altered the entire demographic balance and the geographical center of gravity of the Jewish communities in the Empire during the fifteenth and the early sixteenth centuries. As noted above, most of the Jewish communities during the fifteenth and sixteenth centuries numbered a few score of families (according to census data), and only rarely more than 100-150 families. The removal of two or three score families meant the liquidation or decimation of the local Jewish community.

In contrast, the transfer of 60 families to a town such as Sofia created a new community which included an absolute majority of the new Hungarian immigrants. From this perspective, the exile to Istanbul during the first years after the conquest of Constantinople caused a revolution in the history of Byzantine Jewry. Since it would seem that these population transfers were carried out firmly and consistently, most of the Romaniot Jews of the kingdom shifted from the towns of the Balkans and Anatolia to Istanbul, where a large and variegated Jewish community made up of migrant Jews from the towns of the Empire came into being. The Jews expelled from the Iberian Peninsula arrived only to find in Istanbul a firm, strong community enforcing its views upon its public. The status of the Romaniots in the city was not weakened even after the great migration of Spanish and Portuguese emigrés who became a majority among the Jews of the city as early as the onset of the sixteenth century. Only during the second half of the seventeenth century was there a significant decrease in their numbers and strength.[174] As a result, the process of assimilation of the Romaniot Jewry of Istanbul was far slower and far more complex than in other parts of the Empire.

Just as the exiling process led to the development and the flourishing of Jewish Istanbul, so it also led to the decay and eventual obliteration of many Jewish communities throughout the Empire, particularly in Anatolia and the Balkans. In fact, many towns of the kingdom were emptied of their Jewish population, including places where Jews had resided from very early times. Thus, for instance, in towns such as Salonica[175] or Manisa[176] (Magnesia), the Jewish community ceased to exist. In others—Thebes, Mistra, Negroponte— it thinned out a great deal.[177] When immigrants from Central Europe, Italy and the Iberian Peninsula arrived at the close of the fifteenth century, they often settled in towns which could show no existing Jewish community. There were a few surviving Romaniot communities, either because the town had surrendered peaceably, having been promised that its population would neither be exiled nor its youth sent to the *devşirme* or for some other reason (see, for example, Yanina, Mistra, Arta, etc.). These continued to exist later, as well, in separate, autonomous Romaniot frameworks. When the Iberian emigrés arrived *en masse*, with a strong sense of belonging to their own culture and their origins, they found in the vast majority of places in the Empire where they settled no other communities or different customs with which they would have to contend. It is thus no wonder that they quickly achieved predominance over their neighbors and began to dictate their culture and their customs. Only in those communities which had Romaniot population concentration and strength, such as Istanbul and Edirne, did the Romaniot ways continue to determine the general public customs. In other places, even when the Romaniots succeeded in drawing together and maintaining a separate community in the town, they were neither the ones to lay down the law nor to lead in matters pertaining to the entire Jewish population of the city.

3. Yet another feature, also central to the lives of the Jews of the Empire for a considerable period of time, is their dividing up into congregations in accordance with their town or land of origin. It is universally accepted that this feature, so familiar to us in Jewish history from Second Commonwealth Period Egypt, from the medieval communities of the East and from modern American Jewry, is the consequence of the migration of the Jews of the Iberian Peninsula to territories of the Empire and their adherence to their brethren of common culture, language, past and origin. However, as the topic of *sürgün* became clearer, so it became more evident that the communities which Mehmet II had exiled to Istanbul had been forced to settle there in the area set aside for them, and that they had been exiled there in groups. As early as the 1460's, we find the Romaniot Jews in Istanbul organized in congregations according to their origin, long before the arrival of the Spanish migration waves. It is impossible at the present to know if this resulted from official decree, if it was the consequence merely of the desire of the migrants to congregate together, or whether both of these factors contributed to the evolution of such a situation. Either way, it is no longer possible to claim so confidently that the feature was initiated by the emigrés from Spain and Portugal. This Romaniot settlement pattern and organizational framework in Istanbul, a large town spread out over a broad area, may quite possibly have served as a model for imitation, from which the organizational system of the communities of the Empire developed. Since this organization was well suited to the needs and mood of Iberian Jewry, they adopted it wherever they settled. The tension between particularistic elements in Romaniot society and those who wished to unite them and impose upon them uniform customs accepted throughout the city becomes apparent at the very onset of the process, just as, later, the tensions and contrasts within the Sephardic Jewish community came to the fore in the sixteenth century.[178]

We have thus seen that even before the Spanish and Portuguese Jews arrived, the organizational framework had already crystallized, an arrangement which was to be maintained for hundreds of years. Organization around the settlements of origin was, in fact, the central organizational phenomenon of this Jewry and was undoubtedly influenced by the fact that large population groups arrived together in their new home. The Iberian emigrés who arrived in large numbers may have perceived an organizational model which worked well, and needed only to adopt it, for it suited their needs admirably.

4. The manifold influence of the *sürgün* policy upon the life and future of Empire Jewry had yet another central result. When a person was registered by the authorities as a *sürgün*, and when he had been sent to his new place of residence, this *sürgün* status adhered to him and to his offspring until "the end of time." No one was able to free himself of this status, which obligated him—first and foremost—to be a vassal of his place of residence, without the ability to leave it before first having obtained the permission of the authorities. This limitation had decisive effects on the lives both of the individual and of the general public. This topic comes up quite a few times in the sources available, both with respect to the individual and regarding the public. Concerning the individual, the subject is mentioned with regard to brides and bridegrooms who were *sürgün*: one of the parties involved considered this to be justification for cancellation of the wedding.[179] People were also unable to leave their place for either the purpose of bearing witness or for a legal session elsewhere.[180] However, the more complex subject which surely left its impression on the lives of these Jews is that of double taxation. The *sürgün*'s status as a vassal to his place of residence was expressed on occasion not so much by virtue of his physical presence in his place of exile as by his registration in the authorities' taxation books. The individual was sometimes permitted to leave the city for a limited or lengthy period of time, on condition that he pay his taxes at the place where he was registered.[181] This arrangement would lead to the community where he actually resided (lived and worked there) demanding that he pay his taxes to the authorities and to the community in his place of active residence. And though, at first glance, he was exempt from this by Ottoman law (at least insofar as paying taxes to the authorities), the communities refused to concede, for in their opinion the taxes were determined by the tax collectors according to the quantity of the economic activity and the number of people in the community. They claimed that the authorities imposed their taxes on the community without taking into consideration the fact that a person was *sürgün* and paid his taxes elsewhere.[182]

As a result, those Romaniot Jews exiled to Istanbul in the fifteenth century, who asked for permission to leave the town for economic activities, had to receive permits for that from the authorities (either from the *subaşı* or his assistant, or by agreement of the directors of the *vakıf* to which they paid their taxes, for the money was earmarked for this *vakıf* from the very earliest of times, when they were exiled to Istanbul). When they received their permit to leave or when they left without a permit, and operated in another town, the community in which they lived would not agree to give up its portion of the taxes in their new place. Thus, every such person was obliged to pay double taxes. From the available Hebrew sources it would seem that this demand remained valid as late as the seventeenth century; it may even have grown stronger and more vigorous as the Romaniots left town in larger and larger numbers.[183] It was a serious economic obstacle for the descendants of the Romaniots, most of whom were *sürgün*, and for the descendants of those Spanish and Portuguese emigrés who became *sürgün* as a result of one of the sixteenth-century conquests.

From a letter by the scholars of Istanbul[184] written between 1601 and 1605 to assist a Romaniot Jew of Istanbul, we learn that about one hundred and fifty years after they became *sürgün*, this status was still an obstacle for their descendants. And though "individuals became many and [the authorities] no longer distinguished between Romaniot and Spaniard," the Romaniot congregations responsible for the payment of their members' taxes in Istanbul did not facilitate a person's leaving "unless he guaranteed his congregation by means of a certain guarantor who would pay for him any tax requirement and levy imposed by the crown." This encumbrance of being a vassal to a place, or at least this heavy financial obligation to one's previous place of residence, was a burden endured by the vast majority of Romaniots, and it seems that only a few Spanish Jews were encumbered by it. The problem was well known, and suffices to explain somewhat the Romaniot inferiority, whose legal and economic status was inferior to those of the migrants from Europe (even though they were the more ancient population group). This is a surprising situation whereby it was preferable to be a migrant Jew from a foreign land than to be a long-time Jewish resident of the Empire as early as the fifteenth century.

Furthermore, from a quarrel which has surfaced between the congregations of the town of Gallipoli (Gelibolu) in the sixteenth century, it would seem that the Romaniot community of this important town originated in "about ten *sürgün* Romaniots[185] in Constantinople from the time of Sultan Mehmet who are inscribed in His Majesty the King's lists, and there [in Istanbul] they pay all kinds of taxes and a heavy burden...."[186] In other words, at some date in the fifteenth century, this group moved to Gallipoli with the permission of the authorities and in the economic interest of the kingdom. And then, despite their move having been legally authorized, *they were still paying their taxes in Istanbul in the year 1591*, as shown by the reply there. That is to say, people whose ancestors had left the city some four or five generations before and who may never had laid eyes on it, *still had to pay their taxes* there. This led to a situation where the Sephardic majority in the town compelled the Romaniots, little by little, by means of quarrels and various and sundry acts of pressure and compulsion, to pay taxes in Gallipoli, too, despite the fact that according to Ottoman law and order they were actually exempt from this. This led to constant and unceasing quarrels and tensions between the Spanish Jews and the Romaniots, and all because the Romaniot community was *sürgün*.[187]

It is thus clear that we have before us a problem relating to an entire population group, a long and drawn out problem lasting over hundreds of years. But whenever the authorities ceased their supervision, because of their inability to identify them, the communities were compelled, by virtue of their own economic interests, to see to the recovery of their debts. This caused injustice to the Romaniots both as a group and as individuals, and had long term effects upon their ability to compete economically and to develop and move freely, at least until the seventeenth century. Thus, in the seventeenth century, as well, when—according to the testimony of the scholars of Istanbul and other sources[188]—less attention was paid to the status of the *sürgün*, and imperial policy was less rigid (whether because the authorities found it difficult to implement or because of administrative corruption), the main beneficiaries of the new situation were the "new" *sürgün*, i.e., mainly the Spanish and Portuguese emigrés, and not the Romaniots.[189] Nevertheless, the fact that it was the leadership of the Jewish community that determined the identity of the exiles undoubtedly bred severe tensions and feelings of enmity among the migrant population.[190] As an external sign of the degree of influence the *sürgün* phenomenon had on the Jews of Istanbul, as late as the eighteenth century, one might consider the fact that the term came to be accepted as a familial name for the Jewish community, though it bore negative connotations.[191]

It will thus not be surprising when it becomes evident that the opinion of the Romaniots regarding the Empire and its rulers was less enthusiastic than that of the Spanish emigrés, not only just after the resettlement of Istanbul but also at a later period; however this has still to be studied. It is clear that the emigrés of Spain and Portugal, together with those of other lands, were ensnared by the *sürgün* in its later stages. However, this policy had less decisive an influence upon them, for only a modest portion of them suffered from it, and they tended to see more the positive aspects of Ottoman policy, at least until the end of the third quarter of the sixteenth century. In contrast, their view changed in the seventeenth century, but the reason for this shift is quite complex, and is not a consequence of the subject of our discussion here.

NOTES

1   This article is based partly on a chapter of my doctoral thesis, "The Jewish Community of Salonica from the Fifteenth to the Sixteenth Century - A Chapter in the History of the Jews in the Ottoman Empire and their Relations with the Authorities" (Doctoral thesis, The Hebrew University of Jerusalem, 1978), 17-18, 62-98, Appendices, xiii-xxix, lxxii-lxxiii.

I have discussed the topics dealt with in this article in several places. The main conclusions relating to Istanbul have been discussed in my article, "Ottoman Policy toward the Jews and Jewish Attitudes toward the Ottomans during the Fifteenth Century," in *Christians and Jews in the Ottoman Empire*, vol. 1, eds. B. Braude and B. Lewis (New York and London, 1982), 118-21, 124-25. The phenomenon of *sürgün* and its influence on the Jewish community was discussed by me in a lecture during the IV. Internationaler Kongress für Türkische Wirtschafts- und Sozialgeschichte (1071-1920), Munich, 4-8 August 1986.

2   For the phenomenon of *sürgün* as a punitive measure, its commonplaceness and its significance, see the monograph by M. Çağatay Uluçay, "Sürgünler—Yeni ve Yakın Çağlarda Manisaya ve Manisadan sürülener," *Belleten* 15, no. 60 (1951): 507-592, 685-690; and B. Braude and B. Lewis, eds., *Christians and Jews in the Ottoman Empire*, vol. 1 (New York and London, 1982), 11-12.

3   So it is in the dictionary of J. W. Redhouse, *Turkish and English Lexicon* (Constantinople, 1921), 1089; see also, J. Deny, *Grammaire de la langue turque* (Paris, 1921), 570.

4   Common places of exile were the town of Manisa (Magnesia) in Anatolia or the island of Rhodes. With *sürgün* of this kind and of the kind referred to below—of individuals—see M. Çağatay Uluçay, "Sürgünler." He examined the cases of exiling to Manisa in the seventeenth and eighteenth centuries found in the local archives. His examination of 105 cases and his study of the official causes of this exiling produces an instructive picture of causes of the exiling, the limitations imposed, the life and status of a *sürgün* in exile in a given place, discharge procedures, etc.

The exiles also included Jews who had committed offenses (economic, moral or political in nature) or who had been accused falsely of such offenses, as they included Muslims and Christians as well. See for example, Document A in U. Heyd, "Ottoman Documents on the Jews of Safed in the

Sixteenth Century" (in Hebrew), *Jerusalem* vol. 2/5 (1955): 128-32, which deals with Jewish offenders in Safed in 1573; and Document No. 6 in M. Çağatay Uluçay, "Sürgünler," 554, which deals with the two Jewish *sürgün* in Manisa in 1739. See Moshe Fresco, *Yadav shel Moshe* (Salonica, 5572 [1812]), *Hoshen Mishpat*, no. 30 ("Question. The king made Reuben a *sürgün* to Eretz Israel, may it be speedily rebuilt, because of his guilt. What is he to do with regard to settling his debt to the city and the tax for three years to come, as is customary?"). Examples of false accusations leading to exile, and of threats to bring them against the rich so as to prevent them from retiring from the community, can be found in the community of Bursa in the first half of the sixteenth century. Broad strata of the congregation made use of the Ottoman "system" in order to compel the rich to support the community according to the stipulations of the "system." See R. Eliyah Halevi, *Responsa Zekan Aharon* (Constantinople, 5494 [1734]), no. 180; R. Tam Ibn Yahya, "Responsa Oholei Tam," in *Tummat Yesharim* (Venice, 5382 [1622]), nos. 140, 186 ("some people threatened to testify before the [Muslim] court how they cause the city a loss, so they would exile them to Rhodes or to some other place"); R. Yaakov Berav, *Responsa* (Venice, 5423 [1663]), no. 3.

    5 An example of that kind of punishment applied to a Muslim courtier at the royal court appears in the Hebrew sources. For example, see Yehoshua Ben Ban Benesht, *Shaar Yehoshua* (Husiyatin, 5664 [1904]), no. 27 (5401-1641), [reprint, Yehoshua Ben Ban Benesht, *Responsa Shaar Yehoshua, Hoshen Mishpat*, vol. 1 (Jerusalem, 5742 [1982]), no. 27], where affairs of the Jewish agents of a Muslim official in Istanbul and Egypt are discussed.

    Jewish courtiers serving in central positions sometimes "earned" similar fates. See for example, the fate of R. Moshe Ben Ban Benesht in F. Braudel, *The Mediterranean and the Mediterranean World in the Age of Philip II*, vol. 2 (New York and London, 1973), 1143-85; C. M. Kortepeter, *Ottoman Imperialism during the Reformation: Europe and the Caucasus* (New York and London, 1972), 214-16; M. Benayahu, "R. Moshe Ben Ban Benesht and a Poem about his Exile to Rhodes by R. Yehuda Zarko" (in Hebrew), *Sefunot* 12 (1978): 123-43.

    On the other hand, leaders of the Jewish community also made use of the *sürgün* system in order to cause harm to persons of status with the community. For example, in the sixteenth century, David Fasi was exiled to Rhodes after his quarrel with Don Yoseph Nasi. See R. Eliyah Ibn-Hayyim, *Responsa Mayim Amukim*, pt. 2 (Venice, 1647 [5407]), no. 54; C. Roth, *The House of Nasi, the Duke of Naxos* (Philadelphia, 1948), 204-12. For a later example from the nineteenth century, see R. Hayyim Falaji, *Tikvat Hayyim* (Izmir, 1873 [5633]), *Hoshen Mishpat*, no. 91, p. 126a (the *sürgün* came as punishment for insulting rabbis).

For other examples in which, apparently, influential persons in Istanbul, also affiliated with the Jewish establishment, arranged for people either hated or violent, with strong connections with local authorities, to be punished by exile as *sürgün* in order to relieve the communities of their yoke, see M. A. Epstein, *The Ottoman Jewish Communities and their Role in the Fifteenth and Sixteenth Centuries* (Freiburg, 1980), 73-74, 99 (Baruh of Salonica is exiled to Cyprus), and see below, note 170.

  6 See notes 4-5 above.

  7 For the Ottoman colonization policy see Ö. L. Barkan's articles "Osmanlı İmparatorluğunda bir İskân ve Kolonizasyon metodu olarak sürgünler," *İktisat Fakültesi Mecmuası* 11 (1950): 524-61; 13 (1953): 56-79, and 15 (1955): 202-37; idem, "Les déportations dans l'Empire ottoman," *Revue de la Faculté des Sciences Economiques de l'Université d'Istanbul* 11 (1949-50): 67-131; idem, "Osmanlı İmparatorluğunda bir İskân ve Kolonizasyon Metodu Olarak Vakıflar ve Temihler," *Vakıflar Dergisi* 2 (1942): 279-386; H. İnalcık, "Ottoman Methods of Conquest," *Studia Islamica* 2 (1954): 103-29 [reprint, *The Ottoman Empire: Conquest, Organization and Economy*. Collected Studies (London: Variorum Reprints, 1978), no. 1]; idem, "The Policy of Mehmed II toward the Greek Population of Istanbul and the Byzantine Buildings of the City," *Dumbarton Oaks Papers* 23 (1979): 233ff.

  For the expression of this policy under Bayezid II, see I. Beldiceanu-Steinherr, "Déportation et pêche à Kilia entre 1484 et 1508," *Bulletin of the School of Oriental and African Studies (BSOAS)* 38, no. 1 (1975): 43-50; N. Beldiceanu, "La conquête des cités marchandes de Kilia et de Cetatea-Alba par Bayezid II," *Südost Forschungen* 23 (1964): 72-83; idem, "La Moldavie ottomane à la fin du XVe siècle et au début du XVIe siècle," *Revue des Etudes Islamiques* 37, no. 2 (1969): 243-48.

  For the effects of the *sürgün* policy upon the cities, see N. Beldiceanu, *Recherche sur la ville ottomane au XVe siècle* (Paris, 1973), 36-44; H. W. Lowry, "'From Lesser Wars to the Mightiest War': The Ottoman Conquest and Transformation of Byzance Urban Centers in the Fifteenth Century," in *Continuity and Change in Late Byzantine and Early Ottoman Society*, eds. A. Bryer and H. Lowry (Birmingham and Washington, 1986), 323-38.

  8 For the policy of Islamization, see S. Vryonis, *The Decline of Medieval Hellenism in Asia Minor and the Process of Islamization from the Eleventh through the Fifteenth Century* (Los Angeles and London, 1971); idem, "Religious Changes and Patterns in the Balkans, 14th-16th Centuries," in *Aspects of the Balkans*, eds. H. Birnbaum and S. Vryonis (The Hague and Paris, 1972), 164ff.; D. Angelov, "Certains aspects de la conquête des peuples balkaniques par les Turcs," *Byzantinoslavica* 17 (1956): 261-74.

9 See Vryonis, *The Process of Islamization*, 49, 55, 169ff., 183-84; Barkan, "Les déportations dans l'Empire ottoman," 86ff.; *Recherche sur la ville ottomane au XVe siècle*, 36ff; F. Thiriet, "Venise et l'occupation de Ténédos au XIVe siècle," *Mélanges de l'Ecole Française de Rome* 65 (1953): 219-45 [Reprint, *Etudes sur la Romanie gréco-vénitienne (Xe-XVe siècles)* (London, 1977), no. 2, 219-27]; idem, "A propos de personnes 'déplacées' au XIVe siècle. Le transfert des Ténédiotes en Romanie vénitienne (1381-1385)," *Travaux et Mémoires* 8 (1981): 521-29; idem, "Recherches sur le nombre des 'Latins' immigrés en Romanie gréco-vénitienne aux XIIIe-XIVe siècles," in *Mélanges Ivan Dujčev* (Paris, 1979), 421-39, esp. 427; idem, ed., "Mouvements de population et problèmes de colonisation en Romanie gréco-latine du Xe au XIIIe siècles," *Byzantinische Forschungen* 7 (1979).

10 I am referring, for example, to the appointment and coercion of people into occupations vital to the authorities in Istanbul—for instance, the appointing of meat suppliers (*kasap*) or butchers who were defined as *sürgün* and, consequently, the rules and legal status of *sürgün* applied to them. Jews, too, were included among these at various times and in various areas, but this is not the place to deal with this topic. See, for example, S. Faroqhi, *Towns and Townsmen of Ottoman Anatolia* (Cambridge, 1984), 231-32, 380.

Other activities performed under compulsion which caused large sectors of the population to be transferred to new regions for prolonged periods, involved the construction of walls, mosques or ships. Such tasks, however, were not included within the formal framework of *sürgün*, and do not concern us here, though they are in some ways similar to *sürgün*. For a description of the vast construction projects of a number of the mosques and their surrounding complexes in Istanbul, see Ö. L. Barkan, "Fatih Câmi ve İmareti Tesislerinin 1489-1490 Yıllarına Ait Muhasebe Bilânçoları," *İktisat Fakültesi Mecmuası* 23, nos. 1-2 (1962-63): 297-341; idem, "Süleymaniye Câmi ve İmareti Tesislerine Âit Yıllık bir Muhasabe Bilânçosu 993/994 (1585-1586)," *Vakıflar Dergisi* 9 (1971): 109-61; idem, "L'organisation du travail dans le chantier d'une grande mosquée à Istanbul au XVe siècle," *Annales* 17 (1962): 1093-1106.

11 For the resettlement of the city, see H. İnalcık, "Istanbul," *Encyclopedia of Islam²*, vol. 4 (1973), 224-48; idem, "The Policy of Mehmed II," 213-49; Ö. L. Barkan, "Quelques remarques sur la constitution sociale et démographique des villes balkaniques au cours des XVe et XVIe siècles," in *Istanbul à la jonction des cultures balkaniques, méditerranéennes, slaves et orientales au XVIe-XIXe siècles* (Istanbul, 1977), 279-81, 284-88; Lowry, "The Ottoman Conquest," 323-38; T. Gökbilgin and M. C. Şehâbeddin Tekindağ, "Istanbul," *İslâm Ansiklopedisi*, vol. 5, no. 2 (1950): 1180-1214,

esp. 1205-1207; R. Mantran, *Istanbul dans la seconde moitié du XVIIe siècle* (Paris, 1962), 43ff.

12 See notes 7, 11.

13 On Venice in general and the Jews in particular, see, for example, D. Jacoby, "Jews under Venetian Protection in Constantinople in the Fourteenth and Fifteenth Centuries" (in Hebrew), *Zion* 27 (1962): 30-34. See also idem, "Les quartiers juifs de Constantinople à l'epoque byzantine," *Byzantion* 37 (1967): 214, 216-21 [reprint, idem, *Société et démographie à Byzance et en Romanie Latine* (London, 1975), no. 2]; idem, "Les Vénitiens naturalisés dans l'empire byzantine," in *Travaux et Mémoires du Centre de Recherche d'Histoire et Civilisation Byzantines*, vol. 8 (Paris, 1981), 230.

14 For all of these see, Ö. L. Barkan, "Osmanlı İmparatorluğunda bir İskân ve Kolonizasyon metodu olarak sürgünler," *İktisat Fakültesi Mecmuası* 11 (1950): 524-61; 13 (1953): 56-79; and 15 (1955): 202-37; idem, "Les déportations dans l'Empire ottoman"; İnalcık, "Istanbul," 234-35, 239; Beldiceanu-Steinherr, "Déportation et pêche à Kilia entre 1484 et 1508," 43ff; Beldiceanu, *Recherche sur la ville ottomane au XVe siècle*, 37, 42-43.

15 Eliyah Kapsali, *Seder Eliahu Zuta*, eds. A. Shmuelevitz, M. Benayahu, S. Simonsohn, parts 1-2 (Jerusalem, 1976-77).

16 For all these see J. Hacker, " 'The Chief Rabbinate' in the Ottoman Empire in the Fifteenth and Sixteenth Centuries" (in Hebrew), *Zion* 49 (1984): 226-36, 256-59.

17 Kapsali, *Seder Eliahu Zuta*, 81.

18 Kapsali makes use of the phrase, "And he had an announcement made throughout his kingdom, as well as in writing, saying . . . " to denote the royal edict he is quoting. See, for example, Kapsali, *Seder Eliahu Zuta*, 64 (Edict of Constantinus), 218 (Edict of Bayezid II), 222 (Edict of the King of Portugal), 239 (Edict of Bayezid II), 240 (The "epistle" of the King of Spain). For the attitude toward Cyrus in Jewish literature, see E. E. Urbach, "Cyrus and his Declaration in Talmudic Sources" (in Hebrew), *Molad* 19 (1961): 368-74. B. Lewis, *History Remembered, Recovered, Invented* (New York, 1975), 4ff.

19 By contrast, Kapsali, *Seder Eliahu Zuta*, 98: "And the king reigning over the entire kingdom of Yavan [Greece] liked the Jews, and they were fruitful and multiplied greatly, and dwelt in Constantinople, of which goodness and beauty is endless, and it is also flowing with milk and honey, and such is its fruit." Here the emphasis would seem to be on their multiplying in Istanbul, which is closer to the truth.

20 Kapsali adopted a much more "positive" wording when he began to sum up Mehmet's deeds: "The Jews mention him most favorably for he was a lover of the seed of Abraham. And some of the Gentile kings were led

astray by the wickedness of their hearts . . . and they drove us out of their territory and spoke of us cruelly. But this king, may his soul rest in goodness, not only did he not drive the Jews out before him—he gathered them together from the distant towns and brought them to the capital of the kingdom. And he said to the children of Israel: You shall dwell with me and trade land—as we have written in chapter 16." Kapsali, *Seder Eliahu Zuta*, 131.

From his description of the conquest of Kafa, we can deduce that he was clearly aware of the exiling of the Genovese and the local population to the Empire: "And when he conquered Kafa he brought to Constantinople all the aristocrats who were there, while transferring the people to the cities." Ibid., 114. The editors' notes on pages 81 and 114 also contribute to the obscuring of the fact that what was involved here was enforced exile; it is presented as a matter of voluntary transfer in which, as it were, "they moved to the Ottoman State where their brethren had already been living in a number of places," although this was not the case.

21 See Hacker, "The Jewish Community of Salonica," 69-72; idem, "'The Chief Rabbinate'," 227, has a short review of the approach adopted by nineteenth and twentieth century historians to the question of the Jewish-Ottoman encounter in the fifteenth century, and the influence of the romantic picture sketched by the sixteenth- and seventeenth-century writers with their viewpoint. Included are H. Graetz, S. Dubnow, S. Rozanes, M. Franco, A. Galanté, S. Baron, and H. Z. Hirshberg.

In the meantime, S. W. Baron's *Social and Religious History of the Jews*, vol. 18 (New York, Philadelphia, 1983), has been published. In this volume, Baron mentions the forced exiling and deals with the fate of the Jews in Istanbul at the time of the conquest and after. See pp. 22-23, 31, 51-53, and in the notes, pp. 450-51, 463-64. Although Hacker, "The Jewish Community of Salonica," and idem, "Ottoman Policy," and other studies were available to Baron, he made only marginal and occasional use of the data included in these works.

22 See Hacker, "'The Chief Rabbinate'," and idem, "The Jewish Community of Salonica."

23 See, for example, S. Runciman, *The Fall of Constantinople* (Cambridge, 1965), 148ff., 159, 176; F. Babinger, *Mehmed: The Conqueror and his Time* (Princeton, N.J., 1978), 102ff. (for the exilings, pp. 103-104, 161, 212, 220, 272, 274, 283, 286, 315, 345, 354); H. İnalcık, "Mehmed the Conqueror (1432-1481) and his Time," *Speculum* 35 (1960): 408-16; idem, "Istanbul," 224ff., 238ff.; idem, "The Policy of Mehmed II," 233ff.

The main descriptions of the fall of Constantinople and the reactions of the Christian world to its fall have been collected in A. Pertusi, *La caduta di Constantinopoli*, vol. 1, *Le testimonianze dei contemporanei*, vol. 2, *L'eco nel mondo* (Milano, 1976). Similarly he refers there to a list of sources not included in this broad anthology. The editor, however, took no interest in the question of the resettlement of the city and omitted the central texts relevant to this topic from his collection. See also K. M. Setton, *The Papacy and the Levant (1204-1571)*, vol. 2 (Philadelphia, 1978), 133ff.

24 See note 23, and also Jacoby, "Jews under Venetian Protection," 31-33.

25 N. Jorga, *Notes et extraits pour servir à l'Histoire des Croisades au XVe siècle*, vol. 4 (1915), 67; Pertusi, *La caduta di Constantinopoli*, 1:230, 426. The writer is Samile (Samuel?), a bishop (?) who fled to Wallachia where he wrote a letter on 6 August 1453 to the mayor of Hermannstadt.

26 Doukas (Doucas), *Decline and Fall of Byzantium to the Ottoman Turks*, trans. H. J. Magoulias (Detroit, 1975), ch. 42, 3, p. 241. On p. 243, he discusses the exiling of 4000 people from the Balkans, and on pp. 257-58, the exiling of 2000 families from the Peloponesos.

Confirmation of large-scale resettlement activity in September is also to be found in the letter from the head of the order of knights from Rhodes to Pope Nicholas V. See Pertusi, *La caduta di Constantinopoli*, 1:xc, 2:426.

27 H. İnalcık and R. Murphy, *The History of Mehmed the Conqueror by Tursun Beg* (Minneapolis and Chicago, 1978), 37, 51b-61a; Pertusi, *La caduta di Constantinopoli*, 1:330-31. For Tursun as a historian and his sources, see the aforementioned studies by H. İnalcık.

28 See, for example, the lament of Abraham of Ankara over the fate of Armenian families in Pertusi, *La caduta di Constantinopoli*, 2:410-19, 491-93 (The Expulsion, p. 416); A. K. Sanjian, "Two contemporary Armenian Elegies on the Fall of Constantinople, 1453," *Viator* 1 (1970): 223-61. On this matter, Abraham writes (p. 248):

> He also issued a stern order
> Causing anguish to all who heard it
> To all the cities in Rum
> Which were under his dominion.
> He said to remove men with their families,
> To bring and settle them in this city;
> This brought great grief to the Turkish nation,
> Who are lamenting with bitter tears.
> For they separated fathers from sons,
> They separated daughters from mothers,
> They separated brothers from one another
> They deprived many of their ancestral homes.
> Not only *Tačiks* but also
> Christians they brought here;
> On the twenty-eighth day of October
> They brought four Armenians from Ankara.

29 M. Kritovoulos, *History of Mehmet the Conqueror*, trans. C. T. Riggs (Princeton, N.J., 1954), 93. For the author, see Pertusi, *La caduta di Constantinopoli*, 2:228-51, 461-62.

30 The text can be found in W. Gèrard, *La ruine de Byzance (1200-1453)* (Paris, 1958), 344. For the author, see Babinger, *Mehmed: The Conqueror and his Time*, 45, 283-86.

31 U. Heyd, "The Jewish Communities of Istanbul in the Seventeenth Century," *Oriens* 6 (1953): 299-314. In this article, Heyd printed a list of communities based on the censuses of 1623 and 1691/2, with supplements from other censuses. By contrast, H. Gerber, *The Jews of the Ottoman Empire in the Sixteenth and Seventeenth Centuries: Economy and Society* (in Hebrew) (Jerusalem, 1983), 117-19, reproduced the 1688/9 census in its entirety.

32 Heyd, "The Jewish Communities of Istanbul in the Seventeenth Century," 305-306.

33 H. İnalcık intends to publish and analyze them in detail. See H. İnalcık, "Jews in the Ottoman Economy and Finances, 1450-1550," in *The Islamic World. Essays in Honor of Bernard Lewis* (Princeton, N.J., 1989), 513-14, 527-28; idem, "Istanbul," 224, 238.

34 This refers to the *Vakıfs* of Mehmet II, who channelled the head tax payments made by various population groups to the needs of the *Vakıfs*. In 1540, there were 1,542 Greek households, 777 Armenian households and 1,490 Jewish households. To maintain these religious funds and to finance their activities, he devoted other revenues as well. See Barkan, "Fatih Câmi ve İmareti Tesislerinin 1489-1490 Yıllarına Ait Muhasebe Bilânçoları." See mention of a Jew belonging to the *Vakıf* in the facsimilie in ibid., opp. 304. Note has already been taken of this by Gerber, *Economy and Society*, 27 and n. 68.

For these *Vakıfs* in 1540 and 1545, and the Jews obligated to pay them their taxes, see Ö. L. Barkan and E. H. Ayverdi, *Istanbul Vakıfları tahrîr defteri, 953 (1546) tarihi* (Istanbul, 1970), XIV-XVI; İnalcık, "Istanbul," 238; Epstein, *The Ottoman Jewish Communities*, 178-80. Epstein includes there a list of communities and the number of their members in 1540 and 1545, who paid their taxes to the *Vakıfs* of Mehmet II in Istanbul. Lowry, "The Ottoman Conquest," 325, 334.

For Mehmet II's system of financing the *Vakıfs* and his use of them as a means of development, see Barkan, "Quelques remarques"; İnalcık, "The Policy of Mehmed II."

35 İnalcık, "Istanbul," 238.

36 A. Danon, "Documents Relating to the History of the Karaites in European Turkey," *Jewish Quarterly Review*, n.s. 17 (1927): 168-69. Already referred to by J. Mann, *Texts and Studies*, vol. 2 (Philadelphia, 1935),

296-97, no. 7, and the emendations to the text are his. On page 292 and n. 15, Mann hesitates concerning the contradiction between this paragraph and the version by Eliyah Kapsali, (see above, note 17) and notes: "This point of the real motives of the government still needs clarification."

37 See Z. Ankori, "The House of Bashyatsi and its Regulations" (in Hebrew), in *Aderet Eliahu* (Ramla, 1966), 5-6.

38 See the summary of the matter in Mann, *Texts and Studies*, 292-315, which is generally correct, though a number of details are to be amended. Furthermore, additional information has in the meantime come to light regarding a number of the personages involved in that debate. For R. Isaiah Messini (of Messene), for example, see J. Hacker, "Some Letters about the Expulsion of the Jews from Spain and from Sicily and about the Fate of the Exiles" (in Hebrew), in *Jacob Katz Jubilee Volume* (Jerusalem, 1980), 71-73.

39 M. Frankl, "Karaische Studien," *MGWJ* 31 (1882): 270-71. Referred to in Mann, *Texts and Studies*, 299, n. 11.

40 Unlike Ankori, "The House of Bashyatsi and its Regulations," 9, who views him as opposing the extent of the rabbinic influence only. Mann argues that the extent of the reform in "Ner Shabbat" is a result of their move to Istanbul. See Mann, *Texts and Studies*, 298-99.

41 See below, note 178, for a parallel feature in the Romaniot communities.

42 See, for example, Danon, "Documents Relating to the History of the Karaites in European Turkey," nos. 25, 26, 29, 44, 48, 61, 80, etc.; Heyd, "The Jewish Communities of Istanbul in the Seventeenth Century," 301; Epstein, *The Ottoman Jewish Communities*, 180, 187.

43 His work was described by M. Steinschneider, *Hebräische Bibliographie* 17 (1877): 110-11; 19 (1879): 30-32. And following him, others such as Zvi Hirsch Yaffe in the addenda to the Hebrew edition of Graetz, Part 4, Warsaw, 1899. I intend to deal with him and his work once again in another framework. Mention and use of him to describe the Spanish exile of 1492 was brought up by H. H. Ben-Sasson, "The Generation of Spanish Emigrés Speak of Themselves" (in Hebrew), *Zion* 26 (1961): 28 and n. 23. He does not belong to this generation and his description refers to the Jewish Diaspora in Istanbul. See now I. Ta-Shema, "R. Joseph Caro Facing Ashkenaz and Sepharad—On the Propagation of the *Zohar*" (in Hebrew), *Tarbiz* 59 (1990): 167.

44 A manuscript of the British Library, 379 in the Margoliouth Catalogue, part 2, 42-43. Film No. 5963 in the Institute of Microfilms of Hebrew Manuscripts, at the National and University Library, Jerusalem (hereafter cited as IMHM, NUL).

45 Ibid., leaf 2b: 210 or 215 (1450 or 1455).

46 Ibid., leaf 346a: 215 or 220 (1455 or 1460). Many homilies were written so as to be delivered publicly, though only some of them were actually delivered. The writer continued amending his work for many years; he corrected it, completed it and added addenda. The work throws light on several of the stages of the writer's life and on his movements from place to place. Of his birthplace he wrote (leaf 75b): "I shall tell of my people and my birthplace to the wise. The name of my town is Veroia, in the land of the Turks. . . . " For his education and his studies, see ibid., leaf 99b-100a. Veroia is the Ottoman Karaferia, and for it, see *Encyclopedia of Islam*, vol. 4 (1927), 731.

47 Film no. 5963, IMHM, NUL, leaf 2b.

48 Ibid., leaf 236b and 187a.

49 Ibid., leaf 98b. There, he relates: "And when I arrived here, in the city of Constantinople, I asked for the children of my mother, my brethren . . . and I came from Zeitun, part of the land of Turkey."

50 Ibid., leaves 344b-345a.

51 Ibid., leaf 30b, etc.

52 Ibid., leaves 2b, 99b, etc.

53 Ibid., leaf 289b.

54 He relates that in 1455 or 1460, when beginning to put his work in writing, in Negroponte: "I lived amongst them a little time." See ibid., leaf 2b.

55 Ibid., leaf 245b-246a.

56 Ibid., leaves 96b-97a.

57 The Song of Songs 3.6.

58 According to Leviticus 25.34.

59 The end of a line, and the word was written below in its entirety.

60 According to Joel 1.2: "Was there such a thing in your days."

61 According to Isaiah 55.3. To this point, this has been a kind of opening to the description.

62 *Kittim*—"*kittoth*", groups of people. See Tosephta Moed, *Tractate Pesahim*, ed. S. Lieberman (New York, 1962), chapter 4, section 10; chapter 8, section 7, etc.; *Shir Ha-Shirim Rabba*, pericopee 8, sec. "*Im homa ani*" (If I am a wall): " . . . in that I am about to set up many *kittim* (groups) of righteous men like me"; *Bereshit Rabba*, pericopee 8, sec. 5: "At the hour that the Holy One, Blessed be He, set about creating the first man, the angels of service formed *kittim* (groups)."

Kittim maroth—I have found no usage of this phrase, which is reminiscent of poetic usage, like "*kittei shemayya*" *et sim.*; the speaker seems to have broken *ketimroth* (like columns) into *kittim*, *maroth*, doubling the "m".

His use of the term *midbar* (desert) as if it were related to *dibbur* (speech) was common among the Spanish emigrés at a later date, and cf. a similar usage found in the writings of the poet Israel Najara. See Y. Yahalom, "R. Israel Najara and the Revival of Hebrew Poetry in the East after the Spanish Expulsion" (in Hebrew), *Peamim* 13 (1982): 107 and n. 45; see also Appendix 2 of Hebrew version of this article, *Zion* 55 (1990): 79-82, in the letter of Yosef Mataron of Safed.

Avkath Rokhel - dust rising from the dirt, see Shir Ha-Shirim Rabba, 3, sec. *"mi zoth olah min ha-midbar."*

63   Ibid., leaf 46b, another homily on *mekuttereth*: "Another explanation: *mekuttereth mor*—this is Ishmael who was bitter (*mar*) in his actions like this myrrh (*mor*) which has a bitter taste, *ulevonah*—this is Eliezer, Abraham's servant, and of these two Abraham the Patriarch said: sit yourselves down here with the ass. . . . "

64   A silver coin—*akçe*.

65   *Gematria*—the numerical equivalent of the letters. This is so if we read "*levonah*" as spelled *Ibnah*, for otherwise the numbers do not match.

66   See İnalcık, "Istanbul," 238 (42 families from Lamia); Heyd, "The Jewish Communities of Istanbul," 301 (Veroia); Epstein, *The Ottoman Jewish Communities*, 179 (Lamia, Veroia).

67   See notes 50, 74 and 97.

68   His attitude towards "the homeland" is very interesting, as he reveals something of the attitude of late Byzantine Jewry to their dwelling places. See, for example, film no. 5963, IMHM, NUL, leaf 172a: "and this was certainly a great trial for, by nature, it is difficult for a person to leave a country to which he has grown accustomed and where he has lived for some time, even if it is not the land of his birth. This is far more so if it is the land where he was born, for his temperament is attuned to the atmosphere of the country, and when he leaves it he is weakened. This is so even though he may have no family there; how much more so when his forefathers live there - then it is extremely hard for him to leave them. . . . " And see also what he says about the sense of insult felt by a scholar dying in exile, away from his home, in his stereotyped homily on the death of a scholar (a sermon he gave in the end about Rabbi S. Bueno in Istanbul): "just as happened to this respected man, who was our teacher and rabbi, and died abroad, not having succeeded in returning home; despite the fact that he gathered a praiseworthy and respected community, when the righteous man died he still felt hurt because he could not return home, but rather died in exile," ibid., leaf 183a. This statement reflects a metamorphosis from the question of "dying outside of Eretz-Israel" to that of "dying outside of one's birthplace." That is, he died in Istanbul, rather than among his fellow congregants—this being his "outside of Eretz-Israel." Elsewhere, when discussing "the reason a person begets righteous sons who sanctify the name of Heaven," he refers to rabbinic sayings concerning one's obligation

to sanctify oneself during sexual intercourse, and adds: "This is even stronger if the woman is worthy of him, stemming from the proper root, *of his language and his land*...." Ibid., leaf 224b.

This may well be a case of environmental influence, for the devotion of the early Greeks and Romans to "the homeland" is well known. For the development of the concept in their culture, see M. Bonjour, "Terre Natale. Etudes sur une composante affective du patriotisme romain" (Thèse, Université de Lille III, 1976). For the conception of climate, geography, homeland and matching the population to the land in Jewish medieval thought, see A. Altmann, "R. Judah Ha-Levi's Conception of Climates" (in Hebrew), *Melila* 1 (1944): 1-17; Y. Heineman, "The Relationships between a People and its Land in Hellenistic Jewish Literature" (in Hebrew), *Zion* 13-14 (1948-49): 1-9; A. Melamed, "The Land of Israel and Climatology in Jewish Thought" (in Hebrew), in *The Land of Israel in Medieval Jewish Thought*, M. Hallamish and A. Ravitzky, eds. (Jerusalem, 1991), 52-78.

69 It is interesting to note that in this context nothing was said about the separation of families. On the other hand, he does hint about this elsewhere (see, for example, note 68). Perhaps this stems from the fact that in these Balkan communities all the members of the community were exiled to Istanbul, no Jews remaining behind. The subject requires further study.

70 For the 1458 march of Mehmet II and his army from the region of Negroponte, see Babinger, *Mehmed: The Conqueror and his Time*, 161. Cf. there pp. 283-286 on the march of Mehmet II's army and the exiles after the conquest of the island.

71 Jacoby, "Jews under Venetian Protection," 31-33.

72 On the other hand, D. Jacoby's description of the conditions in Istanbul, based on the accepted views of the relations of the Jews and the Ottomans and the "Chief Rabbinate" of the city cannot be accepted. See Jacoby, "Jews under Venetian Protection," 32; and Hacker, "The Chief Rabbinate in the Ottoman Empire," 225-63.

73 See Hacker, "The Jewish Community of Salonica," 96-97 and nn. 134-137. It is not clear whether this community of emigrés from Negroponte, which settled in the city *voluntarily*, was included officially among the Negroponte emigrés exiled to the city after its conquest who apparently made up the *sürgün* community. This question requires further study. For the people of Negroponte being included in the *sürgün*, see also a document from 1585-86 in Gerber, *Economy and Society*, 90.

74 Film no. 5963, IMHM, NUL, leaf 344b, and see note 97. Not uninteresting is the fact that one of the Latins taken captive at Negroponte when it was conquered in 1470, Angiolello, left behind a detailed description including parallel items regarding both the exiling and the general situation in the Empire. See notes 30 and 70 above.

75 The content of Hebrew ms. Vatican 105 (film no. 217 in IMHM, NUL) has been described a number of times by several leading scholars of Judaism ever since Assemani's faulty list. It was first considered at length by M. Steinschneider in his article on the Jews of Candia, which was printed in installments in the journal *Mosé*, vols. 2-6 (1879-1883), according to information he had received from Abraham Berliner and others. This manuscript was recently described in great detail by M. D. Cassuto in his catalogue of Hebrew manuscripts in the Vatican Library, Vatican City, 1956. N. Ben-Menahem, *From the Jewish Archives in the Vatican* (in Hebrew) (Jerusalem, 1954), 63-68, ignores the description of most of the manuscript. Several sections of the manuscript, letters and documents, were printed by A. H. Freimann, "Emissaries and Immigrants" (in Hebrew), *Zion* 1 (1936): 194-207. See also the other extracts he cites in his introduction, pp. 185-93; idem, "A Document Relating to Captive Redemption in Southern France in the Fifteenth Century" (in Hebrew), *Kovetz al Yad*, n.s. 6 (16), part 1 (1966): 247-57. For Kabbalistic and philosophical texts in this manuscript, see E. Gottlieb, "The Reincarnation Debate in Candia in the Fifteenth Century" (in Hebrew), *Sefunot* 11 (1971-1978): 45-66 [Reprint, *Studies in Kabbalistic Literature* (Tel Aviv, 1976), 370-96, and see note 3, ibid.]; A. Ravitzky, *The Passover Sermon of R. Hisdai Crescas and Studies in his Philosophical Doctrine* (in Hebrew) (Jerusalem, 1989), 21-2 (and the literature referred to there), 128ff.; J. Hacker, "The Immigration of the Jews of Spain to Eretz-Israel and their Attitude towards It, from 1391 to 1492" (in Hebrew), *Shalem* 1 (1974): 137-47.

76 For his birthdate see Hebrew ms. Cambridge 35 (Catalogue Schiller-Sineshi, 61), leaf 122a. For him, see Z. Malachi, *Kiryat-Sefer* 41 (1966): 392-93; M. Beit-Aryeh, *Kiryat-Sefer* 42 (1967): 274.

77 The last dates mentioned in the manuscript are 1474, 1475, 1476. See ms. Vatican 105, leaves 189a, 193a. However, the ms. does include other late material, such as a document relating to the Yoseph Kolon-R. Moshe Kapsali dispute, or documents connected with emissaries from Eretz-Israel.

The letter collection begins on leaf 149 of the manuscript—although there are a number of letters by and to Michael Balbo before this leaf as well—after copying the scholarly exchange between him and other contemporary scholars (leaves 116b-149). It continues until approximately leaf 188b. From 189a onward, his sermons were copied down (occasionally, writings of R. Moshe Ashkenazi "twenty-four" are incorporated), as well as his argument with R. Moshe Cohen Ashkenazi about reincarnation.

78 These letters and other literary fragments have not been described properly in the various listings devoted to this manuscript (see note 75). Some were described defectively, while some texts—including the most important of them—were completely ignored in descriptions of the

manuscript. Some of them were printed in Appendix B of my doctoral dissertation. See Hacker, "The Jewish Community of Salonica," 13-25, and I shall yet discuss them, together with other texts, in my study of the Jewish reactions to the fall of Constantinople.

79 Ms. Vatican 105, leaf 167a-b.

The letter has a long and literary opening (lines 1-27), full of phrases taken from the Book of Daniel, the Book of Yetzira and the Zohar, which describes the fate of the Jewish people and their general situation; the attitude of God toward the Jews; the feelings of the people; and the status of Israel in contrast to that of the Muslims and the Christians. In the second part of the opening—from the end of line 20 to line 27— the author goes on from this general description to that of a particular situation: the fate of the Jews in light of the Ottoman expansions. This opening provides the background for its continuation, a request for assistance for "this downtrodden man" (line 27), of good family and learned, who has been harmed by all of these and is in need of aid. Our interest in this letter is more in the opening section, and less in the man and his fate.

80 See ibid., leaf 167b: "and this man is known to be of the most important of the generation. His family was most hospitable, and when the honored R. Ezra of Rhodes saw him, while visiting here in *the community of the town of Korfu*, he became excited" (emphasis mine). R. Ezra of Rhodes was also mentioned in the manuscript in a letter written to him by Michael Balbo. See leaf 165a. He was on a mission to Venice, and seems to have been one of the leaders of the Rhodes community.

81 "Sons of the lady ... children of the maidservant"— contrasting phrases appearing often in medieval Jewish poetry, referring to the Jews as opposed to the Muslims, and especially in the poetry of Spanish Jewry. See N. Aloni, "Sarah and Hagar in the Poetry of Spain" (in Hebrew), in *Ben-Zion Luria Jubilee Volume* (Jerusalem, 1980), 179-84; idem, "Zion and Jerusalem in the Poetry of Spain" (in Hebrew), in *The Heritage of the Jews of Spain and the East*, ed. Y. Ben-Ami (Jerusalem, 1982), 244-45. See also, E. Fleischer, *The Poems of the Anonymous* (in Hebrew) (Jerusalem, 1974), no. 64.

82 This would seem to raise a difficulty. If "the sons of the lady" are the Jews, why does he distinguish between "us", "the sons of the lady" and "the sons of the maidservant" in the following sentence? It is similarly unclear who the cause was; that is, who "brought them down" to the chasm, in the *singular,* when the Muslims are described in the *plural* in the previous sentence. Is it God, who is mentioned further on ("the Almighty")? It is, of course, possible to assume that the phrase "sons of the lady" hints at the Christians and their defeat, in which case he is expressing a wish to heaven, and everything falls into place. In such a case, this wording must be considered deliberately ambiguous, which is not surprising with a letter

leaving Korfu for Crete, two islands under Christian rule. An overt expression of happiness at the fall of the Christians might have endangered both the community of Korfu and of Crete, had the letter fallen into undesirable hands. It is known that the Jews (including communities of the colonies of Genoa and Venice) were later accused of assisting the Ottomans in their conquests, of being a fifth column. (See note 101 for an opposing view.) Yet, I have never encountered such a use of the phrase "sons of the lady" in Jewish sources. The subject requires additional study.

83 Genesis 21.20; Ishmael.

84 For the term "daughter of Edom" (Lamentations 4.21) as applied to Constantinople, see, for example, Hacker, "The Immigration of the Jews of Spain to Eretz-Israel," 120, 124-25, 147 and nn. 53, 65; and see Kapsali, *Seder Eliahu Zuta*, 80.

85 According to Exodus 21.13: "And one who did lie in wait, but God caused it to come about."

86 Isaiah 51.19-20: "These two have befallen you; who shall lament you? Desolation and ruin, famine and war; how shall I console you? Your sons have been wasted, they lie at the head of all the streets. . . . "

87 Ibid., 13.

88 Deuteronomy 32.36.

89 The use of expressions suitable for referring to God when speaking of the supreme ruler, of flesh and blood, is to be found metaphorically in Jewish sources of the period. See, for example, the way Eliyah Kapsali writes in *Seder Eliahu Zuta*, 78. There, Mehmet II is "the king of kings . . . who can tell him what to do" (cf. Daniel 4.32).

90 See V. L. Ménage, "Devshirme," *Encyclopedia of Islam*[2], vol. 2 (1965), 210-13; idem, "Some Notes on the Devshirme," *BSOAS* 29 (1966): 64-78; B. Papoulia, *Ursprung und Wesen der "Knabenlese" im Osmanischen Reich* (Munich, 1963); see also the review of this work by S. Vryonis in *Balkan Studies* 5 (1964): 145-53; Cl. Cahen, "Note sur l'esclavage musulman et la devshirme ottomane, à propos de travaux récents," *JESHO* 13 (1970): 211-18.

91 The known example is that of the Genovese in Constantinople, about whom much has been written. See, for example, K. M. Setton, *The Papacy and the Levant (1204-1571)*, 2:135-36, and the literature referred to there. And see İnalcık, "The Policy of Mehmed II," 234-35.

92 See Papoulia, *Ursprung und Wesen der "Knabenlese" im Osmanischen Reich*, the index; N. Beldiceanu, "Un acte sur le statut de la communauté juive de Trikala," *Revue des Etudes Islamiques* 40 (1972): 133, n. 5, 137-38. From the document published by Beldiceanu, it is evident that in Trikala, in July 1497, the children of the Jews were not drafted into the *devşirme* under normal conditions.

93 Whether his captors are Christian or Muslim is unclear. There exist letters from that period relating to the fate of the Christians and their goods who have left Istanbul and fallen into the hands of Christians. See, for example, F. Thiriet, *Délibérations des Assemblées vénitiennes concernant la Romanie*, vol. 2 (1364-1463) (Paris and The Hague, 1971), no. 1494 (14 August 1454). And cf. idem, *Régestes des délibérations du Sénat de Venise concernant la Romanie*, vol. 3 (Paris and The Hague, 1961), no. 2959 (13 March 1454), telling of the robbing of a Salonican trader and of the way debts are collected from the property of Venetians in Salonica.

For Christian appeals to release their brethren who had been captured during the conquest of Constantinople, see J. Darrouzès, "Lettres de 1453," *Revue des Etudes Byzantines* 22 (1964): 72-124 (29 July -13 December 1453).

94 Ms. Vatican 105, leaf 161a-b. Reprinted in Hacker, "The Jewish Community of Salonica," Appendix B, 24-25.

95 See his opinion in his introduction to Abraham Ibn Ezra's book, *Yessod Morah*, ms. Vatican 105, leaf 8b: "When I was in captivity in a foreign land, in the town of Adrianople." In his commentary on the Torah, the writing of which was completed in 1460, he writes: "A scholar asked me when I had been in Adrianople for about ten years . . . "; see H. Graetz, *The History of Israel* (in Hebrew), ed. Shmuel Pinchas Rabinowitz, part 4 (Warsaw, 1899), 487-88.

The captives taken prisoner during the conquest of Constantinople are known to have been brought to Edirne. See, for example, İnalcık, "The Policy of Mehmed II," 236-38; idem, "Istanbul," 295. And perhaps that is where Comtiano was kept captive?

Jean-Christophe Attias, "Savoir et pouvoir à Constantinople. Mordekhai Comtino, exegete-enseignant (XVe siècle)" (Thèse de Doctorat, Université de Paris VIII Vincennes à Saint-Denis, Paris, 1989), 31-74.

96 Ms. Vatican 105, leaves 147b, 164a.

97 Film no. 5963, IMHM, NUL, leaf 344b, and see note 74 above.

98 98.For the use of "Romi" for Istanbul, see above, note 97: "Reish-Romans," referring to the "wicked daughter of Rome." For examples of the use of "Rome" for Istanbul, see Hacker, "'The Chief Rabbinate'," 246, n. 93.

99 See above, note 97. According to the Babylonian Talmud, *Tractate Sukkah* 29a. And see *Rashi* to Exodus 12.12 and the Midrashic explanation of this verse. The version here is very similar to that of Exodus Rabba 21.5: "That the Holy One, blessed be He, does not cause a nation to collapse until He causes their lord to collapse first." And see Kapsali, *Seder Eliahu Zuta*, 131. For the dependence of the Gentiles upon constellations and angels, see Hacker, "The Immigration of the Jews of Spain," 144, n. 62 and the literature there.

100 Manuscript of the British Library, film no. 5963, IMHM, NUL, leaf 322b. The sermon is about Ecclesiastes 11.2. See note 44 above.

101 Perhaps in this light one can understand what we are told about the behavior of the Jews in Crete in 1471. According to the tale, they set out to fight together with the Venetians against the Ottomans; see Kapsali, *Seder Eliahu Zuta*, 102. And for their deeds in Kafa in 1481, see Beldiceanu, "La conquête des cités," 72, n. 217.

102 Kapsali, *Seder Eliahu Zuta*, 64-70, 75-80.

103 Ibid., 80; and see note 84 above.

104 Ms. Vatican 105, leaf 162a; Hacker, "The Jewish Community of Salonica," Appendix B., 16. It was first published by S. B. Bowman, following Steinschneider's note, in "The Jews in Byzantium, 1261-1453" (Ph.D. dissertation, Ohio State University, 1974), 428-29. This work was published in an expanded format as *The Jews of Byzantium, 1204-1453* (Alabama, 1985). The final chapter deals with the events of 1453 and their consequences (pp. 177-95, 314ff., 341-43). There he made use of a small part of the material discussed here; partly according to what was known to him in his doctoral thesis and partly according to what he heard in the seminar which I ran in Jerusalem in 1979-80, in which he took part. See J. Hacker, *Jewish Society in the Ottoman Empire [1453-1660]* (in Hebrew) (Jerusalem, 1980), 85-122. Unfortunately, he did not see fit to state this information; furthermore, he only mentioned my doctoral thesis, which he received in 1980 for study purposes, in the Addenda, on p. 374, among other material which he had encountered only after completing the manuscript of his book in 1984.

105 Many laments have been written of the fall of Constantinople to men of different nations and cultures. See Pertusi, *La caduta di Constantinopoli*, 2:293ff., 509ff. To the variegated literature on the subject there must now be added S. Stoicova, "La chanson de la chute de Constantinople dans le folklore bulgare," *Balkan Studies* 25, no. 2 (1984): 475-83. See also note 28 above.

106 Kapsali, *Seder Eliahu Zuta*, 79, 80.

107 Ibid., 10.

108 Ibid., 42, 51, 53, 73, and many more.

109 See, for example, ibid., 131, 240, 272. He adopts the false opinion common among many sixteenth-century Christians that the Jews were the ones who taught the Ottomans how to make use of cannons and heavy shells.

110 And see below, and also, Hacker, "The Jewish Community of Salonica," 65ff., 156-58; idem, "Ottoman Policy," 123. I intend to reconsider this topic in detail elsewhere.

111 See Kapsali, *Seder Eliahu Zuta*, 81, and see above, note 17.

112 Ibid., 131.

113 Ibid., 141-42. And cf. what he says on p. 218: "And Sultan Bayezid, king of Turkey, heard of all the evil perpetrated by the king of

Spain against the Jews, and that the latter seek a place to rest—and he took pity on them, and sent men before him, and proclaimed aloud and in writing throughout his kingdom that no governor of his cities had permission to repulse the Jews and to drive them away; on the contrary, everyone was to receive them cordially ... and thousands and tens of thousands of Jewish exiles came to Turkey, and the land became full of them."

114 As has been shown in detail in Hacker, "The Jewish Community of Salonica," 127-58, there were considerable differences in the policy followed by these two towards the Jews, just as there were similarities as well.

115 Kapsali, *Seder Eliahu Zuta*, 11.

116 Ibid., 239-49.

117 This has already been noted in C. Berlin, "A Sixteenth-Century Chronicle of the Ottoman Empire: The *Seder Eliahu Zuta* of Elijah Qapsali and its Message," in *Studies in Jewish Bibliography ... in Honor of E. E. Kiev* (New York, 1971), 21-44.

118 Eliyah Kapsali's unwillingness or inability to present a variegated picture of rulers whose attitudes towards the Jews were complex is a problem of its own, with weighty consequences for his stature as a historian and for the way he worked, but this is hardly the place to expand on this topic (see note 110).

119 As we have already seen, he was aware of events as they occurred, yet his evaluation of the facts was different and the way he viewed the Sultans as emissaries of God to save Israel is what determined his one-sided standpoint. It is thus interesting that in the book's table of contents (Kapsali, *Seder Eliahu Zuta*, 13), in the manuscript, chapter 16 (which was one of the texts analyzed above) is said: "to tell how the king *imprisoned* the Jews in Constantinople and what happened to him with them" (emphasis mine). Did the writer suffer a slip of the pen, or, perhaps, wasn't it he who penned this table of contents, the person who did so being the one who was aware of the facts and called the spade a spade? We are likewise unable to say that he was unaware of the Romaniot situation in the fifteenth century, for he himself admits he had good sources which enabled him to be familiar with Romaniot history in fifteenth-century Istanbul. See Hacker, "'The Chief Rabbinate,'" 228-32. Cf. also below, notes 127-131, his method in describing the conquest of Egypt. This demonstrates that his motive was not only the confrontation between Christains and Ottomans, for he adopts a stance similar to his anti-Christian views against the Mameluks as well. The merit of the Ottomans was so great in his eyes—because of their attitude towards the Jews of the Iberian Peninsula—that all their actions against the Muslim-Mameluks were justified as well, and he describes the attitude of the Mameluks towards the Jews as a hostile one.

120 See Hacker, "The Jewish Community of Salonica," especially 150ff.

121 Kapsali, *Seder Eliahu Zuta*, 272-73. For a detailed discussion of this, see Hacker, "The Jewish Community of Salonica," 150ff.

122 See note 21 above. For a similar feature which took place in his description of the Chief Rabbinate as well, I have expanded the discussion in Hacker, "The Chief Rabbinate."

123 For his policy, see İnalcık, "Ottoman Methods of Conquest"; idem, "The Policy of Mehmed II."

124 For Bayezid II's *sürgün* policy, see Beldiceanu-Steinherr, "Déportation et pêche à Kilia entre 1484 et 1508," 43-50; Beldiceanu, "La conquête des cités," 72-83; idem, *Recherche sur la ville ottomane au XVe siècle*, 243-48.

From these studies it has not become clear to me whether there were Jews among the exiles or not.

125 Ibn Iyas, *Taarikh Misr*, Bulaq 1312 to the *hijra*. Ibn Iyas, *An Account of the Ottoman Conquest of Egypt in the Year a.h. 922 (A.D. 1516)*, trans. W. H. Salomon (London, 1921).

126 Scholars have already noted his description. See Barkan, "Quelques remarques," 287-88; M. Winter, "Egyptian Jewry in the Ottoman Period according to Turkish and Arabic Sources" (in Hebrew), *Peamim* 16 (1983): 6-7; idem, "Relations of the Jews with the Authorities and with Non- Jewish Society" (in Hebrew), in *The History of Egyptian Jewry in the Ottoman Period (1517-1914)*, ed. J. M. Landau, (Jerusalem, 1988), 375-76.

127 Kapsali, *Seder Eliahu Zuta*, part 1, 315-96.

128 Ibid., 340-42, 349-50, 360, 364, 375-76, 391-93.

129 Ibid., 373, 398-99.

130 Ibid., 398-99. The entire passage is located in the chapter describing the causes of the Ottomans' war with Rhodes, and not in the description of events in Egypt and their effects. Here, too, as in his descriptions of the fall of Constantinople and the resettlement of Istanbul, his silence regarding the fate of the Jews—whenever this involved suffering or tribulations—is noteworthy. His intention in concealing all acts of the Ottoman Sultans which caused the Jews any distress and in glorifying any event or policy of those Sultans which were beneficial to the Jews is entirely clear.

131 Ibid., 11.

132 Levi Ibn Habib, *Responsa* (Venice, 1565), no. 25. And see there, in a responsum, paragraphs quoted from the endowment fund registry of the Jerusalem community, which demonstrate that the property was rented out in 1518: "It is furthermore written there: six days of the month of Tammuz in the year 5278 [1518] the Jews of the Jerusalem community mortgaged to Rabbi Yaakov Ibn Ezra, known as Vaena, the courtyard in which he dwells."

133 Ibid., no. 73.

134 David Ibn Zimra, *Responsa* (Warsaw, 1882), no. 995: "You asked me to inform you of my opinion concerning a widowed woman who has been living for a few years in the house of a Gentile, and she has possession, according to the law of the land, so that no other Jew can remove her. And now, Shimon, her nephew, is suing her, saying that this house used to belong to his grandfather, and that when they went into exile, to Istanbul, they rented the house out to Gentiles on condition that whenever they return, the house reverts to them. And so it was. Joseph, this Shimon's grandfather—who was the father of our widow—and Judah—they were brothers—came back and resided in the house; Joseph even married off his daughter to the son of Judah, his brother, in this house. Then the old people, Joseph and Judah, who were both partners and brothers, died, whereupon the sons of the old men came before the judges in connection with the inheritance, including the possession of the house, but failed to complete the process before they, too, died—but the widow, the daughter of Joseph who was the wife of Jacob, Judah's son, has been living in the house. And now Shimon is suing his father's sister and her son, Levi, who are the grandchildren of the old men, for possession of the house; he has witnesses to testify that the house belonged to his grandfather who lived in it for a long time, whereas the widow and her son claim that she had been in possession for a long time and it is her husband's possession...."

135 Hebrew Ms. Cambridge T-S Misc. 28.143 (film no. 19667 in IMHM, NUL). I am grateful to Avraham David for having directed my attention to this document. Another document reveals that in the year 1515, Meir Saragos was a member of the rabbinic court in Egypt. See A. David, "Biographical Notes on Avraham Talmid the Sephardi, a Notable of the Jewish Community of Egypt" (in Hebrew), in *Yehuda Ratzhabi Jubilee Volume* (Bar-Ilan University, Ramat Gan, forthcoming), 183-89, and esp. 185, 188.

136 The lists are included in the Hebrew ms. Microfilm 1916, leaves 116a-117a, in the Jewish Theological Seminary of America in New York. They were discovered by A. Marx, who was himself responsible for the first-time printing of the main paragraph regarding our question. See A. Marx, "The Expulsion of the Jews from Spain," *Jewish Quarterly Review*, o.s. 20 (1908): 269 [reprint, *Studies in Jewish History and Booklore* (New York, 1944), 99, n. 4]. They were copied over in full in Hacker, "The Jewish Community of Salonica," Appendices, 77-81, and some of them were also discussed in J. Hacker, "Pride and Despair: Polarity in the Spiritual and Social Atmosphere of the Spanish and Portuguese Emigrés in the Ottoman Empire" (in Hebrew), in *Culture and Society in Jewish History in the Middle Ages. The H. H. Ben Sasson Memorial Volume* (Jerusalem, 1989),

554-55. M. Benayahu, "R. David Ben Ban Benesht of Salonica and his Letter to R. Abraham Ibn Yaish of Brusa" (in Hebrew), *Sefunot* 11 (1971-78): 290-91 reproduced three fragments from the lists, including the two fragments relevant to our cause. And see below.

137 This is the correct reading as deduced from the abbreviations. Previously Marx and Benayahu erred and misinterpreted them.

138 Written.

139 Hebrew ms. Microfilm 1916, leaf 116b. Yitzhak Ibn Farash would seem to have written the entire matter because his son-in-law was one of those about to become *sürgün* (as he writes: "In the year 5283 [1523], when they led off 150 homeowners of Salonica to Rhodes and R. David Albargi and my daughter, his wife Clara, were supposed to go with them . . . "). Benayahu's proposal, that he gained exemption from this obligation because his father died on the very same day that the ships sailed, is acceptable (in the lists we find: "That very day R. Shem Tov Albargi, of eternal memory, passed away.")

140 For the number of Jews in the cities of the Empire in 1523, see the data of the population censuses held in the sixteenth century in the Empire and their significance in Ö. L. Barkan, "Essai sur les données statistiques des registres de recensement dans l'Empire ottoman aux XVe et XVIe siècles," *Journal of Economic and Social History of the Orient* 1 (1957): 9-36; idem, "Quelques observations sur l'organisation èconomique et sociale des villes ottomanes des XVIe et XVIIe siècles," *Recueils de la Société de Jean Bodin* 7 (1955): 289-311; idem, "Quelques remarques," 279-301.

141 See, for example, N. Todorov, *The Balkan City, 1400-1900* (Seattle and London, 1983), 52-54, 57-58, 63, 67-68, 311-13; M. Sokoloski, "Aperçu sur l'évolution du certaines villes plus importantes de la partie méridionale des Balkans au XVe et au XVIe siècles," in *Istanbul à la jonction des cultures balkaniques, méditerranéennes, slaves et orientales au XVIe-XIXe siècles* (Istanbul, 1977), 81-89 (out of a list of 26 cities and towns in the Balkans, there are over 150 Jewish households in only two of them; Barkan, "Quelques remarques," 283, 293-99 (on Sofia and Üsküb-Skoplija). The high numbers of Jews in these years stem from only two towns: Istanbul, 8,070; and Salonica, 4,143 households.

142 This according to Todorov and Lowry's count. See Todorov, *The Balkan City, 1400-1900*, 68; H. W. Lowry, "Portrait of a City: The Population and Topography of Ottoman Selanik (Thessaloniki) in the Year 1478," in *Diptycha* (Athens, 1980-81), 281. However, Gökbilgin, on the basis of the very same source, counted 3,174 families. See, T. Gökbilgin, "Selânik," *Islâm Ansiklopedisi*, c. 10 (Istanbul, 1964), 342-43; idem, "Kanunî Sultan Süleyman devri başlarında Rumeli eyaleti livaları şehir ve kasabaları," *Belleten* 20, no. 78 (1965): 265-66, no. 49. For data concerning the number

of Jews in Salonica in the fifteenth and sixteenth centuries, see Hacker, "The Jewish Community in Salonica," 167-75; Lowry, op. cit.

143 Tam Ibn Yahya, "Responsa Oholei Tam," no. 153.

144 David Ibn Zimra, *Responsa* (Warsaw, 1882), no. 1316.

145 Samuel de Medina, *Responsa* (*Hoshen Mishpat*, Salonica, 1598), no. 253.

146 Ibid., no. 226.

147 See note 144 above. Continuing, he writes: "And if you say that he is unaware or that she left against his will—Salonica is a big Jewish city and it has great scholars and lay leaders in each community. How could they let her leave, and how could they not have informed the community at Rhodes that a woman rebelled against her husband and took everything he owned, and she is present dwelling amongst you. . . . "

148 David Ibn Zimra, *Responsa* (Warsaw, 1882), nos. 34, 906. For the *kehaya*, see Hacker, "'The Chief Rabbinate,'" 251, n. 124.

149 See Tam Ibn Yahya, "Responsa Oholei Tam," no. 75: "that a Jew arrived from Rhodes and stated before the court in Constantinople: Be aware, gentlemen, that I have a suit against a person who resides in Rhodes. He is a *sürgün* there, while my witnesses are here in Constantinople, as I found them here. Now they may possibly go to a foreign land . . . for they are not residents of Constantinople, and so I ask of you to summon the witnesses to court. . . . " And see below, note 180.

150 See note 143 above.

151 Yoseph Hacohen, *Emek Ha-Bakha* (in Hebrew - ed. Leteris) (Krakow, 1895), 112. And cf. Yoseph Hacohen, *History of the Kings of France and the Kings of the House of Ottoman the Turk* (in Hebrew) (Amsterdam, 1733), leaf 72a: "And of the Jews in the cities of his kingdom Süleyman sent to Rhodes, where they lived securely until this very day." I do not know what Yoseph Hacohen was relying on when he wrote "in the cities of his kingdom." At present we know only of Salonica.

152 The question whether the Jewish exodus from Buda in 1526 was carried out voluntarily or under compulsion has been discussed at length. See N. Katzburg, "On the History of the Jews in Hungary under Turkish Rule" (in Hebrew), *Sinai* 31 (1952): 340: "With him went many of the Jewish residents of Buda, perhaps the entire Jewish population. According to Christian sources, the Turks took the Jews against their will, according to Jewish and Turkish sources, the Jews went with the Turks voluntarily. It would be closer to the truth to say that the Jews went voluntarily with the retreating Turks."

This description, which sums up the picture drawn by the research into the history of Hungarian Jewry as accepted in the writings of most Jewish scholars, is inaccurate. Firstly, according to Turkish sources, the Jews left as *sürgün*, and secondly, we have encountered no sources written by contemporary Jews describing their exodus as a voluntary one. For contemporary Christian sources, see F. Grunwald and S. Schreiber, *Magyar Zsidó Okleveltár*, vol. 5, no. 1 (Budapest, 1959), nos. 330-335; for statements made by Yoseph Hacohen, see, for example, *History of the Kings of France and the Kings of the House of Ottoman the Turk*, leaf 76a: "and the leaders of the community went out to him, and they threw themselves before his feet, and gave the city over to him . . . and he did not take even a shoelace of their property on that day. Süleyman's eye fell upon them and he dispatched them in boats to his country, where they have been living to this very day."

153 Students of the Ottoman Empire and of the history of Hungary under Ottoman rule have all agreed, on the basis of Ottoman sources, that Süleyman took the Jews of Buda as *sürgün*. See also L. Fekete, "Buda, Pest és Óbuda nem mohamedán polgári lakossága 1547 ben és 1580 ban," *Tanulmányok Budapest történetébol* 6 (1938): 116; idem, "La vie à Budapest sous la domination turque, 1541-1686," *Cahiers d'histoire mondiale* 8 (1964): 530; E. Vass, "Zsidók a hódoltságkori Török forrásokban," in *Magyar-Zsidó Oklevéltár*, vol. 18 (Budapest, 1980), 11; Gy. Kaldy-Nagy, "Contribution to the History of the Jews of Buda in 1526: Banishment or Resettlement?" in *Occident and Orient. A Tribute to the Memory of A. Scheiber* (Leiden, 1988), 257-60.

154 The main points are adduced in Kaldy-Nagy, "Contribution to the History of the Jews of Buda in 1526."

155 See Heyd, "The Jewish Communities of Istanbul," 303; Gerber, *Economy and Society*, 118; Epstein, *The Ottoman Jewish Communities*, 188 (in the year 1603, 59 lives).

156 B. Lewis, "Judaeo-Osmanica," in *Thought and Action, Essays in the Memory of Simon Rawidowicz* (Tel Aviv, 1983), III-IV; Epstein, *The Ottoman Jewish Communities*, 218; H. Gerber, "Jews in Edirne (Adrianople) in the Sixteenth and Seventeenth Centuries" (in Hebrew), *Sefunot*, n.s. 3 (18) (1985): 48-49.

157 See Heyd, "The Jewish Communities of Istanbul," 306-307; Gerber, "Jews in Edirne," 49.

158 Unlike Gerber, "Jews in Edirne." See R. Samuel de Medina, *Responsa, Even Ha-Ezer* (Salonica, 1596), no. 15: ". . . for now there came from Hungary more than sixty families at once, twice as many as the inhabitants of the city [Sofia]"; idem, *Yoreh Deah* (Salonica, 1596), no. 129: "since they were a community, and they seemed to have come there altogether . . . "; ibid., no. 40: "and when the king conquered the kingdom of Hungary, the Jews who the king brought came and settled, a large number of them, in the aforesaid city of Sofia . . . and when the aforesaid Hungarians went away to the town of Cavalla. . . . "

159 See R. Samuel de Medina, *Responsa, Even Ha-Ezer*, nos. 14, 17; R. Moses Alsheikh, *Responsa*, ed. Y. T. Porges (Bnei Braq, 1982), no. 55: "Reuben, one of the people of the town of Cavalla ... the residents of which are *sürgün*, i.e., they are dictated to by the Crown not to leave the place in order to live elsewhere, they themselves and their offspring ... with the disadvantages of that land and its weaknesses—the water is poor and the land is bereaved, and fear of the troops and *sürgün* trouble ... and fear of captivity and of being in *sürgün* imprisonment...."

160 Referred to in Gökbilgin, "Selânik," 343.

161 A. Cohen and B. Lewis, *Population and Revenue in the Towns of Palestine in the Sixteenth Century* (Princeton, N.J., 1978), 158, 160-61.

162 Ö. L. Barkan, "Osmanlı İmparatorluğunda bir İskân ve Kolonizasyon metodu olarak sürgünler," *İktisat Fakültesi Mecmuası* 11 (1950): 524-61; there are full details of the craftsmen required. See also, H. İnalcık, "Ottoman Policy and Administration in Cyprus after the Conquest," in *The Ottoman Empire: Conquest, Organization and Economy. Collected Studies* (London, 1978), no. 8.

163 B. Lewis, *Notes and Documents from the Turkish Archives* (Jerusalem, 1952), 28-34.

164 See Heyd, "Ottoman Documents on the Jews of Safed," 128-32; idem, *Ottoman Documents on Palestine 1552-1615* (Oxford, 1960), n. 111, 167-68.

165 Heyd, "Ottoman Documents on the Jews of Safed," 131.

166 Ibid., 131-32.

167 See H. Bentov, "Autobiographical and Historical Notes of R. Yosef of Trani" (in Hebrew), *Shalem* 1 (1974): 208, 217.

168 See J. Hacker, "Disaster Comes to this World only for the Ignorant" (in Hebrew), *Shalem* 4 (1984): 92-96.

169 The document was published and analyzed in Appendix 2 of the Hebrew version of this article which appeared in *Zion* 55 (1990).

170 See Epstein, *The Ottoman Jewish Communities*, 73-74; Heyd, "Ottoman Documents on the Jews of Safed," 128-29, Document A. In my opinion, there is no connection whatever between this document and the other documents dealing with the transfer of Jewish families from the city. Here the subject is lawbreakers, and the document refers to the kind of *sürgün* dealt with at the opening of this article (see note 4). It has, as already noted, no connection with the mass resettlement. The attempts to exile the Jews of Safed are not, accordingly, to be dated earlier than 1576.

171 Epstein, *The Ottoman Jewish Communities*, 42-43.

172 R. Samuel de Medina, *Responsa, Hoshen Mishpat*, (Salonica, 1595), no. 364; and see B. Lewis, "The Privileges Granted by Mehmet II to his Physician," *BSOAS* 14 (1952): 550-63.

173 See my notes 163-169, 171 above and 182 below. See also, for example, R. Hayyim Ben Ban-Benesht, *Knesset Hagedola Hoshen Mishpat*, 2nd ed. (Izmir, 1734), *Hilkhoth Shuttafim Be-karka* [Rules of Partners in Land], no. 163, section 68: "People from a certain town who settled in another town, and others from the town where they would at first take the initiative to drive them out of the second town where they had settled and to bring them back to their land to bear together with them the yoke of taxation and land levies. They issued a royal edict in this connection. Now when the people who have settled in the second town saw this they paid out a lot of money to cancel that royal edict to save themselves and their money. They asked some of those people from the same city, where they had been living earlier, to assist them in bearing the expense they incurred in working for the cancellation of the *sürgünlik*, for they, too, would enjoy this success: if they were to drive them out, the tax burden would grow heavier on the city residents. The city residents claim that they saved themselves only: for if the tax on them was to grow heavier, their trade would expand as well. . . . " And see also section 74.

174 Heyd, "The Jewish Communities of Istanbul," 313-14, and see note 189 below.

175 See Hacker, "The Jewish Community of Salonica," 58-60, 92-8; idem, "The Ottoman Policy towards the Jews," 118; Lowry, "The Portrait of a City," 261-64; Lowry, "The Ottoman Conquest," 333-35.

176 See R. Eliyah Mizrahi, *Responsa* (Constantinople, 1560), no. 28. In a responsum dated after 1504: "But in our case, when in the town of Magnesia the only people from these places stay there only occasionally, whereas the Sephardim came and settled there by themselves without any strangers with them."

177 The fate of the Romaniot communities and their development after the mid-fifteenth century is a weighty subject in its own right, and this is not the place to expand on it.

178 See what I wrote of the activity of R. Moshe Kapsali in this field in Istanbul in the fifteenth century in Hacker, "'The Chief Rabbinate'," 244-45.

179 See, for example, R. Eliyah Mizrahi, *Responsa Mayim Amukim*, part 1 (Venice, 1647), no. 1: "Since all the community leaders gathered together in the synagogue of old Pulia . . . in that from the very beginning you would claim you took her only on condition that she is not a *sürgün*, so that she would go with you wherever you go, and now that you have heard that she is *sürgün* you no longer desire her. . . . " And see note 159 above.

180 See responsum by R. Yosef Taitazak, in R. Yitzhak Aderbi, *Responsa Divrei-Rivot* (Venice, 1587), no. 164; R. Samuel de Medina, *Responsa, Even Ha-Ezer*, no. 92; M. Benayahu, ed., *Piskei Ha-Gaon Mahrit* [Yosef Taitazak] (Jerusalem, 1987), 205-206: "And the aforementioned

sister-in-law [*yebama*] is unable to leave the town because she is *sürgün*, and the brothers are all in a foreign land, and she cannot go to them...." On p. 206, n. 1, the editor does not understand the significance of the matter, and thinks that *sürgün* meant Jews registered as residents of Istanbul; cf. also his statement on p. 220, n. 2 (This is a mistaken reference and should read: no. 50). See also, in section cited in note 149 above: a Jew who is unable to leave Rhodes.

181 See, for example, *Piskei Mahrit* (above note 180), 220: "Reuven was in possession of a shop in this town [Salonica], and a number of times he was taken under compulsion to Constantinople because he was one of the residents called *sürgün*, and he always used to leave a Jew in this town in charge of his property, to pay the rent constantly to the Turkish owner of the shop ... and whenever Reuven took his leave of the Gate [i.e., the authorities in Istanbul; "the supreme Gate"—Porte] to set out from Constantinople, then, too, he would always arrange his business affairs and return immediately to this town ... "; R. Levi Ibn Habib, *Responsa* (Venice, 1565), no. 132: "the king's men would come in search of the *sürgüns*...." See also Appendix 1 of the Hebrew version of this article in *Zion* 55 (1990): 76-9.

182 See, for example, R. Yosef Ibn Ezra, *Massa Melekh* (Salonica, 1601), leaf 22b [Reprint, ed., I. S. Spiegel, Jerusalem, 1989, p. 86]: "Reuven who for some reason had been expelled by His Majesty, the King, from his happy home to another land in his kingdom to be *sürgün* there, as there are in a number of places; and the residents of that place wanted to impose on this Reuven the community yoke just as they, too, pay the king—Reuven apologized, saying that he arrived there because of the king's decree, that they could not stop him from trading in their land, and force him to go back to his own country. This situation has not been discussed by the Halakhic authorities, neither explicitly nor implicitly. It seems to me that he is obliged to pay his tax with them...."; R. Yosef Iskapa, *Sefer Avodat Massa* (Salonica, 1846), no. 48, leaf 44b, and the literature discussed there. Cf. also, concerning the double taxation, R. Moshe Ben Ban-Benesht, *Pnei Moshe*, vol. 2 (Constantinople, 1674), no. 111; R. Hayyim Ben Ban-Benesht, *Responsa Baey Hayey* (*Hoshen Mishpat*, part 1, Salonica, 1791), no. 108.

183 See notes 181-182 and the variegated literature adduced in the works cited there. See in detail Appendix 1 of the Hebrew version of this article which appeared in *Zion* 55 (1990).

184 See Appendix 1 of the Hebrew version of this article which appeared in *Zion* 55 (1990).

185 It should be corrected according to this reading in Gerber, *Economy and Society*, 163.

186 R. Shelomo Hacohen, *Responsa*, part 2 (Venice, 1586), no. 145. We know of Jews in Gallipoli and of their economic activities prior to 1453.

The Sürgün System and Jewish Society in the Ottoman Empire / 65

They, however, were transferred as *sürgün* to Istanbul, since they are not mentioned in the 1488-89 census, either. Ö. L. Barkan, "894 (1488/89) Yılı cizyesinin tahsilâtına âit muhasebe bilânçoları," *Belgeler* 1 (1964): 35.

187 This feature is problematic, and has considerable effect on the interpretation to be ascribed to the Ottoman censuses, for these Jews are clearly registered in the censuses as residents of Istanbul and not Gelibolu (Gallipoli) a fact true, too, of other groups throughout the Empire, but this is not the place to investigate this topic.

188 See Appendices 1-2 of the Hebrew version of this article in *Zion* 55 (1990), and note 173 above.

189 Perhaps the decrease of Romaniot Jews in Istanbul in the second half of the seventeenth century (see note 174 above) is to be ascribed not only to the disintegration of these circumstances under Sephardic pressure, but also to the fact described in the letter of the Sephardic Rabbis of Istanbul. This letter suggests that the Romaniot Jews left the city and set up separate communities for themselves in other cities. See Appendix 1, Letter A, in the Hebrew version of this article, *Zion* 55 (1990). At the same time, the supervision of the *sürgün* grew more lax, and it would seem that those leaving the city for other towns grew greater in the seventeenth century. The subject requires further study.

190 See Appendix 2 in the Hebrew version of this article in *Zion* 55 (1990): 79-82, for the testimony of R. Yosef Mataron on sixteenth-century Safed.

191 See W. J. Fischel, *The Jews in India* (in Hebrew) (Jerusalem, 1960), 112-19; idem, "The Jewish Merchant-Diplomat Issac Surgun and the Dutch-Mysore Conflict 1765-1791," *Revue des Etudes Juives* 126 (1967): 27-53.

Jean-Christophe Attias
Centre d'Etude des Religions de Livre
C. N. R. S. / Ecole Pratique des Hautes Etudes, Paris

Intellectual Leadership:
Rabbanite-Karaite Relations in Constantinople
as Seen through the Works and Activity of
Mordekhai Comtino in the Fifteenth Century

With what power is the scholar endowed by virtue of the knowledge he holds? What knowledge is he entitled to pass on to others? Who may claim the right to this knowledge and under what conditions? What place does the scholar occupy in the society in which he teaches and writes, and to what controls by the communal establishment should or should not his activities be subjected to? At certain junctures in medieval Jewish societies, these questions were at the center of violent controversies whose sociopolitical dimensions are significant. Such was the case, for example, in Provence from 1230 to 1233, and again from 1303 to 1306, during the period of great controversy provoked by the Maimonidean works and by philosophical and scientific studies in general.[1] This was also the case two-and-a-half centuries later in Constantinople during a troubled period in the history of the Jewish communities, after the fall of the city to the Ottomans (1453) and before the mass arrival of the Jews expelled from Spain (1492), when a little studied controversy broke over the rapprochement between certain Rabbanate and Karaite scholars.

The history of conflict in the relations between the Rabbanites and the Karaites is marked, perhaps more than others, by these problems. According to one of the traditions which account for the emergence of the Karaite dissidence in eighth-century Babylon,[2] Anan ben David was led to found an independent sect in reaction to the appointment of his brother to the position

---

This article was translated from the French by Barbara Pieroni. It has benefited from the aid of the Memorial Foundation for Jewish Culture.

of Exilarch, in spite of the fact that this appointment was ratified by the Muslim authority. This tradition holds that Anan ben David adopted the calendar characteristic of his sect, based on principles similar to those of the Muslim calendar, only to please the Caliph who had thrown him into prison. Whatever the historical accuracy of this tradition, its symbolic importance is beyond dispute. Furthermore, it is precisely the question of the transmission of knowledge which is at the heart of the age-old conflict between the two groups; the Karaites accepted exclusively the text of the Scriptures while rejecting the authority of the oral tradition embodied primarily in the Talmud.

In fifteenth-century Constantinople there was a turning point in the history of Rabbanite-Karaite relations, marked by efforts toward reconciliation.[3] The literary and pedagogical activity of a writer like Mordekhai Comtino (1402-1482)[4] is one manifestation of this little studied development. Even though Comtino had no formally defined communal responsibilities, he was nevertheless an important intellectual leader of his community, and his scholarly work and other activities ran headlong into prejudices and reservations of the socio-economic establishment.

Comtino's work, like the work of other medieval Jewish authors, is composed almost entirely of commentaries—whether the commented text was canonical, as with the Pentateuch, or whether it was a "profane" scientific or philosophical text, such as the writings of an Abraham Ibn Ezra[5] or a Moses ben Maimon.[6] As such, his work is primarily a re-writing or a re-elaboration of a pre-existing literary heritage. Comtino's "debts" are many.[7] His texts are filled with citations, borrowings, and allusions, especially in reference to the Sephardi exegetic and philosophical production. His writing is nevertheless the work of a particular time and place. It is "indebted" as much to the history, conflicts, and personal experiences of its author as it is to his "sources". The exegetic work is also a conjunctural work. It is the product of a given situation, written in answer to given questions in the framework of a historically defined set of tensions.

The study of Comtino's commentary on the Pentateuch reveals the conjunctural nature of his work particularly well. This commentary both informs and is informed by the issue of the relations between knowledge and power as they were viewed by the Rabbanites and the Karaites of Constantinople in the second half of the fifteenth century.

The Ottoman conquest of Constantinople in 1453 marked a turning point in the history of Byzantine Judaism. In particular, this event was followed by considerable migratory movements, both voluntary and imposed. Mehmet II, the Conqueror, wished to re-populate the city and, within the framework of this policy, many Byzantine Jews of the provinces were transplanted there. Karaites originally from various regions of the former Byzantine Empire,[8] from Asia, the Crimea or southern Poland,[9] who had first flocked to Adrianople, also began to settle in the new Ottoman capital.[10] This conjuncture created a favorable setting for the Karaite-Rabbanite rapprochement.

Byzantine Karaism, in a certain way, had intellectually prepared itself for this development. Aaron ben Yosef *Ha-Rofe* (the Physician), called "Aaron the Elder" (c. 1250-1320),[11] had suggested much earlier that every good Karaite had the duty to study the *Mishna* and the *Talmud*. These were the great texts of an oral tradition which was precisely the tradition in reaction to which Karaism had been established. In the introduction to his commentary on the Pentateuch, the *Sefer Ha-Mivhar* (The Book of Choice), Aaron the Elder stated that he himself would not hesitate to turn to the explanations of the commandments given in the *Mishna,* provided these were not in contradiction to the letter of the text.[12] Byzantine Karaism had even opened up to the Jewish philosophical tradition of Aristotelian inspiration. Even an Aaron ben Eliahu of Nicodemia, "Aaron the Younger" (1328?-1369),[13] no longer held fast to the integral nature of the philosophical heritage of the *Kalam*.[14] In fact, contrary to what one may be given to understand upon a first analysis, this author had broken with the atomist physics of the *Kalam* and had adopted the principles of the peripatetic structure of the universe, one composed of matter and form.[15] These two major trends, the reappropriation of the rabbinical heritage and the spreading of Jewish peripatetics, were to become even more pronounced among the later Karaite authors such as Eliahu Bashyazi (c. 1420-1490), author of the great Karaite legal code *Aderet Eliahu* (The Mantle of Eliahu),[16] and Kalev Afendopolo (1454?-1525), brother-in-law and successor to Bashyazi.[17] They were both students of Comtino.

This opening up of the Karaite world, which some have attributed to a "weakness" and a need for renewal,[18] had its counterpart among the Rabbanites. Comtino was often cited as one of those who had most demonstrated a respect for the Karaite school of exegesis.[19] It has even been pointed out that the title under which Comtino's Biblical commentary is sometimes cited is also the title of the Karaite Aaron the Younger's commentary: *Keter Tora* (The Crown of the Torah).[20] This somewhat idyllic image is confirmed by a Karaite author of the first half of the sixteenth century, Yosef ben Moshe Begi. According to him, Comtino held the intellectual qualities of his Karaite contemporaries in highest esteem.[21]

The reading of his commentary on the Pentateuch[22] reveals the intensity of his relations with Karaism, although these relations are by no means without ambivalence and tension. It would be impossible, in fact, to fully grasp the import and the scope of Comtino's enterprise without taking into account one of its essential dimensions, the confrontation with the Karaite exegetic tradition. This confrontation is, on a first level, open and direct when it is linked to the discussion of limited questions, points of traditional contention between the Karaites and the Rabbanites. On another level the confrontation is veiled, indirect. In this guise, the confrontation is a constant, one of the major preoccupations of Comtino's exegesis. The confrontation was not only a literary one. It also had a social and human dimension, for Comtino was also a teacher and among his students there were Karaites. Obviously, these three levels of confrontation are intertwined and inseparable; they clash with and illuminate each other.

THEMES AND FORMS OF THE ANTI-KARAITE POLEMIC IN COMTINO'S WORKS

Comtino often invokes the two major Byzantine Karaite commentators mentioned above, Aaron the Elder and Aaron the Younger. He cites both of them often, sometimes at length. When he cites them openly, that is, when their names appear in his text,[23] they are systematically refuted, sometimes ironically, often vehemently. Though Comtino is given at times to remark with satisfaction that the Elder and the Younger both learned, exceptionally, not to persevere in their errors and to "waken from their sleep,"[24] he more often reproaches them for having "opened their mouths in vain"[25] and for having been smitten by God "with madness, blindness, and astonishment of heart."[26] Certainly the two Karaite commentators are not always so fiercely attacked nor are they the sole objects of his attack. Even Ibn Ezra, whom Comtino particularly revered and whom he had chosen as master and guide,[27] sometimes receives the brunt of a criticism which is ironic, to say the least.[28] This being said, to find in Comtino a vehemence equal to that which is felt in certain of his anti-Karaite attacks, we must look in another direction, to his responses to the objections of Shabtai ben Malkiel Ha-Kohen.[29] This is, however, a case of an explicitly polemical work against a living contemporary (here a Rabbanite) with whom Comtino may well have had personal contact. One might wonder whether the vigor of certain attacks aimed at the long-dead Byzantine Karaite commentators (of whom

Comtino could only have had a literary acquaintance) is an echo of the real, personal, comtemporary debates between Comtino (or other Rabbanites) and the Karaites of Constantinople.

It is true that a writer may argue vehemently across the centuries without necessarily associating his vehemence to a contemporary context. Polemical exchange between the Karaites and the Rabbanites was traditionally virulent. It may be that Comtino was only following in this tradition. In addition, the moderation of certain of his criticisms is equally worthy of attention. Often he would merely note in passing that the Karaite commentator had made a mistake, that his point of view was erroneous. Therefore, it is appropriate to consider with caution the injurious qualifiers with which he regularly designates the Karaites: *ha-makhhishim* ("the nay-sayers"),[30] *ha-zedokim* ("the Sadducees").[31] We know that the latter term, which is frequently found along with the former in the writing of Abraham Ibn Ezra, Comtino's model,[32] was considered particularly insulting by the Karaites.[33] This may have been but a rhetorical tic, a habit Comtino had acquired from the practice of earlier commentators. It is also possible that these terms, when he wrote them, were deliberately charged with injurious connotations. In any case, the Karaite cited above, Yosef ben Moshe Begi, who would later undoubtedly exaggerate the respect in which his fellow Karaites were held by Comtino, still resented Comtino for having identified the Karaites, as had Abraham Ibn Ezra, Moshe Kapuzato,[34] Shelomo ben Eliahu Sharvit Ha-Zahav ("the Golden Sceptre")[35] (c. 1420-c.1501-2) and others, with the Zadokite and Boethusian sects and for having characterized them as "naysayers" and as "perverse."[36]

The analysis of the rhetoric employed in his anti-Karaite attacks does not necessarily reveal the true nature of Comtino's relation to the Karaite school of exegesis; nor does it bring any decisive evidence of the impact of contemporary debates between the Karaites and the Rabbanites in Constantinople on the elaboration of the commentary. The objections he raises concerning principles and methods may be more revealing. There is of course the classic objection: "In conclusion, their words neither add nor retract a thing, for they have no tradition [to support them]."[37] Elsewhere in his work, be it in the framework of a challenge or, on the contrary, of a reappropriation of the rabbinical heritage, Comtino reproaches the Karaites for insufficient knowledge or understanding of this heritage. Thus he holds that Aaron the Elder is unaware of the principle of *notarikon*.[38] He claims further that the Karaites, in their refutation of certain traditional interpretations, forget that these interpretations are not, strictly speaking, exegeses of the text of the Scriptures (whose true meaning they would reveal), but are orally transmitted traditions whose right to legitimacy is self-contained. He holds that these traditions only use the text as asmakhta, as "foundation" or as "support."[39] Generally speaking, the "ways of the Talmud" have remained closed to them and what the Karaites say about these ways has more to do with "bird-chirping" than with any "authentic knowledge."[40]

The principal questions which afford Comtino the occasion to attack his Karaite predecessors are of course those which have been at the center of polemics between Karaites and Rabbanites for generations. These are more or less lengthy investigations into the problems of the calendar (primarily concerning the method for establishing the neomenia and the determination of embolic years),[41] of the extent of the interdiction concerning the consumption of certain animal fats,[42] of forbidden unions,[43] of the number of daily prayers, and others.[44]

We might ask whether Comtino brings new developments to the debate on these classic questions, and whether that was even his intention. It is certainly true that, although he may be following a tradition, he does not hesitate to make his own contribution to the work. He explicitly states as much in the introduction to his commentary on the expression *mimohorat ha-shabat* ("the day after the shabat"):[45] "And so, having seen Abraham Ibn Ezra cite Saadia Gaon in order to prove this truth and to contribute himself in establishing it,[46] and to respond to the 'nay-sayers' (*ha-makhhishim*) who say that that it is Saturday (*shabat be-reshit*), I said to myself that I, too, could offer my contribution (*amarti eene gam ani helki*)." Comtino does indeed see himself as a link in a chain. Nevertheless, he actualizes the debate, cites the later Karaite exegetes, responds to objections they might have raised against A. Ibn Ezra or others.[47] This literary "updating" of an ancient debate may be the sign of its renewal in the midst of the Jewish community of Constantinople. The questions which Comtino addresses, in themselves not new, may reflect issues of concern for his contemporaries.

The fact is that Comtino's commentary on several of these questions is cited, and refuted, by Eliahu Bashyazi who, after having been Comtino's student, became one of the leaders of the Karaite community in Constantinople. Bashyazi cites Comtino on the setting of the neomenia,[48] on the meaning of the word *aviv*,[49] on the meaning of *shabat* in Leviticus 23.11,[50] and on the problems associated with the *shehita* (ritual slaughter).[51] Comtinian exegesis did not remain without echo. It immediately became the object of analysis and refutation in the Karaite world.

PSHAT AND *KABALA*

It may not be sufficient to indicate, as has been done thus far, only instances of explicit confrontation with the exegetic heritage of Byzantine Karaism. It may be that the relation of Comtino to Karaism is more apparent elsewhere, in an indirect, allusive confrontation, and that it is in the most subtle nuances of his writings that the man and his milieu are to be discovered.

One fact is worth noting. Unlike his model, Abraham Ibn Ezra,[52] Comtino does not particularly explore Karaite exegesis in his own introduction to his commentary. He simply states that he holds the *pshat* (the obvious meaning) as his main concern and announces his intention not to stray from it.[53]

Any interpretation which is not governed by the *pshat* must, if it be cited, have its source in the oral tradition (*kabala*). Even in this case, the *pshat* will be noted first. The *pshat* will not be set aside except in cases where it would be in contradiction to rules of logic and common sense (*shikul ha-daat*).[54]

The *pshat/kabala* problematic is immediately mentioned as central. Comtino underscores the ambivalent nature of relations between the *pshat* and "handed-down" or "traditional" (*mekubal*) meanings. The *pshat* may be compatible with a traditional interpretation (may "support" it). It is also possible that the *pshat* "support" more than one interpretation. Finally, the *pshat* may be thoroughly incompatible with a given interpretation. Obviously, the third and final case is the most problematic. In fact, a traditional interpretation incompatible with the *pshat* "uses" the text of the Scripture as "support" (*asmakhta*); in no case does such an interpretation claim to be derived from Scripture.[55]

In no instance could oral tradition, in a global sense, be understood as a "commentary" or an "interpretation" (*perush*) of written tradition. Together they form "one and the same Tora with its interpretation."[56] The content of the oral tradition is independent of the text of the Scriptures; there is no extracting it from the Scriptures, it is not latently present in the text; it has been independently transmitted and received *al pe* ("orally").[57]

Having accepted this, it remains one of the commentator's tasks to confront the oral tradition with the text of the Scriptures. This comparison will then allow "in return" (*ahoranit*) a better grasp of the meaning of the oral tradition itself.[58] Paradoxically, the understanding of the text of the Scriptures is no longer an end in itself. It becomes an instrument for the development of a better understanding of the laws of the oral tradition.

In Comtino's project, then, *pshat* and *kabala* maintain a complex rapport. Comtino refuses to sacrifice one to the other; he praises both of them. This tension is found throughout his commentary. Entire passages are marked, so to speak, with the stamp of this dialectic. Formulas of this type are repeated in a sort of leitmotif: "Our Elders, blessed be their memory, have said ... But the way of the *pshat* is different";[59] "The point of view of our Elders, blessed be their memory, is well known. ... But according to the way of the *pshat* ... ";[60] "Tradition (*kabala*) holds that ... although according to the way of the *pshat*. ... "[61] From one example to the next, the level of tension between the two concurrent interpretations may vary. They are nevertheless always clearly distinguished, and Comtino does not necessarily seek to resolve each conflict. It also happens that Comtino personally aligns himself on the side of the *pshat:* "In my opinion, according to the way of the *pshat*. ... Our Fathers however have passed on to us (*heetiku*)[62] that. ... "[63]

Comtino often transcends the contradiction, as he announces in his introduction, appealing to the notion of *asmakhta*.[64] He nevertheless insists on the fact that the Elders' use of the *asmakhta* by no means negates their profound knowledge of the *pshat:* "They used this verse as *asmakhta*, for they knew through *kabala* that ... just as they had done in numerous other places for they knew the *pshat* better than all who came after them."[65]

Another type of expression merits equal attention. In a different manner, this formula actually reflects the same problematic: "We need the *kabala* to know ... ";[66] "We could not ... without the *kabala*";[67] "Without the kabala we would say that ... ";[68] "Without the *kabala*, we would think that. ... But it was passed down (*kiblu*) to our fathers that. ... "[69]

Certainly Comtino never lets pass an opportunity to emphasize his faith in the truth and in the necessity of the oral tradition: "We know that the commandments require (*zrikhot*) the kabala";[70] "And we will favor their opinion though the *pshat* be different";[71] "And we will believe what was handed down to our Fathers, for he who strays from it is as if he were straying from his life."[72] Such professions of faith, however, must not be taken at face value. They serve, rather, to underscore the tensions between the *pshat* and the *kabala* repeatedly acknowledged and rendered explicit by Comtino. Obviously, the presence of these tensions is particularly evident in the legislative passages of scriptural text. The simple *heetiku ha-maatikim* (literally: "the transmittors [the Masters of the oral tradition] have transmitted") which runs through entire sections of the commentary is enough to alert us. The repetitive and almost systematic nature of this phenomenon calls for explanation and study.

Intellectual Leadership: Rabbanite-Karaite Relations / 75

We could, in fact, suppose that Comtino has constantly in mind the question or the objection which might, at each step, be formulated by a contradicting opponent who is ignorant of, or who rejects, the oral tradition. This opponent is never explicitly designated; he is nonethless always there, always present between the lines. It is not difficult to identify him.

These passages may often be profitably compared to parallel commentaries of Aaron the Elder or Aaron the Younger. This type of comparison reveals that the problematic *pshat* is often none other than one of the interpretations chosen by the Karaite, or that the reaffirmed *kabala* is precisely the one which was contested or discussed by him. One example will suffice here, intentionally selected from one of the *a priori* less controversial narrative passages: "It came to pass (. . .) that Reuben went and laid with Bilhah, his father's concubine . . ." (Gen. 35.22). The text is apparently clear as to the nature of the act because it contains the expression *va-yishkav* (he laid). Here is what Comtino says about it:[73]

> Our Fathers, blessed be their memory, interpreted (this passage by saying) that he had disturbed (*bilbel*) his bed and that the Scriptural text had reproached him as if he had slept with her.[74] But according to the way of the *pshat* he did (in fact) sleep with her.

And here is what Aaron the Younger says:[75]

> The text must be understood in its obvious sense, and what the *drash* (non-literal, homilectic interpretation) says about it is known to be [and appears] far-fetched.

By itself, this one example may not be significant. However, many more could be provided.[76] Certainly, a convincing parallel could not be found for every one of the passages in question. It is not necessary that Comtino have always in mind the commentary of one or another precisely identifiable Karaite. It may also be that his only intention is to anticipate the objections or to respond to the questions of his Karaite students or readers.

The debate also surfaces at times and is expressed openly: "Here, our Ancestors, blessed be their memory, passed down (*heetiku*) that. . . . Contrary to the opinion of the Sadducees according to which . . . ";[77] "Our Ancestors, blessed be their names, passed down (*heetiku*) that. . . . And the nay-sayers (*ha-makhhishim*) have said...and their words are in vain. Let us put aside the *kabala* and [try to answer them] by following the laws of logic and of common sense (*shikul ha-daat*). . . . "[78]

The parallelism of vocabulary and structure between these explicit confrontations and the passages analyzed above, support the proposed hypothesis, which is that when Comtino articulates his propositions concerning the *pshat/kabala*, it is likely that he is doing so in anticipation of a potential Karaite opponent, student, reader, or commentator. The confrontation with the Karaite world appears, then, as a constant in Comtino's enterprise. It constitutes an essential dimension of his work. The confrontation goes beyond the limited framework of passages explicitly directed against Karaism on the subject of major, traditionally debated questions. It is also at work, implicitly but consistently, throughout the whole of the commentary.

COMTINO, TEACHER AND ASTRONOMER

The constancy of this preoccupation is surely not fortuitous. It can be wholly understood only if the social milieu in which Comtino's exegetic work appeared and Comtino's own status in this milieu are taken into account.

As has been noted, Comtino was writing in a heterogeneous Jewish society in which the Karaites and the Rabbanites coexisted and at a time when a rapprochement of the two groups was taking place. Through his agreement to offer his teaching to the Karaite public, Comtino became personally involved in this rapprochement. His literary production cannot be separated from his role as teacher. It was, in part, to comply with his students' request that Comtino composed his commentary on the *Guide for the Perplexed* of Moses Maimonides.[79] His commentary on the *Logical Terminology* of the same Moses Maimonides[80] was dedicated to his student, Isaac Zarfati.[81] His commentary on the Yesod Mora of Abraham Ibn Ezra was dedicated to another student, this one a Karaite, Yosef Revizi.[82]

No dedication of this kind is found heading the commentary on the Pentateuch. It remains more than likely that the drawing up of such a text was, to Comtino's mind, but a natural extension of his teaching activities and that his commentary was destined for an audience as diverse as were his students. Consequently, the ever present concern that we have uncovered in his work is more easily understood—the more so since the rapprochement of the two communities was not without conflict and the very idea of Rabbanite instruction for Karaites was not always unanimously accepted.

These very questions were at the origin of one of the crises which marked the internal history of the Jewish community in Constantinople at the end of the fifteenth century. There was even a *herem* (ban) pronounced to forbid Rabbanite teachers from accepting Karaite students.[83] The interdiction applied not only to the teaching of oral law but also to the written law and to the literal interpretation of the Scriptures as well as to the whole of the secular sciences (logic, physics, metaphysics, arithmetic, geometry, astronomy, music, and ethics).[84] Such a measure, no doubt legitimized as the rejection of religious dissidence, also had a political dimension—for the Chief Rabbi of the city, Moshe Kapsali, had put his position at risk[85] in this confrontation between the "intellectuals" and a group of leading citizens. Later, when he in turn had become leader of the Jewish community in Constantinople, Eliahu Mizrahi was called upon to judge the validity of this *herem*.[86] To justify his decision invalidating the *herem,* Mizrahi was to invoke the authority of his master, Comtino,[87] who was among those who had accepted Karaite students who had pledged themselves to respect the Rabbanite masters, living and dead, and not to profane the feast days of the Rabbanite calendar. Mizrahi did not neglect to point out that the previous warnings of Moshe Kapsali, including the *herem,* had had very little effect on the activity of these teachers. This demonstrates the relative independence of the latter from a weak central authority without any real means of coercion.[88]

It is in such a context, and within such a perspective, that Comtino writes his abundant and diverse work. The commentary on the Pentateuch is but one part of it, along with several philosophic commentaries and numerous scientific works.[89] The diversity of his production reflects that of his teaching. We have seen, however, that the pronounced interdiction applied to all teaching, including that of the secular sciences.

In fact, for Comtino as well, knowledge is indivisible and he draws upon the whole of knowledge in his exegesis. Comtino considers that a knowledge of secular science is indispensable to whoever would penetrate the meaning of the Scriptures. This is why he announces in his introduction that he intends to call upon, when necessary, the sciences of grammar, logic, physics, astronomy, arithmetic, geometry and metaphysics.[90]

Such a profession of faith is not, of course, original. It takes on a particular meaning, however, in the socio-historical context within which it is expressed. Secular sciences could indeed play a mediating role between the Karaites and the Rabbanites. It has already been noted that a Karaite such as Aaron the Younger, in as early as the fourteenth century, was cognizant of the progress in science and philosophy, notably in the Rabbanite world, and considered that the Karaites could participate in this progress without renouncing their identity or breaking with their ancestors. Later Eliahu Bashyazi, one of Comtino's Karaite students, would even insist that mastery of the secular sciences was a necessity and would offer a description of the course of study to be followed which is not without parallel to the fields of study covered in the work of his teacher.[91]

In Comtino's commentary, sciences often play a mediating or neutralizing role in the debate between the Rabbanite and the Karaite exegeses. An example will illustrate this.

Commenting on Leviticus 12.2 ("If a woman has conceived seed [*ki tazria*] and born a man-child"),[92] Comtino recalls the idea of the Fathers of the oral tradition according to which "if the woman is the first to emit the seed, then she conceives a boy."[93] He next applies himself to responding to the objection raised by the Karaite, Aaron the Elder:[94] "If it is so, then why [do we find a little further]: 'But if she bear a maid-child [verse 5]?'" In a third movement he remains not at all within the confines of the polemic and re-examines the factors which determine the sex of a child, this time from a resolutely "scientific" point of view. In particular, he emphasizes the influence of the stars: it is the celestial configuration at the moment of conception which determines the sex of the child. Returning then to the contested opinion of the Fathers of the tradition, Comtino offers the hypothesis according to which the astral configuration which determines the sex of the child may also cause a precocious emission of seed on the part of the woman. In this case, "the opinion of our Elders, blessed be their memory, would be correct." What Comtino forgets to indicate is that at the conclusion of his argument, the element considered the cause by the Elders has become rather a sign or an epiphenomenon; the primary and essential cause lies elsewhere.

Such an example clearly demonstrates the neutralizing function which the secular sciences could fill, becoming a sort of "common ground" where Karaites and Rabbanites could meet and transcend the habitual limits of the debates in which they were opposed.

That the *herem* forbidding the Rabbanites to disseminate knowledge to the Karaites included the "Greek" sciences is completely comprehensible. Eliahu Mizrahi was correct when he recalled that the sciences could be considered the common property of all, Jews, Christians (*goyim*) and Muslims (*yishmaelim*)—the pronounced interdiction thereby striking down what might be considered an ancient and respectable tradition of cultural and intellectual exchange.[95] Comtino himself seems to have been one of the great Rabbanite teachers of the time who did not reserve their teachings for Jews alone (Rabbanite or Karaite) but opened it to all, Jews, Greeks, and Muslims.[96]

One of the sciences most often employed by Comtino in his commentary was astronomy (or astrology, there is no real distinction made between the two).⁹⁷ Discussions of astronomy are numerous and lengthy in his work.⁹⁸ This phenomenon could be accounted for in many ways. It could even be explained as simply indicative of a personal penchant on the part of the author for this science.⁹⁹ In the socio-historical context with which we are dealing, however, it assumes a very particular significance.

In fact, one of the sciences particularly privileged by Comtino in his teaching was the science of astronomy. It is worthy of note that he taught astronomy to two highly important individuals, both of whom were to be called to leadership roles, one in the Rabbanite community and the other in the Karaite community. The first was the Rabbanite Eliahu Mizrahi, author of a commentary on the *Almagest* of Ptolemy¹⁰⁰ and successor to Moshe Kapsali as head of the Jewish community in Constantinople. The other was Eliahu Bashyazi,¹⁰¹ himself head of his community and author of the legal code *Aderet Eliahu*.

We know that in the Karaite world the knowledge of astronomy and a mastery of the problems of the calendar—one of the principal areas of discord between the two communities¹⁰²—was considered a source of power. According to the Karaite, Abraham Bali (second half of the fifteenth century, early sixteenth), if Yosef Revizi, who was one of Comtino's Karaite students, was one of the great men of his generation, it was because it was "according to his instruction that the neomenia was fixed."¹⁰³ In the same way, for Kalev Afendopolo, astronomy is the "superior science" and Comtino, his teacher, is the "astronomer sage" (*ha-hakham ha-tokhen*)¹⁰⁴ par excellence.

It is a fact that Comtino's exegetic work takes into consideration—if only to reject it—the intellectual heritage of the Byzantine Karaite school. But above and beyond the polemical treatment of traditionally litigious questions between the two communities, there is also a constant, implicit, but altogether perceptible and perhaps more profound preoccupation with the confrontation between the *pshat* and the *kabala* which is no doubt the echo of an intimate debate between the Rabbanite teacher and his Karaite students. In this debate, secular, philosophical, and scientific knowledge may act as mediator and neutralizer.

These three lines of force in Comtino's exegetic work reflect a social reality which in turn illuminates the work. To our knowledge, Comtino had no specific communal responsibilities. Any leadership he held was an intellectual one. The fact remains that he was the teacher of each of the leaders of the two large communities which formed Jewish society in Constantinople at the end of the fifteenth century, the Rabbanite and the Karaite communities. Comtino the exegete cannot be separated from Comtino the teacher. In the same way, the whole of his activity, literary and pedagogical, cannot be separated from one of the great debates of ideas which moved Jewish society in his time. This debate of ideas was also a political debate because it revolved around the question of the legitimacy of and the potential restrictions of the transmission of knowledge—all transmission of knowledge (written law, oral law, religious science, secular science) being at once a manifestation of power and a transmission of power. In the final analysis, the debate once again puts the spotlight on the place and the independence of the Jewish scholar vis-à-vis the community and its institutions.

NOTES

1 See especially Charles Touati, "La controverse de 1303-1306 autour des études philosophiques et scientifiques," *Revue des Etudes Juives* 127 (1968): 21-37. See especially what is said about the social status of Levi ben Abraham (pp. 31-32) and of the interference of the Spanish Jews in the community affairs of southern France (p. 33).

2 On the origins of Karaism one might consult, among others, Samuel A. Poznanski, "Anan et ses écrits," *Revue des Etudes Juives*, 44 (1902): 161-87, 45 (1902): 50-69, 176-203. See also Martin A. Cohen, "Anan ben David and Karaite Origins," *The Jewish Quarterly Review*, n.s. 68, nos. 3-4 (1978): 129-45, 224-34.

3 On Byzantine Karaism, see the now classic work of Zvi Ankori, *Karaites in Byzantium. The Formative Years, 970-1100* (New York and Jerusalem, 1959).

4 Since the pioneering work of Hayim Yonah Gurland, (*Ginzei Yisrael be-St. Petersburg* 3 (1866) and *Talpiot* 1 (1895): 1-34 (special pagination of the *Toledot anshe shem* section), Mordekhai Comtino or Khomatiano (on this name see: Steven Bowman, *The Jews of Byzantium, 1204-1453* (Alabama, 1985), 149 n. 68 has not been the subject of a specific, in-depth study, although certain authors came to be interested in him indirectly and even to publish short extracts of his works. For the latest work, see Jean-Christophe Attias, *Le commentaire biblique. Mordekhai Komtino ou le herméneutique du dialogue* (Paris, 1991).

5 Of this author Comtino wrote commentary on the *Yesod Mora* [The Foundation of Fear], the *Sefer Ha-Shem* [The Book of the Name], and the *Sefer Ha-Ehad* [The Book of the One].

6 Comtino wrote a commentary of the *Logical Terminology* (the only one of his works ever to be printed in its entirety, *Beur Milot Ha-Higayon* (Warsaw, 1865)). He also commented on the *Guide for the Perplexed*.

Intellectual Leadership: Rabbanite-Karaite Relations / 81

7 See Attias, *Le commentaire biblique,* chapter 4.

8 Abraham Danon, "The Karaites in European Turkey," *The Jewish Quarterly Review* 15 (1924-25): 298-99.

9 Heinrich Graetz, *History of the Jews,* trans. from the German (Philadelphia, 1894), 4:269.

10 Joseph Hacker, "Ottoman Policy toward the Jews and Jewish Attitudes toward the Ottoman," in *Christians and Jews in the Ottoman Empire,* eds. Benjamin Braude and Bernard Lewis, (New York and London, 1982), 1:120.

11 Literally, "the first Aaron," in Hebrew, Aharon *Ha-Rishon.*

12 Introduction, folio 9a, *Sefer Ha-Mivhar* (Gozlow, 1834). Also cited by Z. Ankori, "Eliahu Bashyazi, the Karaite. A Study of the Traditions He Recorded Relative to the Beginnings of Karaism in Byzantium" (in Hebrew), *Tarbiz* 25 (1956): 201. On this reevaluation of the Talmudic heritage by the Byzantine Karaites, see Ankori, *Karaites in Byzantium,* 239-45.

13 Literally, "the last Aaron," in Hebrew, Aharon *Ha-Aharon.* On this author one might consult Isaac Husik, *A History of Mediaeval Jewish Philosophy* (Philadelphia, 1941), 362-87.

14 On this heritage see Colette Sirat, *La philosophie juive médiévale en terre d'Islam* (Paris, 1988), 53-93.

15 See Daniel Y. Lasker, "Nature and Science in the Thought of Aaron ben Eliahu, the Karaite" (in Hebrew), *Daat* 17 (1986): 33-42.

16 See A. Ankori, "The Bashyazi Family and its *Takanot*" (in Hebrew), introduction to *Aderet Eliahu,* by Eliahu Bashyazi (reprint of the Odessa edition, 1870), 11-13. See also Daniel Y. Lasker, "The Maimonidean Influence on the Philosophical Thought of the Karaite, Eliahu Bashyazi" (in Hebrew), *Mehkerei Yerushalayim be-mahshevet Yisrael* 3 (1984): 405-25.

17 See Ankori "Eliahu Bashyazi," 309.

18 Danon, "The Karaites," 309.

19 Danon, "The Karaites," 310-11.

20 A. Ovadia, "Rabbi Eliahu Mizrahi" (in Hebrew), Sinai 3(1939): 77, n. 191.

21 Jacob Mann, ed., *Karaitica,* vol. 2 of *Texts and Studies in Jewish History and Literature* (1935; Reprint, New York, 1972), 305-306.

22 Completed in Constantinople on 13 Av 5220 (1460): Commentary on the Pentateuch, Bibliothèque Nationale de Paris (hereafter cited as BN) ms. Hebr. 265, folio 173v.

23 Aaron the Elder is cited by name twenty-two times, Aaron the Younger, eleven times.

24 BN ms. Hebr. 265, folio 42r (on Gen. 38.26).

25 According to Job 35.16.

26 According to Deut. 28.28. These accusations appear in BN ms.

Hebr. 265, folio 85v (on Exod. 22.3); the entire passage is written in the same vein. See also, on Aaron the Younger, BN ms. Hebr. 265, folio 18v (on Gen. 9.12) and folio 94r (on Exod. 18.15). On Aaron the Elder, folio 73r (on Exod. 17.16) and folio 74r (on Exod. 18.1).

27   See BN ms. Hebr. 265, folio 3r (Introduction).

28   See for example the way Comtino deals with A. Ibn Ezra's interpretation of certain proper names: BN ms. Hebr. 265, folio 22v (on Gen. 14.3). The admiration Comtino held for his model did not preclude critical appraisals (folio 3r: "And when it appears to us that he has followed another path (than that of the *pshat*) then we will turn to the right or to the left, according to the case"). It was his independence of mind that was at the origin of the violent conflict which opposed him to his contemporary, Shabtai ben Malkiel ha-Kohen.

29   University Library of Leiden, ms. Or. 4779, folio 297v-324v. See note 30.

30   See: BN ms. Hebr. 265, folio 112v (on Lev. 8.16); folio 113r (on Lev. 9.10); folio 114v (on Lev. 11.11) and folio 160r (on Deut. 14.22).

31   See for example BN ms. Hebr. 265, folio 64r (on Exod. 11.6) and folio 120v (on Lev. 16.13).

32   See Ezra-Zion Melammed, *Commentators of the Bible* (in Hebrew), 2nd ed. (Jerusalem, 1978), 2:676-78.

33   On this subject, see Poznanski, "Anan," 169-71 and D. Lasker, "The Ultimate Goal of Man in the Philosophy of the Karaites" (in Hebrew), Daat 12 (1984): 5.

34   On Moshe Kapuzato *Ha-yevani* ("the Greek"), who was himself often cited (and contested) by Comtino, see Mann, *Texts and Studies*, 2:709.

35   See Bowman, *The Jews of Byzantium*, 147.

36   Mann, *Texts and Studies*, 2:305.

37   BN ms. Hebr. 265, folio 128r (on Lev. 23.24).

38   BN ms. Hebr. 265, folio 107r, on Exod. 35.22: "And they came, both men and women, as many were willing-hearted and brought bracelets, and earrings, and rings, and tablets (*kumaz*) all jewels of gold...." The debate was about the meaning of the term *kumaz*. Aaron the Elder contested that, in conformance with a traditional interpretation (*The Babylonian Talmud, Shabat*, 64a. See Rashi ad loc.), this word might be linked to the expression: *kan mekom zima* (literally: "here [is the] place [of] debauchery," an allusion to the place on the body where this jewelry was to be worn): "the *zain* would have had to precede the *mem*" (*Sefer Ha-Mivhar*, Exodus 70r-v, compare with A. Ibn Ezra, *Perushe Ha-Tora* [Commentaries on the Pentateuch], published, presented and annotated by Asher Wiezer, (Jerusalem, 1976), 2:228 (long commentary on Exodus)) in the word *kuMaZ* in order that the last two letters of the name of the jewelry would also be, in

exact order, the first two letters of the term *ZiMa* (debauchery). To which Comtino responds that Aaron the Elder would not have made such an objection had he known the principle of *notarikon* which authorizes the breaking down of a word and the reading of a word as an acronym—the principal letters of the word *kumaz*, (*kaf, mem,* and *zain*) become, in that order, the first letters of each of the words which form the expression *Kan Mekom Zima.*

39 See for example BN ms. Hebr. 265, folio 85v (on Exod. 22.3).

40 BN ms. Hebr. 265, folio 110v (on Lev. 3.9).

41 See, among others, BN ms. Hebr. 265, folio 61v-63r (on Exod. 12.1) and folio 126v-128r (on Lev. 23.11). On the importance and the meaning of these debates concerning the calendar, see Ankori, *Karaites,* 288. On Comtino and the Karaite calendar, one might consult Jean-Christophe Attias, "Un temps pour enseigner, un temps pour apprendre. Karaites et Rabbanites à Constantinople au XVe siècle," in *Politique et religion dans le Judaïsme ancien et médiéval,* ed. Daniel Tollet (Paris, 1989), 187-98.

42 See for example BN ms. Hebr. 265, folio 110r-111r (on Lev. 3.9) and 159v (on Deut. 12.15). On the importance attached to this question, see Ankori, *Karaites,* 288.

43 BN ms. Hebr. 265, folio 121v-122r (on Lev. 18.11-22).

44 BN ms. Hebr. 265, folio 32r (on Gen. 24.63).

45 BN ms. Hebr. 265, folio 126v-127r (on Lev. 23.11): "[and he the high priest] shall wave the sheaf before the Lord, to be accepted for you; on the morrow after the *shabat* [*mi-mohorat ha-shabat*] that the priest shall wave it." The entire question centers on the meaning which should be attributed to the word shabat: "Saturday" (according to the Karaites) or "feast-day" (according to the Rabbanites). The date of the Sukot depends on the exegetic choice made (see Lev. 23.15).

46 See Abraham Ibn Ezra, *Perushei Ha-Tora,* 3:83-85.

47 See, for example, BN ms. Hebr. 265, folio 110v-11r (on Lev. 3.9).

48 *Aderet Eliahu,* folio 5r-6r.

49 *Aderet Eliahu,* folio 33v. For the Karaites, each spring, it is the observation of the maturation of the barley in Holy Ground—the so-called system of the *aviv*—which allows the beginning of a new annual cycle to be determined and the intercalation of a supplementary month to be decided (see Ankori, *Karaites,* 292).

50 *Aderet Eliahu,* folio 68v-69v.

51 *Aderet Eliahu,* folio 119v-121v.

52 Abraham Ibn Ezra, *Perushei Ha-Tora,* 1:2-6 (Hebraic pagination).

53 Comtino, "*U-mi-derekh ha-pshat lo azuz,*" BN ms. Hebr. 265, folio 3r (Introduction).

54 Comtino, "*U-mi-derekh ha-pshat,*" BN ms. Hebr. 265, folio 3r (Introduction).

55 BN ms. Hebr. 265, folio 2r (Introduction).
56 BN ms. Hebr. 265, folio 2v (Introduction). Compare with A. Ibn Ezra, *Perushei Ha-Tora,* 1:6 (Hebraic pagination): "for there is no difference between these two *Tora.*"
57 Comtino, BN ms. Hebr. 265, folio 2r (Introduction).
58 Ibid.
59 Comtino, BN ms. Hebr. 265, folio 18r (on Gen. 8.13).
60 Comtino, BN ms. Hebr. 265, folio 19v (on Gen. 10.8).
61 Comtino, BN ms. Hebr. 265, folio 103v (on Exod. 34.6).

62 On the concept of *haataka* (transmission), on the word itself and its usage in the Rabbanite world (especially in the works of A. Ibn Ezra) and in the Karaite world, see Poznanski, "Anan," 182. See also Ankori, "Eliahu Bashyazi," 195 and Ankori, *Karaites,* 224-39.

63 Comtino, BN ms. Hebr. 265, folio 110r (on Lev. 2.13). One may also consult, on the same theme, among others: folio 39v (on Gen. 35.22); folio 70r (on Exod. 15.25); folio 113r (on Lev. 9.1); folio 125v (on Lev. 21.14); folio 133r (on Lev. 27.29); folio 137r (on Num. 8.2); folio 138r (on Num. 10.3); folio 160v (on Deut. 15.12), etc.

64 See for example Comtino, BN ms. Hebr. 265, folio 32r (on Gen. 24.63); folio 95v (on Exod. 29.14); folio 82v (on Exod. 21.8); folio 98r (on Exod. 30.38); folio 150r (on Num. 27.11); folio 159r (on Deut. 12.4).

65 Comtino, BN ms. Hebr. 265, folio 83v (on Exod. 21.9).
66 Comtino, BN ms. Hebr. 265, folio 115r (on Lev. 11.32).
67 Comtino, BN ms. Hebr. 265, folio 118r (on Lev. 14.6). See also: folio 115r (on Lev. 11.29); folio 116v (on Lev. 13.12); folio 119r (on Lev. 15.25); folio 120r (on Lev. 16.8); folio 122v (on Lev. 19.10); folio 123r (on Lev. 19.19); folio 123v (on Lev. 19.27); folio 124r (on Lev. 20.8); folio 125r (on Lev. 21.2); folio 125v (on Lev. 21.14); folio 126v (on Lev. 22.23 and 23.10); folio 128r (on Lev. 23.15); folio 128v (on Lev. 23.40); folio 129r (on Lev. 24.8), etc.

68 Comtino, BN ms. Hebr. 265, folio 65r (on Exod. 12.18).
69 Comtino, BN ms. Hebr. 265, folio 85r-v (on Exod. 21.37). See also, among others, folio 109v (on Lev. 1.4); folio 119r (on Lev. 16.17).

70 Comtino, BN ms. Hebr. 265, folio 2r (Introduction). Compare with A. Ibn Ezra, *Perushei Ha-Tora,* 1:5 (Hebraic pagination): "And all of these commandments require (*zrikhot*) the *kabala* and the tradition (*masoret*)."

71 Comtino, BN ms. Hebr. 265, folio 76r (on Exod. 19.15).
72 Comtino, BN ms. Hebr. 265, folio 108v (on Exod. 40.17).
73 Comtino, BN ms. Hebr. 265, folio 39v (on this verse).
74 Compare with the *Babylonian Talmud, Shabat,* 55b. See the commentaries of Rashi and of A. Ibn Ezra, *Perushei Ha-Tora,* 1:104 (Hebraic pagination).

Intellectual Leadership: Rabbanite-Karaite Relations / 85

75 Aaron the Younger, *Keter Tora* [The Crown of the Tora] (Gozlow: 1866). Gen. folio 74v (on this verse).

76 Compare, for example, Comtino and Aaron the Younger on Gen. 9.21. (BN ms. Hebr. 265, folio 19r and *Keter Tora*, folio 39r); on Exod. 21.3 (BN ms. Hebr. 265, folio 82r and *Keter Tora*, folio 69r); on Exod. 30.23 (BN ms. Hebr. 265, folio 97v and *Keter Tora*, folio 104v); on Exod. 30.38 (BN ms. Hebr 265, folio 98r and *Keter Tora*, folio 105v); on Num. 27.11 (BN ms. Hebr. 265, folio 150r and *Keter Tora*, folio 42r); on Deut. 19.17 (BN ms. Hebr. 265, folio 162v and *Keter Tora*, folio 22v); on Deut 20.10 (BN ms. Hebr. 265, folio 162v and *Keter Tora*, folio 23r); on Deut 21.11-12 (BN ms. Hebr 265, folio 163r and *Keter Tora*, folio 24r).

77 Comtino, BN ms. Hebr. 265, folio 120v (on Lev. 16.13).

78 Comtino, BN ms. Hebr. 265, folio 82r-v (on Exod. 21.7).

79 Trinity College Library, Cambridge; ms. Hebr. 126, folio 2r.

80 Moses Maimonides, *Beur Milot Ha-Higayon*, Introduction by Comtino.

81 He wrote the famous letter calling the Jews of Germany to come settle in Ottoman territory are one in the same, see J. Hacker, "The Jewish Society of Salonica in the 15th and 16th Centuries. A Chapter in the History of Jewish Society in the Ottoman Empire" (in Hebrew) (Diss., Hebrew University of Jerusalem, 1978), Appendices 2-12.

82 Gurland, *Ginzei Yisrael*, 10.

83 On this affair one might consult Meir Benayahu, *Rabbi Eliahu Kapsali of Candia* (in Hebrew) (Tel Aviv, 1983), 42-45.

84 Cited in this order by Eliahu Mizrahi, *Responsa* (in Hebrew) (Jerusalem, 5698 [1938]) *Responsum*, 57:176.

85 Ibid.

86 Which he did in ibid., *Responsum*.

87 On Comtino as teacher of E. Mizrahi, see Avraham David, "Rabbi Mordekhai Comtino teacher of Eliahu Mizrahi" (in Hebrew), *Kiriat Sefer* 45, no. 2 (Adar 5730 [1970]): 299.

88 Mizrahi, *Responsum* 57:179-80.

89 On Comtino the mathematician, see M. Silberberg, "Ein handschriftliches hebräisch-mathematisches Werk des Mordechai Comtino," *Jahrbuch der Jüdisch-Literarischen Gesellschaft* 3 (1905 [5666]): 277-92, and 4 (1906 [5657]): 214-237; and P. Schuib, "A Mathematical Text by Mordecai Comtino," *Isis* 50 (1932): 55-70. On Comtino the astronomer, see note 100.

90 Comtino, BN ms. Hebr. 265, folio 3r (Introduction).

91 Bashyazi, *Aderet Eliahu*, folio 82r. Compare this passage with Comtino, BN ms. Hebr. 265, folio 53r (on Exod. 3.13).

92 Comtino, BN ms. Hebr. 265, folio 116r.

93 Compare with *Babylonian Talmud, Berakhot* 60a, *Nida* 28a and 31a. Compare with A. Ibn Ezra, *Perushei Ha-Tora*, 3:35. See also the commentary of Nahmanides on the same passage.

94 See *Sefer Ha-Mivhar*, Leviticus, folio 19r.

95 Mizrahi, *Responsa*, 176.

96 According to the testimony of Yosef ben Moshe Begi (J. Mann, *Texts and Studies*, 2:311).

97 On astronomy and astrology in medieval Jewish thought, see Ron Barkai, "L'astrologie juive médiévale: Aspects théoriques et pratiques," *Le Moyen-Age. Revue d'Histoire et de Philologie* 93 (1987): 319-48.

98 See especially, Comtino, BN ms. Hebr. 265, folio 8v-9r (on Gen. 2.4); folio 13v-14r (on Gen. 4.7); folio 31r (on Gen. 24.3); folio 36v (on Gen. 31.19); folio 64v (on Exod. 12.12); folio 88v (on Exod. 23.25); folio 104r-106v (on Exod. 34.10); folio 129v (on Lev. 25.8).

99 Comtino is the author of opuscules on the method of building a sundial, an astrolabe, and the astronomical instrument called *al-zafiha* as well as of a *Commentary on the Persian Tables* (see Gurland, *Ginzei Yisrael*, 3-5).

100 Ovadia, "Rabbi Eliahu Mizrahi," 79.

101 As is recalled by a Karaite author of the eighteenth century, Simha Yizhak Luki (Mann, *Texts and Studies*, 2:1418).

102 See note 42.

103 Gurland, *Ginzei Yisrael*, 32.

104 Gurland, *Ginzei Yisrael*, 14-15.

Leah Bornstein-Makovetsky
Bar Ilan University

Jewish Lay Leadership and Ottoman Authorities during the Sixteenth and Seventeenth Centuries

The Ottoman Empire supervised the economic activities of the *dhimmi* and insured the fulfillment of their fiscal and civil obligations. The Empire granted the Jewish communities throughout its cities the authority to run their own communal institutions by themselves, preserving a separate Jewish identity. The authorities in the sixteenth and seventeenth centuries negotiated with each Jewish community separately, for neither an umbrella communal structure in the Ottoman Empire nor a Chief Rabbinate existed. The government authorities only interfered with Jewish communal life when members within the community appealed to the government, requesting their active involvement. The lay leadership of the Jewish communities, called *memunim* (appointed ones) or *parnasim*, stood parallel to the religious authority headed by the rabbis. As a matter of principle, the Jewish lay leaders drew upon Ottoman governmental authority to manage Jewish community affairs and, in times of need, were actually aided by the government in enforcing their authority.[1]

The central power designated a central role for the lay leaders, essentially in their main functions: the fiscal and organizational management of the communities and their representation in negotiations with the various authoritative bodies of the Ottoman Empire. These roles were filled by both the leaders of the communities (*cemaat, kehilla*) and the leaders of the synagogal congregations (*mahalle, kahal*) which were similar to independent communities within the larger municipal ones. These congregations were established by emigrés from various countries or cities who had settled in the different cities of the Empire and wished to preserve their ancient traditional communal life and ritual.[2]

The present article will survey, analyze and draw the essential characteristics of the complex relations between the lay leaders of the communities and congregations and both the central and provincial Ottoman authorities at their varying ranks during the sixteenth and seventeenth centuries. This essay will not deal at all with the authority of the communal leaders within the communities in matters not requiring government intervention. The period under discussion includes the sixteenth century, with its economic, cultural, social, and organizational growth and flourishing of Jewish society throughout the Ottoman Empire, as well as the period of decline which began in the last quarter of the sixteenth century and continued throughout the entire seventeenth century in most communities. This research is based upon publications and studies of Ottoman documents and upon the vast rabbinical literature of the period, especially utilizing responsa that were penned by Ottoman community rabbis.

This article will also discuss the conflict between Ottoman authorities' demands and the community's needs. The Ottoman authorities held the Jewish lay leaders responsible for the fulfillment of their communities' obligations to the government. The lay leaders, as shall be demonstrated, financially and physically guaranteed the Jewish communities' debts to the Ottoman government. For their part, the *parnasim* tried to perform loyally their duties toward both the Jewish community and the Ottoman authorities. This monograph describes how they operated under varying circumstances in order to prevent clashes between the obligations to the Empire and the personal good of the community and its members. Preference given to the interests of the community which clashed with the interests of the state was liable to shake the status of the community in the eyes of the Ottoman authorities. Yet, at times, the lay leaders did not fulfill all of the government's demands. Often, they could appease the authorities with bribes or compromise. Indeed, the Ottoman authorities often looked the other way instead of enforcing the laws concerning the *dhimmi*. It will be demonstrated, mainly through reports of state law enforcement regarding individual members of the Jewish communities in economic and financial matters, that the lay leaders generally preferred the good of the community, attempting to thwart all government schemes against it. Sometimes this caused tension between them and different groups or individuals within the communities. These leaders were aided in their endeavors by the rabbinical courts and by communal regulations. Only as a last resort did they turn to the Muslim courts. It is clear that such appeals to gentile courts were kept at a minimum in order not to damage the autonomy of the Jewish communities.

Another aspect presented here is the influence of the Ottoman officials on the authority of the lay leaders in internal community matters. The lay leaders received their authority to deal with internal and external financial and organizational matters from the Jewish communities themselves, a practice rooted in longstanding tradition and Jewish law. It will be demonstrated that the support given to them by the Ottoman government enhanced their authority with even greater power. The ability to punish offenders or challengers to the regulations that they initiated within the community tended to halt all opposition. This conclusion raises the question: Did the lay leaders use this authority for their own personal interests? From the sources on hand, the lay leaders, with few exceptions, did not utilize their authority for personal gain or revenge. This was due to the guiding principle that their position was to represent the Jewish communities, their activities having the status of a good deed and a religious obligation; hence, they tried with all their might to act within the norms of the *Halakha*.

Another topic discussed is the degree of success that the lay leadership had in their dealings with the government. It will be shown that with many difficulties in their negotiations, they employed various devices in order to function properly and to achieve their goals. The question of how successful they were will be analyzed.

The lay leaders of the community and congregations were generally called *memunim* (appointed ones) or *parnasim*, yet in many sources they are referred to as the following: men of distinction, *zekanim* (elders), *berurim, manhegim* (leaders), *tovei ha-ir, tovei ha-kahal, gevirim, hashuvim* (the important ones), *pekidim* (functionaries), *roshim* (heads), *murshim, nihbadim* (the honored ones), *gedolei ha-ir* (the great of the city), *nivrarim*.[3] These appellations were used without any specification in the areas under discussion. However, the terms *sheikh* or *sheikh al yahud* are found in Arab areas of the Empire, in such places as Baghdad, Aleppo (Haleb), and Jerusalem.[4] The term *kâhya*, meaning *parnas*, is rarely found in Hebrew sources, but is frequently found in Ottoman documents and generally meant the Jewish leader appointed by the government to represent the Jewish community in negotiations with it; all his authority and activities were solely confined to this realm. These leaders had no authority at all in internal community affairs. Ottoman sources also contain the following terms: *naib* (in the community of Kastorya), *yayabaşı* (in Sofia), and *ser-i mezkurin* (in such places as Edirne)[5] M. A. Epstein best summarized the situation: "The Jewish officials performed functions which in the Muslim community were fulfilled by the government and religious bureaucracies."[6]

THE RELATIONSHIP BETWEEN THE LAY LEADERS AND THE GOVERNMENT: APPOINTMENTS, DUTIES AND METHODS OF IMPLEMENTATION

Relations between the *parnasim* and the Ottoman authorities were intricate and delicate. The Ottoman government held the Jewish leaders responsible for the actions of the community, and in many cases this heavy responsibility caused individuals to refuse appointments to these offices. Hence, a *parnas*, Matitya Sarfati, in Thebes (Istifa), Greece, during the sixteenth century, took an oath "not to attend the communal needs to negotiate with the 'ministers' (governors and other Ottoman bureaucrats) and judges of the country, nor to attend the needs of an individual."[7] From his words, one may deduce the exact duties that he had performed as a *parnas* and that he wished to free himself of. Since the *parnas* was the local community's representative to outside officials, he was sometimes referred to as the "spokesman."[8] The *parnasim* were in contact with the local government in *vilayets* and *sancaks*, and attempted with all their might to finalize all communal affairs with these local officials. Only on rare occasions and when there was no choice did the communities outside of Istanbul turn to the Sublime Porte.[9] Without a doubt, the communal leaders conducted the diplomacy from a position of weakness, a position which worsened as the political status of the Jewish communities of the Empire weakened, especially from the end of the sixteenth century onwards.[10]

All the communities strongly opposed the appointments of leaders with low moral stature, and in particular protested the appointment of informers to leadership positions. An example is found in Chios, in 1619, where the following statement was made: "Since we have seen the power of their informing and tale-bearing which they have done, causing us distress and financial loss. . . ."[11] Sixteenth-century Ottoman sources published by Epstein show that the leaders of the Jewish communities of Irbil and Sofia were accused by their communities of perfidy, oppression and ruthlessness, and were summoned to Muslim courts.[12] A famous case was the attempt to dismiss Isaac Asiao, a well-known leader in Salonica around 1625. The poor artisans, the weavers of Salonica, during a period of crisis in the city's wool industry, mistakenly suspected him of informing upon them to the government. He was required to take an oath before them that he would conduct no communal affairs at all before the "ministers of the city," *i.e.* the *sancak* and his functionaries, and that he would not serve in any public capacity in the community. They also prepared a legal document against him in the Muslim courts that might have led to the death penalty. It appears that he wanted to relieve himself of this oath when certain authorities demanded that he appear before them as the community leader. He was fearful that if he refused he would be in danger, for those authorities would have accused him of contempt of court. The spiritual and lay leaders of the community supported his cause.[13]

Often the *parnasim* were forced to pay the high taxes and the duties out of their own pocket until the money from the community members was successfully collected. This fact facilitated the attempts of the wealthy to rule over the Jewish communities.[14]

Both the rabbis and the *parnasim* recognized the necessity of constant dealings with the government and expressed this both in words and deeds. For example, Rabbi Shlomo Le-Beit Ha-Levi, a famous rabbi from Salonica, wrote in the sixteenth century in his book *Lev Avot*: "Since the people who deal in communal affairs and the leaders must constantly enter the courts of the ministers, judges and kings of the countries. . . . " He also pointed out that these ministers and kings become close to the leaders for their own personal benefit.[15]

In order to prevent the refusal of appointments as lay leaders, different communities during the sixteenth and seventeenth centuries passed regulations that an individual could not refuse to accept the appointment of any communal position, no excuse being valid.[16] There were communities that through regulations promised to insure the security of the *parnasim* against informing by members. Hence, the community of Negroponte in the sixteenth century passed a regulation that all the Jews, personally and financially, were obligated to aid the *parnasim* should private individuals inform the government authorities that the *parnasim* served also as the court in the Jewish community. In this case, the community obligated itself to save the *parnasim* and to excommunicate the informers.[17]

It is not clear whether the Ottoman authorities intervened everywhere in the appointment of *parnasim* or whether official approval was required for appointments. In rabbinical literature, there is no information that sheds light on this question, but it is evident that the communities reported the appointments to the authorities. Hence, in April 1605, four Jews appeared before the *kadı* of Sofia and announced that they had elected "the Jew Shaban ben Yunas as the supreme leader of the community."[18] Similarly, the documents of the *şeri* court in Jerusalem demonstrate that in the sixteenth century the *sheikh al yahud* was appointed by the *kadı* of the city in an official public session of the *şeri* court. This was based upon a list of Jews that had been received earlier.[19] Rarely is it found that the *parnasim* received their appointments with the aid of the government officials, nor is it always mentioned explicitly.

This is reflected in the example of the two Mustaarab congregations in Aleppo who, in the sixteenth century, passed a communal ordinance to depose their *sheikh* because of his libels against them. They forbade him to return to his post for a period of three years "neither willfully or unwillfully... or through intrigues, persuasion or through force with the aid of the nations...." In this same ordinance they forbade the taking of office "through the powers of the state to become *sheikh*." However, the same person, through threats, evil deeds and chicanery, returned to office.[20] More information from the middle of the sixteenth century reveals that the community of Rhodes passed a communal ordinance which stated that if the ruler or the *sancakbeyi* should want to appoint a *kâhya*, the community would try to cancel the appointment, for only a *parnas* appointed by the Jewish community could run public affairs. The background for this was the attempt to run communal affairs autonomously, and the bitter experiences with the previous *kâhyas* in this community.[21] It appears that the essential reasons for such meager information concerning the aid of the state in receiving posts for the lay leadership of the community are: 1) the positive attitude on the part of the Jewish communities toward this leadership; and 2) the desire to involve the state government as little as possible in community affairs. The lack of enthusiasm for this post is reflected in rabbinic sources, as one notes in the responsa which discuss the many appeals of the rabbis made to the authorities in order to dominate the local rabbinate.[22]

The roles of leadership *vis-à-vis* the government expressed itself essentially in financial matters and the responsibility for law enforcement of state statutes.

Taxes were the primary link between the community and the Ottoman authorities. The practice was that heads of the *kehilla* offered the government, according to its demands, information concerning taxes, and they were responsible for the collection and transfer of the money to the state treasury. Sometimes, all the congregations in one community jointly centralized the collection of the money; other times, each congregational leader did it separately. The method was determined in conjunction with the governmental authorities. Information concerning this matter is found in the responsa literature, Ottoman documents, and many other sources. At present, the subject has only been partially researched. A concise summary is found in the words of Professor A. Shmuelevitz:

Jewish Lay Leadership and Ottoman Authorities / 93

> Within the autonomy system, the Jews managed to establish a consolidated autonomous organization for taxation, which seems to have been quite efficient both for internal tax collection and its relations with the Ottoman authorities in general and the tax collectors and tax farmers in particular. It was possible because of the community's discipline, mutual assistance, and an ability to preserve internal well-organized tax administration, which managed to maintain a just division of the tax burden among its members and to maintain cordial relations with the state tax collectors, with the help of gifts and cash payments. . . . [23]

As those responsible for the payment of the Jewish communal taxes to the authorities, the *parnasim* were the first to be injured if the financial and taxation demands were not met. This could happen quite frequently, as for example, in the case of Congregation Shalom in Salonica in the second half of the sixteenth century, when their lay leaders were incarcerated by the *sancakbeyi* who demanded that they pay him the tax; the final outcome was a compromise.[24] In other instances, the *parnasim* were forced to pay the amount of the tax out of their own private pockets and to collect it from the public later. At times they had to borrow money from the gentiles at interest. Consequently, they enforced the collection of the money from the community with all means at their disposal.[25] The lay leaders were also forced to lend money to the Ottoman rulers who did not always pay back their debts.[26]

In Jerusalem during the sixteenth century, the *sheikh al yahud* was responsible for all marriages; later the *parnasim* of the community continued to hold this responsibility. They had to receive the approval of the *kadı* in all cases of marriage so that he could secure the collection of the marriage taxes which were levied with the granting of each formal authorization to marry.[27] However, it appears that in most of the Jewish communities throughout the Ottoman Empire, in accordance with autonomy granted to them, the rabbis of the various communities were appointed to rule over all marital and family laws within the communities.[28] Some sources attest to the fact that the Jewish judge (*dayan*) had to receive authorization from the *kadı* in order to rule and carry out Jewish family laws.[29]

THE JEWISH *KÂHYA* AND THE OTTOMAN AUTHORITIES

The appointment of the Jewish *kâhya* or *kethüda* by the Ottoman government as its contact with the local Jewish community was practiced only in a few communities in the Empire. Some scholars view the *kâhya* as the Eastern equivalent to the European *shtadlan*.[30] Nonetheless, there really is no comparison between the contemporary *shtadlan* of Christian Europe and the Muslim countries' *kâhya*; whereas the former was appointed by the community and received a salary, the appointment of the latter came directly from the authorities. The *shtadlan* also did not deal with tax collection. The roles of the *shtadlan* in the Christian countries and of the *kâhya* in the Muslim countries were similar only in their lobbying efforts for more rights or the cancellation of decrees that injured the welfare of their constituents. One must also emphasize that the *kâhya* operated only on the local level of a specific community, whereas the *shtadlan* in Christian countries represented many communities at one and the same time, and their activities were spread over a number of countries.[31]

The *kâhyas* were most active during the sixteenth century. The most famous among them was Shealtiel, known as Salto, a member of the Spanish community, and, from the days of Bayezid II onwards, he was the administrative and financial leader of the Jewish community of Istanbul. He was appointed by the authorities, and his appointment was almost certainly confirmed by the community. After twenty years of service, he was ousted from office by the community leaders on the fourteenth of *heshvan*, 5279 (19 October 1518), after many complaints of bribery and the illegal collection of arbitrary taxes were lodged against him by the Jews. He was returned to office on the eleventh of *Sivan*, 5280 (29 April 1520), by the leaders of the congregations and the spiritual leader of the community, Rabbi Eliahu Mizrahi. One may surmise that, on the one hand, the Ottoman authorities pressed for his return to office, and on the other hand, the community suffered from his absence, for no one capable of arranging the tax collecting was found to replace him. It appears that his sons also aided him in his efforts.

During his absence, certain individuals called *mahlabsidis* filled his role.[32] However, they did not have his status or influence in the Sublime Porte. They feared the authorities, and according to the claims of the lay leaders of the congregations of Istanbul and Rabbi Eliahu Mizrahi, they caused more harm than good. Thereupon, Shealtiel accepted the community's stipulation not to accept the appointment from the authorities without first requesting permission from the community leaders. Among his duties, Shealtiel kept a list of Jewish businesses and reported their activities to the government, together with the incomes and payments of the most significant Jewish tax-farmers serving the Ottoman Empire. In addition, within the scope of his authority were the various taxes that the Istanbul Jewish community paid to the government. He kept a list of the Jewish communal taxes that were brought before the government functionaries after comparing them to the lists found in the imperial treasury. Consequently, his influence was enormous both within the Istanbul Jewish community and outside it. He was obligated to prove his unquestioned loyalty to the Ottoman government, while preserving his personal and family private interests. This was a source of complaint, as is revealed by reports that the whole community was angry with him concerning an inheritance. Nonetheless, the community feared complaining or testifying against him before the authorities.[33]

After the death of Shealtiel, no successor replaced him, perhaps for the simple reason that no one capable was found, or perhaps the community feared such a concentration of power in the hands of a single individual. In the seventeenth and the eighteenth centuries, one finds at times among the Jews of Istanbul someone called *kâhya*, and this refers to the *kâhya* of a village or quarter of the city, and not the representative of the total Jewish population of the city.[34]

There are also two documents, from the year 1600 (1009 according to the *Hegera*) and 1747 (1160 according to the *Hegera*) in which the *kâhya* as the head of the Rabbinate community in the city, is mentioned with regard to the collection of taxes from the Karaites of Istanbul. The first is Shmuel ben Moshe and the second is Yaakov.[35] Certainly, they were involved in tax collection only.

There was no *kâhya* in any other great Jewish communities of the Ottoman Empire with power and authority similar to those held by Shealtiel.[36] However, there was a *kâhya* who held office in the sixteenth century in Rhodes. He caused damage to the community, and hence it made a regulation forbidding anyone to enter this office, and in his place was appointed three *parnasim*. After a while, the deposed *kâhya* was appointed as one of these three. The Jews referred to him as *parnas*, while the authorities continued to refer to him as *kâhya*.[37] This office had no continuity in Rhodes, as far as the sources reveal.

In the community of Izmir, in 1672-73, during its economic heyday, the *kâhya* even received a salary from the Jewish community. He would intervene in communal judicial matters, and from one source it appears that he intervened in the investigation of Jewish merchants who were suspected by the *parnasim* of possessing forged coins. Such a suspicion could bring trouble to the Jews. Without a doubt, the *kâhya* was Rabbi Shlomo Ibn Ezra (d. 1688), whose offices as community representative to the government did not interfere with the offices that he served concurrently as a rabbi and judge (*dayan*). It is not clear how long he served as *kâhya*.[38] He describes his office as *kâhya* without noting that he was *kâhya*, but by reading between the lines, it is quite obvious that this was the case: "Because of the burdens of time . . . I am weakened by the community yoke upon me, that I must stand at the gates of ministers and judges. . . . "[39] As mentioned above, there are two references of a *kâhya* in two Turkish documents from the sixteenth century: one referring to the Jewish community leader and his chief functionary in Nikopoli, and the other to the *kâhya* in Irbil.[40]

ACTIVITIES OF THE LAY LEADERS IN APPROACHING THE GOVERNMENT AT THE COMMUNITY'S INITIATIVE

The activities the lay leaders conducted for the benefit of the Jewish community were generally to guarantee the community's autonomy and the security of the individual members. Together with the local religious leadership, they frequently made communal regulations, the majority dealing with delicate topics, such as the enforcement of the Ottoman Empire's fiscal laws and regulations concerning the *Iltizam*. Hence, in the communal regulations of Patras and Bursa of the sixteenth century, one finds that no individual could be the *Mültezim* of a certain tax.[41] The community of Bursa during the sixteenth century even forbade with a regulation its members to act as tax farmers of certain taxes, including the leasing of the Alamal house, in order to prevent any act that could cause damage to the Jews.[42] They faced different governors, bureaucrats and functionaries, significant and insignificant, who did not always make it easy for them to arrange the affairs of Jewish community. Fortunately for these lay leaders, they generally did not encounter any religious enmity or anti-Semitism on the part of the government officials. However, in many cases they did encounter demands of payment of large sums of money for an easy and tolerant attitude, and almost every action cost the community huge sums.

The leaders used to bring the complaints of the Jews before the local authorities. Most of these dealt with the damage done to Jews by thieves, robbers and murderers. The number of complaints concerning the internal affairs of the community and Jewish society are infrequent and have no implications; the community throughout all the centuries preserved its autonomy and would not involve the authorities in internal matters. Various rabbinical sources deal with the war against *malshinim* (informers) who complained to the government about members of the community, or about the local Jewish leadership. These treacherous men also offered internal information which Jewish society did not want outside circles to know about. Consequently, they caused loss and damage to their fellow Jews and to the community, and the leaders attempted to stop these informers.[43]

Frequently, the lay leaders were challenged by the discriminatory laws practiced by the Ottoman government toward the *dhimmi* and toward Jews in general, laws which disturbed daily life. The Jews were aware of the scrupulous enforcement of these laws. Nonetheless, the authorities completely ignored them, for their enforcement or lack of it, was a direct result of local conditions, the policies of central and provincial governments, and the need for Jewish money and services. Certainly, communal leaders everywhere received from the Ottoman authorities orders to enforce these laws, and they were well aware of the necessity of observing them completely or partially.[44] Among the most striking discriminatory laws was the prohibition of building new synagogues or to rebuild, renovate and refurbish old ones. The leaders of many communities were requested by their constituents to prevent any scheming against existing synagogues and to receive authorization from the Sultan to build new ones or renovate existing ones when necessary.[45]

The lay leaders everywhere worked for the establishment of a Jewish cemetery, and when problems arose concerning these cemeteries, they arranged matters with the authorities. An example is found at the end of the sixteenth century when the authorities demanded that the Jewish community of Istanbul sell its cemetery to the Muslims in order to make it into a public park.[46]

The suppression of blood libels was also one of the lay leaders' many tasks. Sultans such as Mehmet II, Süleyman I, the *Kanuni* (the Legislator), and his successors, wrote firmans prohibiting blood libels within the Ottoman Empire. The last known firman before the famous one published in 1840 was written in 1602, during the reign of Mehmet III.[47]

As a result of mutual denunciations within the community, the leaders often had to aid members of the *kehilla*.[48] The leaders worked hard to appease the *kadıs* when someone informed upon them or other Jews, thereby risking the welfare of the entire community. An example is found in Izmir, during the 1660's. One member of the community denounced a number of Jews in the *şeri* court while one of the accused was visiting a neighboring village. The *kadı* summoned him to court and the Jew went into hiding. In the meantime, the leaders of the community gathered and agreed to spread bribes liberally "in order to remove the libels of slander and denunciation."[49]

The lay leaders also saw to the release of Jewish prisoners who were incarcerated for the non-payment of taxes or other debts owed to either the government or private individuals, or for some minor infraction of state law. They operated according to the rule that the individual was quite dependent upon the community, for the community defended the individual and without this defense, the individual was as good as lost.[50] The leaders also redeemed their colleagues who were arrested for delays in the payment of taxes.[51] One should note that in many cases they dealt with the release of Jewish prisoners who were private individuals and not community leaders.[52] One may surmise that in accordance with their policy to avoid confrontation with the authorities, and with the passing of communal legislation on this matter, the lay leaders did not deal with the liberation of Jewish prisoners who had committed severe crimes against state laws.

There are sources that demonstrate the intervention of the lay leadership in Muslim courts on behalf of religious leaders and members of the communities and congregations. For example, in Arta, during the 1520's, Rabbi Binyamin ben Matitya, the rabbi of the community, had his court excommunicate a man who had insulted the lay leaders. As a result, the man with a number of allies, brought the rabbi to the *kadı* and denounced him for judicial activities among the Jews. The lay leaders of the community appealed to the *kadı* and their pleas prevented the flogging of Rabbi Binyamin.[53]

Often the leaders defended the livelihood and income of members of the community against gentile competitors. A few examples from sixteenth- and seventeenth-century Salonica will suffice. In the sixteenth century, they passed regulations to protect the raw wool market in order not to damage the essential livelihood of Salonican Jewry. Among other regulations, maximum prices were set for the price of wool. Similar regulations were passed in Larissa and Trikkala. Moreover, the lay leaders appealed to the Ottoman authorities and requested the publication of official firmans to halt competition. The authorities acquiesced to these pleas.[54]

It appears that there was seldom any willingness to involve the authorities in internal communal economic competition. One may cite the *Halakha* query sent from the community of Yanina to Rabbi Shmuel de Medina to Salonica, which asked if they were permitted according to the *Halakha* to appeal to the *sancakbeyi* to aid them in preventing foreign Jewish merchants from entering the city and encroaching upon their markets.[55] The dearth of information concerning this subject almost certainly means that the lay leaders of the communities managed to overcome such problems in the majority of cases without involving outside intervention from the government.

CONFLICTS BETWEEN THE LAY LEADERS AND THE AUTHORITIES

A classic example of the conflicts and tensions found in the lay leaders' responsibilities is best portrayed in the relationship with the *beytülmal*. As is well known, the leaders were obligated to report each death of a community member to the authorities, not only for the payment of a burial tax, but essentially because of the existence of the *beytülmal*. The Jewish communities were obligated, like other citizens of the Ottoman Empire, to transfer any estate of a deceased Jew without any heirs to the *beytülmal*. The Jewish community leaders were themselves obligated to pay the fine should the absence of a report be discovered.[56] Sometimes the leaders did not fulfill these regulations, and buried their dead without first notifying the authorities and without the necessary permits from the *beytülmal* or the local *kadı*. For example, one may cite the reports concerning the *sicil* of Jerusalem in the sixteenth century.[57] The general practice was that upon the notification of death to the functionaries of the *beytülmal*, a permit for burial was given to the lay leaders. However, sometimes investigations were conducted and cases of evasion and misconduct were discovered. To prevent evasion of the law, the Ottoman authorities of Jerusalem during the 1550's established a separate body responsible for the *beytülmal* of the Jews. The first one who "leased" this function from the governor of Jerusalem was a Jewish apostate to Islam. After his term ended and until the end of the century, most of these functionaries were Jews, usually the *sheikh al yahud*. This was a source of income for the general needs of the Jewish community and gave the *sheikh* great powers.[58] This manner of leasing the position by the lay leaders was also done in other communities.[59] It appears that the Ottoman authorities were not aware of the community's leasing the *beytülmal* on a personal basis; they thought that only private individuals were involved.[60] The communities' concern that the *beytülmal* might become a source of trouble found expression in communal regulations forbidding the leasing of the *beytülmal* by Jews, as in the case of the Jewish community of Bursa in the sixteenth century.[61] One may conclude that the *parnasim* frequently walked a tightrope, on the one hand scrupulously following the letter of the law lest they and their constituents suffer dire consequences, while on the other hand utilizing every legal loophole in order to benefit their communities. The lack of a systematic and consistent policy of enforcing the administrative acts concern all the *dhimmi*, including the Jews, frequently forced lay leaders into a conflict between the strict observance of state laws, and the obligation to preserve the good of the Jewish community which demanded a lenient fulfillment of those laws.

THE AID GIVEN BY JEWISH COURTIERS AND THEIR ALLIES AND COMMUNITY REPRESENTATIVES

Appeals by the communal leaders to the Sublime Porte were always made through the services of Jews who were favorites of the court or the Ottoman establishment in Istanbul. From the days of Murad II in the fifteenth century onwards, there were always Jewish courtiers in Istanbul. They filled diplomatic and economic roles for the Sultans and for the higher echelons of the government. One should note that in the courts of provincial governors throughout the Empire one could find Jewish courtiers. They were for the most part statesmen, physicians, translators, *mültezims*, *sarrafs*, suppliers to the army, and businessmen. Many were the object of appeals by Jewish communities who utilized them both for philanthropic activities and as middlemen between them and the authorities. These persons had the power to greatly influence their own communities' affairs, especially the Jewish community of Istanbul. At times, when appealed to by a faction of an outside community, they would intervene in the affairs of that community as well.

Jewish sources inform us that all applications to the Sublime Porte by communities of the Ottoman Empire were made through the offices of these Jewish courtiers and through the services of other Jews who constituted a Jewish lobby in Istanbul by virtue of their intellectual capabilities or financial positions. Rozen has proven that these Jews influenced favorites of the court to intervene on behalf of the Jews of Jerusalem in the seventeenth century. One may surmise that these Jews operated in a similar manner for other communities throughout the Empire, although there is no extant evidence for this. In addition to their widespread philanthropic activities, the lay leaders attempted to arrange through them matters of taxation, the removal of despotic, hostile governors and the return of beneficial governors to office or the retention of those who were favorable to the Jews, the prevention of blood libels, permission to build synagogues, and the renewal of firmans with the succession of new Sultans.[62] Appeals to these personages of Istanbul were made when there was no choice—when the communities through their own efforts could not settle their own controversial affairs with the local and provincial authorities.[63]

Usually in emergency situations, when there was a crisis with the local authorities, the lay leaders sent their own emissaries to Istanbul. Belonging to the lay or religious establishment, these emissaries had well-defined tasks for their solitary singular mission. They *received* no salary, but their expenses were covered. One such emissary from a community containing two congregations (Larissa?) was sent to Istanbul in 1576 to abolish the heavy duty renewed by the Sultan Murad III (1574-1595), known for his oppressive attitude towards the Jews. This emissary was successful in his endeavors and brought about the publication of a firman from the Sultan to abolish the oppressive tax. The community promised the emissary that it would cover all his expenses by granting him profits amounting to two percent of all merchandise that the community members would export until he would be totally reimbursed. However, just as the emissary was about to complete the negotiations, the community sent another emissary who completed the transaction with the Sultan. Although wealthy, the first emissary had neglected his private enterprises and had spent large sums of his own money in order to succeed in his mission. He took the community to the Jewish court to force it to fulfill its contract with him, and the community tried to release itself from fulfilling its side of the agreement.[64]

There is also evidence of an emissary from the community of Lepanto in the first half of the seventeenth century, who came to complain before the Sublime Porte about the *sancakbeyi* and to forestall his appointment to this office for a second term.[65] During this same period, an emissary of the community of Kezriye (Kastorya) was sent to Istanbul to lobby for the reduction of the taxes that burdened the community. A wealthy Jew, the emissary spread bribe money quite liberally.[66]

The most famous of Jewish community emissaries to the Sublime Porte was Moshe Almonsnino who managed to receive in 1576 the *müselemlik*, the renewal of the wide-ranging privileges of the Salonican Jewish community. After five failures, he was finally successful on his sixth trip to the Ottoman capital—success due to the great lobbying efforts by Jewish courtiers and members of the Ottoman government in Istanbul together with the huge sums of money paid by the community of Salonica to bribe the Ottoman authorities. This firman was published in exchange for the obligation of a large annual payment to the authorities.[67] Another Salonican emissary, well known because of his tragic fate, was Rabbi Yehuda Covo, who led a delegation from his community to Istanbul in 1637. The delegation's letter of appointment was signed by the rabbis, lay leaders, elders and the honored men of Salonica. Apparently, the authorities decided upon his execution in order to frighten the Jews so that they would no longer come to request the reduction of the tax burden. The Turkish public proclamation at the time of the execution of Rabbi Covo stated that "this was the manufacturer of the worst clothing."[68]

THE RELATIONS WITH AUTHORITIES OF ALL RANKS IN ISTANBUL AND THE *VİLAYETS*

The lay leaders of the communities usually initiated their liaison with the Grand Vezir, the Ottoman Prime Minister,[69] through the Jewish lobby in Istanbul. From the sixteenth and seventeenth centuries there are many reports of appeals to him by the leaders of the community of Jerusalem through the offices of the Jewish courtiers and wealthy Jews of Istanbul.[70] A source from the first half of the seventeenth century reports that the Grand Vezir, on his way to war, incarcerated the lay leaders of one of the communities in the house of the *voyvoda*. The *voyvoda* stipulated that their release was dependent upon the receipt of five hundred *gassim* for the war chest.[71]

The Jewish communities also had liaisons with the *bostancı başı* in Istanbul. He was the commander of the palace police and was very influential in the Porte. An epistle sent to a wealthy Jew in Istanbul from the leaders of the Jewish community of Jerusalem in the seventeenth century recounts their request that the recipient would wield his influence with the Grand Vezir, the *bostancı başı*, and the *kızlar ağası* (the Head Eunuch in charge of the harem) to procure orders for the governor of Jerusalem to desist his oppression of the Jews of Jerusalem.[72] There are also reports of appeals by the Jews of Istanbul themselves to the *bostancı başı*. In 1703, the wife of a Jewish merchant who had disappeared five years earlier, heard from a gentile that her husband had died. She requested the *bostancı başı* to send a man "to investigate [the matter] in the villages and to avenge the death of her husband."[73] One may assume that community leaders made many such requests. As derived from testimony gathered in a Jewish court in Istanbul in 1744, the men of the *bostancı başı* executed murderers who had killed Jews.[74]

At the beginning of the sixteenth century, the *defterdar* in Istanbul learned of a regulation passed by the leaders of the city's congregations concerning the minting house, and ordered them to abolish it, threatening them if they refused. The congregational leaders were wary of appearing before him with the famous Rabbi Eliya ha-Levi. Clearly this fear resulted from earlier negotiations, records of which no longer exist.[75] It is also known that the *defterdar* of the *vilayet* of Damascus negotiated with the lay leaders of the Jerusalem community concerning the head tax that was levied upon the Jerusalem's Jews.[76]

The lay leaders also had rare contacts with the *müfti* of Istanbul who was known as the *şeyhülislam*. In a seventeenth-century letter to a wealthy

Jew of Istanbul, the *parnasim* of Jerusalem asked him to exert his efforts in obtaining an order from the *müfti* of Istanbul to the governor of Jerusalem to permit the building of a courtyard in which the Jews of Jerusalem would be able to rent apartments. The governor had already prepared building materials, but he was wary of the reactions of the Muslim *sheikhs*.[77] In another missive, the Jerusalem lay leaders requested a wealthy Jew in Istanbul to have the *müfti* send a letter to the *kadı* ordering him not to oppress the Jews.[78] The Porte required the opinion of the Şeyhülislam many times concerning the enforcement of the Covenant of Omar upon the Jews and especially for permission to build synagogues that had burned down. One may surmise that the leaders of the communities involved in these requests attempted to open contacts with him in order to further their interests in these cases.[79]

The communal leaders also had liaisons at times with each of the two *kadıaskers* who sat in Istanbul. For example, the leaders of the Jerusalem community attempted to secure letters from each new *kadıasker* who took office in order to initiate ties with him. Similarly, they sent letters to a wealthy man in Istanbul requesting that he apply his influence upon the *kadıasker*, *müfti* and *ulema* to send a missive to the *kadı* of Jerusalem not to oppress them and to issue a *fetva* concerning the *kısma* (authorization granting the division of an estate) that the heirs of a deceased were obligated to pay.[80]

During the sixteenth and seventeenth centuries, the Jews of Jerusalem and their leaders sometimes presented to the *kadı* of Jerusalem *fetvas* authored by the *müfti* of Jerusalem concerning such matters as usury.[81] The Jerusalem leaders even attempted to support a *sheikh* who had aided the community in his bid to be appointed as *müfti* in Jerusalem.[82]

The Jewish lay leaders everywhere were conscious of the power of the heads of the *vilayets*, usually called *paşa, beylerbey* and *vali*.[83] Although the *paşa* was not completely autonomous—for the sultan could overrule his decisions—he still exerted great authority, and he usually employed it to the utmost, at times increasing his powers by circumventing the limits placed upon him by the central government. The communities attempted to guarantee that only their official representatives negotiated with the *paşa* and *sancakbeyi*. This is the background for the regulation passed in the community of Arta in the sixteenth century, "that no one shall enter the houses of the ministers called *voyvoda*, unless called for explicitly." The aim of the regulation was to "uproot the informers that they should not enter the houses of the ministers. . . ." In reality, many individuals violated the ban and were not punished.[84] There were daily ties between the communal leaders and the *sancak* rulers. The various ministers changed offices at a high rate, and many of them wanted to utilize the different monetary duties to their utmost during their short reigns. Many sources point out the connivance of the *sancakbeyi* and his retainers for the extortion of money from the Jews through false accusations by informers.[85] The extortion was often openly directed to the local Jewish merchants through additional taxation, as in the example of Patras in the beginning of the seventeenth century.[86] As pointed out above, the lay leaders would at times send emissaries to Istanbul in order to prompt the Jewish courtiers to act on their behalf. Sometimes the *sancakbeyis* were fair, while at other times the *beylerbeys* were fair while the *sancakbeyis* were quite negative toward the Jews. Such is the case in the seventeenth century concerning the Avlonya Jews who settled in Berat (Belgrade) who appealed to the *beylerbey* to grant them a *buyuruldu* (a command of a high official to a subordinate) releasing them from paying taxes in this city. However, for a similar authorization they did not turn to his second-in-command, the *sancakbey* himself, who burdened the Jews of the city with heavy taxation.[87]

The lay leaders would also send representatives to hold talks with the *valis* (*paşas*) of the *viyalets*. However, these officials could not intervene much because of the Empire's system of governmental appointments. A Hebrew source from the beginning of the seventeenth century reports that:

> it is well known that the *sancakbeyi* within his city and boundaries was like the Sultan, and so was the *kadı* and any one powerful, especially the *sancakbeyi* and the *kadı* whose power was all-embracing and doing whatever they want, even opposing the sultan, for who could deliberate before such a despotic man, and who could take him to court before the sultan. And should he spend a sum of money . . . he will be sought out, and the complainer will suffer very much. And many times we have seen with our own eyes that someone brought a firman from the sultan, and the *kadı* and *sancakbeyi* do not obey it or enforce it. And how many firmans from the Sultan are in our hands but are useless, and who can tell them what to do . . . consequently nowadays the very natural order has been reversed. . . .[88]

This source notes the weakening of government administration during the beginning of the seventeenth century and the helplessness of the Jewish communities in dealing with despotic chieftains. Subsequently, the communities were forced to appeal less to the supreme rulers, and to settle their problems with those local rulers for huge sums of money.[89] Cohen and Rozen point out that the Jews of Jerusalem during the sixteenth and the seventeenth centuries generally appealed to the *vali* of Damascus and to the Sublime Porte,

Jewish Lay Leadership and Ottoman Authorities / 105

to help them in their times of distress and despair. The authorities would either respond to those who appealed or would demand that the governor of Jerusalem and the *kadı* investigate or improve the situation.

Examples from the sixteenth century demonstrate this. At the end of the sixteenth century, when the local authorities of Jerusalem attempted to expropriate the synagogue located at Nebi Samuel (the burial site of the Prophet Samuel), and the Jews were even enjoined from making pilgrimages to the place, the leaders of the Jerusalem community appealed to the Sublime Porte for help. They received an order in September 1598, commanding the *sancakbeyi* and the *kadı* to see that the Jews were not disturbed in their pilgrimage and prayers at the place. In 1554, the Jerusalem lay leaders complained to Istanbul about plots against those who were making pilgrimages to Jerusalem and the demands of *cizye* from them. Complaints were also *received* from the Jews of Cairo, Damascus and Safed concerning illegal duties levied upon them upon arrival at Jerusalem as pilgrims. The Sublime Porte sent an order instructing the *sancakbeyi* and the *kadı* of Jerusalem to refrain from such illegal acts.[90] Similarly, in 1636, the Muslim population was incited against the Jewish inhabitants because of a false accusation that the Jews wanted to murder a Jewish youth who had converted to Islam and had escaped to Egypt. The lay leaders sent missives to their Damascene brethren imploring them to exert their influence on the *vali* in Damascus so that he would write to the governor and *kadı* of Jerusalem to guard the youth from any harm. The epistles hint that the cause behind the agitation was the Jerusalem governor himself, who wished to extort money from Jerusalem's Jews, and in this he was successful.[91] The lay leaders of Jerusalem presented documentation to the governors to protect the rights of the communities, and in 1556, the governor expropriated a document presented to him concerning the synagogue in Jerusalem. The document was returned to its lawful owner at the end of the affair.[92]

The lay leaders of the communities had to report community individuals who were immoral and transgressed the moral norms, and were thus obligated to be tried in criminal proceedings in the *şeri* court. The dearth of information concerning the extradition of Jews in such cases during the sixteenth and seventeenth centuries demonstrates that the community did its utmost to prevent handing over those guilty to criminal courts, settling these problems quietly. Only when there was no choice were these felons handed over to the authorities. In the eighteenth century, an appeal by the leaders of a Jewish community, probably Izmir, was made to the *sancakbey*. After rumors had spread about a woman throughout the whole city, they reported the case of this adulteress. He sent the *çavuş* to arrest the lady and the adulterer. While the woman was imprisoned, rumors were heard that the *sancakbeyi* wanted to banish the two adulterers from the country, a solution which the community leaders also desired.[93]

In extreme cases, when various *sancakbeyis* made exaggerated attempts of extortion or were unduly hostile through other schemes and plots against them, the Jews attempted to influence the central government to remove them. Nonetheless, the communities generally accepted each governor's demands as a fact of life. It is clear that the central government itself was interested in putting an end to this practice of forced payments, although its success in terminating this was quite limited. The example of Lepanto in the beginning of the seventeenth century demonstrates this. A newly appointed *sancakbeyi* came into conflict with the citizens of the city and the Turkish functionaries until he was forced to leave during the first year of his appointment. He returned to the city with a private army, caused of a number of murders and was subsequently forced to flee the city. He notified the Jews that they should not dare to join the Muslims in their attempt to remove him from office. After he left the city, a *kapıcı* from Istanbul arrived with a firman to prevent that *sancakbeyi* from reentering the city. The Jews informed him of the illegal extortion of funds that the *sancakbeyi* had extracted from them. They also sent an emissary to Istanbul with accompanying documentation against that *sancakbeyi*. Much to his misfortune, the emissary was found by the *sancakbeyi* in Istanbul, who vented his anger upon him, shaving off his beard. Afterwards, he bought his office for a third time and returned to Lepanto. The congregations of the city sent messengers to appease him and bribed him with 2,500 *gassim*. Among the financial complaints that he raised was the blood money for all the murders that had taken place in the city during his absence in the second year of his rule. Since murderers were found in the "*Kahal* street," i.e., in the Jewish quarter, they had to pay the blood money.[94] The Jerusalem community also initiated the removal of extorting and hostile *sancakbeyis*, such as Muhammat Ibn Farouh in the years 1624-1626. However, the community had limited success.[95]

The lay leaders also had ties with the *subaşı* who was responsible for the security of the whole province. The nature of these ties and his attitude toward the Jewish community can be determined by some *sicils* from sixteenth-century Jerusalem in which the sums he collected as marriage tax are described together with other excuses to extract money.[96] He even received a fixed sum from the communal treasury during the seventeenth century.[97]

Everywhere the Jewish leaders had many ties with the local *kadı* whose appointment was fixed to a limited time and was dependent upon the central government in Istanbul, not the local government. In addition to his judicial duties, he was responsible for many administrative roles in the Ottoman city.[98] The local *kadıs* received firmans from the Porte which had direct bearing upon the relations of the government with the local Jews, and upon the enforcement of the segregation laws and the outlawing of libels.[99] There were *kadıs* who acted fairly toward the Jews, such as the *kadıs* of Jerusalem in the sixteenth century,[100] especially the one in 1636, who attempted to prevent a blood libel against the Jews.[101] In one of the communities (apparently in Greece) during the seventeenth century, the Jews refused the request of the *paşa* to sign a petition against the *kadı* who had returned to Istanbul because of a disagreement with him. Informers bore false tales to this same *paşa* that the Jews had aided this *kadı*, sending with him three Jews to accompany him to Istanbul.[102] Rozen points out that the public good was the central factor for the Jerusalem *kadı*'s confirmation of the 1638 request of Shmuel ben Aharon, the Jerusalem officer in charge of the Ashkenazic *vakıf*, to renovate a building belonging to the community that was about to fall down. The *kadıs* of Jerusalem throughout the seventeenth century also revealed tolerance in their judicial decisions concerning the payment of communal debts.[103]

However, there are many cases of many *kadıs* in sixteenth- and seventeenth-century Jerusalem who disappointed the hopes of the Jewish community and took advantage of judicial deliberations concerning the communal debts to Muslim creditors in order to extort more money. In one case in the seventeenth century, the *kadı* decreed that the community immediately pay the debts, and imprisoned the leaders until the sum of five hundred *grossos* was paid. Upon payment, he reached a compromise with the Jews and their creditors, but then changed his mind and continued to hold the leaders as prisoners. Finally, they wrote to Istanbul courtiers to intervene to remove the *kadı*.[104]

There are reports of *kadıs* in other cities of the Ottoman Empire who joined hands with the governors to extort huge sums of money, as in Patras during the seventeenth century.[105] The Jerusalem community also paid the *kadı* a fixed sum to receive a permit to bury its dead. The *kadı* of Jerusalem and his retainers were fixed customers on the community list of bribery payments during the seventeenth century.[106] The Jerusalem community attempted to improve its relationship with the *kadı* by pressuring him from Istanbul, and at times this pressure had positive results.[107] One may assume that a similar situation existed within other communities of the Empire. The community of Jerusalem also gave large sums of money to the *kasam*, one of the *kadı's* bureaucrats. Until he received payment, the *kasam* would halt burial and not grant the *kısma*.[108] The payoffs to the *kadı* for the *kısma* was a common practice throughout the cities of the Empire.[109]

BRIBERY

As mentioned, the lay leaders often offered the authorities bribes. This common practice found expression in the words of Rabbi David Ibn Abi Zimra (Radbaz, 1479-1573), judge of the Jewish community of Cairo for forty years (circa 1513-1553) who later served on the bench in Jerusalem (he died in Safed in 1573), and wrote: "In this Diaspora, we cannot live among them except through bribes and [monetary] losses, for what shall a lamb do among the wolves, for naught will they tear out his wool...."[110] Rabbinic literature shows that this was a common and widespread practice of both individuals and lay leaders.[111] Bribes were given to the central personalities in Sublime Porte by means of the Jewish courtiers and community emissaries.[112] In the cities themselves, the payoffs were given by the lay leaders directly to the rulers and functionaries.

THE *PARNASIM* AS RESPONSIBLE FOR CRIMES OF THE COMMUNITY (IMPRISONMENT OF THE *PARNASIM* AS HOSTAGES, AND TORTURE)

The lay leaders suffered from the crimes of the community because they were held responsible for the community's debts to the authorities. The history of the Jewish community of Jerusalem during the existence of the Ottoman Empire is filled with reports of the imprisonment of lay leaders as a result of almost continual scheming by the rulers against them, essentially due to their desire to squeeze money out of the Jewish population.

There are especially numerous reports from the reign of Muhammad Ibn Farouh (1624-1626) in Jerusalem. He threatened to expel the Jews from the city, wealthy and important community members were incarcerated, and lay leaders and rabbis were tortured by him. It has come to light that when this governor came to Jerusalem, the lay leaders, the physician Yaakov Ibn

Amram and Yitzhak Gaon, gave him a gift, which was customary in the city. However, after three days, the community was ordered to pay 1,300 *grossos*, a sum that no governor had ever levied. The Jerusalem population, including the Muslims and Christians, soon discovered that he was an unscrupulous extortionist. Many Jews fled the city during his reign. In 1626, famous Jerusalemite rabbis and lay leaders went to Istanbul to complain about the situation. The local despot attempted to halt the correspondence with Istanbul. The lay and spiritual leadership of the community also appealed during his reign to the *vali* of Damascus, who sometimes appointed the governor of Jerusalem. In another case in 1636, eight Jerusalem community leaders were arrested and held as hostages until the emissaries of the community, sent to Egypt by order of the *kadı* to Egypt, returned the Jewish youth who had been forced to convert to Islam.[113]

Reports of the imprisonment of lay leaders become numerous in the seventeenth century. In the first half of this century, the Grand Vezir imprisoned the leaders of one community in the home of the *voyvoda*.[114] Another report from that period tells that the lives of the *hahamim*, Yaakov Leon and his son, were in danger in Izmir. The *paşa* had taken both into captivity and sentenced them to death. Eventually, the father was released, but his son remained in prison. Yaakov Leon demanded that the *kollelut ha-ir* (community council) release his son at any price, but the *kollelut* refused. Both sides finally reached a compromise.[115]

Another example from the end of the sixteenth century reports that one of the lay leaders of Patras was arrested by the governor of Morea, Davut Ağa, after he had been commanded to pay the *ispence* tax for two years in the name of four congregations in the city. The ruler tortured and imprisoned him, and afterwards two more Jews were apprehended. The three were forced to take out loans at high interest rates to pay the required tax. Upon his release from prison, the *parnas* demanded that his colleagues collect the necessary amount, and they were forced to comply with his demands.[116]

As already mentioned, the imprisonment of leaders for non-payment of taxes was a common occurrence.[117] In one community (probably in Greece) during the seventeenth century, the *paşa* took into custody eleven Jews who were not leaders, in lieu of the leaders who had hidden themselves. He did this because he claimed that the *parnasim* allowed a certain Jew to serve the *kadı*, with whom the *paşa* was feuding. These Jews paid the sum of ninety-eight *grossos* in exchange for their liberty.[118]

THE HANDING OVER OF INDIVIDUALS BY THE LAY LEADERS AND THE APPEAL TO GENTILE COURTS

Rarely did the Jewish lay leaders hand a colleague over to the authorities in order to force him to comply with their rule.[119] However, with recalcitrant individual community members, the leaders employed this last resort quite often. One may assume that even in these cases they first tried to force him to comply by other means, for any surrender to the authorities was detrimental to their autonomy.[120]

The leaders also handed over individuals when they were guilty of criminal offenses. In such cases, the Ottoman law demanded judgment in the *şeri* courts.[121] Ottoman documents from the middle of the sixteenth century mention the Jewish *kâhya* in the city of Irbil and his trial in a Muslim court. The *yayabaşı* of the community of Sofia were accused of perfidy, extortion, and oppression.[122] Almost certainly they were handed over by the lay leaders or their colleagues to the government authorities. More such cases are found in the seventeenth century onwards than in preceding years because, as had been previously stated a number of times, the political status of the Jews within the Empire was deteriorating. Accordingly, the lay leaders of one community in the seventeenth century were willing to surrender the son of a wealthy Jew to the *voyvoda*, thereby preventing a severe libel that could endanger the community.[123] Hence, the lay leaders observed the Ottoman laws scrupulously, and in this period of political decline, usually did not dare risk circumventing any state law. This position is reflected in their attitude to the *şeri* courts. As a general rule, they negated any appeal to a Muslim court, but in reality they appealed to them in extreme cases and when there was no option, bearing in mind the security of the Jewish communities.

From rabbinical sources it is apparent that the Jewish community leaders throughout the Empire categorically opposed appearing before the Muslim court, the *mahkeme* (referred to Jewish sources as the courts of gentiles—*Arhaot shel Goyim*), except in unique cases where Ottoman law required.[124] Certainly within the community they preferred the rabbinical courts for settling any internal controversy in the leadership management, thus preserving their autonomy. In spite of all this, the *parnasim* at times, as proven above, did surrender Jews to the gentile courts for trial.

There were cases when the lay leaders appealed to the authorities when internal discord and controversy among the leaders threatened the management of communal affairs. In the seventeenth century, one lay leader was a difficult and contentious man, who caused communal strife. Once, in his absence, his colleagues conferred and passed a written resolution not to meet with him any longer, and should he come to the community council meetings (*maamad*), they would leave, or no longer discuss the topic for which they had assembled. Upon learning of this conspiracy against him, the *parnas* appealed to the *kadı* who sent one of his retainers to arrest a relative of one of the other lay leaders with the intention of trying him before the *mahkeme*. The accused denied all knowledge of the secret agreement, and demanded that the *parnas* take him to a rabbinical court, but the *parnas* stubbornly insisted that the matter be tried before the Muslim court. Every Jew present at the time of the arrest admonished the *parnas* not to transgress by handing over a Jew to the Muslim courts, but the *parnas* stubbornly refused. He ordered the *kadı's* retainer to bring the accused to the Muslim court against his will and employed violence to accomplish this.[125]

There is also an exceptional report from a sixteenth-century Ottoman document concerning a Jew whose activities, which included the collective payments of taxes in kind on behalf of the community, incurred the enmity of the council by complaining about it to the Muslim courts. He was excommunicated or was about to be excommunicated by the community. The Ottoman authorities ordered that he be transferred to Cyprus.[126]

The leaders also handed over to the Muslim courts those individuals who opposed the very foundations and values of Jewish society and the community when there was no alternative punishment or manner of enforcing their authority. An instructive example of sixteenth-century Safed is found in the responsa of Rabbi Moses MiTrani, one of the greatest of Safed's rabbinical judges. He recorded that he had been called to a joint rabbinical court of all the congregations of the city which usually dealt with significant topics relating to the whole community. In this case, the joint court was called into session to deal with Yaakov Zarkon who had tendencies toward heresy. The judges granted permission to the lay leaders to punish him through the Muslim court. He was arrested and flogged until he weepingly pleaded the lay leaders to supervise his interests and to try to save him from his imprisonment. However, the leaders told him to leave the city so that he would not soil the community with his evil deeds. His wife's relatives insisted that before he be banished from Safed, he should divorce his wife, which he did. His wife gave him a sum of money that he was obligated to pay the gentiles, and the lay leaders paid the balance in accordance to the compromise made with the gentiles, and he left.[127]

A similar case is found in sixteenth-century Jerusalem where the Jewish communal lay leadership appealed to the *kadı* to arrest a Jew who had acted insanely in his house; to banish another Jew who had acted wildly or insanely, causing damage to the community; and to banish from the neighborhood still another Jew who had converted to Islam and was causing insufferable tension.[128] Without a doubt, the lay leaders supported the handing over of recalcitrant Jews who refused to obey significant judicial decisions of the Jewish courts.[129] A similar case is found in Manisa in 1672: "The following happened in our city. A bad man caused the men of the community to issue a ban and to punish him through the offices of the gentiles, and the man hid himself and the *paşa* searched for him."[130] As mentioned above, only on rare occasions did the lay leaders report cases of adultery among members of the community, and only when the adulterers refused to accept the judicial decisions of the Jewish court, or when the gentiles heard of the case. In such cases, the Ottoman authorities demanded to punish the guilty parties according to Ottoman law.[131] From the meager reports of applications to the authorities in cases of adultery, one may conclude that the majority of these cases were dealt with in accordance with Jewish law, such as the prohibition of the adulteress to cohabit with either her husband or her lover.[132]

In conclusion, the status of the lay leaders *vis-à-vis* the Ottoman authorities influenced their own authority within Jewish society itself. Their status granted them power in domestic affairs, and Jewish society recognized the need for a lay leader to administer internal affairs.[133] There is no proof that they used this power for their own personal gain, except on rare occasions. Without a doubt, they are noted for their flexibility and ability to reach decisions for the public good in their negotiations with the Ottoman governmental authorities. The topic should be further investigated as more research based upon Ottoman archives is published and more information is revealed.

NOTES

1 Amnon Cohen, *The Jewish Community of Jerusalem in the 16th Century* (in Hebrew) (Jerusalem, 1982), 7-16 [hereafter: Cohen, *Jerusalem*]. This article does not deal with the scholarly controversy whether the *Millet* system was in use from the very beginning of the Ottoman Empire or only from the nineteenth century. See B. Braude and B. Lewis, eds., *Chris-*

tians and Jews in the Ottoman Empire, 2 vols. (New York, 1982). See also H. Gerber, *Economic and Social Life of the Jews in the Ottoman Empire in the 16th and 17th Centuries* (in Hebrew) (Jerusalem, 1982), 9, 35; Z. Ankori, *Encounter in History: Jews and Christian Greeks in their Relation Through the Ages* (in Hebrew) (Tel Aviv, 1984), 158ff.

2 Leah Bornstein, "The Jewish Communal Leadership in the Near East From the End of the 15th Century Through the 18th Century" (in Hebrew) (diss., Bar-Ilan University, Ramat Gan, 1978), 215-38 [hereafter: Bornstein, Dissertation]; Leah Bornstein-Makovetsky, "Cooperation and Conflict Between the Religious and Political Leadership (Relations Between *parnasim* and Rabbis in the Communities of the Ottoman Empire During the 16th and 17th Centuries)," in *Conflict and Consensus in Jewish Political Life* (in Hebrew), eds. S. A. Cohen and E. Don-Yehiya (Ramat Gan, 1986), 15-30; idem, "Tendencies of Separation and Unification in Greek-Jewish Communities during the 16th and 17th Centuries" (in Hebrew), *Bar-Ilan Annual* 20-21 (1983): 242-70. These articles contain a comprehensive bibliography on this topic.

3 One should note that sometimes these appellations referred to other offices of the community, *e.g.* the leaders of the Talmud Tora, *hekdeshot* (*vakıfs*), social societes, etc. Bornstein, Dissertation, 215.

4 Rabbi Yitzhak Idrabi, *Divrei Rivot Responsa* (Venice, 1587), no. 395; Rabbi Moses miTrani (Mabit), *Responsa*, III (Venice, 1630), nos. 32, 188; Cohen, *Jerusalem*; Minna Rozen, *The Jewish Community of Jerusalem in the Seventeenth Century* (in Hebrew) (Tel Aviv, 1984), v. index.

5 M. A. Epstein, *The Ottoman Jewish Communities and Their Role in the Fifteenth and Sixteenth Centuries* (Freiburg, 1980), 75.

6 Ibid., 54-55.

7 Rabbi Shmuel de Medina (Rashdam), *Responsa, Yoreh Deah* (Salonica, 1597), no. 128.

8 Rabbi Moses Galanti (Ramag), *Responsa* (Venice, 1608), no. 47; *Divrei Rivot Responsa*, no. 99.

9 See below for the discussion on the aid given by court Jews and special representatives and see notes 63-68.

10 See below for the discussion about the local government, especially the *sancakbeyis*.

11 Rabbi Yosef mi-Trani (Maharit), *Responsa*, II, *Yoreh Deah* (Furth, 1768), no. 14.

12 Epstein, *The Ottoman Jewish Communities*, 74-75.

13 Rabbi Haim Shabtai, *Torat Haim Responsa*, III (Salonica, 1722), no. 34; Bornstein, Dissertation, 62-63.

14 See below the discussion concerning tax-collecting on the part of the *parnasim*.

15 J. Hacker, "Israel Among the Nations as Described by Solomon Le-Beit Ha-Levi of Salonica" (in Hebrew), *Zion* 34 (1969): 72-73.

16 Regulations of the Sixteenth Century: Rabbi Eliya ha-Levi, *Zekan Aharon Responsa* (Constantinople, 1734), no. 36; Mabit, *Responsa*, I (Venice, 1629), no. 44.Concerning the oath taken by a member of the community not to serve as *parnas*, see the Responsa of the Sages of Egypt of the seventeenth century, Bodleian Library ms. 845, opp. add. 4-1, fol. 108a. A case that happened in Egypt at the end of the seventeenth century or the beginning of the eighteenth century is recounted in the responsa of Joshua Shababu Yedia Zayin, Jewish Theological Seminary, New York, ms. Adler 1319, fol. 228a: "Reuben who swore not to be Gabai and the trusted officer (Neeman) of the community, and now he wants to annul the oath...."

17 Rabbi Shmuel Kalai, *Mishpatei Shmuel Responsa* (Venice, 1599), no. 54.

18 H. W. Dudda and G. D. Galalov, "Die Protokollbücher der qadiamtes Sofia," *Südosteuroäpische Arbeiten* 55 (Munich, 1930), no. 407.

19 Cohen, *Jerusalem*, 44-46.

20 Mabit, *Responsa*, no. 32.

21 Rabbi David Ibn Abi Zimra (Radbaz), *Responsa*, III (Furth, 1981), no. 906. See also below for the discussion of the *kâhya*.

22 See Bornstein-Makovetsky, note 2.

23 A. Shmuelevitz, *The Jews of the Ottoman Empire in the Late Fifteenth and the Sixteenth Centuries* (Leiden, 1984), 126. See also the basic research articles on this subject by: B. Lewis, "The Privilege Granted by Mehmed II to his Physician," *BSOAS* 14 (1952): 550-63; Gerber, *Economic and Social Life of the Jews in the Ottoman Empire*, 36-45; Shmuelevitz, ibid., 14ff., 81-127; A. Shohat, "Taxation and its Administration in Greek Communities in the 16th Century" (in Hebrew), *Sefunot* 11 (1971-77): 299-340; idem, "The King's Clothing in Salonica" (in Hebrew), *Sefunot* 12 (1971-78): 169-88; J. R. Hacker, "The Payment of Djizya by Scholars in Palestine in the Sixteenth Century" (in Hebrew), *Shalem* 4 (1984): 63-118; Bornstein, Dissertation, 91-94; Cohen, *Jerusalem*, 25-59, 70-79.

24 Rashdam, *Responsa, Yoreh Deah*, no. 152.

25 Rabbi Yaakov Beirab, *Responsa*, no. 22; Rabbi Yaakov Tam Yahya, *Ohalei Tam Responsa* (Venice, 1622), no. 205; Mabit, *Responsa*, III, nos. 188, 228; Ramag, *Responsa*, no 7; Maharit, *Responsa*, II, *Yoreh Deah*, no 39; Rabbi Meir Melamed, *Mishpat Zedek Responsa*, I (Salonica, 1615), no. 20; Rabbi Aharon Ha-Cohen Perahya, *Parah Mateh Aharon Responsa*, III (Amsterdam, 1703), no. 118.

26 Rabbi Shlomo Gaon, *Mishpatim Yesharim Responsa* (Salonica, 1732), no. 22; *Mishpatei Shmuel Responsa*, 24; see also below for the discussion about the *parnasims*' responsibility for the sins of their communities.

27 Cohen, *Jerusalem*, 44.
28 Bornstein, Dissertation, 204 for the responsa literature.
29 J. Hacker, "Jewish Autonomy in the Ottoman Empire: Its Scope and Limits" (in Hebrew), in *Transition and Change in Modern Jewish History: Essays Presented in Honor to Shmuel Ettinger* (in Hebrew), eds. Shmuel Almog, Yisrael Bartal, Michael Graetz, et al. (Jerusalem, 1987), 366ff.
30 Shmuelevitz, *The Jews of the Ottoman Empire*, 24-26.
31 See Bornstein, Dissertation, 129 and the sources listed there, n. 40.
32 Shmuelevitz, *The Jews of the Ottoman Empire*, 27 identifies them with the *mahalle-başı* Muslims who kept an eye on the Jewish quarter when there were no leaders. However, from the context, it appears that the subjects are Jewish leaders who replaced Shealtiel after his ouster.
33 Rabbi Eliahu Mizrahi, *Responsa* (Jerusalem, 1938), nos. 14-15; Epstein, *The Ottoman Jewish Communities*, 62-67; Shmuelevitz, *The Jews of the Ottoman Empire*, 62-68.
34 An example from the year 1744 is found in Rabbi Abraham Meyuhas, *Benei Avraham Responsa, Even Ha-Ezer* (Constantinople, 1773), nos. 3, 7.
35 A. Danon, "Documents Relating to the History of the Karaites in European Turkey," *Jewish Quarterly Review*, n.s., 17 (1926-27): 264, 293.
36 The claims by the historians S. A. Rozanes, *History of the Jews in Turkey* (in Hebrew), 6 vols. (Sofia and Tel Aviv, 1907-45), 2:56-59; J. Nehama, *Histoire des Israélites de Salonique*, vol. 3 (Salonica, 1936), 125ff; I. S. Emmanuel, *Histoire des Israélites de Salonique* (Paris, 1936), 116; and also Epstein, *The Ottoman Jewish Communities*, 74, that Baruh, one of the rich men in Salonica during the sixteenth century, served as a *kâhya* has no real basis.
37 Radbaz, *Responsa*, III, no. 906.
38 In the 1650's and 1660's, he was one of the important congregational heads and a central figure in the Izmir community. In 1669 he was already well known as a rabbi, and in the 1670's and 1680's his position was more important than the chosen rabbis of the community. The sources also mention his thorough knowledge of Turkish. See Rabbi Haim Benveneste *Baey Hayey Responsa, Hoshen Mishpat*, II (Salonica, 1791), no. 78; Rabbi Moshe Benveneste, *Penei Moshe Responsa*, III (Constantinople, 1719), no. 58; *Parah Mateh Aharon Responsa*, I (Amsterdam, 1703), no. 64; and the introduction by Rabbi Shlomo Ibn Ezra in Rabbi Haim Benveneste, *Sheyarei Knesset Ha-Gedolah, Orah Haim* (Izmir, 1671); Rozanes, *History of the Jews in Turkey*, 4:168; J. Barnai, "A Document from Izmir Concerning the History of Sabbateanism" (in Hebrew), *Jerusalem Studies in Jewish Thought* 2 (1982): 118-31.

39 See the introduction by Rabbi Shlomo Ibn Ezra in *Sheyarei Knesset Ha-Gedolah*; J. Barnai, "A Document from Izmir Concerning the History of Sabbateanism" (in Hebrew), *Jerusalem Studies in Jewish Thought* 2 (1982): 118-31.

40 Epstein, *The Ottoman Jewish Communities*, 74-75.

41 *Mishpatei Shmuel Responsa*, no. 74; Rashdam, *Responsa, Yoreh Deah*, no. 225; Rabbi Meir Gavizon, *Responsa*, edited by E. Shochetman (Jerusalem, 1985), nos. 12, 27; Maharival, *Responsa*, IV, no. 15; Gerber, *Economy and Social Life of the Jews*, 143.

42 Rabbi Abraham di Boton, *Lehem Rav Responsa* (Izmir, 1740), no. 67.

43 See below.

44 Concerning the regulations of Omar and their actual enforcement, see Bornstein, Dissertation, 29-36; M. Winter, "The Relations of Egyptian Jews with the Authorities and with the Non-Jewish Society," in *The Jews in Ottoman Egypt (1517-1914)*, ed. J. M. Landau (Jerusalem, 1988), 390-95; Epstein, *The Ottoman Jewish Communities*, 30ff; Gerber, *Economy and Social Life of the Jews*, 9-20; Cohen, *Jerusalem*, 80-114.

45 This has already been discussed by many scholars. See A. Galanté, *Documents officiels turcs* (Istanbul, 1931), 50-54, 163-66; Bornstein, Dissertation, 30-31; Epstein, *The Ottoman Jewish Communities*, 29ff.; Cohen, *Jerusalem*, 34-35; Rozen, *The Jewish Community of Jerusalem*, 187. For an example of the scheming against a synagogue in Egypt during the seventeenth century, see Rabbi Mordechai Ha-Levi, *Darhei Noam Responsa, Hoshen Mishpat* (Venice, 1697), no. 21; Yosef Sambari, *Divrei Yosef* (Bodleian ms. 2410, opp. 34), 75. For Istanbul in the sixteenth and the seventeenth centuries, see Rabbi Eliahu Ibn Haim (Ranah), *Responsa* (Venice, 1610), no. 60; Danon, "Documents Relating to the History of the Karaites," 253-54. A question in a manuscript to Rabbi Shmuel Pinto, ms. Ginzbourg-Moscow 398, fol. 21a, reveals that the Jews of Marmara Ereğlisi in Turkey, were told to evacuate their synagogue. The local gentiles expropriated all the books, prayer-books, and prayer-shawls in the synagogue, using the claim, "You have no permission to build a synagogue." For the sum of 50 *grossos* paid by the Jews to the city judge, they redeemed their books.

46 Ranah, *Responsa*, no 81; idem, *Mayim Amukim Responsa*, II (Venice, 1647), no. 11. Concerning the problem of the Jerusalem cemetery and the proceedings in the Muslim court as a result of difficulties in the renewal of the contracts to lease the land where the Jewish cemetery stood, see Cohen, *Jerusalem*, 96ff.; Rozen, *The Jewish Community of Jerusalem*, 171-73 which includes an extensive bibliography.

47 U. Heyd, "Ritual Murder Accusations in 15th and 16th Century Turkey" (in Hebrew), *Sefunot* 5 (1961): 135-50; H. Jacobsohn, "Testimony

Jewish Lay Leadership and Ottoman Authorities / 117

from Salonica on an Unknown Blood Libel in Greece in the Seventeenth Century," in *Then and Now* (in Hebrew), ed. Z. Ankori (Tel Aviv, 1984), 67-72. On attempts to accuse the Jews of Jerusalem in the sixteenth century of blood libels, albeit without the usual claim that the blood was needed for rituals, see Cohen, *Jerusalem*, 138-39.

48 Rabbi Yaakov Castro, *Ohalei Yaakov Responsa* (Livorno, 1783), no. 47, offers an example from Egypt at the end of the sixteenth century and the beginning of the seventeenth.

49 *Baey Hayey Responsa, Hoshen Mishpat*, I (Salonica, 1788), no. 229.

50 There is plenty of information on this subject within the responsa literature, e.g., Mabit, *Responsa*, I, no. 22; *Parah Mateh Aharon Responsa*, III, no. 12. Ottoman documents from the 1470's recount Jewish leaders who acted for the release of Jewish guarantors from prison. See Epstein, *The Ottoman Jewish Communities*, 114-17, 124.

51 *Mishpat Zedek Responsa*, I, no. 20. See below for the collection of taxes.

52 There is much material in rabbinic literature from the period.

53 Rabbi Binyamin ben Matatya, *Binyamin Zeev Responsa* (Venice, 1539), no. 249. Concerning the appeal to gentile courts, see below the discussion about the handing over of individuals to the authorities and the use of the leaders of gentile courts.

54 These were published by H. Sahillioğlu, "Yeniçeri Çuhası ve II Bayezidin Son Yıllarında Yeniçeri Çuha Muhasebesi," *Güney Doğu Avrupa Araştırmaları Dergisi*, vols. 2-3 (Istanbul, 1974), 420-21. A summary of the literature is found in R. Cohen, "Socioeconomic Development in Salonica in the Wake of the Portuguese Marrano Immigration" (in Hebrew), in *From Lisbon to Salonica and Constantinople* (in Hebrew), ed. Z. Ankori (Tel Aviv, 1988), 53-68. See also M. Z. Benaya, "Moses Almosnino and the Influx of Portuguese Jewish Immigrants to Salonica" (in Hebrew) in *From Lisbon to Salonica and Constantinople*, 95-120.

55 Rashdam, *Responsa, Hoshen Mishpat*, no. 407.

56 Gerber, *Economy and Social Life of the Jews*, 35; Shmuelevitz, *The Jews of the Ottoman Empire*, 76-78, 156-57.

57 Cohen, *Jerusalem*, 67. There are reports of observing this law on the part of the communities together with cases of evasion of the law in responsa literature; see Shmuelevitz, *The Jews of the Ottoman Empire*.

58 Cohen, *Jerusalem*, 66-70; J. Barnai, *The Jews in Eretz Israel in the Eighteenth Century* (in Hebrew) (Jerusalem, 1982), 272-74.

59 See for example, Mabit, *Responsa*, III, no. 183; Gerber, *Economy and Social Life of the Jews*, 35.

60 Gerber, ibid.

61 *Lehem Rav Responsa*, no. 67.
62 Rozen, *The Jewish Community of Jerusalem*, 27.
63 Epstein, *The Ottoman Jewish Communities*, 78-81; Gerber, *Economy and Social Life of the Jews*, 61-66; U. Heyd, "Moses Hamon Chief Jewish Physician to Sultan Süleyman the Magnificent," *Oriens* 16 (1963): 152-70; L. Bornstein-Makovetsky, "Portuguese Jews at the Sultan's Court of Constantinople in the Sixteenth Century: Don Josef Nasi" (in Hebrew), in *From Lisbon to Salonica and Constantinople*, 69-94; Rozen, *The Jewish Community of Jerusalem*, 23ff.; idem, "Influential Jews in the Sultan's Court in Istanbul in Support of Jerusalem Jewry in the 17th Century" (in Hebrew), *Michael* 7 (1981): 394-430; S. Baron, *A Social and Religious History of the Jews*, vol. 18 (New York, 1983), 74-147; J. Hacker, "Some Letters on the Expulsion of the Jews from Spain and Sicily" (in Hebrew), in *Studies in History of Jewish Society...Presented to...Jacob Katz* (in Hebrew), eds. E. Etkes and Y. Salmon (Jerusalem, 1980), 71-73. All these articles contain a general bibliography on the topic, including the works of Rozanes, Benayahu, Galanté, Danon, and Roth.
64 Maharival, *Responsa*, IV, no. 14.
65 *Torat Haim Responsa*, III, no. 93.
66 *Magen Geborim Responsa*, no. 40.
67 Benaya, "Moses Almosnino and the Influx of Portuguese Jewish Immigrants to Salonica," 95-120.
68 *Torat Haim Responsa*, I, no. 94; Maharit, *Responsa and Decisions*, ed. Rabbi Tzvi Leitner (Jerusalem, 1978), no. 27; Rozanes, *History of the Jews of Turkey*, 3:396-98.
69 In Hebrew sources he is known as the *Mishne* or *grand Mishne*.
70 Rozen, *The Jewish Community of Jerusalem*, 23-28. Concerning the applications of private individuals to the Grand Vezir and/or the *defterdar* in Istanbul, see Rashdam, *Responsa, Hoshen Mishpat*, no. 58; *Torat Haim Responsa*, I, no. 26.
71 *Mishpatim Yesharim Responsa*, no. 22
72 Rozen, *The Jewish Community of Jerusalem*, 351, letter 214.
73 Rabbi Eliahu Alfandari, *Seder Eliahu Raba ve-Zota Responsa, Even Ha-Ezer* (Constantinople, 1719), no. 2.
74 *Bnei Avraham Responsa, Even Ha-Ezer*, no. 3.
75 *Zekan Aharon Responsa*, no. 158.
76 Cohen, *Jerusalem*, 27-29.
77 Rozen, *The Jewish Community of Jerusalem*, 323.
78 Rozen, *The Jewish Community of Jerusalem*, 349.
79 Gerber, *Economy and Social Life of the Jews*, 122; Shmuelevitz, *The Jews of the Ottoman Empire*, 36ff., 44-45, based upon the *fetvas* published by A. Refik Altınay, *Onuncu asr-ı hicride İstanbul Hayatı* (Istanbul,

1333h), 61-63, 72; P. Horster, *Zur Anwendung des Islamischen Rechts im 16. Jahrhundert* (Stuttgart, 1935); F. Selle, *Prozessrecht des 16. Jahrhunderts im Osmanischen Reich* (Wiesbaden, 1962); and upon sources found in responsa literature.

80 Rozen, *The Jewish Community of Jerusalem*, 351. For information concerning its payment to the *kadı* in cities in the Empire during the seventeenth century, see *Parah Mateh Aharon Responsa*, II, no. 83.

81 Cohen, *Jerusalem*, 77; Rozen, *The Jewish Community of Jerusalem*, 137.

82 Rozen, *The Jewish Community of Jerusalem*, 73. For the attempts to obtain the support of the *müfti* of Jerusalem, see ibid., 306.

83 In the responsa literature they are referred to as the *sar ha-ir* (the minister of the city) which also applied to the *sancakbeyis* and their many functionaries. The *sancakbeyi* was also called *daglan*, see *Torat Haim Responsa*, III, no. 94.

84 Mahariv, *Responsa*, I, no. 38.

85 Ramag, *Responsa*, no. 63. See below for the discussion on bribes.

86 *Torat Haim Responsa*, II, no. 101.

87 *Parah Mateh Aharon Responsa*, III, no. 52.

88 *Torat Haim Responsa*, III, no. 101.

89 A similar situation existed with the Greeks. See *Torat Haim Responsa*, III, no. 101.

90 Cohen, *Jerusalem*, 120.

91 Rozen, *The Jewish Community of Jerusalem*, 52-53.

92 Cohen, *Jerusalem*, 86.

93 Rabbi Yosef Hazan, *Hikrei Lev Responsa*, 2nd ed., I (Salonica, 1853), *Even Ha-Ezer*, no. 3. There is a similar case in Izmir in the nineteenth century when an immodest woman committed adultery with a guest. See Rabbi Rafael Isaac Zuriano, *Tair Neri Responsa, Even Ha-Ezer* (Izmir, 1875), no. 1. See also the discussion of appeals to gentile courts concerning the handing over of an adulteress to the authorities by the Jewish court at the end of the seventeenth or beginning of the eighteenth century. See also Rabbi Abraham Israel Zevi, *Urim Gedolim Responsa* (Izmir, 1758), no. 124; Rabbi Yuda Diwan, *Hut Meshulash Responsa* (Constantinople, 1739), no. 6. See also below for the discussion concerning the handing over of individuals to the Ottoman authorities by the lay leaders.

94 *Torat Haim Responsa*, III, no 94. Ottoman criminal law determined the payment for blood money when the murderer was not located or known. It was paid by the Jews living on the street where the body was found; see U. Heyd, *Studies in Old Ottoman Criminal Law*, ed. V. L. Ménage (Oxford, 1973), 114-15.

95 Rozen, *The Jewish Community of Jerusalem*, 37-50; idem, *The*

Ruins of Jerusalem (in Hebrew) (Tel Aviv, 1981). See also below for the discussion of the lay leaders being held as hostage.

96 Cohen, *Jerusalem*, 88, 90.

97 Rozen, *The Jewish Community of Jerusalem*, 182. No other information is available concerning the leaders of other communities.

98 H. A. R. Gibb, and H. Bowen, *Islamic Society and the West*, part 2 (Oxford, 1969), 121ff.; Stanford J. Shaw, *History of the Ottoman Empire and Modern Turkey*, vol. 1 (Cambridge, 1976), 126ff.; Cohen, *Jerusalem*, 123ff. The representatives of the Jewish communities turned to the Muslim courts to abolish oppressive orders. See, for example, U. Heyd, *Ottoman Documents on Palestine, 1552-1615* (Oxford, 1960), 167-68.

99 See the discussion concerning the enforcement of the segregation laws.

100 Cohen, *Jerusalem*, 126-27.

101 Rozen, *The Jewish Community of Jerusalem*, 52-53.

102 *Magen Giborim Responsa*, no. 42. See also below, note 118.

103 Rozen, *The Jewish Community of Jerusalem*, 60.

104 Rozen, *The Jewish Community of Jerusalem*, 60-63. On the arrest of lay leaders as hostages, see below, note 113.

105 *Torat Haim Responsa*, III, no. 101. See the discussion above concerning the *sancaks*.

106 Rozen, *The Jewish Community of Jerusalem*, 182. There are many Hebrew sources of bribing the *kadıs* throughout the Empire, although this did not always help. For examples, see *Zekan Aharon Responsa*, no. 62; *Baey Hayey Responsa*, *Hoshen Mishpat*, I, nos. 227, 229; *Torat Haim Responsa*, III, no 107.

107 Rozen, *The Jewish Community of Jerusalem*, 62.

108 Rozen, *The Jewish Community of Jerusalem*, 62, based upon a seventeenth-century epistle from Jerusalem. See also note 80.

109 *Parah Mateh Aharon Responsa*, II, no. 83. See also note 80.

110 Radbaz, *Responsa*, III, no. 467; II, no. 638; Rozanes, *History of the Jews in Turkey*, 2:152-53.

111 Examples are found in: *Divrei Rivot Responsa*, no. 313; Rashdam, *Responsa, Hoshen Mishpat*, nos. 193, 207, 348, 442; *Torat Haim Responsa*, III, no. 93; *Parah Mateh Aharon Responsa*, III, no. 87; *Mishpetei Zedek Responsa*, III, no. 63. One may conclude that the *kadıs* and local rulers did not always give receipts for these payments or duties which they secretly demanded from the Jews—*Parah Mateh Aharon Responsa*, III, no. 118.

112 See the discussion above.

114 Rozen, *The Jewish Community of Jerusalem*, 51-54; idem, "The Incident of the Converted Boy - A Chapter in the History of the Jews in Seventeenth-Century Jerusalem" (in Hebrew), *Cathedra* 14 (1980): 65-80;

see also above concerning the discussion about the relationship between the heads of the *vilayets* and *sancakbeys* and note 91. Concerning the imprisonment of *parnasim* in the sixteenth century, see Cohen, *Jerusalem*, 47; and note 104.

114 *Mishpatim Yesharim Responsa*, no. 22.
115 *Torat Haim Responsa*, II, no. 38.
116 *Mishpat Zedek Responsa*, I, no. 20.
117 See above; see also Ramag, *Responsa*, no. 7; Rabbi Shmuel Vital, *Beer Mayim Haim Responsa* (New York, 1968), no. 38.
118 *Magen Giborim Responsa*, no. 42.
119 For the sixteenth century: Maharshah, *Responsa*, IV, no. 10. For the end of the seventeenth century or the beginning of the eighteenth century: Rabbi Avraham Yitzhaki, *Zera Avraham Responsa, Hoshen Mishpat* (Constantinople, 1732), no. 16.
120 See also the discussion above concerning complaints by the lay leadership against the high rate of taxes.
121 Bornstein, Dissertation, 173-75; Hacker, "Jewish Autonomy in the Ottoman Empire," 349-88. See also above for the relations with the *kadıs*.
122 Epstein, *The Ottoman Jewish Communities*, 40-41.
123 *Mishpatim Yesharim Responsa*, no. 22.
124 Shmuelevitz, *The Jews of the Ottoman Empire*, 41-80; Hacker, "Jewish Autonomy," and the up-to-date bibliography therein.
125 Rabbi Yehoshua Benveneste, *Shaar Yehoshua Responsa, Hoshen Mishpat*, mss. Warsaw, fol. 295a. In this matter Rabbi Benveneste decided that the Jewish court must admonish, punish and fine the stubborn *parnas*.
126 Epstein, *The Ottoman Jewish Communities*, 73, n. 38.
127 Mabit, *Responsa*, I, no. 22.
128 Cohen, *Jerusalem*, 129-31.
129 As found in the beginning of the seventeenth-century responsa: Maharit, *Responsa, Yoreh Deah*, II, no. 21; *Mishpat Zedek Responsa*, II, no. 71.
130 Rabbi Haim Benveneste, *Responsa, Tur Orah Haim* (Constantinople, 1743), II, no. 21.
131 Concerning the Ottoman law, see Heyd, *Studies in Old Ottoman Criminal Law*, 41, 48, 95ff., 134, 146, 181, 263, 277.
132 For examples, see Rabbi Moshe Alashkar, *Responsa* (Sabionite, 1554), nos. 88, 94; Radbaz, *Responsa*, IV, no. 277; see also the chapter on the *sancakbeys*.
133 Bornstein, Dissertation, 229-35.

Minna Rozen
Tel Aviv University

Strangers in a Strange Land: The Extraterritorial Status of Jews in Italy and the Ottoman Empire in the Sixteenth to the Eighteenth Centuries

STRANGERS

It is in the nature of states to impose their authority and laws on persons living within their territory. Such persons are of two kinds. Most of them have personal ties with the state; consequently the state regards such people, wherever they may be—even outside the country's borders—as owing obedience to its laws. By the same token, such persons fully expect the state to protect their interests both at home and abroad. In a word, they are subjects of the state. Yet in any country there are nearly always people with no personal allegiance to the state, or whose ties to the state are purely circumstantial, e.g., they may be touring or traveling, trading or studying there, and in more extreme cases, they may have entered with the intention of harming the state and its citizens. The latter are foreigners. The foreigner is usually the subject of some other country, but may also lack any nationality or allegiance. Except for the aforementioned circumstantial tie, foreigners are not subjects of the state, either normatively or in practice. Generally, when the state agrees to the foreigner's stay within its borders, it creates special norms for this status, and sometimes separate norms prevail for each category of foreigner.[1]

The status of subjects from the Ottoman Empire who later settled in the Italian states, and that of Italian subjects residing in the Ottoman Empire, acquires an unusual and interesting dimension when one examines

---
This article was translated from the Hebrew by Goldie Wachsman.

the position of Jews. There were Jewish subjects of the Ottoman Empire in Italian states, as well as Jewish subjects of the Italian states inhabiting the Empire. The unconventional dimension arises from the fact that such Jews were considered foreigners no matter where they lived, whether in the Italian states or in the Empire. As subjects of another country, they were naturally deemed a foreign element in the new lands they reached. However, they were also considered foreigners, or at best held some interim status, in the countries of origin from which they emigrated. In the Ottoman Empire, their legal status was inferior to that of Muslims. Even in the Italian states, Jews did not possess a status equal to that of Christian subjects. In fact, for such Jews, one might legitimately question if the term "subject" is at all appropriate when dealing with at least part of the era under analysis.[2] The inferiority of Jews in these domains, both Christian and Muslim, was apparent not only in their legal status but also in the concept that a Jewish presence was tolerated as an act of magnanimity by the rulers of the land—a generosity displayed with varying degrees of good will.[3]

I have chosen to dwell on two issues arising from the aforementioned state of affairs. First, how and to what extent did the special status of Jews in their countries of origin affect their legal standing in the host country they subsequently inhabited? Second, did the fact that a Jew in his country of origin possessed fewer rights than the majority of his compatriots, influence his status once he left his mother country? By extension, did the special status accorded the indigenous Jew in a given country affect the treatment extraterritorial Jews may have received in that same country?[4]

EMIGRATION AND SETTLEMENT

The presence of Jewish-Ottoman subjects in Italian states, and that of Italo-Jewish subjects in the Ottoman Empire, was primarily connected to the expulsion of Jews from Spain in 1492, and to a two-hundred-year Inquisitorial process that led to the migration of Jews to the southern and eastern shores of the Mediterranean.[5] The social fabric of this Jewish community was destroyed, but later reconstituted wherever the refugees from the Iberian peninsula decided to settle. In their new homes, these fugitives created a society of "citizens of the Mediterranean," whose primary emotional allegiance was to the Ibero-Jewish "nation," wherever it was scattered. Political borders and geographic obstacles played only a marginal role in their consciousness. This rule remained in force for close to three hundred years, although some reservations and nuances, connected with the passage of time and changing circumstances, do apply. Beyond the primary link with an insular group, these Jews also identified with the Jewish people as a whole and felt a certain bond with the country which had given them shelter.[6]

There is no need to elaborate on the reasons why these Jewish fugitives preferred to immigrate to the Ottoman Empire. In 1492, it was the only country that agreed to accept them without imposing restrictions of a religious or economic order. The expressions these Jews used to describe the Ottoman Empire were laudatory in the extreme; its leaders were extolled as "Kings of Mercy,"[7] and because the Empire restored to the Jews a possibility of living a more secure religious life, residence within its borders was likened to "living under the wings of the Divine Presence."[8] The choice of Italy as a haven was less natural. In the Italian states Catholicism reigned supreme. Their social climate was anti-Jewish, and in most of them Jews were not warmly welcomed. Yet many "New Christians" fled from the Iberian Peninsula to Italy, especially after the forced conversion in Portugal (1497). Their motives were varied: some already had some financial investment in Italy;[9] others lacked the funds to continue their journey; and there were even those, particularly the second and third generation of Jews following the conversion, who concluded that living under a dual identity was a viable option.[10]

Under such circumstances, Jewish life in Italy was not without risk. A Jew who openly returned to Judaism after having lived as a Christian was considered a heretic, which placed him under the jurisdiction of the Inquisition. Similarly, the life of a Jew practicing a dual identity was none too secure. Although the Inquisition in Italy was not all-powerful as it was in Spain or Portugal, it posed an undeniable threat after the ascent of Pope Paul IV to the papal throne. This Pope, the standard-bearer of the Counter-Reformation, launched his campaign in the Church with an order aimed at harassing and degrading Jews (1555) according to the rulings of the Church fathers,[11] and he energetically pursued the goal of eradicating Jewish heresy among the "New Christians" in his domain.[12]

The choice of Italy as a permanent residence in the mid-sixteenth century aroused a heated debate among the Jewish emigrants who had already settled in the Ottoman Empire. After the burning in 1556 of the Portuguese Jews of Ancona,[13] a rabbi in Istanbul, Yehoshua Soncin, expressed the opinion that one who had escaped the "catastrophe" and then chose to settle in Christian lands was risking his life; that if disaster struck him anew, only his own stupidity was to blame; and such a person should not be mourned or avenged. It should be noted that this rabbi was not of Sephardic origin, and his lack of sympathy for the Iberian Jews in Italy may have stemmed, in part, from communal considerations.[14] However, close to that time, Rabbi Shemuel de Medina, the leading Sephardic rabbi in Salonica, advised the *anusim*[15] in Ferrara to depart for safer shores "under the protection of Our Master, His Majesty the King, King of Mercy, for he and his fathers before him have treated us with extraordinary munificence." The rabbi also pointed out the danger of living in Italy, "the land of Edom."

> For we see the frequent misfortunes which befall these people [the Jews], and even if they cease for a day or two, there is no safety from the perversity of wicked Esau.[16]

Under such circumstances, one might have expected increased emigration from Italy into the Empire, but such was not the case. Migration of this sort did occur, but there was also a movement in the opposite direction, i.e., from the Empire to Italy. The emigrants from the Empire to Italy established congregations of *Levantini* in places such as Ancona and Venice. These groups were considerably reinforced by emigrants from Portugal.[17] Among the latter, migration often took a zig-zag course: a Jew would arrive from Portugal to Italy, whereupon he learned that his Christian past might complicate his life. He therefore left for a short period, for example, to Salonica, and returned to Italy as a *mercante levantino* (the proper noun *Levantini* refers in this paper to Levantine Jews in Italy), a "Levantine merchant" who, of course, had no idea what his parents or grandparents had done many years earlier in the Iberian Peninsula. For many of these emigrants, a brief sojourn within the Empire was therefore a way of "laundering" past sins.[18]

LAW AND ACTION: THE SIXTEENTH CENTURY

A typical picture of sixteenth-century Jewry would depict the erstwhile Jewish inhabitants in the Ottoman Empire in the process of settling in one of the Italian states. Hebrew sources show practically no evidence of Jews who came from Italy to the Ottoman Empire, while retaining their allegiance to the Italian state they left behind.[19] To understand the reasons underlying this situation, we must explore the legal status of Jews both in their countries of permanent "residence," and in those countries where they lived as foreigners.

The legal status of a Jewish subject of the Ottoman Empire was determined by rulings of classic Islam. He was a *dhimmi*, i.e., a protected person. In return for paying the poll-tax and adhering to a number of rules and restrictions designed to stress his inferiority to the Muslim, a Jew enjoyed the *dhimma* (protection) of Islam. The *dhimmi*'s obligation to obey the norms of the Muslim state made him a part of *Dar al-Islam*; guaranteed his life, liberty, and property; and afforded him a considerable measure of freedom of action.[20]

The Jew who entered the Ottoman Empire therefore became a subject whose status was inferior to that of Muslims, but from a legal standpoint he was a permanent part of the "Muslim order." However, even if the incoming Jew or his ancestors did not hail from somewhere outside the Ottoman Empire, they were perceived as "belonging" to the Muslim order by virtue of Islamic mercy alone, and they remained branded as aliens in the eyes of the Muslim state and society.[21]

What was the status of Jews in the Italian states? Their position, of course, differed from one state to another. The Ottoman Empire was a politically monolithic bloc and, in contrast, Italy was a political mosaic. In some parts of Italy the residence of Jews was not tolerated at all; in others, Jews were permitted to live under specific conditions; and sometimes, in the very same place, each "type" of Jew was accorded a different status. Aside from political conditions, there was another reason for this state of affairs. Islam regarded the "protected person" as living in error but accepted his right to exist, whereas Christianity viewed the existence of Judaism and Jews as an expression of the latter's obstinacy. Jews, Christians claimed, knew the truth but were too wicked to acknowledge it. Hence, the existence of Judaism was an interim and temporary state. This attitude greatly influenced the legislation concerning Jews in the Italian states, particularly when the economic benefit brought by their presence was not outstanding. Thus, for example, when the activities of Jewish money-lenders in the Veneto cities no longer yielded the anticipated benefit for their Christian neighbors, a wave of legislation began in the 1540s and 1550s, aimed at removing the Jews from the area. The inspiration these cities received from papal activities merely complemented their prejudicial inclinations, which were reinforced by sheer pragmatism.[22]

The two most important states for out purposes are the Papal State and the Venetian Republic. Ancona and Venice, the two principal ports where the Jews conducted their trade, were located in these states, and the bulk of commerce between Italy and the Ottoman Empire flowed through them. Naturally, these two cities also became major residential centers for Ottoman subjects in Italy.

The community of Venetian Jews included several groups, each accorded a different status. The oldest sector of the community comprised the descendants of German-Jewish immigrants and a few *Italiani*—autochthonous Italian Jews. This group of Jews sought refuge in the city during the Cambrai War, and following the war they asked to remain in the city. In 1516, the Republic acceded to their request but with obvious reluctance and great misgivings. The Jews' stay was predicated on certain conditions: they were to live in a special quarter on the outskirts of the city, in the Ghetto Nuovo, and restrictions were placed on their economic activity. Among other things, they were prohibited from engaging in international trade. Permission granting them a right of domicile in the city was renewed every few years.[23] These, then, were the unwanted and barely tolerated "subjects" of the Most Serene (*Serenissima*) Republic. The reasons why there were no Jews from the Republic who retained their allegiance to it while residing in the Ottoman Empire are twofold: First they were not truly Venetian subjects in the full sense of the word, since in Venice they were regarded as aliens as well. As a result, they arrived with no extraterritorial rights granted by Venice. Second, they could not engage in international trade. Even if we assume that their previous residence in Venice did indeed confer upon them certain extraterritorial privileges, this last restriction must have convinced them to waive the hypothetical "citizenship."[24]

What was the status of Ottoman-Jewish subjects in the Venetian Republic? In theory, it should have reflected the status of Venetian subjects in the Empire. The Ottoman state's legal solution determining the status of foreigners from the *Dal al-Harb* in its borders was based on classical Islam. The central idea was to grant the *harbi* safe conduct (*aman*) upon entry, on the condition that his stay would be of benefit to Islam and that he promise to behave in a friendly and peaceable manner. When such an *aman* was granted to a group of people from a given country, it was understood, by implication, that the special rights conferred (*imtiyazat*) would be answered in kind by European and other states harboring Ottoman subjects. In other words, the Ottoman state anticipated that its protection of foreign subjects would result in reciprocal protection of Ottoman subjects in foreign lands. Here it should be noted that in the history of relations between the countries of Christian Europe and the Empire, the former held these rights to be bilateral agreements, but Ottoman rulers did not view things the same way. In their view, the rights conferred were a function of the Sultan's grace. To the Ottomans, a respectful attitude on the part of the Christian country towards Ottoman subjects entering the *Dar al-Harb* was a prerequisite in a relationship of good will that determined the extent of the Sultan's grace.

Privileges granted the *harbi* entering the borders of the Empire were largely based on the arrangements customary in the Byzantine state. In the main they included the freedom of trade, freedom of movement, the right to independent management of the group members' internal affairs, exemptions from several taxes (particularly the poll-tax), and exemption from certain regulations of the *Sharia* courts pertaining to laws of evidence and inheritance, which applied to the *dhimmis* in the Empire.[25]

Hence, an Ottoman-Jewish subject residing in Venice was entitled to freedom of trade, freedom of movement, exemption from certain taxes imposed on his coreligionists in the Republic, the right to independent management of internal affairs, and exemption from certain restrictions imposed on his brethren in the Republic because of their religion. In a word, the Venetian *salvo conducto* should have corresponded to the Sultan's *aman*. But what did the Jew in fact obtain? And to what degree did the Empire support him when his rights were infringed?

It stands to reason that Ottoman merchants would have been free to conduct their business in Venice as soon as the Ottoman rulers granted reciprocal rights to Venetian merchants in the Empire. Yet until the end of the fifteenth century, the Venetian Republic enacted various legislative measures to prevent Levantine merchants from trading freely within its domain.[26] It is unclear how these restrictions were reconciled with the symmetrical concept of reciprocity binding the two states, and one can only surmise that if the Ottoman Empire failed to appreciate the importance, or insist upon the implementation, of these rights, it was because only a minority of their merchants traded in Venice. In any case, no later than the second decade of the sixteenth century, Ottoman subjects traded openly in Venice, and in 1524 the question of their commercial rights was explicitly addressed.[27] This process was intimately linked to the Republic's realization that its commerce was suffering as a result of the Ottoman Empire's territorial expansion, and that the Venetians themselves had lost interest in trading. To a degree, this capitulation to pressure meant that the *patrizi* and *cittadini* were ready to give up their monopoly of Levantine commerce in order to preserve the preeminence of Venice as an emporium of Mediterranean trade.[28]

According to D. Cooperman, the legal standing of Levantine merchants in Venice was not consolidated before 1518 and was influenced by the rights these merchants obtained in Ancona in the same year. These rights, he maintains, caused the Venetian government to consider the possibility that henceforth Levantine trade might flow through Ancona rather than Venice, and the government consequently decided to extend official recognition of these merchants' activities.[29] In addition to this development, one should also note that in the twenty years that elapsed since the expulsion from Spain, a group of Jewish merchants had become active in the ports of the Ottoman Empire, and much of their attention was directed toward the Italian states. Conceivably, the increasing commercial activity of this group may have pressured the Ottoman government into taking greater political interest in the rights of its subjects abroad. In any case, by 1537, when war broke out between the two states, Levantine merchants significantly expanded their trade in Italy. By the end of that war (1537-1540), they had exploited the opportunity to broaden their privileges to the hilt.

Until 1541, no particular mention is made of the rights of Ottoman-Jewish subjects trading in Venice. In that year, a group of these Jews turned to the Republic's Chamber of Commerce, complaining that living space in the Ghetto Nuovo had become too cramped for their personal and commercial needs. They also asked for their own residential quarter. Thus, in the summer of 1541 their request was granted, and a number of buildings were allotted for their personal and commercial use: the Ghetto Vecchio.[30]

Until recently, the prevailing view has been that the *Levantini* were not included in the original order calling for the establishment of a ghetto, and that it was only in 1541 that they were forced to move into a special, enclosed district adjacent to the Ghetto Nuovo.[31] Yet following his research into the archives of the Venetian Republic, B. Ravid claims that it was the *Levantini* themselves who requested the transfer, and that until 1541 they had lived together with other Venetian Jews in the Ghetto Nuovo. In other words, the establishment of the Ghetto Vecchio in no way interfered with the rights of the *Levantini* but actually enhanced them.[32] The establishment of a special district implied a clear and direct recognition of their importance as a group and improved their living conditions and commercial opportunities. That same summer, all customs on goods imported to Venice from the Ottoman Empire were waived, as were those on goods from the West, which in Venice were exchanged for goods from the East.[33]

This picture of events does not coincide with the objectives to which the Venetians and Italians subscribed in the mid-sixteenth century in their relationship with Jews and Judaism.[34] But studies of the archives of the Republic can resolve the conflict completely. During the war between Venice and the Empire (1537-1540), the importance of Venice in the Levant trade declined precipitously, and Jews generally dominated the trade. In order to attract the Jews and their goods to Venice, something had to be done.[35] The steps taken in the summer of 1541 were thus another legislative expression of an existing economic reality: the growing importance of Ottoman Jews in the Levant trade.[36]

Nevertheless, if we rely exclusively on Italian sources, it would seem that this assessment of the motives underlying the formal recognition of Levantine Jews' trading rights in Venice, ignores another factor: the bilateral relationship between the Ottoman Empire and the Venetian Republic. It should be recalled that the decision of the Venetian Chamber of Commerce to establish the Ghetto Vecchio and waive the customs was reached on 2 June 1541, approximately seven months after the Ottoman Empire granted new trading rights to the Republic in the wake of a peace treaty concluded between the two states on 3 October 1540.[37]

The Ottomans' signature of the peace treaty with Venice was done from a clear position of strength. They had crushed Venice, and their military superiority in the Mediterranean was assured. Their agreement to the peace was in large measure a concession to the interests of the French, their ally.[38] In fact the treaty itself was not a document drawn between two equal parties, but an enumeration of privileges Sultan Süleyman (hailed as the "ever-triumphant") conferred upon the Venetian state in his mercy and kindness, after he agreed to put an end to the war.

The implicit understanding concerning reciprocal trading rights was expressed chiefly in matters of maritime travel and guarantees of life and property.[39] It was after the end of war in 1540 that questions about the exercise of these rights were first raised. This fact supports the view that the conferral of privileges upon the *Levantini* had as much to do with political pressure as with the decline of Venetian commerce. These privileges were not only a result of economic calculations but were an expression of the "friendship and loyalty" that *harbi* states were expected to show the Muslim government in exchange for the peace the Muslims had concluded with them. One can safely assume that from the Ottoman point of view reciprocity was both self-understood if not mandatory. At that time the role of Jews from the Ottoman Empire in Levantine trade had become sufficiently important to render the expressions of reciprocity more forceful than they had been in the beginning of the sixteenth century.

A glimmer of this perspective is preserved in the Hebrew documentation of the period and reflected in a query sent in the late summer of 1559 to the renowned rabbi of Safed, R. Moshe Mitrani. The query was sent from Venice and dealt with a complicated affair involving a property dispute between a Jewish doctor and the local residents; both parties to the dispute were members of the local Jewry, i.e., the Ashkenazim and the *Italiani*. The contested property included a house, a garden and several residential buildings located in the Ghetto Vecchio, i.e., in the *Levantini*'s district. Between the lines we glean that the story was reconstructed by R. Moshe Mitrani himself on the basis of contracts and letters he received from the doctor in Venice, the plaintiff. The reconstruction therefore reflects the orientation of a Jewish rabbi, a resident and subject of the Ottoman Empire, and that of local Venetian Jews, with respect to the motives that encourage the Republic to establish the Ghetto Vecchio. The query was worded thus:

> In the reign of this renowned kingdom, there is a large district for the residents of the state. The merchants arriving from without, called the Livanitani [sic], dwelled with them. After a few years, when the number of merchants grew and there was not enough space for them, they asked the authorities for special quarters where they might live and trade. The government agreed *out of love and respect for the potentate of their land, who is greater and more powerful than all the kings of the earth* [emphasis mine]. In recent days they have received permission to rent an area of two houses adjacent to the residential district, on the condition that they not engage in the same work as the local residents. They rented the area and lived in it for five years.[40]

These words indicate that the parties involved in the formulation of this text understood that the government's agreement to the establishment of the Ghetto Vecchio stemmed from larger causes having to do with relations between Venice and the Ottoman Empire. Especially interesting is the use of the words "love and respect," which allude to the terms of "friendship and loyalty" under which the rights of *harbis* were guaranteed under the Muslim state. The recognition of the Ottoman ruler's supremacy is equally blatant. One should, of course, recall that these hyperbolic expressions issued from a subject of the Ottoman state and that, in all probability, he alone was responsible for their formulation. It should come as no surprise that he extolled the ruler of the state at a time when Jews in the Empire underwent a cultural and economic efflorescence and enjoyed a considerable measure of security. Be that as it may, there are other aspects of the case which indicate that in Venice itself the status of the *Levantini* rested on solid ground.

Five years after the establishment of the ghetto, the *Levantini* renewed their lease with the landlord of the buildings. The latter stipulated that he reserved the right to rent a house and garden, which were part of his property, to a non-Levantine Jewish family. This clause was ratified by the Venetian government, provided that the "alien residents" would not engage in activities permitted for the *Levantini* and forbidden to local Jews, i.e., traffic in international trade. Another proviso stated that the right of domicile was granted to the aforementioned family only so long as "the *Levantini* dwelled in the area." This last dictum underscored the temporary basis of the *Levantini*'s residence in the city.

At this point the doctor who sent the query to R. Moshe Mitrani enters the picture. The doctor had argued with his fellow congregants, the Jewish residents of the city, and sought refuge with his family among the *Levantini*. The landlord allowed him to remain in one of his houses under the same conditions granted to the other Jewish family. In the interim, the other family moved from the city, and the doctor and his family rented the former tenants' house and garden. As it happened, there were other local Jews living in the Ghetto Vecchio, and one day a Venetian Jew decided to inform the government about this violation of the rules. As a result, all the local Jews residing in the Ghetto Vecchio had to return to the Ghetto Nuovo, except for the doctor and his family, whose rights of domicile had been guaranteed by the authorities. The houses which the local Jews vacated now stood empty, and the landlord complained about this loss to the leaders of the Jewish community. As a consequence, they were obliged to rent out the houses themselves and had to obtain permission to do so from the authorities. Among the properties in dispute was the doctor's house. Ultimately the leaders of the community obtained the right to rent out the houses for a specific duration of time, i.e., for the duration of their *condotta*. But the doctor refused to cooperate and would have nothing to do with them. He claimed that he had rented the house directly from the landlord, that his lease was approved by the authorities, that it remained in effect so long as the *Levantini* resided in Venice, and that the community had no right to question the validity of his lease. The leaders of the community remonstrated, inter alia, that the privilege they had obtained from the Venetian Republic took precedence over the doctor's since their rights were guaranteed for the duration of their *condotta* (five years), during which time the Venetians could not evict them. They maintained that the *Levantini*'s position was inferior, because the authorities had the power to evict the *Levantini* "whenever they pleased." In other words, the Venetian Jews understood that the distinction between their own and the *Levantini*'s status was rooted in the element of time, a component in the privileges the Venetian Jews obtained. They, after all, possessed a *condotta* permitting them to reside in Venice under certain conditions for a period of five years. During that period, their right to reside in the city was guaranteed. By contrast, the right of the *Levantini* to reside in the city depended on the state of relations between the Ottoman Empire and the Venetian Republic. The *Levantini* were not accorded a conditional, interim status and were essentially strangers that the Republic could expel at any moment. Yet in reality, the position of the *Levantini* was the stronger one, since they had the backing of a great power. As a result, in his reply to the leaders of the community, the doctor stated that "it is clear they [the *Levantini*] will not be expelled."

The aforementioned dispute raises other issues connected to the status of the *Levantini* in Venice. One fundamental issue concerns restrictive housing of Jews in an enclosed district. It is not without reason that Cecil Roth erroneously maintained that in the beginning the *Levantini* could live wherever they wished and that it was only later that they were relegated to the ghetto.[41] The *Levantini*'s involvement in an aspect of trade that was forbidden to local Jews clearly indicated that their legal status was better than that of the local Jews. But since the ghetto was perceived as a limitation of freedom and as a discriminatory policy against Jews, it was easy to conclude that a "superior" status entailed the right to live where one wished. The essential question to be raised in this context is the following: to what extent were the *Levantini* considered different from other foreigners in Venice, and more important, what was the status of Venetians in the Ottoman Empire with respect to their rights of domicile?

In truth there were other groups of foreigners in Venice who resided in separate districts. This situation obtained for the Luccans, the Florentines, and the Armenians. Yet their neighborhoods were not legally restricted or enclosed. It would appear that they were established merely to facilitate trade. B. Ravid discusses the similarity between the restrictive housing of Jews and of German merchants,—especially after the Reformation—prostitutes, and Muslim merchants from the Ottoman Empire. The rationale underlying these restrictions was to prevent the "contamination" of Venice by the "evil malignancies" these groups might unleash against the general populace. Such views clearly owed much to prejudice.[42]

And yet, Venetian merchants who traded in the Ottoman Empire were also restricted in their housing and could not always live where they wished.[43]

Hence, one cannot say that the restrictive housing of the *Levantini* in Venice was due to the Ottoman Empire's neglect of its subjects. Rather, it resembled the living conditions of Venetian subjects themselves in the Empire. At the same time, one can also state that by relegating the *Levantini* to a ghetto, the Venetians not only adhered to the concept of reciprocity but evinced a specific attitude toward the *Levantini* as Jews. The housing restrictions affecting Muslim merchants in Venice were not enacted until thirty years after the establishment of the Ghetto Vecchio, and the Venetians never seriously considered the possibility of allowing the *Levantini* to dwell wherever they pleased.[44] On the one hand, the establishment of the Ghetto Vecchio did not restrict the rights of the *Levantini* but enhanced them. On the other hand, to a degree, the restrictive housing of Levantine Jews was a reflection of discriminatory measures practiced against the local Jews.

Another limitation can be derived from the same source and is corroborated in others. This concerns the ban prohibiting the settlement of Levantine families in the city. Until 1589 the Republic did not entitle these merchants to immigrate with their families.[45] They were not only aliens but "transients" (*viandanti*). At first they were allowed to remain in Venice for a period not exceeding four consecutive months, and in September 1541 this period was increased to two years.[46]

One can safely assume that between 1541 and 1589 at least part of the "transient" merchants started families in Venice, but such families were not recognized by law. In any case, when the landlord in the Ghetto Vecchio secured the permission to rent out a house and garden—the disputed property—to a local Jew, it was with the proviso that only "*one* Hebrew family" could occupy the house. The emphasis on the single family recurs in the discussion.[47] The permission granted therefore imparted both an affirmative and negative message. By granting the right to only one Jew and his family to reside in the Ghetto Vecchio, the government also implied that its decision was the exception that proved the rule. The rule was that the *Levantini* were forbidden to live in the district with their families.

Limitations in time and restrictive housing were also the rule for Venetian merchants residing in the Empire. Time-bound restrictions were legally entrenched in the Islamic religious code, whereby a *mustamin* who resided in the Empire for more than a year automatically became a *dhimmi* and had to pay the poll-tax. In the Capitulations the French proposed to the Ottomans in 1536, this time period was extended to ten years.[48] In practice, however, the Ottomans did not enforce the rule too strictly, since these merchants were wont to come and go at all times.[49] For the same reason, one can therefore assume that even the law curtailing the *Levantini*'s stay in Venice to two years was something of a paper tiger.[50]

The frustration of Venetian merchants living without family in the Ottoman Empire was discussed in a letter written in 1553 by *Bailo* Bernardino Navagero, in which he described the problems of Venetian merchants in Istanbul. Among other things he especially noted that as a last resort the Venetians were becoming involved with local women, a phenomenon he viewed as a necessary evil.[51]

We have already mentioned that a key aspect governing the Ottoman Empire's relationship with Venice was the mutual recognition of maritime rights and safe conduct at sea. Was this reciprocity in effect even when the rights of Jews, the subjects of the Sultan, were violated?

An example from the rabbinic literature affords us a general idea in this matter. The incident in question occurred in the sixteenth century. A number of Jewish merchants sailed from Patras, Greece, to Venice. En route their ship was captured by pirates from Malta. From the wording of the source, it is clear that the ship and its cargo belonged to Jews. Under pressure from the Ottoman government, the Venetians overtook a Maltese vessel and its passengers were held captive in Venice until the Jewish merchants were freed. The cargo, however, was never returned.[52] In this case, injury was done to the interests of both the Ottomans and Venetians, a fact that undoubtedly influenced the course of action taken. In any event, the merchants' *dhimmi* status was not a factor in the decision of the Empire to work towards their release.

In the same spirit, when the Grand Vizir Rüstem Paşa wrote the Republic to warn them that infractions of the rules governing safe maritime travel would lead to the suspension of privileges accorded to Venetians in the Empire, he did not refer to the protection of Muslim merchants' rights but to those of "subjects and merchants from my *Padishah*'s felicitous domain."[53]

One should also take note of the assumptions the Venetians made with respect to the attitude of the Ottoman Empire towards its Jewish subjects trading in Venice. In a letter written in 1560, *Bailo* Marino Cavalli expressed his concern over the decline of Venetian commerce in Istanbul. He made special mention of the fact that Jewish merchants negotiating with the Venetians consistently earned a fifty percent profit on every transaction concluded. As a way of reducing Jewish control of trade with Venice, he wrote that the economic losses incurred by Venetian merchants were due to a misinterpretation of the Capitulations. He claimed that a distorted interpretation of the Capitulations enabled Jewish merchants to sail on Venetian ships and galleys as if they were bona fide Venetians, and he insisted that the Capitulations assured no such thing. At bottom, Cavalli was right; the Capitulations did not mention Jews at all. But the Ottomans' assumption of reciprocity governing their treatment of Venetians was the basis for the guarantees allowing Jewish subjects of the Sultan to trade and travel on Venetian vessels. In his summation, Cavalli wrote that indeed "one cannot foresee every eventuality when concluding a contract, for insofar as the Jews are concerned, the Turk is not at all perturbed about them."[54] This last sentence truly reflects the expectations Venetians had of the Ottomans when it came to the treatment of Ottoman-Jewish subjects. According to Cavalli, when the Venetians accepted the Capitulations, they never imagined that Jews might exploit them to their own advantage and gain certain rights. Now he proposed to the Venetians that they behave toward the Jews as if they had no part in the Capitulations. Cavalli believed the Sultan would not object, since in his view the Sultan's intent was to protect his Muslim subjects. Cavalli therefore perceived the Jews *in toto* as persons of an inferior status and insisted that the Sultan's agreements with foreign countries were designed to protect his subjects and were never meant to protect the Jews. We have already seen that in reality things were different, and the Ottomans reacted with all seriousness to violations of agreements even when the injured parties were Jewish.

Better still, when the interests of people close to the Sultan's court were not respected, Ottoman intervention was forceful. Thus, when the interests of the firm owned by Aaron di Segura, a relative of Don Yosef Nasi, were at stake, the resulting altercation heightened tensions between the two states in 1566-1567. Significantly, when tensions peaked, the *Bailo* and the senate wrote each other about the possibility of expelling all the Jews of Venice! This is interesting because it proves that Venetians saw Jews in both states as a single entity, whereby each individual was tied to another, and it was assumed that the Jews would sooner respond to the needs of their people as a whole than to the needs of a solitary Jew.[55]

Between the lines of this diplomatic correspondence, one can infer that the perception of Jews was that international law should not apply to them; further, the implication was that wherever they may be, Jews ought to be subject to a different set of rules. Yet in practice the Venetians were cautious in this regard. The reason is obvious. The Venetians, too, had their own interests to safeguard in the Ottoman Empire, and despite all they said and wrote about the Ottoman attitude towards Jewish subjects, they were uncertain how the

Ottomans would react if put to the test. Experience had already taught them that the Empire did not always respond according to Venetian expectations.

For this reason, when war broke out between the Republic and the Ottoman Empire in 1570-1573, the Venetians were careful in their treatment of Levantine merchants in their midst, because there were Venetian subjects trapped in the Ottoman Empire. At the same time, the Venetians distinguished between Christian Levantines, Jews, and Muslims. The first were not arrested, nor was their property confiscated, whereas the latter two were imprisoned. The authorities of the Republic housed and fed these prisoners by drawing on the proceeds of their confiscated goods. Following negotiations for their release, the goods were returned, minus the amount used to house and feed the prisoners.[56]

The Venetian merchants in Ottoman territory were also arrested and their property was confiscated. When negotiations began in 1571 over a prisoner exchange and the return of property, the Venetians claimed that Jewish merchants had sabotaged the agreement, because the latter maintained that their merchandise had been sold against their will and at less than the market price. The Venetians also complained that these Jews, with the help of Don Yosef Nasi, had succeeded in convincing the Sultan not to return the Venetians or their merchandise before the Jewish merchants received their due. The Ottomans insisted that it was up to the Venetians to take the first step, and justified this stance by declaring that the Empire was a far more powerful and important state than the Venetian Republic, and that it was beneath the Sultan to take the first step.[57]

An event that occurred towards the end of the sixteenth century, and certainly no later than 1639, points to a certain erosion in the link between the Empire and its Jewish subjects abroad. In the incident in question, a foreign state, most probably the Venetian Republic, imposed a tax on goods sent by Jewish merchants to the Empire, and on goods received from the Empire. This tax was not imposed on Christians or Muslims. In other words, the Jews received "special treatment" because they were Jews. But the Empire did not intervene to revoke the tax, and from the language of the Jewish source, it would seem that the Jews did not even attempt to enlist the aid of the Ottoman government. The reasons for this are not clear and we can only conjecture about the cause. Perhaps the Jews did not turn for help to the Ottoman government because they knew their request would be denied for reasons connected to the state of relations between the Empire and the Republic. Alternatively, perhaps the Jews felt it was pointless to turn to the Ottoman Empire because it was mired in internal problems. But there is another possibility. At the end of the sixteenth century, the *Levantini* in Venice were accorded the status of residents, independent of their protection by the Sultan, and perhaps this prompted the Jews to remain silent. Whatever the case may be, the Jewish merchants who were residents of the Empire sent an envoy to Venice and empowered him to spend liberal amounts of money to rescind the tax.[58]

The minutiae of the privileges of Ottoman-Jewish subjects residing in the Venetian Republic can almost make one forget what was so attractive about Ottoman protection in the first place. We have already mentioned that when Jews resided in the borders of the Empire, the government allowed them to practice their religion freely, and when such Jews went abroad, the Sultan's protection removed these Jews from the jurisdiction of the Church in all matters related to their religious past.

Until 1589, a "New Christian" who left the Iberian Peninsula in order to reside in the Venetian Republic could lead his life in one of several ways. It was not always the desire to return to his Jewish roots that motivated such an individual to leave, but rather the pressure and persecution of the Inquisition that may have spurred him on. In such a case, a "New Christian" might reside outside the ghetto and continue living as a faithful Christian. So long as no one had reason to accuse him before the *Sant' Uffizio*, i.e., the Inquisition, his life, it would seem, could continue unhindered along a "normal" path.[59]

Nevertheless, sometimes our hypothetical immigrant might have been moved to leave because in some way he continued to practice his Judaism in secret. Such a Jew had three options. He could continue living with a "dual identity"—to all appearances a devout Christian, but in secret a Jew—while residing outside the ghetto, maintaining various relationships with both Jews and Christians, and presenting himself on different occasions as the bearer of either identity. The motives behind such a choice were manifold. First, people are creatures of habit. Those who had become accustomed to living a double life found it "natural" to continue and may not have wished to give up the benefits. For example, there was the matter of such a Jew's social standing among Christians of a certain economic class, or his ability to have social relations with Christian women.[60] Sometimes these people could not return quietly to the practice of Judaism because of their fame or wealth, as was the case of the Nasi family. This option necessarily entailed the risk of an entanglement with the Inquisitorial network and all the consequences of arraignment by the Church.[61] The government of the Republic, alerted to the existence of these Jews, decreed their expulsion in 1497, and when such Jews became a significant presence in the city once again, they were ordered to leave in 1550.[62] In the years following the latter expulsion, there were only a few cases involving *Giudaizzanti* (lit., "Judaizers") in Venice, which indicates that hardly any "New Christians" of doubtful religious affiliation, who had immigrated to the city, remained in Venice.[63]

Another possibility, one to which we have already alluded, was for such a Jew to travel to the Ottoman Empire, remain there for a time, and then return to Venice as a *mercante levantino*. This method afforded the greatest protection from the Inquisition. Although technically such Jews were also heretics because they returned to their Judaism after having been baptized, the Inquisition could not touch them, since they were protected by their Ottoman status.[64]

Our hypothetical immigrant could pursue yet another course of action. Though it yielded the same results as the preceding one, its legality was doubtful from every point of view. Upon his arrival to Venice, the immigrant could settle in the Ghetto Vecchio, discard his Iberian clothes and don those of the *Levantini*, declare himself a Jew and a *mercante levantino*, and conduct himself as one who had been born and bred in the Jewish faith. So long as such a Jew did not enter situations that might compromise his Jewish identity, i.e., if he avoided close social interaction with Christians and did not mix with Christian women, the chances of his being caught and tried as a *Giudaizzanti* were slim.[65] This strategy enabled Jews from the Iberian Peninsula to acquire the Sultan's protection and extraterritorial privileges without stepping foot in the Ottoman Empire and without recourse to legal action.

Like other developments in the history of Venetian Jewry, eventually the aforementioned process was officially sanctioned. At the end of 1573, the *Consiglio dei Dieci* and the *Zonta*, the committee of senators attached to the *Consiglio*, granted Portuguese Jews and "New Christians" the right to settle in Venice for a two-year period, on the condition that they remain in the ghetto. This decision soon caught the attention of the Pope's envoy in Venice, Giambattista Castagna, and in a letter he wrote on 23 January 1574 to Tolomeo Galli, the secretary of state and cardinal of Como, Castagna described the problem of Ibero-Jewish immigration to Venice. He claimed that sheer greed, i.e., economic need, had motivated the authorities of the Republic to permit the settlement of such Jews in its borders. In truth they were Marranos—baptized individuals who returned to their ancestral faith— and assumed the mantle of the *Levantini* even though they came from the West, and they were exploiting the opportunity to live in Venice unscathed by the Inquisition. If one permitted them to live as Christians outside the ghetto, this was tantamount to allowing the establishment of a Church whose members were counterfeit Christians, for they were really Jews. And if these people remained in the ghetto, they profaned the act of baptism.[66]

Nevertheless, since the inclinations of the Venetians had long been more mercantile than theological, and the Republic sorely needed the economic boost these immigrants would provide, Castagna's aims were foiled. The Venetians did their utmost to prevent Jewish settlement from becoming anchored in Venetian law, but in the end the scales were tipped in favor of reality and pragmatism. One aspect of this pragmatism owed its existence to the efforts of other Italian states to attract Levantine trade.

What was the situation in the Papal State? There were three groups of Jews in the port of Ancona: the autochthonous Jews, the *Italiani*, and a few Jews of German extraction. These groups constituted a class unto themselves and some of the Jews engaged in money-lending.[67] Next to these Jews were the Levantine merchants, many of them Jews from the Ottoman Empire, who engaged in trade with the Empire. This last group could trace its roots in the city all the way to 1518, and in Ancona the *Levantini* were granted a variety of commercial privileges in that year.[68]

In 1532 Ancona became part of the Papal State. From the year 1534, the papal throne was occupied by Pope Paul III. Even among the Popes, there were those whose inclinations were more mercantile than theological. It was Pope Paul III who ultimately sanctioned a nationwide Inquisition in Portugal, after much hesitation and repeated efforts by "New Christians" to avert the decree—attempts accompanied by substantial offers of money. Yet this same man issued a *salvo conducto* to merchants of all nations, including the "Turks" (i.e., the Muslims) and the Jews, enabling them to trade and live in Ancona along with their families. Jews and other heretics were also allowed to dispense with the wearing of the stigmatizing yellow patch. The rights accorded the *Levantini* on 23 December 1534 essentially legalized a status quo that had prevailed for decades. The Papal State's ardent desire to maintain Ancona's status as an important conduit to the Levant was expressed in the renewal of these rights on 4 December 1535. After a few months, on 12 April 1535, the Pope himself took everyone trading in Ancona under his protection and exempted them all—the Levantine merchants, the Christians, the Jews, and the "Turks"—from all taxes, and he also revoked the special tax imposed on Jews.

The economic considerations that prompted the Pope to grant privileges to the *Levantini* were also the basis for the rights he granted to Jews who hailed from other parts of the world. Thus, on 7 January 1542, the Pope allowed a number of Jews, expellees from Sicily, to reside in Ancona. An edict issued six months later referred to "all the Jews who arrived from Sicily and other parts of the world." The reference to Jews from "other parts of the world" was apparently directed toward Jewish refugees from the Iberian Peninsula, for immediately afterward we hear of the arrival in Ancona of the first Jews from that region. After a year, in 1544, a charter of expanded privileges was given to the *Levantini* who reached Ancona and other areas under the jurisdiction of the Church. Underlying the charter of privileges was the realization that the public had much to gain from increased economic activity, and the hope that greater contact with devout Christians would induce these merchants to accept the true faith. On 21 February 1547, the charter granted to the *Levantini* was extended to the "Portuguese, even if they are 'New Christians' of Jewish extraction or if they were of the Jewish nation, whatever their origin may be."

The rights of the "Portuguese" in Ancona were preserved and subsequently expanded by Pope Paul III. In 1552, the rights of the *Levantini* and of the "Portuguese" in Ancona were renewed by Pope Paul's successor, Julius III. But the "Portuguese," still dissatisfied, requested and received a special confirmation of their privileges, issued on 20 March 1553.[69]

This picture of events resembles the one in Venice and even preceded it. The privileges of the non-local Jews were granted in two stages. At first they were extended to the *Levantini* in the city; in the second phase they incorporated the "New Christians" in the city who returned to their Judaism as well as the Jews expelled from other places because of their faith.

In Ancona there arose a group of "Portuguese" Jews who traded under papal protection. The Nasi family was commercially affiliated with this group, and four members of the Portuguese group represented the family's interests in the city. On the basis of the rights they obtained, and in view of their contribution to the economic life of the city, "Portuguese" Jews mistakenly assumed they had finally achieved a state of tranquillity and peace. In 1555, a new Pope, Paul IV, occupied the papal throne. As noted earlier, his views with respect to the status of Jews in general, and Jewish heresy in Ancona in particular, differed from those of his predecessors. The one hundred "Portuguese" Jews in the city were arrested and arraigned by the Inquisition. A number of them escaped from prison, and thirty-eight confessed the error of their ways after having been tortured, and then re-embraced the Christian faith. One of the prisoners committed suicide, and twenty-four who refused to renounce their Jewish faith were burned at the stake in the town square in Ancona in 1556, in the months of April and June. During this blood-soaked episode, not one *Levantino* was in the least bit harmed, although it was common knowledge that the sole difference between the "Portuguese" and most *Levantini* was that the latter had gone to the trouble of passing through the Ottoman Empire before settling in Ancona.[70]

The only explanation that can account for the differential treatment of the two groups of Jews is the diplomatic crisis that would surely have arisen had both groups received identical treatment. Such a crisis would have undermined Ancona's status in the Levant trade, and that was precisely what the Nasi family had in mind. A propos this subject, one should note the attempt of Dona Gracia to intercede on the prisoners' behalf. Pressure was applied in various ways, principally through the French embassy in Istanbul. Among other things, a personal letter of Süleyman the Magnificent was sent to the Pope. The letter stated that subjects of the Sultan were under arrest and that their detention was causing the Sultan appreciable economic damage. The Sultan requested a redress of his grievance and a return to the status quo. The end of his letter contained a passage that should have interested the Pope even more than the fate of the incarcerated Jews.

> By doing so [freeing the prisoners] you will make it possible for us to behave generously toward your subjects and toward other Christian merchants trading in this part of the world.

The caveat, of course, alluded to the principle of reciprocity that determined the treatment and guaranteed the rights of people from the *Dar al-Harb* in Ottoman territory. If the Christian ruler reneged on his promise of friendship and good will, the *aman* would be similarly revoked. Yet the root of the problem was that a good part of the Jews in question could not really prove they were subjects of the Sultan, and the Pope therefore refused to accede to the Sultan's demand for their release.[71]

The tragedy of the *anusim* in Ancona did not subvert the policy of other Italian cities with Jewish inhabitants. They followed the pattern of granting rights to the Levantine-Jewish merchants and of expanding them to include Jews of any origin, and promised protection from any investigation of their past. In 1549, the Grand Duchy of Tuscany granted similar rights to anyone who settled in Firenze, and these were renewed in 1551. Ferrara followed suit in 1550, 1555, and 1559, as did Urbino in 1550 and 1551, and Savoy twenty years later.[72]

In summation, until the end of the sixteenth century, one can discern a marked trend: Ottoman-Jewish subjects residing in Italy ordinarily retained their Ottoman identification. The reason is self-evident—at the time, Ottoman identification represented protection from a hostile world. It does not seem that the Jews' inferior status in the Empire itself affected the treatment they received once they left its borders. On the other hand, the inferior status of local Jews, at least in Venice, affected that of foreign Jews.

LAW AND ACTION: THE SEVENTEENTH AND EIGHTEENTH CENTURIES

At the end of the sixteenth century, a number of changes occurred in the status of Jews in Italy. Throughout the sixteenth century, "New Christians" continued to immigrate to Italy. They exploited the political mosaic of the country and would wander from one state to another whenever the local ruler made an issue of their Christian past. The experiences of these immigrants in the Venetian Republic continued to follow the dictates, or rationale, of the Republic's economic needs. There was a tacit agreement that the legal standing of anyone who arrived from the West (the *Ponentini*) and settled in the Ghetto Vecchio was identical to that of a Levantine merchant. However, since the *Consiglio dei Deici*'s decision in 1573 concerning the settlement rights of such Jews was not confirmed by the Senate, the *Ponentini* still feared for their life and property, and they continued to present themselves as members of the Levantine community.[73]

This state of affairs was altered by one individual whose initiative and imagination have only recently earned adequate recognition. He was one of the "New Christians" who settled in Venice, and his immense contribution to the city's commerce helped pave the way for his brothers and assure their safety. The man was Daniel Rodriga. In a proposal to the authorities of the Republic, he suggested that they establish a free port in territory held by Venice in the northeastern part of the Adriatic Sea, in Spalato (known today as Split, in Yugoslavia). The objective of the proposal was to attract Balkan trade from the city of Ragusa (Dubrovnik), whence a large quantity of goods was shipped to Ancona. The rerouting of trade via Spalato was suggested to ensure that the goods continued on their way to Venice.[74]

In 1589 the Republic became convinced of the idea's importance and approved Rodriga's plan. At the same time, a charter of privileges formulated by Rodriga was also ratified. This charter allowed Levantine merchants to bring their families to Venice and prolonged their right of settlement in the city by linking it to a time clause in the charter, i.e., they could remain in the city until the last day the charter was in effect. This charter also applied to all the Levantine merchants who dwelled in the city or who arrived there from any port in the Levant, and it thereby embraced recent emigrants from the Iberian Peninsula in the Ottoman Empire. Finally, the charter also applied to Jews who arrived in Venice directly from the West. All these people were allowed to reside in Venice and freely engage in international trade. Although the charter was slated to remain in effect for only ten years, it appears that its beneficiaries saw it as a turning point. It altered their status, for now they were no longer residing in Venice as foreign Ottoman subjects, but were accorded the interim status of Venetian residents with rights anchored in Venetian law.[75] Two years later, in 1591, Rodriga proposed that the *condotta* embrace all Venetian Jews, regardless of origin, and guarantee their residence for a ten-year period; a "grace period" of two years was appended in the event the *condotta* was not renewed. In exchange, all the Jews would be obliged, regardless of origin, to support the banks in the ghetto. According to this proposal, merchants among the *Levantini* who were considered *viandanti* were exempt from the aforementioned obligation. The actual charter granted in 1591 required *all* the Jews in Venice to support the existing banking network; hence, at least in theory, all the Jews in Venice were placed under the same status.[76]

Although significant parts of Rodriga's proposal were not ratified at the time, an understanding that the charter represented a watershed decision is reflected in the internal relations between various groups in Venice. Prior to the charter, the *Ponentini* were part of the Levantine-Jewish community, for obvious reasons. Such an affiliation protected them from investigation by the *Sant' Uffizio*. But two years after the charter was obtained, the *Ponentini* left the aforesaid community and established their own congregation, which they named *Talmud Torah*. The property shared by the two groups was divided, and the *Levantini* continued to pay their share of the maintenance for the House of Study, which served both communities.

From the agreement drawn between the two communities in 1606, it is amply clear that the differences between them were minimal, that members could choose rather freely between the two congregations, and that they cooperated to a significant degree. Although their status was no longer as precarious, a fact reflected in the creation of the new congregation, members of both groups exercised caution and never mentioned the words "Sephardim" or "Portuguese" in their internal communications. Instead, they referred to themselves simply as the "*yehidim* of the Holy Congregation of *Talmud Torah*."[77]

Nevertheless, it is clear that as individuals the *Ponentini* felt quite secure. A few years after the attainment of privileges, some of the *Ponentini* who had arrived in Venice remained and bore Portuguese-Christian names, either in part or *in toto*.[78] Their security proved well founded when some of the *Ponentini* were accused of being *Giudaizzanti* in 1608. Relying on the rights they had obtained previously, the accused parties turned to the doge, who interceded on their behalf.[79]

The problems confronting the "New Christians" who wished to return to their Jewish faith were resolved. They no longer needed the Sultan's protection to dry their skins from baptismal waters. When Rodriga proposed that the Republic extend a ten-year *condotta* to all the Jews, he also reminded the authorities that the Grand Duchy of Tuscany had recently invited one and all to trade in Livorno without fear of investigation into their past. At the same time, Rodriga subtly alluded to the fact that a war cannot be fought without soldiers, nor can a port exist without merchants. Thus, a series of privileges was accorded in succession, and not without a certain logic: Venice in 1589, Tuscany in 1590, Venice in 1591. Finally, in 1593, the dukes of Medici invited the "New Christians" to settle in the port of Livorno. This privilege, known as the "Livornina," was far more liberal than any granted to Jews in other Italian states. The privilege included a pledge that no Jew's religious past would be investigated. The Livornina was also somewhat limited in time—twenty-five years—and this constraint kept those arriving in Livorno in something of an interim status. It was better than anything they had known elsewhere, but was still not equal to the status of other subjects of the Duchy.[80] The granting of these privileges soon yielded dramatic results. In short order, a community of "New Christians" who returned to Judaism began to flourish in Livorno. By the mid-seventeenth century, the small fishing harbor of Livrono grew into a major center of trade on the Mediterranean Sea.[81]

The aforementioned privileges granted in Venice and Tuscany naturally reduced the value of, and need for, Ottoman identification in the Italian states. Furthermore, it helped create a new class of Jews from the Iberian Peninsula who could now live in Italy, secure in the knowledge that their rights were formally guaranteed without recourse to a foreign political power.

In the interim, a number of states in Europe received *imtiyazat* from the Sultan, which are otherwise known in the history of European diplomacy as the Capitulations. The French obtained a renewal of rights in 1569,[82] and England and Holland obtained rights in 1580[83] and 1612,[84] respectively. Once the French proved willing to protect Jews from Italian states who wished to trade in the Empire, they created an unprecedented situation. French patronage of Jews sailing and trading in the aforementioned areas implied that these Jews were entitled to the protection of their country of origin, a fact that strengthened Jewish loyalty to these states. French protection provided the Jews with a status far superior to that of *dhimmi*s in the Muslim state, a status legally equivalent to that of any French or Italian merchant who was a Christian. Until the end of the sixteenth century, we hear mainly of Ottoman-Jewish subjects residing in Italy, particularly in Venice, but as of the 1620s, we see a significant increase in the number of Jews bearing identification from an Italian state while trading in the Empire under French protection.[85]

The request for French protection is especially noticeable in the years 1670-1673, and was apparently linked to two developments in French trade in the Levant. First, the port of Marseilles was awarded a special status in 1669. Second, France received substantial Capitulations in 1673. The special status given the port of Marseilles and the formation of a company of French trade in the Levant greatly boosted this avenue of commerce. Jewish merchants were keen to become a part of it, even though it was monopolized by French merchants.[86] The Capitulations of 1673 were also pivotal in the annals of French trade in the Levant. After years of paralysis, the French finally succeeded in lowering their tariffs to the same rate paid by the English and Dutch.[87] The French agreed to provide the same benefit to Jews who traded under their protection—rights equal to those the French themselves had obtained from the Ottomans.

What drove the French to grant such rights to the Jews from the Grand Duchy of Tuscany and in other Italian states, at a time when no Jews were permitted to settle in France itself? There are two answers. First, the privileges given to the Jewish merchants were a vestige of exclusive rights the French had once enjoyed in the past: the right to protect the subjects of states from the *Dar al-Harb* who lacked diplomatic representation in the Ottoman Empire. Thus, the rights in question reinstated a prestigious status that had since become obsolete.[88]

A more decisive factor behind French patronage was their management of consular affairs. The French consuls were heavily dependent on the taxes they levied from their *protégés*. The funds at their disposal never sufficed to maintain the kind of lifestyle they deemed appropriate for consular officials of the French nation. To achieve that standard, they borrowed money, sank into debt, and constantly sought new sources of revenue. Taxes levied from Jewish merchants represented a major source of income for consulates in the Levant.[89] In addition, their *protégés* furnished French vessels with cargo for shipment between the Levant and Livorno.[90] In brief, the consulates had a vested interest in extending their protection. French merchants, however, did not share in the enthusiasm. As for the Jews, they were none too eager to pay the consular taxes and tried to avoid them in legal and extralegal fashion. French sources are filled with complaints against Jews who were accused of resorting to fraud to avoid paying the taxes and of engaging in unfair competition with French merchants. The Jews were forbidden to trade directly with France, but found a way around this. They would "borrow" the names of French merchants, for a fee, and sometimes they would enter into real or bogus partnerships in order to trade. Despite all the complaints, the evidence shows that there were always French merchants and consular officials willing to work around French law in order to do business with the Jews.[91] This French connection with the Jews was not sentimental; it was a business relationship based entirely on the profit motive. If a consul's ties with the Jews yielded a profit, he would send a communiqué off to Paris to inform the French that it was worth their while to protect the Jews. Just such a letter was sent on 10 July 1699 by the French consul in Aleppo, Jean Pierre Blanc, to the secretary of state, the Comte do Pontchartrain.

> As for the twenty-five Italian or Spanish Jews under the king's protection, they tend to wear hats according to the French fashion. They are not required to pay the *haraj* to the Grand Seigneur, nor do they pay him a share of duties, in accordance with Item 45 of the Capitulations which permits the Portuguese (as the Jews of Turkey are called) and other nations hostile to the Porte, who are protected by the French king, to pay the same duties as the French. As a result of [in exchange for] this privilege, these Jews pay two percent to the consul, which benefits the Chamber of Commerce in Marseilles for all the merchandise received on foreign vessels. They engage and load all the French vessels completing their journey to Italy. Lastly, by virtue of these taxes, the *nation* is able to cover its expenses and pay the salaries of clerks who serve His Majesty in these ports, and of the *pashas,* without whose help we could not live here in peace.[92]

French protection of Jews was certainly not brought about by a revaluation of the Jews' qualitative worth. To wit, a French consul in Aleppo who failed to obtain the desired benefits from his Jewish *protégés,* so informed the minister of maritime affairs in a letter sent on 22 August 1696.

> The *juifs francs* [European Jews from Christian lands] who have settled in Aleppo with French protection have harmed the pursuit of trade in this port.

Not content with paying an impost of only three percent like all other Frenchmen, they now demand an exemption from consular as well as other taxes they are required to pay. I take the liberty of informing your grace that the only way to remedy the situation is to withhold our patronage and leave them to the protection of the Grand Seigneur, for throughout the world they are but subjects of the rulers in whose lands they live.... Thus shall they bear the mark of slavery on their very clothes and pay the poll-tax like all the subjects of the Grand Seigneur.[93]

Obviously, Consul Chambon posited that the status of Jews was unlike that of the rest of mankind. Jews did not possess rights *iure sanguinis*, and those they did possess were acquired *iure soli*. His claim was a typical reflection of the view Christian Europeans held of the Jews, a prejudice entrenched for generations.

Discriminatory practices against Jews trading under French protection were evident not only in the matter of consular taxes. Whenever the Jews became embroiled in a case of *avania*, i.e., extortionate demands by the Ottoman government, monies were collected exclusively from the Jews, and the French contributed nothing toward the payment. In the same vein, French merchants refused to allow the participation of Jewish *protégés* in official ceremonies of the consulate.[94]

There were two factors that helped the Italian Jews trading under French protection become wealthy in a relatively short period of time: their legal status as *mustamin* and their connections to the Jews of the local community. Naturally their self-confidence increased along with their wealth, and at a certain stage they felt secure enough to confront the French with various demands. Some of them concerned the reduction of taxes, but others were of an entirely different ilk. The Jews wished to obtain a social recognition of their economic stature, and they therefore requested permission to participate in formal ceremonies of the French consulate. Such functions were held to welcome visiting dignitaries or took place in the Ottoman governor's residence.[95] The above demand represented a radical departure on the part of Jewish society in the Ottoman Empire. It indicated that, no longer satisfied with intramural recognition within their own community, these Jews now sought the prestige afforded by an external acknowledgment of their status! When the French refused to comply, the Jews threatened to leave them and seek the protection of the English. At the beginning of the eighteenth century in Salonica, for example, a spokesman for the Jewish merchants warned the French consul that if he did not lower the taxes, the Jews would abandon him. He argued that just as the extension of patronage was motivated by pragmatism, so was its acceptance. In a cynical vein, he also remarked that if the French took great pride in the patronage of their king, the Jews, by contrast, were mere merchants who had come to Salonica in order to trade. He added that the Jews had not sought French protection out of loyalty to the king, but because they had been instructed to do so by their partners in Livorno. Finally, the consul was informed that if he interfered with the Jews' trading activities, they would seek better conditions elsewhere or return to Livorno.[96]

In general, until the mid-eighteenth century, the threat to seek English protection was an empty one, since the British were not eager to patronize the Jews.[97] In fact, the British did not accept Jews into the Levant Company of England until 1753, for fear that they would be dispossessed in the Levant trade by Jews who had close ties with their Sephardic coreligionists.[98] On the other hand, once the British agreed to protect a foreign or local Jew, they proved willing to spend considerable sums to back it up as a matter of principle and honor.[99]

In the mid-eighteenth century, events transpiring outside the Ottoman Empire led to a turnabout in the status of Italian Jews trading in the Empire. First, in London there was mounting pressure to incorporate Jews into the Levant Company. This pressure was the result of progress achieved in the qualitative and legal standing of Jews in England.[100] In Italy, things did not remain static either. Most of the Italian Jews who traded in the Empire were the subjects of the Grand Duchy of Tuscany. In 1737, the last heir to the Medici dynasty in Tuscany died, and the dukedom was transferred to Francçois de Lorraine. This duke married Maria Theresa of Austria, the heiress to the throne of the Holy Roman Empire. Following the War of Succession (1740-1748), the duke was proclaimed emperor of the Holy Roman Empire, and the ducal title was conferred upon Leopold, the son of Maria Theresa and Francçois de Lorraine, who ruled from 1745 to 1790. Thus Tuscany became part and parcel of the Habsburg dynasty.[101]

In 1747, the Capitulations granted to the Holy Roman Empire in the Treaty of Passarowitz were extended to Tuscany as well.[102] In that year most of the British consuls in the Ottoman Empire obtained the right to protect Jews who were former *protégés* of the French. The majority of French *protégés* switched to the protection of the English, much to the astonishment and dismay of the French. It should be noted that such crossovers did not always take place quickly or voluntarily, and local conditions played an important role in the process.[103]

In most of the ports, the withdrawal of Jewish merchants had a severe economic impact on the French consulates, and the archives are replete with anxious reports about the decline in trade.[104] But British trade flourished. In 1758, the British consul in Aleppo reported that in order to accommodate the number of merchants under his protection, he was compelled to hire another interpreter and to acquire additional housing in the port of Iskenderun.[105] In 1755, British merchants in Iskenderun wrote that the Jewish group of merchants was the most prominent in the city, both in its size and scope of commerce.[106] The magnitude and success of Italian-Jewish finance eventually led to the social and political recognition of these Jews. If in the beginning of the eighteenth century the British in Aleppo were unwilling to protect Jews from Christian lands,[107] and the French snubbed the Jews in their consular ceremonies,[108] by the end of the century a *volte-face* occurred. In 1784, the Austrians were granted new Capitulations and an Austrian consulate was established in Aleppo. In charge of the consulate was a Jew of Livornese descent, Señor Raphael Piccioto. Most of the Jews trading under British protection became *protégés* of Austria. Initially the British were unsure how they should respond, but the wealth of the Piccioto family and their influence in the city decided the issue, and the British consequently maintained good relations with their former *protégés*.[109] In this context, a personal letter of a Mr. Abbott, written in 1791 following his appointment as British pro-consul in Aleppo, is of particular interest. The letter was sent to his brother Peter in Galata, Istanbul, and in it Mr. Abbott expressed pride in his appointment. He was certain the position would be offered to his rival, Moshe Piccioto.[110]

The French, too, began to treat their Jewish *protégés* differently, whether they were of Livornese or local descent. The change was due not only to the Jews' economic power but to the altered status of Jews in France itself after the French Revolution.[111] The Jews of Salonica, who in the 1740s demanded the right to join the *cortège* of Frenchmen accompanying the Marquis d'Antin on his visit to the city,[112] were invited to accept French citizenship after 1791 and transfer their affairs to Paris. The French consul was surprised, if not incensed, to receive a polite refusal.[113] It should be noted that the improvement of the Jews' legal standing did little to enhance their social image in France itself or in the Levant. True equality was achieved slowly, and many years were to pass before the legal and social status of Jews reached some kind of balance in French society.[114]

How did the Ottoman Empire perceive the status of Jews in their midst, the subjects of Tuscany and Venice, who traded under the protection of European consulates? At this juncture, I must stress that this study does not deal with the phenomenon of Ottoman Jews who relinquished their Ottoman identification in favor of European protection, although the subject is a fascinating one. Our analysis is confined to foreigners, and their ancestors, who came from the *Dar al-Harb*.

At least three issues are noteworthy in this regard. First, the evidence shows that the Ottoman Empire did not single out Italian Jews in its borders for particular harassment or animosity, i.e., they were not treated any worse than the French or Italian Christians. In general, the available documentation yields the opposite impression: Jews adapted well to the local lifestyle and customs and therefore had good relations with the Ottoman government and the local residents. A good part of this success was due to their extensive contacts with local Jewish communities.[115]

The second issue is of special interest and involves certain inconsistencies on the part of local Ottoman authorities towards the Jews in diverse places. In theory, these Jews should have received the same treatment as the French; in reality, this did not occur. Differential treatment was evident in the issue of taxes. In Salonica and Iskenderun, Italian Jews paid the same duties as the French: three percent.[116] Yet in the ports of North Africa, the Jews had to pay ten percent,[117] the rate paid by other *dhimmi*s trading in the Empire. We have not found that the Jews attempted to reverse this state of affairs by compelling local authorities to respect the law. Pressure could only have emanated from Istanbul, and Istanbul's authority in North Africa was tenuous to begin with. Furthermore, the French, primarily interested in making the Jews pay their consular duties, were not about to go out of their way to help Jews benefit from the achievements of French diplomacy. Thus, the French made no efforts to assist their *protégés* in this regard. The Jews found a solution to the problem by "renting" the names of French merchants. By 1697, the practice was so widespread that the *bey* of Tunis warned the French that he would raise their duties to ten percent as well. The inspector in charge of French Levantine trade forbade the abuse in no uncertain terms—to no avail. Again, theory and practice did not coincide.[118]

In Egypt a similar situation obtained. The duty on goods entering Egypt was very high. It was twenty percent in Alexandria and ten percent in Bulak, the port of the Nile in Cairo. These duties were not reduced by the Capitulations of 1673, and it was only in 1683-1686 that diplomatic and legislative efforts resulted in a reduction to three percent in Egypt, the standard rate. The English and the Dutch, however, continued to pay stiff tariffs for some time to come.[119] Initially the Jews under French protection also paid the lower duties. But when the local authorities saw that a reduced rate boosted French commerce to new heights, they began to argue that the practice of "renting" out names was to blame and sought to revoke the lower rate. Pressure of the local Ottoman authorities and the large sums the French had to pay them in order to protect their rights, led the French to forbid their merchants to rent out names to Jews or Armenians. As can be expected, the French had difficulty enforcing this injunction as well.[120]

The final point worth stressing is that after having settled for several decades in the Levant, fairly permanent groups formed in the ports of the region, of Jews who either possessed or inherited Tuscan and then Austrian nationality. Yet these Jews had never lived in Livorno and certainly had never seen Vienna. This curious phenomenon can be traced to the rise of European influence in the Ottoman Empire during the eighteenth century, a process that seriously weakened the sovereignty of the Empire.[121]

In summation, there was a significant difference between the Jews of the Ottoman Empire who sought to trade in the Italian states in the sixteenth century, and the Jews of Livorno, Venice, or Ancona, who sought to trade in the Empire during the next two centuries. The allegiance of Jews to the Ottoman Empire was not predicated on a time constraint, unlike the situation of Jews in the Italian states. This constraint, even when it was a mere formality, accorded the Jews an interim status similar to that of foreigners, whose right of residence remained in effect for specific periods of time.

The Jews of Italian states residing in the Ottoman Empire during the seventeenth and eighteenth centuries did not receive the same support that Ottoman subjects in Italy received in the sixteenth century. This was not because of their special status in their lands of origin; their flawed status, such as it was, did not prevent them from exercising their rights abroad. The reason for the lack of support is that, for many years, the Jews did not obtain real protection from their own country but from France, with relations between protector and *protégé* built on considerations of mutual benefit.

As the Jews consolidated their economic base, and as Christian Europe began to take a greater interest in the affairs of the Ottoman Empire, states willing to grant protection treated their Jewish *protégés* with greater seriousness.[122] By the end of the eighteenth century, an additional factor reinforced this tendency: the improved status of Jews in various parts of Christian Europe itself.

The attitude of the Ottoman Empire towards this group of foreigners was not uniform. In general, it may be said that the Empire respected the rights arising from their extraterritorial status, but on the subject which interested the Empire more than any other—the rate of customs duties—it attempted and sometimes succeeded to equate the foreigners' status with that of the local Jews. By the end of the eighteenth century, the Ottomans could no longer ignore the influence of those powers that stood behind the Jewish foreigners, nor could they impose any outward signs of inferiority upon them, i.e., the stigmata borne by local Ottoman Jews. On the contrary, in their acquisition of privilege and status, Jews of foreign lands served as an example to the local Ottoman Jews.

When the transformations in the status of Jews during the three centuries in question are surveyed from a certain distance in time, it is difficult not to observe a phenomenon that typifies the entire epoch: In the relationship of the individual to the state, his legal and personal connections to the state were not only tenuous but at odds. No doubt this can be partly attributed to the alienation that was so much a part of life for the subjects of this study. In a very real sense, they were made to feel like strangers in a strange land. Yet another aspect of this tenuousness is linked to the perception of the state concerning relations between itself and the individual. The more powerful state was ready to extend its protection, either as a demonstration of might and glory, or out of considerations of sheer pragmatism, to individuals whose connection to the state was at times purely fortuitous.

NOTES

1 For a definition of the term "subject" and on the differences between "subject" and "citizen," see B. Akzin, *Theory of Governments* (in Hebrew), vol. 1 (Jerusalem, 1964), 64-80. For a theoretical discussion of the term and concept of "foreigner," see 83-91. See also S. Oda, "The Individual in International Law," in *Manual of Public International Law*, ed. M. Sorenson (New York, 1968), 471-74.

2 If by the term "subject" we refer to a person's subjection to, and obligations toward, the government, the sixteenth-century residents of the Italian states can be so considered. But if we bear in mind that in all these states the legal basis of their existence was the *condotta* (a contract revolving about the "right of being"), which was renewed every few years, then these Jews were clearly perceived as foreigners with an interim and tempo-

rary status, whose normative connection to the state was a function of their physical presence in its territory (see not 3). For a comprehensive discussion of the status of Venetian Jews along the Eastern Mediterranean during the thirteenth and fifteenth centuries, and for a clarification of their legal connection to "their" state, see D. Jacoby, "Venice and the Venetian Jews in the Eastern Mediterranean," in *Gli ebrei e Venezia, Secoli XIV-XVII*, ed. G. Cozzi (Milano, 1987), 29-58, hereafter referred to as *Gli ebrei*.

3 On the misgivings of the Venetian Republic concerning the settlement of Jews in its domain, see C. Roth, *History of the Jews in Venice* (New York, 1975), 39-611; B. Ravid, "The Religious, Economic and Social Background and Context of the Establishment of the Ghetti in Venice," in *Gli ebrei*, 211-22. On the status of Jews elsewhere in Italy, especially in Mantua, see S. Simonsohn, *History of the Jews in the Duchy of Mantua* (in Hebrew), vol. 1 (Jerusalem, 1962), 78-83. For the English version, see idem, *History of the Jews in the Duchy of Mantua* (Jerusalem, 1977), 99-118. See also idem, *The Jews in The Duchy of Milan, 1387-1477*, vol. 1 (Jerusalem, 1982), xxvi-xxxvii. On the problematic aspects in defining the legal status of Jews in the Italian states, ibid., xxvi. See also V. Colorni, *Gli ebrei nel sistema del diritto comune* (Milano, 1956), 2.

In the perception of Jews in the Ottoman Empire, particular emphasis was placed on the "mercy" of rulers who permitted Jewish settlement. For a description of the Ottoman Empire's invitation to the Jewish expellees from Spain, permitting their settlement in the land, see R. Eliahu Kapsali, *Seder Eliahu Zuta*, vol. 1, annotated and edited by A. Shmuelevitz, A. Simonsohn, and M. Benayahu (Jerusalem, 1975), 218-21. Though Kapsali's description may not be an accurate account of the facts, it reflects a state of mind he undoubtedly imbibed from those living in the Empire. See also notes 7-8.

4 For a general survey of the attitude of the Venetian states toward the *Levantini*, as influenced by that of other Italian states, see D.B. Cooperman, "Venetian Policy towards Levantine Jews in Its Broader Italian Context," in *Gli ebrei*, 65-84.

15 For a discussion of the Jews with a connection to the Venetian Republic and who resided within the Byzantine Empire, see Jacoby, "Venice and the Venetian Jews," 33-36. Any rights the Jews obtained from this connection had nothing to do with the fact that they had immigrated to these areas from the Venetian Republic; rather, their rights stemmed from the Empire's conquests and domination of these areas. See Jacoby, "Venice and the Venetian Jews," 33-36. One cannot assume, nor is there any evidence, that the Jews held on to this status after the conquest of these areas.

6 See my article, "The Connection of Person to Place: The Sephardic Diaspora in the Eastern Mediterranean from the Sixteenth to the Eighteenth Centuries" (in Hebrew) (forthcoming).

7   R. Shemuel de Medina (Rashdam), *Responsa, Hoshen Mishpat* (Lemberg, 1862), no. 303: "one's body, spirit, and property are immeasurably more secure in this Kingdom whose rulers are Kings of mercy, may their majesty and glory endure forever"; Rashdam, *Yoreh Deah*, no. 124; *Hoshen Mishpat*, nos. 361, 364, 401, 434, and 436; R. Aharon Hacohen Perahiyah, *Parah Mateh Aharon* (Amsterdam, 1703), no. 55; R. Avraham de Buton, *Responsa, Lehem Rav* (Jerusalem, 1968), no. 67.

8   Rashdam, *Responsa, Hoshen Mishpat*, no. 46; R. Yosef Ibn Lev, *Responsa*, vol. 2 (Jerusalem, 1960), no. 23; R. Avraham de Buton, *Responsa, Lehem Rav*, no. 5.

9   On *anusim* who had business holdings in Italy before the immigration, see R. Yaakov LeBeit Halevi, *Responsa* (Venice, 1632), rule 6, no. 52.

10 On an *anus* from Portugal who lived as a *Giudaizzante* in Italy for a number of years before immigrating to the Ottoman Empire, see R. Yosef Ibn Lev, *Responsa* (Jerusalem, 1970), pt. 3, no. 75; R. Hayim Shabtai, *Responsa, Torat Hayim* (Salonica, 1715), no. 13. See also the material on the expulsion decree against the *anusim* in Venice, in D. Kaufmann, "Die Vertreibung der Marranen aus Venedig im Jahre 1550," *Jewish Quarterly Review* 13 (1900): 520-33, esp. 525-27; P.C.J. Zorattini, *Processi del Sant'Uffizio di Venezia contro Ebrei e Giudaizzanti (1548-1560)*, vol. 2 (Firenze, 1980), 26-35. See note 60 of this article.

11 On the growing extremism of the papacy in its attitude towards the Jews in the time of Pope Paul IV (1555-1559), and on the papal bull "Cum nimis absurdum," see J. Sonne, *From Paulus the 4th to Pius the 5th* (in Hebrew) (Jerusalem, 1954); K. R. Stow, *Catholic Thought and Papal Policy, 1555-1593* (New York, 1977).

12 See note 70.

13 R. Yehoshua Soncin, *Responsa, Nahala Liyehoshua* (Istanbul, 1731), no. 39.

14 C. Roth, *The House of Nasi* (in Hebrew) (Tel Aviv, 1953), 101; Sonne, *From Paulus*, 148. For a reevaluation of the boycott affair, see R. Lamdan, "The Boycott of Ancona: Viewing the Other Side of the Coin" (in Hebrew), in *From Lisbon to Salonica and Constantinople* (in Hebrew), ed. Z. Ankori (Tel Aviv, 1988), 135-54.

15 The terms "Marrano" and "New Christians" do not convey the elements of coercion and dual identity that were an integral part of such Jews' experience, and we therefore prefer the term *anusim*, which denotes duress and literally means "the coerced ones."

16 Rashdam, *Responsa, Hoshen Mishpat*, no. 303.

17 See note 65.

18 See note 64.

19 An example of this phenomenon would seem to be the story of

Shelomo Ashkenazi (Salomone Ashkenasi). In Istanbul, he served as the physician of the Venetian nation and as that of the Grand Vizir, Mehmet Sokollu, during the war between the Empire and Venice in 1570-1573. He was born in Udine, within the borders of the Republic, and when the Jews were expelled from Udine, he embarked on a winding journey that ultimately brought him to Istanbul. On several occasions, he reminded the *bailo* of his Venetian birth, as a basis for obtaining a bona fide Venetian status. Certainly Ashkenazi's services as an intermediary in the negotiations between the two states are proof of his deep commitment to the land of his birth. On the other hand, one can legitimately question if he would have obtained Venetian citizenship, notwithstanding his birth in Venice, had the Venetians in Istanbul not required his expertise as a physician and exclusive conduit to the outside world. His Jewishness, after all, was the reason for his expulsion from Udine! A bibliography on the man and his life can be found in B. Arbel, "Venezia, gli ebrei e l'attivita di Salomone Ashkenasi nella guerra di Cipro," in *Gli ebrei*, 189, no. 103, hereafter referred to as "Salomone Ashkenasi." On Ashkenazi's claim and desire to be a Venetian subject, see p. 176.

20 On the concept of the *dhimma* in Islam, see Cl. Cahen's entry in the *Encyclopedia of Islam*, 2nd ed., s.v. "Dhimma". Unless otherwise noted, all references to the encyclopedia are from the second edition. See also C. E. Bosworth, "The Concept of *Dhimma* in Early Islam," in *The Central Lands*, vol. 1 of *Christians and Jews in the Ottoman Empire*, eds. B. Braude and B. Lewis (New York and London, 1982), 37-51.

21 On the distinctions between Jews and Muslims, see A. Cohen, *The Jewish Community of Jerusalem in the 16th Century* (in Hebrew) (Jerusalem, 1982), 8. In the English translation, the book is titled *Jewish Life Under Islam* (Cambridge, Mass., 1984), 2.

22 On the status of Jews in the Italian states, see note 3. For material on anti-Jewish legislation in the Veneto region, see Arbel, "Salomone Ashkenasi," 161 and the accompanying notes. For a more detailed discussion, see B. Pullan, *Rich and Poor in Renaissance Venice—The Social Institutions of a Catholic State, to 1620* (Cambridge, Mass., 1971), 516-37.

23 On this matter, see Ravid, "The Religious . . . Ghetti in Venice," 211-22, 248-50; idem, "The Legal Status of the Jews in Venice to 1509," *P.A.A.J.R.* 58 (1987): 169-202; and Pullan, *Rich and Poor*, 476-509.

24 See Arbel, "Salomone Ashkenasi," 166; idem, "Venice and the Jewish Merchants of Istanbul in the Sixteenth Century," in *The Mediterranean and the Jews: Finance and International Trade, 16th -18th Centuries*, ed. A. Toaff (Leiden, 1980), 93; and F. C. Lane, *Storia di Venezia* (Torino, 1978), 183 and accompanying notes. For the English version of Lane's work see, idem, *Venice: A Maritime Republic* (Baltimore, 1973), 300.

25 On these issues, see H. İnalcık's entry in the *Encyclopedia of Islam*, s.v. "Imtiyazat."
26 Cooperman, "Venetian Policy," 67.
27 Ibid., 70-71.
28 Arbel. "Salomone Ashkenasi," 165-66; idem, "Venice and the Jewish Merchants," 98-100.
29 Cooperman, "Venitian Policy," 67.
30 Ravid, "The Religious . . . Ghetti in Venice," 248-50.
31 Roth, *History of the Jews*, 61.
32 Ravid, "The Establishment of the Ghetto Vecchio of Venice, 1541: Background and Reappraisal." in *Proceedings of the Sixth World Congress of Jewish Studies*, vol. 2 (Jerusalem, 1973-75), 153-67; idem, "The Religious . . . Ghetti in Venice," 222-28, 250-54.
33 Ravid, "Establishment of the Ghetto Vecchio," 162-63.
34 This was discussed by Arbel in "Salomone Ashkenasi," 166.
35 Ibid., 165.
36 Cf. the privileges obtained in the 1530s by the *Levantini* in Ancona (see note 69). On the status and categories of Jews in Levantine trade in general, see Arbel, "Venice and the Jewish Merchants."
37 For a bibliography on the peace treaty, see C. Villain-Gandossi, "Contribution à l'étude des relations diplomatiques et commerciales entre Venise et la Porte ottomane au XVIe siècle," *Südost Forschungen* 26 (1967): 23, nn. 3-5. For the wording of the privileges, see T. Gökbilgin, "Venedik Devlet Arşivindeki Vesikalar Külliyatında Kanuni Sultan Süleyman Devri Belgeleri," *Belgeler* 2 (1964): 121-28.
38 J. von Hammer-Purgstall, *Geschichte des Osmanischen Reiches*, vol. 3 (1828; reprint, Graz, Austria, 1963), 218-20; H. İnalcık, "The Heyday and Decline of the Ottoman Empire," in *The Cambridge History of Islam*, vol. 1A, eds. P. M. Holt, A. K. S. Lambton, and B. Lewis (Cambridge, 1970), 327.
39 *Encyclopedia of Islam*, s.v. "İmtiyazat", Gökbilgin, "Venedik," 248-50.
40 R. Moshe Mitrani, *Responsa* (Lemberg, 1861), part 2, no. 21.
41 Roth, *History of the Jews in Venice*, 61.
42 Ravid, "The Religious . . . Ghetti in Venice," 228-44.
43 Ravid refers to F. C. Lane's description of Venetian housing in Alexandria in "The Religious . . . Ghetti in Venice," 230. This situation obtained not only in Alexandria but elsewhere and among other nations as well. See, for example, P. Masson's description of the French *nation* in Aleppo, Sidon, and Alexandria in the beginning of the seventeenth century, in *Histoire du commerce franççais dans le Levant au XVIIe siècle* (Paris, 1911), 463-66; see also *Encyclopedia of Islam*, s.v. "İmtiyazat."

44 Ravid, "The Religious . . . Ghetti in Venice," 233-44 and accompanying notes.

45 Ravid, "The First Charter of the Jewish Merchants in Venice, 1589," *Association for Jewish Studies Review* 1 (1976): 187-222.

46 Ravid, "Establishment of the Ghetto Vecchio," 166-67 and accompanying notes.

47 See note 40.

48 *Encyclopedia of Islam*, s.v. "Imtiyazat."

49 Ibid.

50 On the time clause attached to the settlement of *Levantini* in Venice, see Ravid, "Establishment of the Ghetto Vecchio," 164 and 166 n. 29. On the circumvention of this clause, see Arbel, "Salomone Ashkenasi," 184 n. 20, and idem, "Venice and the Jewish Merchants," 100.

51 E. Alberi, *Relazioni degli Ambasciatori Veneti al Senato*, vol. 1 (Firenze, 1840), 102.

52 Rashdam, *Responsa, Hoshen Mishpat*, no. 344.

53 Gökbilgin, "Venedik," 161.

54 Alberi, *Relazioni*, 1:274.

55 See Arbel, "Salomone Ashkenasi," 167-68 and accompanying notes.

56 Rashdam, *Responsa, Hoshen Mishpat*, no. 70.

57 See the letter of Jacopo Razazzoni to the Venetian senate, in Alberi, *Relazioni* (Firenze, 1844), 2:83-84, 90-91.

58 R. Yosef Mitrani, *Responsa, Hoshen Mishpat* (Lemberg, 1861), no. 105. The date of the responsum is based on the years R. Yosef Mitrani was active in Istanbul, 1597-1599 and 1605-1639. See the introduction to his *Responsa*; see also H. Bentov, *Autobiographical and Historical Register of Rabbi Josef Trani, Shalem I* (in Hebrew), ed. J. Hacker (Jerusalem, 1974), 195-228. The approximate location of the "power" mentioned in the responsum is based on the names of those rabbis who issued a verdict in the case in that area: Yehiel Basan and Moshe Meshulam Halevi. We are unable to identify them further, but the families were well known in the Veneto region. See, for example, M. Benayahu, *Copyright, Authorization and Imprimatur for Hebrew Books Printed in Venice* (in Hebrew) (Jerusalem, 1971), 133, 136-38, 144-45, 148, 201, 296, 311, 317-19, 321, 346.

59 On the history of the *Sant' Uffizio* in Venice, see P. C. J. Zorattini, *Processi del Sant' Uffizio di Venezia contro Ebrei e Giudaizzanti* (Firenze, 1980), 2:37-46 and the accompanying notes. See also B. Pullan, *The Jews of Europe and the Inquisition of Venice, 1550-1570* (Oxford, 1983). It should be noted that for the decades discussed by Zorattini—a period when the Franciscans were deeply involved in the *Sant' Uffizio* in Venice—there were few cases against *Giudaizzanti* (p. 59). This was not because the number of "New Christians" who had immigrated to Venice was small, for if that were

so, the Republic would not have found it necessary to expel them from the city in 1550. On this question, see P. C. J. Zorattini, *Leandro Tisanio, un Giudaizzante Sanvitese del Seicento* (Firenze, 1984), 57, 59. It appears that the number of "Marranos" in Venice was severely reduced after the expulsion in 1550. See Zorattini, *Processi,* 2:10, 17.

In the 1570s and 1580s, before rights were granted in 1589, one comes across persons from the Netherlands in Venice, whose names were distinctly Portuguese. To all appearances, they were Christians in every respect, and a large number of them were probably "New Christians." In some cases, this can be proven beyond doubt (see note 60). More details can be found in W. Brulez, *Marchands flamands à Venise, 1568-1605*, vol. 1 (Brussels, 1965). A number of the "Flemish" merchants bearing Portuguese names, who are mentioned in the archives cited in this book, also appear in the rosters of the *Sant' Uffizio*, but not all of them were *Giudaizzanti*, and some clearly wanted nothing more than a chance to live in peace. For example, Brulez documents the instance of Guielmus Helman (p. 278), a Flemish merchant who, in his will drawn in 1583, bequeathed a triangle-shaped diamond to his colleague, Ruy Gomez Mendez, as a sign of friendship. For the names of other "Flemish" merchants with Portuguese names, see pp. 25, 52, and 72.

60 The material culled by Brulez and Zorattini, and especially a comparison of their works, in addition to the data found in notary archives and in the archives of the *Sant' Uffizio*, provide a full picture of this lifestyle and of the motives behind it. For example, in the protocols of the *Sant' Uffizio*, a man by the name of Ruy Lopez, also called Ludovicus Lopez, is mentioned several times as a witness against *Giudaizzanti*, but was himself accused of being one. See Zorattini, *Processi . . . 1571-1580* (Firenze, 1985), 6:140. Elsewhere, a witness attests to Lopez's Christian devotion (p. 145). A man by the name of Ruy Lopez, the partner of a brother named Diego Rodrighes, worked outside the ghetto and was involved in various enterprises in 1600 (see Brulez, *Marchands flamands*, 334-35) and 1603 (ibid., 458, 462). Ludovicus Lopez (alias Ruy) also continued to live as a Christian in these years (ibid., 422, 431). Another brother (perhaps the same Lopez, under another name?) of Ruy or Ludovicus Lopez was Michael Vaz, who also bore a dual identity in Venice. Vaz was brought to court in Venice in 1572 (ibid., 49-61). Zorattini also discusses business holdings Michael Vaz owned as a Christian in 1583 (*Marchands flamands*, 23). In 1594, Vaz died a prosperous man in Istanbul, but under the name of Mose Sarfatin (?) (see *Processi*, 6:39). See also the case against the agency of the Mendes-Nasi family, in Zorattini, *Processi*, 2:225-45, 251-62 and that of Ioan Ribiera, who was accused of being a *Giudaizzante*. In Ribiera's case, witnesses testified that "non era ne christian ne ebreo et che non credeva in cosa alcuna" (ibid., 2:171).

The aspect of social relations with Christian women arises in the case of Odoardo Dias, who lived as a Christian outside the ghetto and was married to a Flemish woman named Susana Van de Blum. He was arrested for being a *Giudaizzante*, at which point it was discovered that he had lived as a Lutheran in the Netherlands. For the numerous versions of his wife's last will, see Brulez, *Marchands flamands*, 8-9. For the protocols of the case in the *Sant' Uffizio*, see Zorattini, *Processi*, 6:89-100.

Relations with Christian women were also a factor in the case against Francisco Olivier, a man from Lisbon who was circumcised as a Jew. Olivier divided his time between a Venetian *cartagena* (courtesan) and his friends in the ghetto. See Zorattini, *Processi*, 2:54.

61 Although the punishments meted out by the *Sant' Uffizio* were far more lenient than those of the Inquisition in Spain and Portugal, financial losses could be substantial. See the case of the Nasi family, in Zorattini, *Processi*, 2:29-30, and the attempts of Susana Van de Blum to change her original will in order to safeguard the estate after her husband's imprisonment. In her original will, she had bequeathed her property to her "beloved husband" (see note 60).

62 See note 10, and Zorattini, *Leandro Tisanio*, 56-57.

63 Ibid., 59; see note 65.

64 Most of the *levantino* merchants trading in Venice during the latter half of the sixteenth century, and who are mentioned by Brulez, bore Iberian names. See Leon Abravanello [Abravanel] and Josef [Yosef] Mocato (p. 49), Samuel [Shemuel] Ergas (p. 53), Isaac Namias [Yitzhak Nahmias] (p. 24), Salomon Cabiglio [Shelomo Havilio] (p. 92), Frain [Efrayim] Pichio (p. 153), Begnamin [Benyamin] Bendessus and Salomon Carabun [Shelomo Harabun] (p. 163), and others. It is hard to believe that all of them were Ponentini who "adopted" a Levantine identity (see note 65). As for the relative security provided by Ottoman identification, see the investigation of Giuseppe Margaran by the *Sant' Uffizio* in 1559. He was accused of being a party to the *anusim* in Ancona who returned to their Judaism and were sentenced to forced labor on galleys. When he arrived in Venice, he conducted himself as a Jew. He claimed that he was born in Istanbul and that his real name was Ioseph de Abran Lachar [Yosef ben Avraham Bakhar?]. The court accepted his claim without difficulty (see Zorattini, *Processi*, 2:317-19). Conceivably, the man may have actually "adopted" a Jewish-Levantine identity, which enabled him to claim that he was never baptized. Nevertheless, the readiness with which the court accepted his claim is telling.

65 On this matter, see Zorattini, *Leandro Tisanio*, 67-68.

66 Zorattini, *Processi*, 4:9-11.

67 On the Ashkenazic and *Italiani* Jews in Ancona, see S. Simonsohn,

"Marranos in Ancona under Papal Protection," eds. D. Carpi and S. Simonsohn, *Michael* 9 (1985): 234-35. See esp. 235 n. 2.

68   Cooperman, "Venetian Policy," 70-71.

69   Simonsohn, "Marranos in Ancona," 235-67.

70   On the incident in Ancona, see the bibliography in Simonsohn, "Marranos in Ancona," 234 n. 2. See also R. Segre, "Nuovi documenti sui marrani d'Ancona (155-1559)," *Michael* 9 (1985): 130-233. More detail about the status of *Levantini* in Ancona during this episode are in the responsa of R. Yehoshua Soncin, *Nahala Liyehoshua*, no. 40. In this work, he states that the Portuguese in Istanbul dismissed the testimony of the *Levantini* in Ancona, in which they warned of the dangers awaiting Jews in the city if Ancona would be boycotted. The Portuguese felt that the *Levantini* were not "objective," since their primary goal was to avoid "eviction from a place to which they have become accustomed." Most of the *Levantini* in Ancona were also of Iberian origin. Only one Ashkenazic Jew from Istanbul traded there, and among the Romaniots, not one traded in Ancona (see R. Soncin's responsum).

71   G. Ruscelli, *Lettere dei Principi* (Venice, 1581), 177-78. A Hebrew translation of the letter was done by Roth in *The House of Nasi*. The English translation was done by S. W. Baron, in *A Social and Religious History of the Jews*, vol. 4 (New York, 1969), 39-40. The Pope's response to the letter, and the letter of his nephew, the Duke of Paliano, to Michel de Codignac, the French ambassador to Istanbul, deal with the same problem and were all published by P. Grunbaum in "Un Episode de l'histoire des Juifs d'Ancone," *Revue des Etudes Juives* 18 (1894): 142-46.

72   See Cooperman, "Venetian Policy," 76 and accompanying notes.

73   See note 77, and Arbel, "Salomone Ashkenasi," 180-81.

74   See note 45.

75   Ibid.

76   Pullan, *Rich and Poor*, 569-70. In the privileges of 1591, the requirement to support the banks also included the Levantine *viandanti*. This may have been the tax that elicited the resentment of those merchants mentioned in R. Yosef Mitrani's responsum. See above and note 58.

77   See the documentation in D. Carpi, "The Statutes of the Community of Venice," in *Jubilee Book of Hayim Beinart* (in Hebrew) (forthcoming). I am indebted to Prof. Carpi for allowing me to benefit from the fruits of his research prior to its publication.

78   See, for example, a proclamation of 26 March 1599, in which the name Vidal de Luner appears among those of other *Levantini*, in Brulez, *Marchands flamands*, 299. See also the i.o.u. of 1 October 1599, signed by a Jew named Juan Maria de Ezra (p. 317).

79   Zorattini, *Leandro Tisanio*, 68.

Strangers in a Strange Land / 163

80 On this matter, see A. Milano, "Gli antecedenti della Livornina del 1593," *Rassegna di Mensile Israel* 37 (1971): 343-60; idem, "La constituzione Livornina del 1593," *Rassegna di Mensile Israel* 34 (1968): 394-410; and Cooperman, "Venetian Policy," 84 n. 55.

81 On the demographic increase of the Livornese community, see M. Rozen, "Les Marchands Juifs livournais à Tunis et le commerce avec Marseilles à la fin du XVIIe siècle," *Michael* 9 (1985): 8 nn. 3-4. On the importance of Livorno in the economy of Europe during the seventeenth century, see K. Glamann, "European Trade (1500-1750)," in *The Fontana Economic History of Europe, The Sixteenth and Seventeenth Centuries*, ed. C. M. Cipola (Glasgow, 1981), 507; F. Diaz, *Il Granducato di Toscana*, vol. 13 of *Storia d'Italia*, ed. G. Galasso (Torino, 1976), pt. 1, 259-60; and F. Braudel and R. Romano, *Navires et marchandises dans le Port de Livourne (1547-1611)* (Paris, 1951).

82 *Encyclopedia of Islam*, s.v. "Imtiyazat."

83 A. Wood, *A History of the Levant Company* (London, 1964), 8-9.

84 Ibid., 46-47.

85 This phenomenon is first encountered in North Africa and remained particular to that area for several decades. On the settlement of Livornese Jews in Tunis, see H. Z. Hirschberg, *A History of the Jews in North Africa* (in Hebrew), vol. 2 (Jerusalem, 1965), 120-21. See also H. Avrahami, "Les Juifs de Livourne et leurs relations avec Tunis au XVIIe et XVIIIe siècles" (in Hebrew) (M.A. diss., Bar Ilan University, 1979), 4-15. On the settlement of Livornese Jews in Algeria in the first half of the seventeenth century, see Hirschberg, *A History of the Jews in North Africa*, 54-55.

86 On these issues, see M. Rozen, "France and the Jews of Egypt: An Anatomy of Relations (1683-1801)," in *The Jews in Ottoman Egypt, 1517-1914*, ed. J. M. Landau (Jerusalem, 1988), 444-52. See also Rozen, "Les Marchands Juifs livournais," 104-106 and accompanying notes.

87 On these Capitulations, see François Emanuel Guinard, 1735-1821, Comte de Saint Priest, Ambassadeur de France en Constantinople, *Mémoire sur l'ambassade de Turquie et sur le commerce des Français dans le Levant*, ed. C. Schefer (Paris, 1877; reprint, Amsterdam, 1974), 473. See also R. Paris, *Le Levant*, vol. 5 of *Histoire du commerce de Marseille de 1660 à 1789* (Paris, 1957), 85-87.

88 For a summary of the struggle over the right to represent the states of the *Dar al-Harb* in the Empire, see *Encyclopedia of Islam*, s.v. "Imtiyazat."

89 On the connection between the consulates and the imposts levied from Jewish *protégés*, see the correspondence from Salonica, Consul Jean François Arnaud to Secretary of Maritime Affairs, the Comte de Pontchartrain, 12 August 1699, Archives Nationales de France, Affaires Etrangères, BI 990, hereafter referred to as A.N., A.E. See also Consul

Boismond to Pontchartrain, 10 November 1716, A.N., A.E., BI 991. For Aleppo, see Consul Lemaire to Pontchartrain, 28 December 1710, A.N., A.E., vol. 2, BI 77. For Cairo, see Consul Maillet to Pontchartrain, 10 June 1693, A.N., A.E., BI 313, 225r-v.

90 On this issue, See M. Rozen, "Contest and Rivalry in Mediterranean Maritime Commerce in the First Half of the Eighteenth Century: The Jews of Salonika and the European Presence," trans. Goldie Wachsman, *Revue des Etudes Juives* 147 (1988): 309-52.

91 Ibid.; Rozen, "France and the Jews of Egypt"; idem, "Les Marchands Juifs livournais."

92 Archives de la Chambre de Commerce de Marseille, J 901, hereafter referred to as A.C.C.M.

93 A.N., A.E., BI 76, p. 327v; see also Consul to Echevins et Députés de Commerce de Marseille, 22 June 1692, A.C.C.M. J 900.

94 On the refusal of the consulate to help pay off the extortion involving a Livornese Jew by the name of Belilios, see the letter of the consul in Aleppo, Joseph Arasy to the Echevins et Députés de Commerce de Marseille, 29 July 1774, A.C.C.M. J 908. On the refusal of French merchants in Salonica and Aleppo to allow the participation of Jewish *protégés* in consular ceremonies, see Rozen, "Contest and Rivalry"; idem, "France and the Jews of Egypt."

95 See the letter of the French consul in Salonica to the secretary of maritime affairs, Bayle to Maurepas, 31 October 1734, A.N., A.E., BI 994.

96 Rozen, "Contest and Rivalry."

97 Ibid., esp. the letter of the French ambassador in Aleppo to the secretary of state for maritime affairs, Lemaire to Pontchartrain, 22 July 1711, in A.N., A.E., BI 77, C.C. 1708-1715.

98 Wood, *A History of the Levant Company*, 156.

99 See the volume of correspondence for 1703-1706, much of it containing letters from the British consul in Aleppo, George Brandon Esquire, to various parties in England and the Levant, dealing with the arrest and release of the Jewish interpreter of the consulate, in the Public Record Office of Great Britain (hereafter referred to as P.R.O.), vol. 23, Aleppo papers, 110. See esp. Brandon to William Sherard, the British consul in Izmir, 14 February 1703, P.R.O., F. 63-64.

100 Rozen, "Contest and Rivalry," 340-440.

101 F. Diaz, *Il Granducato di Toscana*, 522-24; see G. Guarnieri, *Livorno e la marina mercantile Toscana sotto i Lorenzi (1737-1760)* (Pisa, 1969), 19-23, 149-55. It should be noted here that between 1732 and 1735, the duchy was under a powerful Spanish influence, since the presumption was that the heir to the Spanish throne would also inherit that of Tuscany. When the government of the Venetian Republic learned of this, they promptly

urged the Livornese Jews to move themselves and their property to the Republic . . . for their own good. The Jews politely declined the offer, having received assurances from the Tuscan authorities that they would come to no harm. When the Spaniards left, they pointedly emphasized their good relations with the Jewish nation in Livorno. See L. Poliakov, "Tentativo di Venezia par attirare gli ebrei di Livorno," *Rassegna di Mensile Israel* 23 (1957): 291-95.

102 *Encyclopedia of Islam*, s.v. "İmtiyazat."

103 Rozen, "Contest and Rivalry," 342-44; idem, "France and the Jews of Egypt," 456.

104 For Salonica, see Rozen, "Contest and Rivalry," 344-49; for Aleppo, see, for example, Consul Thomas to the Ministry of Maritime Affairs, 10 April 1752, A.N., A.E., BI 86, C.C. Alep. 1751-1753, vol. 2, F. 159r-160r.

105 P.R.O., SP 110, vol. 29 (1746-1784). On the need for additional housing, see the letter of the British consul in Aleppo to the vice-consul in Iskenderun, Brand Kirkhouse to Vice-Consul, 5 January 1757, ibid., F. 71v-72r. On the need to hire an additional interpreter, see the letter of the British consul and merchants in Aleppo to the Levant Company in London, 13 July 1758, ibid., F. 74r-v. The correspondence indicates a connection between the aforementioned needs and the extention of British protection to the "Tuscans."

106 Letter of British merchants in Aleppo to the British consul in Aleppo, 7 September 1775, P.R.O., SP 110, vol. 29, F. 184r-187v.

107 See, for example, the letter of the French consul in Aleppo to the secretary of maritime affairs, Lemaire to Pontchartrain, 22 July 1711, A.N., A.E., BI 77, 1708-1715.

108 Rozen, "Contest and Rivalry," 334.

109 See the letter of the British pro-consul in Aleppo, David Hays, to the Levant Company in London, 1 June 1784, P.R.O., SP 110, vol. 29, F. 283v-284r. See also the volume of correspondence between Hays and Baron Herbert Rathkeal, the Austrian ambassador to Istanbul; and between Hays and Sir Robert Ainslie, the British ambassador to Istanbul, Summer 1783 to Summer 1784, P.R.O., SP 110, vol. 24.

110 Letter of pro-consul, 2 May 1791, P.R.O., SP 110, vol. 50 (1791-1793), F. 1v-2v.

111 See Rozen, "France and The Jews of Egypt." On the public controversy over freedom of religion and the rights of citizenship for French Jewry, see A. Hertzberg, *The French Enlightenment and the Jews* (New York, 1968); S. Schwartzfuchs, *Les Juifs de France* (Paris, 1975), 199-240.

112 Rozen, "Contest and Rivalry," 334.

113 F. de Beaujour, *A View of the Commerce of Greece, formed after an annual average, from 1787-1797*, trans. T. H. Horne (London, 1800), 386.

114 For a detailed discussion, see Rozen, "France and the Jews of Egypt, 456-60."

115 Ibid. See also Rozen, "Contest and Rivalry," 326-30.

116 For Salonica, see Rozen, "Contest and Rivalry." For Aleppo, see the letter of French Consul Louis Chambon to the Echevins et Députés de Commerce de Marseille, 22 June 1692, A.C.C.M. J 900.

117 On this, see Rozen, "Les Marchands Juifs livournais," 93-94, and the documents on 123-24.

118 Ibid., 92-129.

119 Rozen, "France and the Jews of Egypt," 426-27.

120 Ibid.

121 On this, see Ali İhsan Bağış, *Osmanlı Ticaretinde Gayri Müslimler, Kapitülasyonlar—Beratlı Tüccarlar Avrupa ve Hayriye Tüccarlar (1750-1839)* (Ankara, 1983).

122 On these developments, see the discussion in B. Lewis, *The Jews of Islam* (Princeton, N.J., 1984), 154-73.

Jacob Barnai
Haifa University

Messianism and Leadership: The Sabbatean Movement and the Leadership of the Jewish Communities in the Ottoman Empire

In 1718, R. Leib, the secretary of the Ashkenazi Jewish community in Amsterdam, wrote the following in his book on Sabbateanism:

> Nevertheless there were very many people in Turkey who continued to believe and were willing to wager with their lives that there was something genuine in Shabbetai Zevi, and according to rumor there are still today many people in Turkey who believe in him: at any rate ten years ago there [were] still many such. . . ."[1]

And indeed, as is well known, the Sabbatean movement was not merely a short episode that lasted only from the time that Shabbetai Zevi declared himself to be the Messiah in Gaza in July 1665 until his conversion to Islam in Edirne in September 1666. Sabbateanism as a religious and social movement continued to exist even after Shabbetai Zevi's conversion and his death (1676) and until the end of the eighteenth century in various parts of the Diaspora. Moreover, even in places and periods in which it no longer exists, its influence on Jewish history remains great.

Since Gershom Scholem published his book *Sabbatai Sebi—The Mystical Messiah*,[2] many important studies have been published and many new sources have been printed, especially on the period after Shabbetai Zevi's death. Worth mentioning are the publications of I. Tishbi,[3] R. Shatz,[4] I. Sonne,[5] Y. Liebes,[6] R. Molcho and A. Amarilio,[7] A. Atias,[8] E. Moyal[9] and others. M. Benayahu[10] performed a particularly important service with his book, *The Sabbatean Movement in Greece*, in which there is an amazing wealth of important sources for the history of Sabbateanism in the Ottoman Empire and in Italy after the time of Shabbetai Zevi. There are also additional sources, some of which are mentioned in this book while others remain concealed in various manuscripts. All these works point to the important place held by Sabbateanism in the seventeenth and eighteenth centuries, and help us draw a broader picture of the Sabbatean movement in the communities of the Ottoman Empire.

The family of Shabbetai Zevi almost certainly arrived in Izmir from Greece in the beginning of the seventeenth century, at the time of the development of the city, and he was born there in 1626.[11] At a young age he already stood out because of his strange behavior, and even then he claimed to be the Messiah. The community of Izmir and its leadership thus knew him quite well and even banished him from the city.[12] This point is important because such knowledge did not prevent many of the leaders and individuals in the community (and also in other places where people were personally acquainted with his strange conduct)[13] from believing that he was the Messiah when he was later declared to be so in Palestine and returned to Izmir.

In September 1666, Shabbetai Zevi converted to Islam in Edirne, and many of his believers converted with him.[14] As a result of this conversion, many of his supporters repudiated their belief, but not a few continued to believe in him and his doctrine for decades. Many of them did so in secret, but there were also overt or "semi-overt" believers.

Two additional events are worthy of being mentioned in this connection. First, in 1683, hundreds of Sabbateans in Salonica converted to Islam and lived there as the *Dönme* sect—a Sabbatean-Islamic sect—until the twentieth century. And second, in 1759, hundreds of Sabbateans in Poland, led by Jacob Frank, converted to Christianity in the final epilogue to this movement.

Immediately after the conversion of Shabbetai Zevi and his supporters, the rabbis of Istanbul issued a proclamation with legal standing in the communities of Israel "not to speak about Shabbetai Zevi, whether good or bad."[15] This stemmed from their great fear of the authorities. Until then, the Ottoman government had reacted with great forgiveness to the events and to the excitement in the Jewish quarters. This proclamation may well explain the absence of source material about the Sabbeatean movement in the official archives of the Jewish communities and in the contemporary rabbinical literature. Because these sources were silenced, we must rely on the material left by the fanatical opposition to Sabbateanism, the circles of the believers and their descendants, and non-Jewish sources.

An analysis of the extent of Sabbateanism among the leadership of a few of the leading Jewish communities of the Ottoman Empire will show the relationship between Jewish society, communal leadership and the

Sabbatean movement. Each community analyzed below—Jerusalem, Izmir, Istanbul, and Salonica—illustrates the variety of reaction to Shabbetai Zevi as well as the common features of the crisis his movement provoked.

JERUSALEM

The first place that Shabbetai Zevi went to after he was proclaimed to be the Messiah in Gaza was Jerusalem. The principal sources for this episode point out that while in Gaza and Hebron he had much support from the rabbis, most of the rabbis and leaders in Jerusalem rejected him.[16] In order to expell him from the city, they brought him to trial before the local *kadı* on the charge of stealing money from the emissary of the community on behalf of which he had traveled to Egypt and returned from there as the Messiah.[17] An examination of these sources arouses many questions, because the story about Shabbetai Zevi's trial before the *kadı* of Jerusalem, his acquittal, and the honor paid him by the *kadı* comes from Sabbatean sources which seek to exalt him. In a painstaking examination completed recently at the *sicil* of Jerusalem, Shabbetai Zevi's trial before the *kadı* was not found.[18] (It is interesting that this also occurred in the other attempts to find official Ottoman documents on Shabbetai Zevi.) Other sources tell that it was the rabbis of Jerusalem who excommunicated Shabbetai Zevi and ordered him to be banished from the city. However, there is also information to the effect that some of the important rabbis of the city were among his enthusiastic supporters, and some of them left the city with him on his way to Izmir.[19] The leadership of the Jerusalem community was thus divided in its attitude toward Shabbetai Zevi during the time of his messianic activity.

Another episode that should be mentioned in this context, and which seems to have been meaningful in other communities, was the inability of the Jerusalem leadership—even those who were opposed to Shabbetai Zevi—to control the masses of enthusiastic believers. One of the Jerusalem sages wrote about the gap between the masses and the Jerusalem leadership at the time of the flourishing of the movement:

> The observance of *Tisha Beav* has been abolished and the king and prophet have forbidden them to fast on that day, but they have made it into a day of feasting and joy just like *Purim*. And this did not happen in the entire world but in all the cities of the Ottoman Empire except for Jerusalem where the community did not abolish the observance of *Tisha Beav* but most of the individuals did not fast.[20]

The attitude of the rabbis of Jerusalem after the conversion and death of the Messiah was no different. Even at the end of the seventeenth century, many believers remained in the city, although most of their activities took place in secret. However, traces of their beliefs and their meetings emerge from various documents. This activity was also known to their opponents. At the turn of the seventeenth and eighteenth centuries, many Sabbateans went to Jerusalem from the various parts of the Diaspora, because they were awaiting the "Second Coming" of Shabbetai Zevi forty years after his first revelation. Many famous Sabbateans, including R. Judah Hassid, R. Haim Malakh, and R. Abraham Rovigo, led groups of hundreds of people to Jerusalem to witness the event.[21] These leaders, whose Sabbatean activities were more far-reaching and partly overt, aroused the opposition of the official leadership of the community. The latter wrote letters to communities in the Diaspora protesting against the Sabbateans arriving in Jerusalem, in part because they suspected that the activities of the Sabbateans there would decrease the donations sent to Jerusalem by donors from the Diaspora. This financial and social crisis which took place in the Jerusalem community at the beginning of the eighteenth century shifted the center of gravity of the controversy from theological problems to the survival of the community itself. After the community was rehabilitated during the 1830's by the "Officials of the Land of Israel in Istanbul," some more remnants of the Sabbateans (mainly from Izmir) went to Jerusalem and even captured key positions in the leadership of the community.[22]

IZMIR

As mentioned above, Shabbetai Zevi arrived in Izmir from Jerusalem as the Messiah. This city, in which he was well known, was divided in its attitude towards him and, at the same time, was embroiled in bitter controversy with respect to the leadership of the community. Shabbetai Zevi took advantage of this situation and within three months he gained control of the community through the use of terror, violence, and the ecstacy of hundreds of his believers. Perhaps more importantly, when one of the two chief rabbis, R. Aaron Lapapa, opposed him, Shabbetai Zevi had him removed from office and appointed the remaining rabbi, a supporter, as sole rabbi of Izmir. This supporter was none other than R. Haim Benveniste, one of the leading halakhic authorities of seventeenth-century Turkey.[23]

The appointment of Benveniste as rabbi of Izmir by Shabbetai Zevi reawakens questions that go beyond the event and Benveniste's appointment. No information has been found which suggests any relation whatsoever between Shabbetai Zevi and Benveniste before his appointment in 1666. Since Benveniste had visited Izmir in the 1640's and lived in the city in 1658, it is possible that he knew Shabbetai Zevi's family. When Shabbetai Zevi appeared as the Messiah in Izmir the day before *Rosh Hashanah* in 1665 (5426), the same complex and tension-filled system described above reigned in the community and its leadership. Nevertheless, Benveniste was not immediately appointed by the believers and supporters of Shabbetai Zevi. On the contrary, he was one of those who met to discuss the episode, and he carried with him the letter from the rabbis of Istanbul protesting against Shabbetai Zevi. Shabbetai Zevi even attacked Benveniste and cursed him in the synagogue together with the other sages who opposed him. What happened then that made Benveniste change his mind? Did Benveniste actually change overnight from a denier of to a believer in Shabbetai Zevi? Did he change his mind for opportunistic reasons, because he realized that this would eventually lead him to the chair of the Chief Rabbinate as sole rabbi? Did Shabbetai Zevi's sympathizers use personal terror against their opponents, thus forcing Benveniste to support Shabbetai Zevi, even though he had been one of his most bitter opponents?

It is clear that the historian must rely upon what the texts tell him or her, and that he or she cannot read people's minds and hearts. The texts indicate that, initially, there was great tension between R. Haim Benveniste and Shabbetai Zevi, but that later there was an overnight change in the situation. However, the sources provide evidence of Benveniste's later attitude toward Sabbateanism. For example, Benveniste did not fast on *Tisha Beav* of that first year after Shabbetai Zevi's departure from Izmir for Istanbul. He himself admitted this in a letter to the Tire community a year later. In this letter, Benveniste warned them not to repeat the mistake of the previous year on *Tisha Beav* (this was already after Shabbetai Zevi's conversion): "Since last year we all went astray like sheep, in that we made the day of *Tisha Beav* into a day of feasting and joy as we relied on the broken reed Nathan of Gaza who pretended to be a prophet. And now we know that it was all lies and falsehood."[24] Thus, according to his own testimony, in 1666 Benveniste had behaved as a believer in all respects. Moreover, in another place he wrote that later, in 1668, he took it upon himself to fast every Monday and Thursday for a whole year, perhaps in order to atone for his belief in Sabbateanism and for his having eaten on *Tisha Beav* the previous year.[25] Isolated reponsa which have survived from this period reveal Benveniste's moderate attitude toward the Sabbateans of Izmir.[26] His name is also not to be found among the signatories of the letter by the sages of Izmir who protested against a Sabbatean prophet in Tunis in 1671. His absence is all the more striking, for among the signatories were R. Isaac de Alba and other rabbis, men who had once been close friends of Shabbetai Zevi, and who had supported him at the time of his appearance as the Messiah.[27] Even in Sabbatean tradition and legends, where the image of Benveniste was sanctified, there is conflicting evidence about his attitude toward Shabbetai Zevi.

The question may be asked why Shabbetai Zevi chose to appoint Benveniste as rabbi of the Izmir community. Although there were many rabbis from which to choose, he chose precisely an outstanding *halakhic* scholar, a forceful person who aroused controversy and antagonism within parts of the community. On the other hand, one of Shabbetai Zevi's most powerful opponents in Izmir was also one of the most important kabbalists of the generation, R. Solomon Algazi. One may speculate about this question, as it is quite paradoxical. In the light of all the data on his personality and on the quarrels in the city, one can assume that Benveniste's motives were mainly opportunistic and not due to a true belief in Shabbetai Zevi.

Clarification of the relationships among the people who were active in this episode reflects to a large extent the totality of problems the Sabbatean movement presented to this generation of Jewish sages. With respect to the Izmir community, it seems that it was not Sabbateanism which brought division and crisis to the community and its leadership, but rather that the crisis already existed and Shabbetai Zevi and his supporters took advantage of this situation. Moreover, this enabled him to successfully gain control over the very city which knew the most about him and his eccentricities.

It seems to me that this sort of investigation into the relationship among society, communal leadership and Sabbateanism should be broadened to include other communities as well, for there was strong agitation in many communities during the years of the appearance of Shabbetai Zevi. From this we can learn about the relations between religion and society, and between ideology and socio-economic factors as nourishers of religious movements. Only a few of the rabbis of Izmir dared to manifest public opposition to Shabbetai Zevi at that time, and they were compelled to hide out of fear of the crowd and the believing rabbis. It is true, however, that not all the believers at this time in Izmir were believers for ideological reasons. Indeed, many were "believers" out of opportunism or fear, and this is also an important aspect in understanding the attitude of the rabbis toward Sabbateanism. Still, without the support of the majority of the leadership of the community, Shabbetai Zevi would not have been able to gain control of the community.

In Izmir, as in other palaces, many became disillusioned with Shabbetai Zevi after his conversion. For example, a year later, one of the leading sages of Izmir wrote: "And all who thirst to see God's salvation . . . should all come running . . . to fulfill the command of the king."[28]

> And even those who were not believers . . . also went because of their fear of the masses, that they should not rise up against them and say, "You are rebelling against the words of the Messiah of the God of Jacob" and they answered "Amen" against their will . . . as the Lord God knows . . . that I believed completely that the day of salvation had arrived and that God had remembered his people . . . and I brought about the sinning of many people who obeyed my authority and took my advice.[29]

In 1671, several of the rabbis of Izmir made a similar admission in a letter to Tunis, stating: "That at the beginning we violated the covenant and in the end we sinned and rebelled against every matter of our God."[30] And yet, Izmir remained an important stronghold of Sabbateanism until the eighteenth century, and famous Sabbateans were continually attracted to that city. At the end of the seventeenth century, they still operated publicly and they apparently were not forced to hide, as was the case in other places. This is not surprising because in the first years after the conversion, the same rabbi whom Shabbetai Zevi himself had appointed still served as the chief rabbi of the city. And even if R. Haim Benveniste had ceased to believe in Shabbetai Zevi (as was apparently the case), he was unable or unwilling to prosecute his former colleagues. He himself wrote in one of his responsa of a "sect of believers" which existed in the city, one of whose members was suspected of celebrating on the Ninth of Ab. This fast day, the most important of the fast days commemorating the destruction of the Temple, had been converted into a holiday by the Sabbateans because "the Messiah had already arrived" and Shabbetai Zevi was born on that date (according to tradition, "On the day that the Temple was destroyed the Messiah was born"). Evidence about many Sabbateans in the city and about their activities can be found in various sources, and visits of famous Sabbateans at the end of the seventeenth and the beginning of the eighteenth centuries, such as Cardozo, Hayun, Vilna and others, also attest to the extent of the belief in Izmir.

After the death of the chief rabbi, R. Haim Benveniste in 1673, an emissary from Palestine, R. Solomon Halevi, was appointed as one of the rabbis of the city; only in recent years was it discovered from various documents that he too tended toward Sabbateanism.[31] Several well-known rabbinical scholars of Izmir during this period and during the eighteenth century were known for their belief in Sabbateanism and for their sympathetic attitude towards it. This was a respected group that served in key positions in the community, both as rabbis of the congregations and as chief rabbis. The peak of their activity was in 1731 with the editing and printing of the three-volume work *Hemdat Yamim* (Delightful of Days), a collection of all types of Jewish literature containing the fundamentals of Sabbatean belief. After the publication of this book, most of the people responsible for its publication emigrated to Palestine.[32]

ISTANBUL

From the beginning of Shabbetai Zevi's activities, it was possible to discern in Istanbul a difference in the attitude of the leadership toward him. Unlike the other communities, a large part of the leadership of the capital expressed open opposition. The reason for this was probably their fear of the Ottoman government and of the heavy responsibility that weighed on the shoulders of the leadership of this community in particular. "However," as G. Scholem points out, "this opposition on the part of the community could not withstand the Messianic storm."[33] Most of our knowledge about the Messianic ferment in the capital comes to us from Christian or Jewish documents which included reports from his supporters, his opponents, and some forgeries. The Ottoman documents for this episode in Istanbul (as in the other communities) have not yet been discovered.

It is probable that the Jewish establishment in Istanbul was divided in its opinion before Shabbetai Zevi's conversion, and each side attempted to spread its opinion in public among the provincial communities. After the conversion, the rabbis of Istanbul disclosed that the catastrophe could have been greater and that actually the crisis was more internal than external. The authorities disregarded the episode and the communal leadership sought to limit the damage within the Jewish communities as much as possible. They did this by calming the people and by attempting to prevent discussion on the subject as much as possible. Since there were so many leaders among the believers of Sabbateanism in the Jewish communities, the leaders of the capital decided to neither attack nor persecute the believers or former believers, but rather to ignore them. In the Istanbul communities, this policy did indeed succeed more than in the provincial communities. There is practically no evidence of Sabbateans in Istanbul at the end of the seventeenth century and during the eighteenth century.

SALONICA

In Salonica, too, Shabbetai Zevi was not unknown when his Messianic role was announced to the Jewish communities. He had lived there for a while when he was banished from Izmir in the 1650's.[34] When he was proclaimed to be the Messiah in 1665, many of the rabbis of Salonica joined the believers, among them several leaders of the community. Some of them even supported Shabbetai Zevi's instructions to change the Ninth of Ab into a holiday.[35] Other communities in the Balkans and in European Turkey, which were traditionally much influenced by events in Salonica (for example, Edirne, Castoria, Sofia, Belgrade and others), followed their example.

An especially important place in the Sabbeatean movement was reserved for Salonica after Shabbetai Zevi's conversion and his death. About a year before his death, he married the daughter of one of the rabbinic scholars of Salonica.[36] In 1683, (the year of the siege of Vienna), as mentioned above, hundreds of Jews in Salonica, including familiy members of the city's leaders, converted to Islam and established the *Dönme* sect.[37] A contemporary source commented:

> Since those who converted were the great sages and especially the sect of kabbalists that existed until our time—"At the time of the approach of the Messiah impudence will increase. . . . "—and this trouble continued even after his death for several years, and they still hope that he will return and deliver them. . . .[38]

And indeed, we know the names of many of those who converted in Salonica during those mass conversions (Benayahu mentions them in his study), among them sages and leaders such as R. Solomon Florentin, author of the *halakhic* work *Doresh Mishpat*, and R. Solomon Ailion, who later returned to Judaism (although he did not necessarily relinquish his Sabbatean beliefs), and fled Salonica, and was appointed rabbi of the Portuguese community in Amsterdam. Many rabbinic scholars who did not convert continued to believe in Shabbetai Zevi at the end of the seventeenth century and during the eighteenth century. Both the *Dönme* sect and the Sabbateans who remained Jewish left, in my opinion, a deep imprint on the social and religious life of this city, for this was a widespread phenomenon, in which members of the elite of the community participated.

* * *

The extent of the belief in Shabbetai Zevi during the time he actively played the role of the Messiah (1665-1666) cannot be disputed in the light of G. Scholem's book and the wealth of sources that he cited there. Scholem's innovation was his identification of the great involvement of the leadership in the belief in Shabbetai Zevi during his life time. This was in opposition to the previous views, which sought to describe the Sabbatean belief anachronistically as the actions of the vulgar masses alone. It is true that among the leaders who supported Shabbetai Zevi there were those who did so for opportunistic reasons and because of their fear of the enthusiastic crowd of believers. After the conversion the situation was different. The conversion of the Messiah caused many people to stop supporting him. From then on, there remained two central groups of supporters of Sabbataenism: Those of his believers who followed in his footsteps and also converted, and those who remained Jews and attempted to explain by means of apologia why it was necessary for the Messiah to convert and who expected him to return even after his death. The converts lived as Muslims externally and as Sabbateans in secret, but the matter was an "open secret" among the authorities, the population and even visitors from the outside. The relatives and friends of converts had remained Jews.

An unpublished document illustrates this point. In a letter sent by the rabbis and community leaders of the community of Tripoli in Libya to a community in Italy in 1669, the activities and Sabbatean beliefs of the famous Sabbatean Abraham Michael Cardozo are defended. Among other things they wrote:

> And our testimony is that we saw in him a valorous man of many activities ... who from the sharpness of his knowledge of *Torah* ... which God gave him ... *acted according to the opinions of the great sages in the belief in our master* [Shabbetai Zevi].[39]

This constitutes support by the establishment for a great Torah scholar who continued to believe in Shabbetai Zevi about three years after his conversion, and this in a community far from the main Jewish centers of the time.

G. Scholem divided the Sabbateans into "moderates" and "extremists" according to the theology they developed.[40] There is room for a new defini-

Messianism and Leadership: The Sabbatean Movement / 177

tion of "Who was a Sabbatean?" in the generations after the conversion of Shabbetai Zevi in the light of our new information. Perhaps now the division can be made as follows: Sabbateans who believed explicitly in Shabbetai Zevi and his Messianic role even after his conversion and his death, and expressed this belief openly; and others who, though defined as Sabbateans, can be called believers only with great difficulty, for they are connected with the movement only because they gathered to study Sabbatean writings, or conducted written or oral discussions with true believers. I therefore tend to categorize them as "sympathizers," "supporters," "interested," "concerned" with Sabbatean theories, and as "collectors" of Sabbatean material. The "sympathizers" and "supporters" were closer to the believers and perhaps differed from them only in nuance. They assisted the believers in their debates, authorized their books, and gave them shelter when they were persecuted. Some of these were trying to understand the phenomenon and wondered greatly about why it all failed and why the Messiah did not succeed in his activity. We learn this from the vast material that was recently discovered, which can explain the great involvement of the rabbinic scholars of the Ottoman Empire with the Sabbatean theories. Sometimes it is indeed difficult to distinguish clearly between the actual "believers" and the "interested ones". Various comments that the latter wrote in the margins of the Sabbatean documents tell us that there was a great deal of "intellectual curiosity" and confusion about the problems of that actual generation and the delayed redemption.

The following examples may serve to illustrate more clearly my categorization of the different types of Sabbateans found at the end of the seventeenth and beginning of the eighteenth centuries:

Believers—R. Meir Rofe, R. Abraham Rovigo, and the members of their circles.[41]

Supporters—The rabbis of Tunis and Tripoli who supported the activities of Cardozo.[42]

Interested people and collectors—The *Hida*, who in the eighteenth century collected important material on the history of Sabbateanism and wrote comments in the margins.[43]

Sympathizers and Students—The editors of *Hemdat Yamim*.[44]

Those who study the diaries of R. Abraham Rovigo and other Sabbateans can find the different types there.[45]

From here we turn to a further definition of G. Scholem, who claimed that after Shabbetai Zevi's conversion, the Sabbatean movement changed from "a mass movement to a sect."[46] Today, however, on the basis of our extensive information about the different types of Sabbateans, it seems that we are speaking of a much wider phenomenon which does not fit the framework of a mere "sect."

The conversion of the Messiah and his believers shocked the Jewish leadership and caused a terrible crisis and a rift in several communities. Before they succeeded in recovering from the fact that the whole business of the Messiah had been discovered to be false, large-scale conversions occurred, especially in Salonica, headed by some important rabbis, such as R. Solomon Florentin and R. Solomon Ailion. It is appropriate to compare the shock that this caused in a community to the shock suffered by the body when a limb is amputated. Whole families, some of them from the elite of the community, converted to Islam, while others were divided between converts and those who remained Jewish.

In the eighteenth and nineteenth centuries, the existence of the *Dönme* sect alongside the Jewish community, among whom many of its members had relatives and friends, certainly constituted a severe problem for the community and its leadership. In the light of this, the absence of Jewish sources on this topic is astonishing. There are only scattered crumbs of information in the rabbinic literature of the eighteenth and nineteenth centuries concerning the *Dönme* sect and the relationships with the Jews. The establishment drew a line around the converts and attempted to hide its dealings with them. One should remember that, at least in the earlier generations, there were many leaders of the community who still believed in various degrees of Sabbateanism, and their attitude toward the Sabbateans was not one-dimensional. These leaders lived in a difficult duality and were torn internally. In their everyday lives they fulfilled their rabbinic tasks in the communities as if there were no problems, but in their inner circles and also privately, they continued to study Messianic ideas and Sabbatean theology, questions of conversion and redemption, and they tried to solve the problems raised by these matters. This inner struggle is illustrated by the editing and printing of the kabbalistic-Sabbatean book *Hemdat Yamim*. In this book they tried to express both the feelings and the thoughts of their generation about the problems of Messianism and redemption. Some of the things they had tried to conceal most of the time burst forth in this book. However, this book was not the only one and it is possible to bring additional examples. But most of the Sabbatean activities remained in manuscript, some of which have reached us recently in the form of personal diaries, letters and theological hermeneutics, and they open a door for us to understand the problematics of many of the rabbinic scholars in the Ottoman Empire in those generations.

Another example of this duality is R. Samuel Primo, who served as rabbi of Edirne until 1708. He was Shabbetai Zevi's scribe, the propounder of his doctrines during his lifetime, and the interpreter of "the secret of divinity" after his death, even during the period when R. Primo was rabbi of one of the central communities in the Ottoman Empire.[47]

In Jerusalem. Sabbatean activity took place both in public and in private, and disturbed the leadership of the city. In many communities in Turkey and the Balkans, Sabbateans roamed around and spread Sabbatean doctrines from city to city. Some of them were persecuted in some communities and others were welcomed with open arms in various places. The phenomenon was widespread and the reactions to it were hesitant and not uniform.

We still lack information about how the rabbis explained the problems to the masses. It is almost certain that the sermons they preached on this topic in the synagogues were not printed. What has been published is more obscure than clear and has not yet been thoroughly researched. It is reasonable to assume that the public requested explanations from the leadership after the failure of the Messiah and the mass conversions. What we have pointed out about the leadership and its attitude toward Sabbateanism certainly made it difficult for them to offer acceptable explanations. From the little that remains of the later sources from the eighteenth and nineteenth centuries, we can perceive a fairly lenient attitude toward the Sabbateans who remained Jewish, while the sharp and aggressive opposition was directed against the converts. This is in contrast to the much sharper reaction of the Jewish establishment in Europe during the corresponding period. The prophet Nathan received a truly sympathetic attitude in later sources,[48] his grave in Skopje (Yugoslavia) became a pilgrimage center for many Jews, and even folktales, legends and praises about his personality were developed. Shabbetai Zevi, in contrast, did not merit compliments from the rabbis of following generations and almost certainly only members of the *Dönme* sect made pilgrimages to his grave (which is also in Yugoslavia).

While some of the Sabbatean books mentioned above were actually printed in the eighteenth century, the anti-Sabbatean spiritual works were often hidden. The rabbis of the Ottoman Empire tried to turn their creativity to non-controversial subjects in order not to excite the public.[49]

SUMMARY

1) The phenomenon of support for Shabbetai Zevi by the establishments of the communities of the Ottoman Empire at the time of his appearance was very widespread.

2) The phenomenon did not die with the conversion of Shabbetai Zevi and the mass conversions which followed it, but took on a more internal and dualistic shape. Some of the rabbis of the Ottoman Empire lived at the end of the seventeenth and the beginning of the eighteenth centuries in a divided, dual internal world.

3) The influence of Shabbetai Zevi and the Sabbatean beliefs penetrated deeply into the eighteenth century and possibly even into the nineteenth century by various means: by evasion and silence on the one hand and tolerance towards the believers on the other.

4) It is possible to distinguish between the Sabbatean activities in Istanbul and the provincial cities.

5) Much of the attitude of the rabbinic scholars of the Ottoman Empire and of what was written on the topic was hidden and did not reach us. Even the spiritual works of the scholars of the Ottoman Empire of the eighteenth century which were printed or are available in manuscript, have not yet been exhaustively researched, and perhaps the answers to some of our questions may be found in them.

NOTES

1 R. Leib Ben (the son of) R. Ozer, *The Story of Shabbetai Zevi*, trans. to Hebrew from Yiddish and ed. Zalman Shazar (Jerusalem, 1978), 126.

2 Hebrew original published in Tel-Aviv, 1957. English translation: Gershom Scholem, *Sabbatai Sebi* (Princeton, N.J., 1973).

3 Isaiah Tishbi, *The Path of Belief and Heresy* (in Hebrew) (Ramat Gan, 1964).

4 Rivka Shatz-Uffenheimer, "Portrait of a Sabbatean Sect" (in Hebrew), *Sefunot* 3-4 (1960): 395-431.

5 Isaiah Sonne, "New Material on Shabbetai Zevi from a Notebook of R. Abraham Rovigo" (in Hebrew), *Sefunot* 3-4 (1960): 39-69.

6 Yehuda Liebes, "Shabbetai Zevi's Attitude towards his own Conversion" (in Hebrew), *Sefunot* 17 (1981): 267-307.

7 Issac R. Molcho and Abraham Amarilio, "Autobiographical Let-

ters of Abraham Cardozo" (in Hebrew), *Sefunot* 3-4 (1960): 183-241.

8 Moshe Atias, Gershom Scholem and Itzhak Ben-Zvi, *A Book of Poems and Praise of the Sabbateans* (in Hebrew and Ladino) (Tel Aviv, 1948).

9 Elie Moyal, *The Sabbatean Movement in Morocco - Its History and Sources* (in Hebrew) (Tel Aviv, 1984).

10 Meir Benayahu, "The Sabbatean Movement in Greece" (in Hebrew), *Sefunot* 14 (1971-77): the entire volume.

11 Scholem, *Sabbatai Sebi*, 103.

12 Ibid., 125ff.

13 Ibid., 371ff.

14 R. Leib Ben R. Ozer, *The Story of Sabbatai Zevi*, 300.

15 R. Haim Palachi, *Kol Hahaim* [All Life] (Izmir, 1874), p. 18/1. One might also consult R. Leib Ben R. Ozer, *The Story of Sabbatai Zevi*, 113.

16 Scholem, *Sabbatai Sebi*, 233ff.

17 Ibid.

18 I would like to thank my student Mr. Itzhak Zisk for his efforts on this issue.

19 Meir Benayahu, "The Status of the Sabbatean Movement in Jerusalem" (in Hebrew), in *Salo Wittmayer Baron Jubilee Volume*, the Hebrew section. (Jerusalem, 1975), 49-70. Jacob Barnai, "On the History of the Sabbatean Movement and Its Place in the Life of the Jews in the Ottoman Empire" (in Hebrew), *Peamim*, no. 3 (1979): 65-67.

20 Gershom Scholem, "Two Fragments of Manuscripts in the Adler Collection Pertaining to the History of the Sabbatean Movement" (in Hebrew), *Eretz-Israel* 4 (1956): 189.

21 Meir Benayahu, "The 'Holy Brotherhood' of R. Judah Hasid and their Settlement in Jerusalem" (in Hebrew), *Sefunot* 3-4 (1960): 131-82.

22 Jacob Barnai, *The Jews in Eretz-Israel in the Eighteenth Century* (in Hebrew) (Jerusalem, 1982), 72-92.

23 Scholem, *Sabbatai Sebi*, 389ff.

24 R. Jacob Sasprotass, *Tzizat Novel Zevi*, ed. Isaiah Tishbi (Jerusalem, 1954), 209.

25 R. Haim Benveniste, *Sheyarey kenesset Hegedda, Orah Haim* (Istanbul, 1729), p. 102/2.

26 R. Haim Benveniste, *Responsa, Orah Haim* (Istanbul, 1743), 34; idem, *Responsa Baey Hayey, Hoshen Mishpat*, part 1. (Salonica, 1789), on. 228.

27 Jacob Barnai, "Two Documents Concerning the History of Sabbateanism in Tunis and Izmir" (in Hebrew), *Zion* 52 (1987): 191-202.

28 R. Abraham Palachi, *Avraham Ezkor* (Izmir, 1889), 35-36.

29 Ibid.

30 Barnai, "Two Documents," 195.

31 Benayahu, "The Sabbatean Movement in Greece," note 10.

32 Tishbi, *The Path of Belief and Heresy*, 108-68; idem, "Hanhagot of Nathan of Gaza" (in Hebrew), *Kiryat Sefer* 54 (1979): 585-610: idem, "The 'Genealogy' of 'My Teacher' and 'My Father Who is My Master and My Teacher' as a 'Pseudonymous Quotation in Hemdat Yamim'" (in Hebrew), *Tarbitz* 50 (1981): 463-514; Barnai, *The Jews in Eretz-Israel in the Eighteenth Century*, 77-84.

33 Scholem, *Sabbatai Sebi*, 433ff.

34 Ibid., 152ff.

35 Ibid., 633ff.

36 Ibid., 882ff. Benayahu, "The Sabbatean Movement in Greece," 167.

37 G. Scholem, "Die Krypto Jüdische Sekte der Dönme (Sabbatianer) in der Türkei," *Numen* 7 (1960): 93-122; idem, *The Messianic Idea in Judaism* (New York, 1971), 142-66; Benayahu, op. cit., 77.

38 Scholem, "Two Fragments," 190.

39 Ben Zion Rubin, "The Sabbatean Movement in Libya" (unpublished paper written at the Hebrew University of Jerusalem, 1987).

40 Gershom Scholem, *Studies and Texts* (Jerusalem, 1974), 28.

41 I. Tishbi, "R. Meir Rofe's Letters of 1675-80 to R. Abraham Rovigo" (in Hebrew), *Sefunot* 3-4 (1960): 71-130; Benayahu, "The Sabbatean Movement in Greece," 449-525.

42 Ben Zion Rubin, "The Sabbatean Movement in Libya"; Barnai, "Two Documents."

43 Tishbi, *The Path of Belief and Heresy*, 227-34.

44 See note 32.

45 Benayahu, "The Sabbatean Movement in Greece," 525.

46 Scholem, *Studies and Texts*, 16.

47 See the indices in Scholem, *Studies and Texts*; Benayahu, "The Sabbatean Movement in Greece." Zalman Shazar (Rubashov), *The Light of Generations* (in Hebrew) (Jerusalem, 1971), 48-73.

48 Palachi, *Kol Hahaim*, 17-18.

49 Benayahu, "The Sabbatean Movement in Greece," 9-16.

Avner Levi
The Hebrew University of Jerusalem

Shavat Aniim:
Social Cleavage, Class War and Leadership in the Sephardi Community—The Case of Izmir 1847

Many Jewish sources mention the existence of social tensions prevailing in the Jewish communities in Turkey from the sixteenth century onwards.[1] These tensions increased during the nineteenth century, often erupting into disputes and bitter quarrels. One of the most serious outbursts was the one concerning the Rabbi Haim Palachi of Izmir. This incident has been studied by different historians who based their knowledge primarily on Palachi's books.[2] During the last two years J. Barnai and H. Gerber have been studying different social aspects of the Turkish-Jewish community in the nineteenth century, revealing very important facts.[3] However, an important source of information has not been used by researchers up until now. This is a booklet entitled *Shavat Aniim* [Cry of the Poor], published by one of the factions during a rift which broke out in Izmir in 1847. It is an eight-page booklet written in Ladino in very small and congested characters. A copy (perhaps the only one) is to be found in the British Museum. A xerox copy is available in the library of the Ben Zvi Institute in Jerusalem. Though mentioned by Abraham Galanté and Moïse Franco,[4] the author is unknown and it has not been used by historians for research purposes. *Shavat Aniim* tells us the story of the 1847 rift, and gives valuable data on former quarrels, and hence it enables us to better understand them. It demonstrates that the *Tanzimat* decree of 1839 was a turning point in the history of the Jewish-Turkish community. In order to better understand the changes caused by the *Tanzimat*, we must remember what the situation was before, as described by *Shavat Aniim*.

THE JEWISH COMMUNITY BEFORE THE *TANZIMAT*

Before the *Tanzimat*, the leadership of the Izmir community was in the hands of the rich, many of whom were *Francos*[5] (foreign citizens), who enjoyed many privileges due to capitulations. One of the main tasks of the leadership was to pay the taxes on behalf of the whole community to the government, the most important of which was the *cizye*[6] (the poll tax). A special census, known as the *Tahrir*, divided the community into three categories according to their financial status: low (*edna*), medium (*vasat*) and high (*ula*). The community as an entity was assessed the total sum. The leaders could collect this sum from the members according to criteria they themselves fixed. The situation in Izmir during the pre-*Tanzimat* era is described by *Shavat Aniim* (p. 1) as follows:

> We the poor of Israel living in the city of Izmir—may God preserve it, slaves of our lord the King, Sultan abd al Macid—May God bless him—are exploited and oppressed by the rich,—may God bless them. Most of them are foreign citizens (*Francos*). During many years we have been maltreated and they have no respect for us. If it happens that a poor person or a person of the middle class refuses to obey them for any reason which may be most insignificant they [the rich] ex-communicate him and surrender him to the authorities. He is arrested and even flogged. They do not fulfill the religious laws (*dinim*). Some of them even violated the sacred law (Torah). The poor people being under the impression that all the expenses and taxes due to the authorities, as well as the expenses required to take care of the sick, the community and its institutions were all paid by the well-to-do, endured their behavior, believing that this is the way of life; one who depends on the help of someone else becomes his subordinate. . . .

THE *TANZIMAT*

The *Tanzimat* brought the principle of equality before the law. Many *ad hoc* taxes, such as the *avariz*, the *cereme,* and the *salgın,* were abolished, together with the notorious tax-farming system *İltizam*. As for the poll-tax, then generally called the *harac* instead of the *cizye*, it was justified by the government as compensation for the exemption from military service that the minorities enjoyed. Illustrative of this is a law promulgated in the year 1847, the very year of the publication of *Shavat Aniim*, which abolished simultaneously both the poll-tax and the exemption from military service. This tax wasn't put into practice but the linkage between the two issues was complete. Any change in the poll-tax was now accompanied by a parallel change in the military service and *vice versa*. The final abolition of the poll-tax gave birth to the *bedel-i askeriye* tax. This, however, was only a nomenclatural change for the so-called new tax was in every way identical to the *harac*.

As for the system of tax collection, it underwent many changes from time to time and from place to place. Thus, for every place and time we need concrete documents showing that the *de facto* application was there and then. Hence the greater importance of *Shavat Aniim*, for it tells us that in Izmir in 1847, the taxes were paid individually and directly to the governor. As a result, the tasks of the communal leaders were limited to internal matters, such as maintaining the charity institutions and the rabbis. Most of the daily services were provided by the synagogues which had their independent management and their own budget. The poor hoped that the communal taxes would now be reduced, but their hope was not realized; on the contrary, the indirect tax paid on the meat, "the meat *gabela*", was increased. The following are the words of *Shavat Aniim*(p. 1):

> Now the poor and the middle-class (*esnaf*) learned that our king, the righteous and the merciful—may God bless him, ordered in his reform edict (*Tanzimat-ı Hayriye*) that there will be no more *cereme* taxes but only *punto*[7] and *harac* and these are paid by every person directly to the governor. The expenses of the community, hospital, cemetery, clothes for the poor (*halbashat aniim*), *talmidei hahamim, asara batlanim*, the rabbis and religious court are covered by the indirect taxes (*gabela*) on the meat, wine and cheese. The wine *gabela* reaches to 25,000 "lions" (*arayot*)[8] the sum of more than 20,000 of which is paid by the poor. The rich pay only 5,000 *arayot*. The same situation exists in the meat *gabela*. There are the expenses for the payment to the slaughterers (*shohatim*) too, the sum of 40,000 *arayot* a year. All the 40,000 *arayot*, including an extra sum for the expenses of the community—is paid by the poor. The *shohet* receives his payment on the spot, so the poor gets the meat for double the price, while the rich does not pay for the *shohet*. The meat *gabela* arrives to the sum of 90,000 *arayot* a year. The poor and the middle-class pay at least 70,000 of the sum, maybe even more. The management and the power are in the hands of the rich. They treat the poor as if they were slaves. They do not have pity on them, they beat them and injure them more than the "Egyptian *galut*." There was only one rabbi in the city, the beloved of God, *Rav* Shelomo Hakim[9] of blessed memory. He was paid 1,200 *arayot* a year. When he passed away, someone else was chosen to replace him. But the rich managers could not reach an agreement since each one of them desired to nominate a relative of his and thus in order to satisfy them all, it was decided to appoint three rabbis—God bless them—and as a result of this agreement, the expenses rose from 1,200 *arayot* a year to 12,000.[10]

Before long, in order to satisfy the other *talmidei hahamim*—God bless them—they, in addition, appointed a religious court which required the payment of four thousand *arayot* per year, thus the poor had to pay these extra expenses by the way of the *gabelas*, while they [the rich] enjoy the power. . . .

THE SPLIT OF 1840 AND THE GREAT FIRE

In 1840, a year after the *Tanzimat* came into force and two years after the death of the *Rav* Shelomo Hakim, there was a serious dispute between the rich and the poor over the *gabela* question. The poor wanted to go through the accounts of the community, but the administrators, all of whom were rich, refused to show them the accounts or to give any explanations. The community split into two enemy parties. The quarrel lasted for two years, during which time the poor even preferred to eat non-kosher meat rather than pay the *gabela*. In August 1841, a great fire broke out in the city causing serious damage to the Jewish community.[11] Thousands became homeless. The people interpreted the fire as divine punishment for eating *trefot unevelot*, taking place in order to "kosherise the instruments."

In 1842, the parties, terrorized by the fire, reached a compromise. The three newly-appointed rabbis of the city sympathized with the poor. The meat *gabela* was fixed at 8 *paras* for an *okka*.[12] A contract (*modaa*) was signed by the parties through the rabbis of Salonica. This was to become a law (*tikun*) for the city. According to this contract, the *gabela* on the meat was to be abolished after a short time and it was explicitly stated that this *gabela* represented an "oppression on the poor" (*gezel aniim*). Thus, three rich merchants, all *Francos*, signed this *modaa* with the poor. It was agreed that the administrative council would include an equal number of representatives from the rich party and from the poor and the *esnaf*. In the future, the expenses of the community were to be divided with half to be paid by the rich and half to be paid by the poor. The first Jewish journalist of Turkey, Raphael Uziel, wrote that after this compromise "peace was on the land for four years."[13]

According to *Shavat Aniim* (p. 2), the rich did not fulfill their obligations. The *gabela* on the meat was not abolished. Initially, representatives of the *esnaf* did participate in the administrative council, but this was only *pro forma* participation; they lacked any real authority and were powerless against the rich who *inter alia* had good connections with the Turkish officials. Moreover, the number of the poor in the council diminished quickly and in no time everything returned to the previous state of affairs. The direct community tax (*pecha*) was not increased. On the contrary, the rich made a great effort to reduce it to five *arayot* a year. Simultaneously, the rich wanted to increase the *gabela* on the meat, pretending that the expenses had increased. Now the poor and *esnaf* remembered the contract signed in 1842, and requested the complete abolition of the meat *gabela*. The rich claimed that the main reason for the increased expenses was their high payments to the rabbis. The poor argued that even without the meat *gabela* and despite the salaries paid to the rabbis, there was no deficit in the budget. The rich pressed, both through the Turkish authorities and the rabbis, but the poor refused to accept any augmentation of the meat *gabela*. In spite of this, at the beginning of the month of *sivan* (1846), the rabbis formerly in sympathy with the poor reached an accord (*haskama*) with the rich which enabled them to increase the *gabela*. According to *Shavat Aniim* (p. 1), the poor and the *esnaf* "were burned deep in their hearts and took an oath before the open ark (*Heikhal ha-kodesh*) to be no more the slaves of the rich, but to separate from them and to serve the God of Israel. . . . " They based their decision on a former responsa by Rabbi Raphael de Yosef Hazan,[14] given during the *Tov ve yashar* quarrel, which said that they could break the partnership.[15]

The dispute with the rich in which the rabbis were now involved, entered a new stage when Rabbi David Hazan, son of the above mentioned Rabbi Raphael Yosef Hazan, returned to Izmir from abroad. At that time he was one of the five *shohatim* of the city. Both parties addressed him and asked him to attain a peace compromise (*shalom bayit*). It seems that the *Beit Din* was the first to request that he take part in the peace-making. The president of the *Beit Din* was Rabbi Haim Palachi, the grandson of Rabbi Raphael Hazan and the nephew of Rabbi David Hazan. Rabbi David Hazan agreed to intervene and requested both parties to submit their claims within eight days. During this period, he asked that the meat be sold once a week, on Sunday, without the *gabela*. The rich categorically refused this suggestion. The rabbis declared that without the *gabela*, the meat was *trefa* (non-kosher), and this declaration was read in the synagogues. As a result, the 1,500 *okkas* of meat without the *gabela* offered to the poor on that Sunday were to be destroyed.

The *esnaf* now lost all hope of reaching a compromise and returned to their earlier decision to separate themselves from the rich. They asked

David Hazan to become their "rabbi". At first he refused. At this point, some of the poor took a drastic step: eighty of them together with their families abandoned Judaism and converted to Protestantism. The missionaries of Izmir, who had been very active since 1839,[16] intensified their efforts. Lots of Protestant religious books were distributed among the Jews, and 2,000 more families became interested in conversion. The rabbis tried to persuade them not to take such a step, but they had already lost their prestige because of their collaboration with the rich. In view of the threat of a mass conversion, together with the memory of the disastrous fire of 1841 (believed to have been caused by the consumption of non-kosher meat), David Hazan and his friends, the slaughterers Hayim Levy and Nissim Cohen, decided to support the poor. They provided kosher meat without the *gabela*. Thousands begged David Hazan to become their rabbi and threatened the possibility of a mass conversion. As a result of this threat, David Hazan agreed to become the rabbi of the poor party which wanted to separate from the rich. But, this was to be only for a limited period of two months. The Protestant propaganda was collected by him and burned.[17]

Both parties wrote to Rabbi Bar David, the Chief Rabbi (*hahambaşı*) of the Ottoman Empire in Istanbul.[18] The poor complained about the oppression they suffered from the rich and the rabbis, and warned that they would renounce Judaism if David Hazan was not ordered to guide them. The three official rabbis of Izmir and the *Beit Din* declared David Hazan a trespasser (*mesig gevul*). Rabbi Bar David, according to *Shavat Aniim* (p. 3), did not take into consideration the arguments of the rich and the rabbis; instead, he accused them of mismanagement and praised Rabbi Hazan. He wrote to the governor (*vali*) of Izmir that the parties had to try to reach a compromise; they were to send two representatives each, and he [J. Bar David] would hear their complaints and render judgement. Meanwhile the proposed separation became a fact. Twelve people were chosen by the poor as administrators (*parnasei ha-kehila*). These, divided into three groups of four, would manage the new community for a period of four months. Representatives (*memunei ha-zaman*) were chosen to deal with the authorities. Six other members were selected to control security, Judaism, and *Kashrut* (*isur ve heiter*).

Rabbi Hazan began to judge disputes between the poor and *esnaf*. Money was collected from different sources, such as the *gabela* on wine and cheese, and the expenses were paid and charity institutions were supported. The poor declared that they accepted the *hahambaşı* of the city, Rabbi Pinhas Raphael de Segura (*Rav* Pardess),[19] the first rabbi of Izmir to be officially appointed to this position by the Sultan. Although in the past he had collaborated with the rich together with his colleagues, the poor claimed that his collaboration had been imposed upon him by the rich, and that they would nevertheless continue to respect him. Now the Rabbi Hazan was the second rabbi of the dissident community, and according to *Shavat Aniim* (p. 3), the Rabbi Pardess actually gave him his blessing and delivered him his authority just as he himself received his authority from Rabbi Bar David of Istanbul. He realized that the rich and the rabbis were pushing the poor towards conversion and that David Hazan was bringing them back to the faith of their fathers.

However, the rabbis, pressed by the rich, wrote a judgement (*maase beit din*) without even holding a *din tora* and without listening to the poor or to David Hazan. David Hazan was once again declared as a *mesig gevul* (trespasser). Rabbi Hazan, in a letter which he wrote to the *Beit Din*, explained the reasons for his conduct and asked why he had been declared to be a *mesig gevul*, stating that he had taken no one's allocations or *midrashim*, or congregation. His letter remained unanswered, and the rabbis decided that no one could be judged by David Hazan.

This decision provoked a counter-declaration by the poor that they would refuse to be judged by anyone other than their rabbi. The party of the rich wrote to Istanbul, denouncing the *Rav* Hazan for causing disgrace and shame. They also submitted the balance of the communal budget which proved that it was impossible to cover the expenses without a meat *gabela* of 20 *paras* an *okka*. A letter from Istanbul was sent to the Chief Rabbi demanding that Rabbi Hazan leave the poor. The poor in their turn wrote back to Istanbul that without Rabbi Hazan, they refused to make peace. Rabbi Hazan wrote again to the *Beit Din* of Izmir, and complained that he had been humiliated. He said that all the Jews of Izmir were in danger because of the constant oppression by the rich, and threatened that a petition signed by 2,000 family chiefs would be sent to the Sultan submitting their complaint. This caused the rich to change their attitude. A committee composed of three rich merchants, Shelomo Chikurel, Shemuel ha-Kohen and Daniel Sidi, brought a letter signed by Haim Palachi (though composed by his son, Avraham Palachi) which suggested a judicial debate on the whole question. Both parties were to send three representatives, and a rabbi representing each side would explain their arguments. If the two rabbis arrived at an agreement, their decision would be binding. Otherwise, both would submit their claims to Rabbi Bar David and his decision would be final.

The poor party accepted the proposition. They wrote a protocol (*zikhron devarim*), signed it and delivered two copies to Istanbul to Rabbi de Toledo[20] and to Avraham Camondo.[21] At this point, the rich made a new request: they wanted to know what the claims of the poor were before the debate took place. The rabbis found this justified. The poor prepared a summary of their claims and delivered it to those concerned. They demanded that half of the expenses of the city be covered by direct taxes—(*pecha*) on the rich—and half by indirect taxes (*gabela*)—paid mostly by the poor. The rich refused this demand, stating that the law of the city (*tikun ha-ir*) required that the expenses be paid by indirect taxes (*gabela*) only. They asked Rabbi Hazan to promise not to increase the *pecha* to more than 6 *arayot* a year. The rabbi refused this request, and the rich ended the negotiations. According to a new request by Rabbi Bar David, the poor formulated all their claims in the form of a question (*sheela*) and sent it to the leaders of the Jewish community of Istanbul. The question contained all the details of the previous and current quarrels. In addition, the poor declared that if their request was refused and the appointment of Rabbi Hazan was cancelled, they would agree to be under the authority only of the *Rav Pardess* who had been honored with the Imperial *Nişan*.

For the problems connected with the *isur ve heiter*, and for all other questions, they would apply to the Turkish courts.[22]

THE QUESTION OF SERMONS

In this situation, a new conflict arose with regard to sermons. According to the tradition of the city, giving a sermon on certain Saturdays was the prerogative of those who held the title of rabbi. The three main sermons were held on Saturdays, called respectively *teshuva*, *ha-gedala* and *halbasha*. Rabbi Hazan was to hold a sermon on the next *halbasha*, but because the Rabbis Palachi and Eliezer declared that they were to give the sermon on that day, David Hazan cancelled his own as a gesture of good-will and declared that he would give a sermon on *shabat shekalim*, a day on which the other rabbis were not in the habit of delivering sermons. At this instant, the rich party appointed a fifth rabbi, one Avraham Eskenazi.[23] At the time of the quarrel of 1840-41, he was one of the young rabbis who believed that the *gabela* represented an oppression on the poor (*gezel aniim*). However, the moment Avraham Eskenazi was appointed by the rich as their rabbi, he took their side and began to attack Rabbi Hazan, *inter alia* declaring that he would hold a sermon on *shabat shekalim*. The rich and the other rabbis used

Shavat Aniim / 191

their pressure on the public and on the *talmidei hahamim* to attend the sermon of Rabbi Avraham Eskenazi. Obviously, the presence of the *talmidei hahamim* at a rabbi's sermon was a question of prestige.

THE END OF THE QUARREL OF 1847

Shavat Aniim ends here, without telling us about the final decision arrived at in Istanbul, or what happened with regard to the question of the sermons. It appears that the story about the conflict was told by different people at different stages. The final pages of *Shavat Aniim* are clearly pessimistic. Nevertheless, they also show determination. It is repeated that the poor refused to be judged by the rabbis of Izmir and would instead apply to the Turkish courts. By collecting bits of information from later sources, one can safely conclude that the coalition of the rich and the rabbis emerged victorious.

In 1855, when Palachi became Chief Rabbi of Izmir, David Hazan left the city and went to Jerusalem, and later became Chief Rabbi and *Rishon le Zion*. In 1855 he held only the title of *shohet* [ritual slaughterer] and he wanted his eldest son to inherit his position. However, Avraham Eskenazi apparently continued to oppose him, and prevented this. In his collection of responsa, Rabbi Hazan referred later to this question.[24] His collection of sermons contains two sermons delivered in Izmir.[25] All the other sermons were delivered in Jerusalem when he became Chief Rabbi. This might possibly mean that he indeed gave at least two sermons in Izmir as the rabbi of the poor party, but that his tenure of the post as a whole did not last long. A letter by an anonymous reader which appeared in the anti-establishment Ladino newspaper *La Vara*, informs us that Hazan officially held the title of Rabbi in Izmir on behalf of the poor party.[26] The rich and other rabbis exiled him for some time to the neighboring Tire. When Hazan returned, he resumed his duties as rabbi, but he was attacked and physically injured by the servants of B. Mosseri, a rich merchant. M. D. Gaon identifies Hazan as the Chief Rabbi of Izmir in his book on the Eastern Jews in Israel; however, he does not give any details or sources.[27] The books of David Hazan have responsa clearly connected with the quarrel of 1847, but all are presented as hypothetical questions and in no way enable us to reconstruct the facts.[28] Nor do the books of Haim Palachi help us. However, the rabbinate of D. Hazan and the division of the Izmir Jews into two communities for a short time was a fact.

THE BUDGET OF THE COMMUNITY

Shavat Aniim (p. 2) gives us details of the revenues and expenses of the Izmir community in 1847. The figures do not include payments of debts and interest or revenue from the meat *gabela*. This budget is important because it is the only one which was presented by what may be called "the opposition."[29]

Revenues (figures are in *arayot*)

25,000	wine *gabela*
5,500	cheese *gabela*
3,000	the mill
2,000	rent
3,000	doweries
<u>10,000</u>	head tax
48,000	Total

As the above figures indicate, 30,500 *arayot*, that is, more than three-fifths of the total revenue, came from indirect and regressive taxes—from the *gabela* paid primarily by the poor. The mill provided 3,000 *arayot* a year. Because the mill supplied the kosher flour for *matzot* (unleavened bread), the cost of the processing was added to the price of the *matza*. Thus, it, too, served as a kind of indirect and regressive tax. The 2,000 *arayot* represented the income from the rent on properties owned by the community. The dowries, meaning the registration and confirmation of marriage contracts (*ketubot*), provided 3,000 *arayot*. We do not have enough information on the rates and fees. It is probable that a fixed fee was paid per contract.[30]

The last entry is the "head" revenue. The term used in the text is "*de kavesa*" meaning by head. This is certainly the *pecha* or the direct tax charged on the rich according to their income and properties. Those who paid the *pecha* were exempt from paying other taxes and fees; for example, they did not have to take part of the *örf*[31] taxes which were paid for the permission of kosher slaughtering nor did they pay any fee to the *shohet*, a sum which amounted to 40,000 *arayot* a year. Thus, the rich paid less for meat than the poor, partly because of the fact that they were foreign citizens and partly because they paid the *pecha*. This data shows that the rich paid only a little more than the fifth of the expenses of the community while the poor paid the rest. In spite of this, the administration of the community was in the hands of the rich. The distribution of revenues explains the reason for the quarrel between the poor and the rich.

The Expenses of the Community

11,300	Payment to the rabbis and maintenance of the Religious Court.
4,000	Salaries to gravediggers and bundles for the poor.
6,000	Support for the poor and the sick
2,500	Salary to a clerk
3,000	Payment of wages to servants
1,777	Rent for *talmidei hahamim* and *iruv*
3,000	*Haluka* to the Holy Land
4,000	Salary to the *asara batlanim*
5,000	Clothes for the poor
6,000	Petty expenses and prison
2,000	Aid to *talmidei hahamim* for their *harac*
48,500	Total

The 11,300 *arayot* to the rabbis represents the largest single item in the list of expenses. In the text, the sum of 12,000 *arayot* is often cited as the total payment to the rabbis and an additional sum of 4,000 *arayot* is mentioned as payment to the religious court. Here we have only 11,300 *arayot*.

Nevertheless, if it is true that Rabbi Hakim received only 1,200 *arayot* as the only acting acting rabbi in 1838, it means that there was a ten-fold increase in less than ten years in this item. The minor rabbis (*talmidei hahamim*) received 2,000 *arayot* as a supplement to their *harac* tax, 4,000 *arayot* as salaries to *asara batlanim*, and 1,700 *arayot*, as an aid for their rent, a total of 7,700 *arayot*. This sum added to the 11,000 paid to the rabbis amounts to 19,000 *arayot*, or almost half of the expenses of the community. That such a large percentage of the budget went to pay the rabbis may well explain why the quarrel between the rich and the poor also became a quarrel between the rabbis and the poor. The salaries of the clerk and the servants were administrative expenses. The rest, only 15,000 *arayot*, or one-third of the budget, went to social assistance and charity; for example, burial expenses and health services for the poor. The aid to the Jewish community in Palestine (*haluka*), which lasted until the middle of the nineteenth century, represented 5% of the budget. This budget also shows that the community maintained its own prison which, when combined with petty expenses, required 6,000 *arayot* a year. This clearly reflects the high degree of autonomy the minorities enjoyed during the Ottoman Empire. At the beginning of the *Tanzimat* period, they had their own means of punishment. The autonomy diminished gradually after the *Tanzimat*.

The budget analyzed above was presented by the poor party. The rich party and the rabbis sent their own version of the budget to Istanbul which claimed that the meat *gabela* was unavoidable. We have no particulars about this. Two important questions must be asked: 1) Are the figures mentioned in *Shavat Aniim* correct? and 2) In what ways did it differ from the budget presented by the rich? Concerning the first question one should remember that *Shavat Aniim* was published and copies of it were sent to prominent personalities and rabbis of the Sephardic communities of Istanbul, Jerusalem, Rhodes, Salonica and Adrianople, including to Avraham Comando and R. Yaacov Bar David and it is understood that the numbers could withstand scrutiny. The budget presented by the rich party would have had an additional item of income, namely, the meat *gabela*, the main reason for the dispute. Thus, it also had to include an additional expense which justified and even obliged the meat *gabela* to be paid at 20 *paras* an *okka*.[32] The only important expense, we can guess is the payment of debts and interest. Haim Palachi mentions the fantastic sum of 500,000 *arayot* as the debts of the community.[33] *Shavat Aniim* also refers to the debts of the community, but does not mention any figure. What was the source of these debts and to whom were they owed? If they were owed to non-Jews, we should have heard about them from different sources. Thus, it may be assumed that they were owed to the rich members, who were at the same time at the head of the community. It is well known that those who managed the community did not like nor were in the habit of giving detailed reports on their activities.[34] It is obvious that they wanted to keep their affairs secret. Haim Palachi maintained that as a result of the quarrel, taxes could not be collected.[35] This may be so. The debt may also have been due to the great fire of 1841 which caused great damage and naturally required enormous sums for reconstruction of public institutions and assistance to the poor. Nevertheless there is an imbalance between a budget which claimed to be less than 50,000 *arayot* a year and the debts which amounted to half a million *arayot*. It seems quite certain that this figure was the result of cumulative interest. The poor did not accept the responsibility of these debts, claiming that they were caused by the extravagance of the rich.

We know that during the later quarrel between the rich party and Haim Palachi, known as the quarrel of *gabeleros*, the rich managed to sell to themselves the meat *gabela*, which amounted 90,000 *arayot*, for the grotesque sum of 10,000.[36] Thus the meat *gabela* was a means of extorting money from the poor. Many efforts were made to abolish this tax but they all failed; until the late nineteenth century, it was the main revenue of the community because the rich refused to pay direct taxes. This situation was not unique to the Jews but was quite common in the whole Middle East. The governmental tax-farming system, the notorious *İltizam*, caused heavy oppression on the poor people as well as economic disaster.

THE *TANZIMAT* OF 1839 AS THE TURNING POINT

In many important issues, the *Tanzimat* appears to be a turning point in the history of the Jewish community in Turkey. The abolition of many taxes and the direct payment of the rest by individuals without the interference of the community administrators has already been mentioned. Another question which should be addressed concerns the authority of the rabbis. In the past, rabbinical authority depended upon personal prestige which was the result of knowledge, publications, connections, even family background. With the *Tanzimat*, the Ottoman government became the most important source of authority. The *hahambaşı* nominated by the government was now supreme. For example, the dispute of 1847 had been handed over to Rabbi Yaacov bar David and his decision was final, because he had been honored with the *Nişan* by the Sultan. By contrast, during the earlier dispute of *Tov ve Yashar*, the parties had to apply for advice, or even judgement, to the rabbis of Salonica.

In Izmir proper the Rabbi Pardess enjoyed a special status as the *haham* of the city, a title given to him by the Ottoman government through the *hahambaşı*, Y. Bar David of Istanbul. Thus, even though he sided with the rich and the rabbis, the poor continued to respect him and his authority because he was *nişanlı*, that is, he held an official appointment.

Thus an official religious hierarchy was established by the government. Rabbi Bar David was the *hahambaşı*; Rabbi Pardess was the *haham* of Izmir. Rabbi Pardess was nominated by Rabbi Bar David and was dependent upon him. Both were Ottoman officials and collaborated with the authorities. Rabbi Bar David reported to the governor of Izmir and even sent him copies of his letters and decisions. All this limited the autonomy previously enjoyed by the community.

MISSIONARY ACTIVITIES

As is well known, the *Tanzimat* was largely the product of foreign pressure, especially pressure from Protestant England. The Christian powers pressed not only for equality for the minorities but also for freedom of action for missionary activities. The *Tanzimat* cancelled capital punishment for abandoning Islam. Although the main objective of the Christian missionaries was to convert the different Christian sects of the East to Protestantism, the conversion of non-Christians, specifically of Jews, was never neglected. Right from the beginning Izmir was one of the chief centers of missionary activity. Various propaganda books in Ladino were printed and distributed free of charge to the Jews. One of the most important of these books was a translation of the Bible, based primarily on Avraham Asa's translation done in eighteenth-century Istanbul. This new edition omitted the *Rashi* commentary and made some changes in significant passages of the Books of Daniel and Isaiah to prove that Jesus of Nazareth was the Messiah. For tactical reasons the place of printing was stated as Vienna, though the book was actually printed in Izmir. The Protestant propaganda enjoyed great success during the serious crisis of 1847; whereas during the earlier crisis the poor had eaten non-kosher meat, they now converted to Christianity. *Shavat Aniim* gives the exact number of 80 families who left Judaism and 2,000 more were in process of conversion. The appearance of Protestant missionaries and the actual conversion of Jews is mentioned in rabbinical sources as well.[37]

THE RABBIS AND THEIR ATTITUDE

There seems to have been a clear case of interdependency between the rich and the rabbis. The rabbis gave moral legitimacy to the administration by the rich party and were paid by these same administrators. J. Barnai has already pointed out that the elder Rabbi de Mayo, who belonged to the establishment, supported the rich faction in the rift of *Tov ve Yashar*, while the young Rabbi Yosef Hazan, who was just beginning his career, sympathized with the poor.[38] At the time of the rift of 1840-1842, the rabbis Haim Palachi, Pinhas de Segura, Shelomo Krispin and A. Eskenazi, were young and new at their jobs. They were awarded their titles after the death of Rabbi Hakim in 1838. They supported the poor and declared that the meat *gabela* was "an oppression of the poor." Soon after that, in 1847, all collaborated with the rich party against the poor. In the meantime, they were paid higher salaries, won the respect of the rich, and became part of the establishment. It was not just a coincidence that support for the poor came from Rabbi Hazan, who at that time held only the position of *shohet*. The rabbis and members of the *Beit Din* also used the means of excommunication in order to oblige the poor to pay the high meat *gabela*. On this point, the attitude of Rabbi Haim Palachi should be mentioned. In 1847, Haim Palachi was president of the *Beit Din*, and he fought for the meat *gabela*. Later, the rich party prevented him from dealing with financial matters. Immediately after that he declared the meat *gabela* was null and void.[39] When the rich appeased him, he regained his authority and forgot completely about the annulment.

THE IMPORTANCE OF THE *SHOHETS*

The *shohets* were instrumental to the application of the *gabela*, and thus their activity was of immense importance. It seems that traditionally they obeyed the rabbis and the managing directors of the community, so that the people either had to pay the *gabela* or be deprived of kosher meat. It was only after the tragic events of 1841-1847—the great fire and the threat of a mass conversion to Christianity—prevailed that some of the *shohets* revolted against the rabbis.

That the job of the *shohet* meant prestige and good income is quite evident from what is stated in *Shavat Aniim*, as well as from the fact that Rabbi Hazan wanted to transfer this job to his eldest son when leaving Izmir. However, the organization of the poor party into an independent community was made possible by the collaboration of three of the *shohets* of the city. In the past they had refused to help the poor, and many of the poor lost all hope and were obliged to eat non-kosher meat. Believing that this had caused the fire, in 1847 Haim Levi, David Hazan and Nessim ha-Kohen changed their minds, fearing a repetition of the disaster.

THE RESPONSA LITERATURE AS AN HISTORICAL SOURCE

The response literature is accepted today as a valuable and reliable historical source.[40] The booklet *Shavat Aniim* raises several important questions about this subject, at least for what concerns the nineteenth century in Izmir.

The most important personalities in the 1847 schism, namely the rabbis A. Eskenazi, David Hazan and Haim Palachi, published several responsa books. However, these works do not permit us to reconstruct the exact events described in *Shavat Aniim*. Moreover, the responsa caused students to arrive at incorrect or undesirable conclusions. Even as notable a researcher as J. Barnai reading Haim Palachi's words says that in Izmir during the 1840's the administration was chosen on a class basis equally by the poor and the rich, and this is taken as proof of the ascendancy of the guilds.[41] In reality, the power remained in the hands of the rich; the participation of the *esnaf* in the management of the community was ephemeral and *pro forma*. Even the latter was part of the compromise reached in 1842, after and because of the great fire, but the rich did not maintain their part of the bargain. This was repeated in 1847. It was only in 1908, after the "Young Turk" revolution, that the *esnaf* and the poor actually participated in the management of the city.

Shavat Aniim contains the complete text of the question (*sheela*) addressed by the poor to the chief rabbi of Istanbul. This is not to say that it is not to be found in the responsa literature, but here it is written in Ladino and this is significant. The responsa of the nineteenth century do not contain questions written entirely in Ladino. This may suggest that what we find in the responsa literature may not be the original but rather a later version by the author, with all the questions that this raises about historically accurate reconstruction of events.

CONCLUSION

The bitter class struggle which occurred within the Jewish community of Izmir could not be resolved through compromise. All efforts to improve the situation of the poor and the *esnaf* failed, and they became so desperate that they began to convert to Christianity. Moreover, in 1847 the community actually split, and the poor organized themselves as a community independent of the rich. This situation lasted only a few years. The rich had many trump cards in their hands, including the support of the Turkish authorities and the religious hierarchy. In no time they succeeded in subduing the poor. Their domination as well as their oppression of the poor went on for many more years.

NOTES

1 Leah Bornstein, "The Jewish Communal Leadership in the Near East from the End of the 15th Century Through the 18th Century" (in Hebrew) (diss., Bar Ilan University, Ramat Gan, 1978), especially 55-60 and sources mentioned therein.

2 A. Galanté, *Histoire des Juifs d'Anatolie, les Juifs d'Izmir* (Istanbul, 1937), 58-62; M. Franco, *Essai sur l'Histoire des Israélites de*

l'Empire Ottoman (Paris, 1897), 197-200; S. L. Eckstein, "The Life, Work and Influence of Rabbi Chaim Pallagi" (in Hebrew) (Doctoral thesis, Yeshiva University, New York, 1970), 71-90.

3 J. Barnai, "On the Jewish Community of Izmir in the Late Eighteenth and Early Nineteenth Century" (in Hebrew), *Zion* 47 (1982): 56-76 and the sources mentioned there in nn. 1-2.

4 Galanté, *Histoire des Juifs d'Anatolie, les Juifs d'Izmir*, 341 (attributed by mistake to Isaac Amaradji); Franco, *Essai sur l'histoire des Israélites*, 270.

5 Barnai, "On the Jewish Community of Izmir," 57 and sources mentioned there in n. 4; M. Rozen "Les marchands Juifs livournais à Tunis et le commerce avec Marseilles à partir du XVIIe siècle," *Michael* 9 (1985): 87-129; Bornstein, "The Jewish Communal Leadership," 68-71.

6 On the taxes and tax reform, see E. Z. Karal, *Osmanlı Tarihi*, vol.5, 2nd edition (Ankara, 1961), 175-80; H. A. R. Gibb and H. Bowen, *Islamic Society and the West*, vol. 2. (London, 1969), 251-52. On Ottoman censuses, see S. S. Shaw, "The Ottoman Census System and Population," *International Journal of Middle East Studies* 9 (1978): 325-38; idem, "The Nineteenth-Century Ottoman Reforms and Revenue System," *International Journal of Middle East Studies* 6 (1975): 421-59. On different Ottoman terms, see M. E. Pakalın, *Osmanlı Tarih Deyimleri ve Terimleri Sözlüğü*, 3 vols. (Istanbul, 1946-56).

7 Literally "points." It was applied for a short period during the first years of the *Tanzimat*. This term appears in different Jewish responsa dealing with this epoch and is treated by J. Barnai who misunderstood it as *"fondo"*; it should read *"punto"*. Barnai, "On the Jewish Community of Izmir," 75.

8 The Ottoman golden *kuruş*, called *arslanlı* or *asadi* because of the lion painted on it. One *kuruş* was equal to 40 *paras*

9 The author of *Kise Shelomo* (Salonica, 1847). He died in Izmir in 1838.

10 The three rabbis were J. Pinhas de Segura, S. A. Krispin and Haim Palachi. On the number of rabbis in Izmir and on the discussions concerning the establishment of a religious court, see Eckstein, "The Life, Work and Influence of Rabbi Chaim Pallagi," 33-34; J. Barnai, "R. Yosef Escapa and the Rabbinate in Izmir," *Sefunot* 18 (1985): 53-82.

11 According to A. Galanté, 90 percent of the damage was in the Jewish quarter and all the synagogues, except the synagogue *Shalom*, were burned. Galanté, *Histoire des Juifs d'Anatolie, les Juifs d'Izmir*, 205. *Puertas de Oriente*, 2 September 1846, reported that two-thirds of the city was burned down in sixteen hours.

12 2.83 lbs. or approximately 1,400 grams.

13   *Puertas de Oriente*, 2 September 1846. Uziel mentions the dispute, but gives few details about it. On this newspaper, see B. Mevorah "*Puertas de Oriente*" (in Hebrew), *Alei Sefer* 6-7: 213-16. On the Ladino press, see the bibliography of M. D. Gaon, *The Ladino Press: A Bibliography* (in Hebrew) (Jerusalem, 1965). On the Jewish press in Izmir, see A. Levi, "The Jewish Press in Izmir" (in Hebrew), *Peamim* 12 (1982): 87-104.

14   The father of David Hazan and grandfather of Haim Palachi, author of the eight-volume *Hikrei Lev*. He was born in Izmir in 1747. In 1794 he was the second rabbi of the community and in 1810 he was the *Rav ha Kolel*. In 1813 he went to Israel and died there in 1821."

15   Y. Hazan, *Hikrei Lev, Hoshen Mishpat* (Salonica, 1832), no. 116.

16   After the great fire of August 1841, they offered relief services to the poor. Galanté, *Histoire des Juifs d'Anatolie, les Juifs d'Izmir*, 205. This gave them an opportunity to intensify their activities

17   Franco, *Essai sur l'histoire des Israélites*, 276, provides a large list of missionary books printed in Ladino, the first of which is the book of psalms printed in Izmir in 1853, a year and a half after the great fire. See also A. Yaari, *Ladino Books in the National Library* (in Hebrew) (Jerusalem, 1934), 102-04. On translations of the Bible into Ladino, see M. Lazar, "The Judaeo-Spanish Translations of the Bible" (in Hebrew), *Sefunot* 8 (1964): 335-75. The aforementioned Bible in Ladino was printed in 1839, the very year of the *Tanzimat*.

18   He was nominated in 1841 and remained in his post until 1854. See A. Galanté, *Historie des Juifs d'Istanbul*, vol. 1. (Istanbul, 1941), 129.

19   On Pinhas Raphael de Segura, see Galanté, *Histoire des Juifs d'Anatolie, les Juifs d'Izmir*, 58.

20   I could not find information about him, nor about the three merchants who represented the rich.

21   A. Camondo—a rich banker of Italian origin who served as president of the Istanbul community at that time. See Galanté, *Histoire des Juifs d'Istanbul*, passim.

22   H. Gerber and J. Barnai, in their research on the Izmir Moslem court discovered that during this period many Jews indeed applied to be judged by the Turkish religious court. H. Gerber and J. Barnai, *The Jews in Izmir in the 19th Century* (in Hebrew) (Jerusalem, 1984), 11.

23   Members of the Eskenazi family have held the title of rabbi since that time. They were associated with the *Bikur Holim* synagogue, and the family archives, which are the archives of the congregation, are now in the possession of The Central Archives for the History of the Jewish People in Jerusalem.

24   D. Hazan, *Nediv Lev*, vol. 2. (Jerusalem, 1866), *Yoreh Deah*, no. 1.

25   D. Hazan, *Heitiv Lev* (Izmir, 1868). The sermons *Halbasha* 4 and

5 were delivered in Izmir, *Talmud Torah* Synagogue, in 1853 and 1854.

26 *La Vara*, 22 December 1905. The letter was written by a man who was 70 years old in 1905. Thus he was a 12 year-old child in 1847, and 20 years old in 1855, the last year David Hazan was in Izmir.

27 M. D. Gaon identifies Hazan as the Chief Rabbi of Izmir in his book on the Eastern Jews in Israel; however, he does not give any details or sources. M. D. Gaon, *Eastern Jews in Israel* (in Hebrew), vol. 2. (Jerusalem, 1938), 249. Gaon, who does not give his sources, is not very reliable. For example, he says that D. Hazan was nominated as rabbi in Izmir in 1840 [!] and kept his title until 1855, the year he came to Jerusalem.

28 D. Hazan, *Nediv Lev*, vol. 1. (Salonica, 1862), nos. 109, 110 (see also no. 89). The hypothetical question posed by D. Hazan discusses a dissident community which chose a rabbi for themselves. After a certain period, both parties arrived at a compromise and consequently, the whole community accepted him as their rabbi. After four months, the parties were divided again and the rich party wanted to nullify the honors accorded to the rabbi. Replying on this subject, D. Hazan says that they had no right to do that. From this we learn that the two parties arrived at a compromise; we may also guess that a contract was signed and the rich party made some concessions to the poor. It is probable that this and similar contracts mentioned by the rabbis made the students conclude that the situation of the poor in Izmir had improved (Barnai, "On the Jewish Community of Izmir," 74), or that the rabbis helped the poor (Bornstein, "The Jewish Communal Leadership," 64). This was not the case. The contracts were not applied, and the rich party did not fulfill its promises. In this case, the peace continued only four months. That is why the disputes continued until 1908, always for the same old reasons. The most notorious were the *Tov umetiv* in 1860 and the *Palachi-Kolel* disputes in the first decade of the twentieth century.

29 Franco, *Essai sur l'histoire des Israélites*, 187-88; Galanté, *Histoire des Juifs d'Istanbul*, vol. 1, part 5.

30 It may also be that there were different categories according to the sum involved. It is difficult to believe that the fee was fixed by percentage.

31 Meaning customary taxes.

32 The poor claimed that the meat *gabela* amounted to 90,000 *arayot* a year when the *gabela* was 8 *paras* an *okka*. The rich wanted to increase it to 20 *paras*, thus making the yearly income from this item 225,000 *arayot*. This is an enormous sum even if the debts of the community amounted to 500,000 *arayot*. The disparity between the burden on the poor and the rich is evident.

33 Cited by Barnai, "On the Jewish Community of Izmir," 59.

34 Franco, *Essai sur l'histoire des Israélites*, 158.

35 Barnai, "On the Jewish Community of Izmir," 59.
36 Franco, *Essai sur l'histoire des Israélites*, 198.
37 Barnai, "On the Jewish Community of Izmir," 59.
38 Barnai, ibid., 65-66.
39 Franco, *Essai sur l'histoire des Israélites*, 198.
40 See the introduction in A. Shmuelevitz, *The Jews of the Ottoman Empire* (Leiden, 1984), 7-8.
41 Barnai, "On the Jewish Community of Izmir," 73-74.

Israel Bartal
The Hebrew University of Jerusalem

From *"Kollel"* to "Neighborhood": Revisiting the Pre-Zionist Ashkenazi Community in Nineteenth-Century Palestine

JEWISH HISTORIOGRAPHY AND THE PRE-ZIONIST COMMUNITY

Writers of modern Jewish history were not indifferent about concepts and descriptions that equated time with value judgements. Concepts such as "old" and "new," or "conservatives" or "innovators," are invoked quite frequently in the historical works of the successors of the Jewish Enlightenment heritage and the *Wissenschaft des Judentums* scholars. The nineteenth-century Eurocentric perspective, well entrenched in the major cultural streams that gave rise to modern Jewish historiography, was unable to render an objective portrayal of the traditional society that was still the mainstay of most of Jewry. Neither did it look favorably upon what it viewed as the vanguard of outmoded values—the Ashkenazi Jewish community in Palestine. Historian Heinrich Graetz, who visited Jerusalem in 1872, regarded the Ashkenazi community of that town as—among other failings—the source of the anti-Jewish prejudices harbored by European society. Graetz believed that the Jews in the civilized countries had succeeded, by virtue of their diligence and talents, to earn the gentiles' respect; they were treated as equals, and advanced to the most exalted positions as warranted by their achievements. Anti-Jewish prejudices were ebbing, on the whole, as long as no new source arose to fuel them. Graetz regarded the Ashkenazim of Palestine as such a source.[1]

Graetz's position is a classic example of the negative attitude of *Wissenschaft des Judentums* scholars toward the value and nature of Jewish society in Palestine. Nevertheless, this movement—and subsequent modern nationalist historiography—sought the origins of the Jewish cultural and spiritual renaissance precisely in the traditional social milieu that it was trying to eradicate. Palestine stood out as one of the focal points of the persistence of this dialectic. The Old *Yishuv* (the old Jewish settlement in Palestine), preceding the modern waves of nationalist immigration in the late nineteenth and early twentieth centuries, evoked (and still evokes) tension among the writers of Zionist national history. On the one hand, this *Yishuv* embodied all the adverse characteristics that modern nationalism strove to uproot by creating a "new" Jewish people. On the other hand, this *Yishuv* was a living testimonial to the unbroken connection between the Jewish people and their land, and the most recent link in the *aliya* endeavor that had been so emphasized in Zionist writings on the Middle Ages and the early modern period.[2] As a consequence of this dualism, patterns of thinking and writing emerged that discovered "Zionist" elements in the pre-Zionist *Yishuv* or that rejected other elements of this community as "non-Zionist."

Although there was some reluctance to invoke the unvarnished truth, the radical nationalist facet of much of this historiography was much more conspicuous than the judiciously weighed, objective one. There were various combinations and permutations of both the trend of "Zionizing" the pre-Zionist *Yishuv* and the Zionist perspective with regard to what deserved to be uprooted and altered. In principle, the historiographic patterns were distinguishable from each other by the degree to which they removed the beginning of "modernity" to the previous century; or, conversely, by the degree to which they presented the "new" (in the Zionist-*Yishuv* sense) as a continuation of the trends already visible in earlier times as part of the "old." The first sense was—and, to a certain extent, remains—a characteristic of the writings of radical nationalist authors who, viewing the immigration of the *Hasidim* and *Perushim* to Palestine, detected signs of social and political activism, along with organizational ability, typical of twentieth-century political movements.[3] The second sense was invoked primarily in some of the writings of the national-religious vein.[4] The search for the roots of the "new" in the "old" (which then appears to have been "renewed") and conversely, the continuation of the "old" by the "new" to the point at which one may deny the existence of the "new" since the "old" is really the "new," manifested itself in the topics selected by scholars as fit for discussion in the history of the pre-Zionist *Yishuv*.

The agrarian aspiration (and the inclination to adopt productive occupations in general) displayed by members of this "Old *Yishuv*" fired the imaginations of Zionist observers and led to a proliferation of writings concerning various land-acquisition attempts, settlement programs, and the activities of societies and organizations with productivist tendencies. By contrast, few studies have addressed themselves to Jewish economic activity in the towns, the complex and ramified economic systems that raised funds overseas and forwarded them to Palestine, and the use to which these monies were put. Even the recent studies on the central fund-raising organization in Western Europe—the *Pekidim* and *Amarkalim* of Amsterdam—make only passing reference to the major purpose for which this body was founded: the marshalling of funds abroad and their transfer to and distribution in Palestine.[5]

The unique type of selection that set the parameters of this research had a spin-off effect on the Orthodox anti-Zionist writings as well. The definitive authors of Orthodox literature on the history of the *Yishuv* reached the conclusion, in a manner typical of their society and spiritual outlook, that they were the true "Zionists." In their opinion, any trend to which members of the New *Yishuv* laid claim had already existed in the Old *Yishuv*—from mass immigration and the building of settlements to the transition to Jewish agrarianism and self-defense.[6]

BREACHING THE RAMPARTS: AN OLD *YISHUV* ENDEAVOR

One undertaking of the Old *Yishuv* whose historic importance cannot be diminished by any shift of historical perspective is the exodus from the walled Old City of Jerusalem, a move that extended the boundaries of Jewish Jerusalem in the second half of the nineteenth century to areas outside the Ottoman ramparts. This exodus has been the subject of systematic geographic and historical research,[7] and has been documented in such extensive detail over the past two decades that the contemporary scholar may trace systematically the initial stages, organizational methods, economic infrastructure, physical planning, and ideological background of the establishment of most of the new neighborhoods. Y. Ben-Aryeh claims that the Old *Yishuv* indeed deserves credit for having founded these neighborhoods, and has sketched the community's demographic and geographic expansion in great detail—from its small core in the walled city to the extramural districts. Ben-Aryeh writes:

> The expansion of Jerusalem beyond its ancient walls and the development of the New City was an entirely internal process, generated by the growth and development of the Jewish community of the Old City—the so-called Old *Yishuv*. The Jewish Quarter of the Old City was simply too small to contain

the "population explosion" of Jerusalem in the nineteenth century, and so the city grew in its new dimensions, outside the walls. Immigrants and new institutions reaching Jerusalem in the nineteenth century came mainly to the Old City, and only from that basis did they later emerge to build the New City. In other words, the new Jewish city of Jerusalem, in the Ottoman period, was built in the main not by people and public bodies from outside Jerusalem, but rather, by people and bodies indigenous to the Old City. The growth and development of the New City were spurred on by changes that occured in the Jewish population of the Old City—its numbers, its composition, its living conditions and world outlook. Put briefly: it was the old Jerusalem that built the new.[8]

Elsewhere Ben-Aryeh writes:

... significant developments were underway in the realm of Jewish settlement in Palestine, and particularly in Jerusalem, even before the period of the First *Aliyah*. Important Jewish neighborhoods sprang up in Jerusalem *before* the inception of the organized Zionist movement: the Jewish community in Jerusalem began to grow, develop and erect a New City—*before* the birth of modern Zionism.[9]

Indeed, the exodus from the walled city, viewed as an example par excellence of the modern Jewish national renaissance by those who espouse the "Zionization" of Palestine's pre-Zionist past, was undoubtedly one of the definitive endeavors of the Jerusalem society identified with the Old *Yishuv*. The ideas that stirred the imaginations of the founders of the new neighborhoods, the modalities of socio-economic organization invoked there, and the neighborhoods' demographic makeup were all classic manifestations of this identity. This notwithstanding, the issue of the nature of this exodus from the walled city should be closely examined since, despite the identity noted above, this historical phenomenon was genuinely novel. And if this step was not taken in the direction of modern Jewish nationalism—as I attempt to demonstrate below—what then was its nature? Moreover, what connection existed between the novel aspects of the establishment of the new Jerusalem neighborhoods and their traditional underpinnings, the continuation of which is now generally acknowledged among scholars? One may arrive at plausible answers to these questions by redefining the nature of the breakthrough represented by the Old *Yishuv*'s undertaking. That is, these were not necessarily steps connected with manifestations of the modern national awakening, but rather classic examples of the Old *Yishuv*'s transformation from a traditional society to an Orthodox one.

WHAT IS ORTHODOXY?

"Orthodoxy," in nineteenth-century Jewish society, was the conscious response of part of the Jewish population to the indigenous and exogenous changes—on the communal, familial, and individual levels—brought about by modernity. This response manifested itself in the adoption of stringent positions on a wide range of aspects of modern life; segregation—practiced with varying degrees of severity—from the spirit, ideas, and opinions of the times; and a controlled, begrudging accommodation with the changing realities. Self-defense coupled with adjustment was in fact the phenomenon that connected the diaspora communities of Eastern and Central Europe, from which the Ashkenazi Old *Yishuv* drew its human and spiritual strength.

The Old *Yishuv* came into being in the towns of Palestine even before Orthodoxy entered its stage of intensive coalescence in Europe. The Eastern European *Hasidim* who reached the country and settled in the Galilee in the late eighteenth century, and the disciples of the *Vilna Gaon* (*Perushim*) who immigrated from Lithuania and founded their communities (*kollelim*) in Safed and Jerusalem in the early nineteenth century, reached Palestine before the Orthodox response to the challenge posed by modernity in their native communities had been formulated, or was in its early stages. It is hard to find Orthodox motives for immigration from the Ashkenazi Diaspora before the 1840's. Later on, particularly in the 1870's and 1880's, the Jewish population of Palestine diversified with the arrival of immigrants from Russia, Prussia, and Austria, whose motives included awareness of the need to fend off modernity and its religious and social ramifications. Orthodox views seeped into the consciousness of the *Yishuv* members themselves during these years, and the impact of these tendencies on the activities of the overseas aid organizations gained strength.

A salient example of this transition which illustrates the developments in the Jewish communities of Europe during this period, was the opposition of the Jerusalem *Perushim* in 1849 to Moses Montefiore's plan to establish a modern school. Their reaction was connected with the "official" (coerced) *Haskalah* controversy that they had recently experienced in Russia, and the struggle of traditional East European Jewry against the establishment of government schools for Jewish children.[10] From the 1840's onward, Orthodox positions became the major factor in forming the focus, the political conduct, and the social behavior of Ashkenazi community of Jerusalem. Admittedly, this posture embraced various gradations—some more moderate toward the adoption of modern values and ways, and some more extreme in rejecting all innovations—but none of these deviated from the position shared by the Orthodox world as a whole: self-defense coupled with adjustment.

Consequently Palestine in general and Jerusalem in particular not only retained their traditional sanctity in the eyes of the traditionalists but also acquired a more innovative significance, even for them. Since this dimension was an outgrowth of modernity, it was unprecedented in Jewish history. The Jewish community in Palestine became the stronghold of the values that Europe was threatening. A nineteenth-century immigrant who joined one of the Jerusalem *kollelim* spared himself the effects of the changes sweeping the European communities. This also explains the gravity of Jerusalem ultra-Orthodoxy's response to anything suspected of transplanting some aspect of European values in Palestine. A school that taught the language of a European country or represented a state that had offered protection to its Jewish subjects; a hospital whose doctors were not observant Jews; proposals for occupational or lifestyle changes in the spirit of *Haskalah* values, all these were threats to the last stronghold of traditional society still unsullied by the pernicious influence of European *Haskalah* in all its manifestations. Among all the texts written during the myriad of polemics waged by Jerusalem Orthodoxy against reformers and innovators, one can hardly find one that does not begin with an exhortation of the following sort:

> Arise to the aid of God, for strangers have met in conspiracy... like the plotting of strangers who know neither Torah nor prayer nor ethics. Now they have reached the gates of Jerusalem and are plaguing the city; they have constructed a siege wall upon the city and piled upon it a rampart so that they may destroy it and bring it down.[11]

The image of Jerusalem as a city under siege, its ramparts guarded by "our" Jews against other Jews out to destroy the last vestiges of the traditional world, was an important element in the collective consciousness of the Old *Yishuv*. The city's Ashkenazi community was also depicted as part of a worldwide front defended by the Orthodox, those faithful to Jewish values. It is therefore no wonder that the participants in the polemics surrounding the character of Jerusalem's education system and spiritual and social life included Orthodox activists known for similar activity in Central and Western Europe. The Lehren family of Amsterdam were not the only ones who combined Orthodox community leadership throughout Europe with support for the existential goals of the Jewish community in Palestine.

Another example was Ignace Deutsch, who lobbied against the establishment of a modern school in the late 1850's as part of his wider involvement in the affairs of the Austrian communities.

Alongside this approach, with its besieged-city image coupled with pan-Jewish activity against all reformers everywhere, there emerged and developed another Orthodox attitude that contemplated modernity in Messianic terms, paradoxically viewing it as a positive phenomenon. Contemporary events were interpreted in terms of traditional beliefs and views and construed as stages in the process of redemption. This approach originated in the teachings of leaders such as Rabbis Yehuda Hai Alkalai and Zvi Hirsh Kalisher, who, in the 1830's and thereafter, put forward various programs for settling Palestine. Although this approach did not attract many adherents in the *Yishuv*, it reverberated clearly in statements by several of the founders of the first extramural neighborhoods in Jerusalem.[12]

THE "*KOLLEL*" AS AN ORTHODOX ORGANIZATION

The two attitudes described above—extreme segregation from modernity and the attribution of positive Messianic significance to contemporary changes—merged in the consciousness of the founders of New Jerusalem neighborhoods and in several settlement plans of the 1870's.

The ideological component of the Orthodox phenomenon ostensibly explains the "old" character of the exodus from the walled city, and even that of the plans to establish an agricultural community (*moshava*) populated by members of the Old *Yishuv*. Whether the expansion of the boundaries of Jewish Jerusalem was viewed (either *a priori* or *a posteriori*) as a stage in the process of Messianic redemption, or as a reinforcement of the Jewish presence in Palestine in the form of a stronghold against modernity, the ideological character of many of the settlement undertakings was clearly stamped wih the Orthodox imprint. J. Rivlin, a leading figure in the Jerusalem *Perushim* community, represented positions of clear-cut objections to modernity and espousal of a need to protect oneself from its dangers.[13] At precisely this point in time, he described the exodus from the walled city in blatantly Messianic terms:

> A wondrous awakening is taking place on our holy soil these very days, one that binds the Children of Israel to this soil. We are being led down a smooth path to the longed-for goal of settling Eretz Yisrael, meaning the building of homes for Jews. Thus far, with God's grace and salvation, the societies have succeeded in a manner far transcending nature. . . . This is the straight and

clear path by which their exalted and sublime destination [the settlement of Eretz Yisrael] will be reached.[14]

Rivlin's very words, however, stress that not all who subscribed to the ideas of the "heralders of Zionism"—Kalisher and Alkalai—necessarily espoused the modern nationalist trends. There were others, such as Rabbi Akiva Yosef Schlesinger, who were strongly influenced by Kalisher's ideas but nevertheless offered little evidence of pro- modernity views in their writings. Those who equate the settlement of Palestine, according to the proto-Zionism attitude, with streams of the modern national movement—an accepted and widely-held view in the study of Jewish nationalism from its inception through the present time[15]—obfuscate the conspicuously Orthodox nature of the activities of those "heralding" the modern movement. This approach also loses sight of the Orthodox identity of those who adopted these views in Palestine.

Accordingly, it seems to me that ideological distinctions alone are unlikely to explain the *Orthodox* nature of the exodus from the walled city; to gain understanding, we must address additional facets of the topic. It would seem that the socio-historic explanation, which links the ideological world of the Old *Yishuv* with the social changes sweeping European Jewry in the eighteenth and nineteenth centuries, may help clarify the historical place of this phenomenon.

The centralized state in Central and Eastern Europe had been threatening Jewish autonomy since the second half of the seventeenth century. The *kehillah*, a framework and way of life in which traditional social values found full expression, was on the decline. Its institutions had been brought under government authority and stripped of their judicial, administrative, and enforcement powers. Concurrently, alternative agencies were gaining strength within or alongside the autonomous framework and did not require official authorization in view of their non-formal nature; they acquired some of the functions of the weakened corporation, or even established a parallel authority of their own. By the time the Old *Yishuv* took shape, the governmental authorities in Central Europe had already taken over most powers of the *kehillot*, thus completely undermining a social system that had facilitated the existence of full Jewish life in its premodern sense. The flourishing of Orthodoxy in Europe was a manifestation not only of the ideological and cultural confrontation with the threat of Reform and *Haskalah* but also of social development that ultimately produced an alternative to the abrogated or transformed *kehillah*. While membership in the premodern *kehillah* was the self-evident duty of any Jew living under the auspices of a

European state, and while existence within a framework other than the Jewish corporation was inconceivable, Orthodoxy was linked with voluntary membership in alternative agencies. Several of the agencies that stepped into the shoes of the *kehillah* had come into being before the emergence of Orthodoxy and now received an infusion of new content. Others were sociopolitical innovations of the modern era. Thus the courts of the hasidic *tzaddikim*, originally supra-communal organizations that sapped the authority of the existing *kahal* (the communal leadership), became major bastions of opposition to the dismantling of the traditional structures and one of the elements around which Eastern European Orthodoxy coalesced.

Similarly—if on a smaller scale—the superordinate Lithuanian *yeshivot* stepped into the role previously occupied by the *kehillah* in Russia during the first half of the nineteenth century. Even the various "societies"—organizations within the traditional *kehillah* that had preceded the modern era—took over the role of the defunct communal organization.

One of the major reasons that the Hasidic movement, the Lithuanian *yeshivot*, and the various societies were able to fill the social vacuum left by the ban on the Russian *kahal* in 1844 was their freedom from the requirement of official license. Their voluntary nature permitted them to survive as the guardians of traditional values without entering into actual confrontation with the centralist government. The *maskilim* of Eastern Europe were well aware of this feature and identified it best with the Hasidic movement, repeatedly alleging in their writings that the *Hasidim* were enemies of the political and social order and were perpetuating Jewish isolationism. What they failed to notice was that the centralist regimes of the Russian and Austrian empires did not share their views on this matter and took little interest in social systems that were not formally recognized.[16]

In areas of Central and Western Europe where the influence of Eastern European movements had not penetrated but the rampart of traditional values had disintegrated, the late eighteenth century witnessed the emergence of a type of Orthodox community that abandoned the since-transformed central *kehillah* and demanded official recognition. In Eastern Europe, society remained largely traditional for quite some time because the voluntary organizations had emerged alongside the *kehillah* and existed within and by virtue of it. In Central and Western Europe, by contrast, these organizations were the products of withdrawal and opposition, as well as a demand for government recognition.

The Orthodoxy of the communal organizations throughout the European Diaspora embraced elements that both preserved the premodern corporative nature of Jewish autonomy and integrated itself into the changing political structure.

Most members of the Ashkenazi Old *Yishuv* in Palestine had originated in the Eastern and Central European *kehillot*, which were engulfed in tremendous change in the late eighteenth and nineteenth centuries. The immigrants reached the Holy Land from countries where relations between the Jews and the authorities were undergoing sweeping reform. Moreover, the Old *Yishuv* emerged and coalesced from nuclei of immigrants who had belonged to movements that had become the social bearers of the new Orthodox identity in Europe. The disciples of the *Vilna Gaon*, the founders of the community known as the *Perushim* in the early decades of the nineteenth century, belonged to the same circles that established the Lithuanian *yeshivot* at approximately this time; the *Hasidim* of Belorussia, Wolyn, and Galicia arrived in Palestine at a point in time when their courts, those of the *tzaddikim*, were engaged in fierce confrontation with the innovations of the modern world.

The core groups of immigrants, with their various affiliations, developed into subgroups of the Ashkenazi community in nineteenth-century Jerusalem, Safed, Tiberias and Hebron. They combined strong socio-economic relations with their communities of origin in Europe with a central idea that had far-reaching social implications: sustaining the Jewish community in Palestine as a congregation of scholars engaged full-time in devotional studies. This idea manifested itself in the formation of the institution known as the *kollel*. The *kollel*—a type of sub-*kehillah* or sub-community (relative to both the community of origin and that in Palestine)—was by nature a voluntary organization. Anyone who chose to settle in the Holy Land and devote his life to devotional studies joined this body. The *kollel* was yet another corporative substitute for the premodern Ashkenazi *kehillah* that had come into being before the coalescence of Orthodoxy. In due course, the *kollel* became a definitive stronghold of Orthodoxy, in a process similar to that which swept the Lithuanian *yeshivot*, the Hasidic movement, and the various societies.

In its original form, the *kollel* was a group of scholars supported for the community by the *kahal* in the communal *beit midrash* (devotional study hall). As with the growth of the supra-community *yeshivot* in Lithuania (and in their direct typological and historical context), the *kollel* was a distant extension of the "parent" *kehillah* or of a group of *kehillot* that had assumed its financial support. It maintained a long-term connection with the *kehillah* of origin and remained dependent on its support and manpower. The "*roznei*

Vilna" ("grandees of Vilna") handled the affairs of the *Perushim* community *kollel* in Safed and Jersalem for decades after the first immigration from Lithuania, and Lithuanian scholars joined its ranks throughout this period. In like fashion, the Hasidic immigrants retained strong ties with their *tzaddik* and with the Hasidic support organization.

The splintering of the *kollelim* in Jerusalem and other Old *Yishuv* centers into dozens of groups based on members' geographic origins strongly reinforced and helped perpetuate relations with the parent communities. In another sense, the *kollel* may be described as a "collegium"—a students' society modeled on those of the mediaeval universities. Here too, the connection with its spiritual and social birthplace persisted for decades after founding, while its geographic separation caused it to develop all the characteristics of a community so that it might provide its members with the requisite services.

It is worth noting that the students' "corporations" were but one manifestation of a type of organization common in the Middle Ages, of which the *kehillah* was another example. It is no coincidence that the surrounding Christian communities referred to the entire Jewish community (*"klal" yisrael*) of a given city or even a kingdom as a *universitas*.[17] That the term *kollel* originated in a Jewish perception that paralleled the Christian one is almost beyond doubt. The *kollel*, a classic mediaeval institution transposed to Jerusalem, maintained its integrity in a period when the traditional frameworks were disintegrating and adapting to the changes of the modern era.

The European immigrants' *kollel*, however, possessed an additional characteristic that emphasized its Orthodoxy. Just as the premodern *kehillah* sought official patronage and protection, so too did the latter-day *kollel*. In modern times, it was the European state of origin that provided this protection; in the premodern era, it had been acquired through an agreement with the crown, the liege lord, or an urban corporative society. When the *Hasidim* and the *Perushim* first began to reach the Holy Land, the *de facto* source of patronage was a Jewish agent acting in the service of a local ruler (a member of the Farhi family in Acre); the *de jure* patron was the local Sephardi community, itself recognized as being under the patronage of the Ottoman regime. Rabbi Israel of Shklov, a leading person of the *Perushim* who settled in Safed, described the situation in the following way:

> The rabbis of the local Sephardim [in Safed] helped him and led him to their *beit midrash*. At that time, the governor and officer of these two towns [Safed and Tiberias] was Rabbi Yitzhak Abulafia, who had been appointed by the government of the honorable, righteous, and saintly

officer, the late Rabbi Haim Farhi . . . who was then the Pasha's financier and a great governor in Acre. . . .[18]

Thus the *Perushim* in Safed enjoyed the protection (administered by a prominent Jew serving the local potentate) of the Sephardi community, which, in turn was under the patronage of this same power. Throughout the nineteenth century, the Ashkenazim in Palestine made great efforts to shift their dependence on the Sephardi community to another source, taking advantage of the presence of European consular agents in the coastal towns and, later, in Jerusalem.[19] By the end of the century, a special connection had evolved between the various *kollelim* and the European consulates in Jerusalem. This relationship, composed of conspicuously modern elements intermingling with patronage reminiscent of the Middle Ages, replaced the protection of the local ruler or potentate.

Therefore the Jerusalem *kollel*, after decades of changes, had become a "corporation" that continued to uphold the traditional values of Ashkenazi society, performing functions of the traditional *kehillah* on a voluntary basis and under the patronage of a European state. The European countries, paradoxically enough, did not subject the corporations' members to the demands that they imposed on Jews in the home communities. While the members of traditional society in Prussia and Austria had to cope with sweeping changes thrust upon them by or with the assistance of the regime, Jews who had emigrated from these lands to Jerusalem were almost completely exempt from a similar intervention in their internal affairs. Consequently, they were able to maintain in Jerusalem a milieu and way of life that the patron-state in their communities of origin had assaulted. The realities of life under Ottoman rule facilitated and further strengthened the conditions that permitted the *kollel* to exist as an alternative to premodern Jewish autonomy, because 1) the citizens of the European countries were not subject to Ottoman law, and 2) centralist trends grew more slowly in the Ottoman Empire than in Europe, and their effect upon the internal lifestyle of the European Jews was weak and insignificant.

It is worth noting that the major spokesmen of ultra-Orthodoxy in Jerusalem and overseas regarded the concept of *kollel* as having a pan-Jewish meaning—not necessarily in the modern national sense, but even perhaps the opposite. It represented a type of expansion of the post-emancipation corporative entity that survived irrespective of any connection with European soil and applied to the Jews as a whole. Thus a conspicuously traditional perception continued to exist, consciously or unconsciously, that persisted in viewing the corporation—or what remained of it—as an inteqral part of the separate, and separatist, community that had preceded the modern era. It is certainly no coincidence that thinkers such as Akiva Yosef Schlesinger, whose ultra-Orthodox doctrines whet their hopes of "rebuilding, in the uniqueness and isolation of Palestine, a Jewish community that would not have to cope with the effects of assimilation and Reform,"[20] invoked the *kollel* concept to describe the Orthodox *halakhic* state that they envisioned. The *kollel*—the order (or corporation) of the scholarly ultra-Orthodox avant-garde—was supposed to spread throughout Palestine and achieve an integration of technological, economic, and administrative innovations with a quasi-corporative organization possessed of an anti-modernist fighting spirit. Although even Schlesinger's inner circle of confidants rejected the most extreme manifestations of his views, their general spirit was attuned to some trends of thought that were current in Jerusalem of the 1870's and 1880's. The founding of *Petah Tikva*, in its first incarnation, suggests that at least some members of the Old *Yishuv* in Jerusalem believed, and accepted upon themselves, the following:

> Above all is the fear of God, to know and make known to others that our entire holy society will act in accordance with the ways of Torah, fear of God, and *Halakha*, as instructed by our sages and teachers. Moreover, our society is entitled to expel any member who disobeys the Torah and the law, so that he not appear with our congregation.[21]

The authors of *Sefer ha-brit ve-ha-zikaron le-hevrat agudat meyasdei ha-yishuv*—the ledger kept by the founders of the "second" *Petah Tikva*—established bylaws prescribing distinctly Orthodox practices meant to lend their community a highly conservative coloration. Their "Rules of Conduct" (*hukei ha-hanhaga*) are concerned chiefly with the appointment of a *Torah* scholar who would "steadfastly uphold our holy *Torah*, overlooking nothing. Whoever disobeys him will surely be punished."[22] The role of the rabbi was expanded and enhanced behind anything known in the premodern *kehillah*—further clear evidence of the defensive nature of Orthodoxy.[23] Other areas covered by the bylaws evoke similar conclusions. Education is a case in point. Whereas traditional society had taken for granted the primacy of religion as a guiding light of children's education, it was now necessary to set explicit boundaries: "In all *Talmud Torahs* and *yeshivot*, Jewish children will learn only God's *Torah* and ethical prescriptions."[24] These trends, so typical of the ultra-Orthodox communities of Central and Eastern Europe, also had a decisive impact on the members of the Ashkenazi community in Jerusalem in the 1870's and 1880's.

THE NEW NEIGHBORHOODS IN JERUSALEM

The neighborhoods established in Jerusalem since the 1860's do not display equal measures of "Orthodoxy," nor do all the texts describing the establishment of the more Orthodox neighborhoods display definitive characteristics of the spirit of Orthodoxy as described above. In fact, however, several ideological and social processes that developed in the various stages of the move to extramural Jerusalem led gradually to a partial association of the new neighborhoods with phenomena associated with Central and Eastern European Orthodoxy. Two of the major stimuli for first phase of the exodus from intramural Jerusalem were demographic pressure and building projects by European and philanthropic agencies, meant to improve the Jerusalemites' living and sanitary conditions. These factors—and not necessarily the utopian vision of an expanded swath of ultra-Orthodox *kollelim*—were the focal causes of settlement activity in the early days of the new neighborhoods. This, however, does nothing to detract from the distinctly Orthodox essence that the "exodus from the walls" acquired. In Europe too, members of traditional society who sought defenses against the political and cultural transformations adopted institutions, devices, and tactics that were not originally identified with Orthodoxy. Some of these actually originated in the camp they so feared.

Thus, for example, an Orthodox press came into being in the mid-nineteenth century, after decades in which this institution had been one of the most potent weapons of the *Haskalah*.[25] Orthodoxy even adopted modern organizational patterns that they filled with an extreme anti-modern content.[26] The first extramural neighborhoods, founded for clearly philanthropical reasons (*Mishkenot Shaananim* in 1860), in response to housing shortages, or by the economic initiatives of private individuals, actually suggested a possible channel of Orthodox activity that was gradually adopted by the agencies in charge of the *kollelim*. Although prominent members of Ashkenazi *kollelim* participated in the founding of *Nahalat Shiva* (1869), several years passed before the establishment of new neighborhoods became an enterprise unequivocally identified with the *kollelim* and with intentions typical of the Old *Yishuv*.

The wide differences in the social and cultural character of the various neighborhoods were clear manifestations of the stages of this process. These were amplified by the heterogeneity of the Jerusalem population, as reflected in its social composition (Lithuanians versus Galicians, Hungarians versus Poles, *Hasidim* versus *Perushim*), issues connected with subgroups and factions within Jerusalem Orthodoxy, and socio-economic factors such as differences in the income and enrollments of different *kollelim*. Thus a socio-geographical phenomenon that began for reasons other than those that would characterize the "Orthodoxization" process in European Jewish society took on a saliently Orthodox flavor.

Moreover, due to the distinctly corporative nature of the Ashkenazi *kollel* in Jerusalem, the new neighborhoods became a modern alternative that facilitated the *kollel*'s continued existence. The "exodus from the walls" opened up a new direction for members of the Ashkenazi *Yishuv*, one that permitted the preservation of values alongside the expansion of boundaries and the diffusion of communal structures.

The bylaws of the more Orthodox neighborhoods (such as Meah Shearim, 1889)[27] rely totally on *Halakha* as a living "constitution," even in the most trivial matters. The grounding of the bylaws in *Halakha*, too, is worth noting. This was one of the most typical manifestations of the difference between traditional and Orthodox society: whereas the traditional bylaws occasionally rested on local custom and displayed organic growth with local features, the Orthodox bylaws derived from the *Shulhan Arukh* only. They attempted, as it were, to "integrate" the sources, notwithstanding their complexity, into an unequivocal base heading in one direction only.[28] Moreover, the bylaws written by the founders of Meah Shearim, repeating a phenomenon mentioned above, empowered neighborhood residents to expel anyone who acted contrary to *Halakha*, who threatened the traditional way of life, or who did not belong to the founders' core group. Several authors writing about Meah Shearim defined this neighborhood—for good reason—as a "voluntary ghetto," and even noticed a tendency to segregate from other factions in the Old City itself.[29] Here two desires—for a *halakhic* way of life and for insularity *vis-à-vis* the rest of the Jewish community—combined to achieve the most complete and extreme manner of preservation.

Neighborhoods of this type, of which Meah Shearim was the epitome and an archetype that served as a paragon for the founders of the other neighborhoods, were autonomous in all respects; they maintained a loose federation based on the umbrella organizations of the Ashkenazi *kollelim*. Decentralization tendencies, originating not only in the aforementioned heterogeneity but also in the Orthodox nature of these types of communities, characterized the relations between the neighborhoods. In this sense, those who left the Old City continued to pursue a process begun by the Ashkenazi *Yishuv* in Jerusalem in the middle of the nineteenth century:

various subgroups set up joint institutions (a committee embracing all the *kollelim*, a hospital, a *yeshiva*),[30] but did not unite under a central leadership that might exercise real authority over the *kollelim*. The development of the Jewish neighborhoods in Jerusalem in the late nineteenth and early twentieth centuries was well suited to the sociological structure of these "supra-*kollel*" organizations in terms of decentralization and slackness of ties, in contrast with the centralistic tendencies of the nascent Zionist movement. The residents of these neighborhoods were therefore typified by voluntary affiliation with their society coupled with a tendency to self-segregation. The Meah Shearim bylaws attest to this combination. The *kollel* invested the neighborhood with an Orthodox ambiance both socially and spiritually. Thus they permitted members of the Old *Yishuv* to adapt to the vicissitudes of the times, which had deprived the premodern *kollel* of its former function as an agent of community cohesion. The establishment and social coalescence of the neighborhoods were therefore a practicable further stage in the transition of pre-Emancipation society from the corporations to modern Orthooxy.

ORTHODOXY AND MODERN NATIONALISM

By depicting the establishment of extramural Jerusalem as part of the conversion of Jerusalem society from "traditionalism" to "Orthodoxy," we invest the discussion of the concepts of "old" and "new" with a new dimension. If the term "old" is invoked as a value and in the manner associated with consciousness, then the neighborhoods of New Jerusalem belong undoubtedly and explicitly to the "old." However, if we take a sociohistorical perspective—as we have thus far—toward the nature of Orthodoxy as a phenomenon of the modern, post-Emancipation era, then the neighborhoods are part of the "new"—assuming, of course, that Orthodoxy is perceived as bearing the attributes of the "new."

Here is the place to point out that the many studies of the past decade on issues of the Old and the New *Yishuvim*[31] and the question of when the modern era in Palestine began,[32] fail to take account of the centrality of "Orthodoxization" as a characteristic of the tension between conservatism and innovation in Jewish society in the Holy Land. In view of this oversight, which originates in ideological attitudes or research considerations, several of the trends discussed above have been disregarded. However, observations rooted in stale polemics and naive analogies—legacies of the *Haskalah* and of Jewish nationalism—abound. Some of these observations have a direct bearing on the historical interpretation of the "exodus from the walls." Below are several questions we wish to ask in connection with these observations, from the viewpoint presented in this article:

A. Is the conventional historiographic model valid as a way of explaining the "retreat" of *Yishuv* leaders such as Israel Dov Frumkin and Yehiel Mechl Pines, after their encounter with the more radical stream of modern nationalism? Do the views of personalities such as Joel Moses Salomon or Joseph Rivlin have anythinq in common with the "nationalist" views? Alternately, might the "Orthodox" element of their activity have been the dominant one in the 1870s, and *a fortiori* in the 1890s? Were the neighborhoods originally "nationalist" in character, and did they become Orthodox only in subsequent years? Or were they perhaps Orthodox from the very outset, having been shaped by explicitly Orthodox tendencies?

B. The role of several modern nationalist anachronisms in our understanding of the pre-Zionist *Yishuv*: equating the geographical expansion of the Jerusalem *Yishuv* with nationalist "activism"; viewing all such activity as "upbuilding the land" at a time when the reasons for such activity were far removed from any nationalist ideology; attribution of modern organization methods, innovative trends, and political intentions to various activists in Jerusalem Ashkenazi society.

C. A particular instance of anachronism: the belief that the establishment of the neighborhoods was a manifestation of a productivization trend. Does innovative urban planning really teach us anything about industrial or agricultural occupational trends? Had not such trends become apparent in Jerusalem only in the early twentieth century, when the philanthropic agencies, which were actually opposed to the ultra-Orthodox ambiance evolving in the Ashkenazi neighborhoods, brought their gospel from overseas?

D. The function and significance of changing social patterns within the neighborhoods: did the neighborhoods' modes of organization presage nothing about socio-political trends that characterized the New *Yishuv* and its institutions? Did such organizations perhaps shape the modern face of Orthodoxy without any direct connection with modern nationalism?

Unequivocal answers to questions raised against historiographic observations are hard to provide. Some of this difficulty arises from the intriguing correspondence between several features of "Orthodoxy" and those of modern nationalism. This correspondence has caused observers to obfuscate the uniqueness of each phenomenon to this very day. Orthodoxy and nationalism are two outgrowths of the challenge presented by modernism to continued Jewish existence; they acted in similar ways for the upholding of similar values. Moreover, there is a large "gray area" between these two streams, where they are virtually identical. This was the case in the Old *Yishuv* too, as the numerous peripheral groups revolving around the solid core of the leading elite trod a fine and ephemeral line between antinationalist Orthodoxy and incipient religious nationalism.

In the final analysis, many channels of communication were formed between modern nationalism and a modernized traditional society, and the exclusivity of the significant manifestations of Orthodoxy had become blurred even before the national movement surfaced. As for the events in Jerusalem, the New *Yishuv* continued to develop not only the *Yishuv* infrastructure installed by members of the Old *Yishuv* in the extramural neighborhoods, but also those trends and intentions that were recognized after the fact as being shared by both *Yishuvim*. The attempt to sustain quasi-corporative existence in the modern era originated in Orthodox intentions and was suited, in part, to corresponding nationalist intentions. The exodus from the walled city was a "new" phenomenon, unrelated to *Haskalah* or nationalism, and its objective, ironically enough, was the preservation of the "old."

NOTES

1 H. Graetz, *Paths of Jewish History* (in Hebrew) (Jerusalem, 1969), 282.

2 I. Bartal, "'Old Yishuv' and 'New Yishuv' - Image and Reality" (in Hebrew), *Cathedra* 1 (1980): 9-11.

3 See for example, B. Dinur, "'Modern Times' in Jewish History: Their Definition, Essence, and Image" (in Hebrew), in *With the Changing Generations* (in Hebrew) (Jerusalem, 1972), 26-29; idem, "The Ideological Fundamentals of the *Aliyot* of 1740-1840" (in Hebrew), in *With the Changing Generations*, 69-79. A contrasting view of these immigration movements is articulated by R. Mahler: "The hasidic immigrations were no different in principle from those of the great talmudists and the kabbalists who preceded them, except that hasidism, as a mass movement, was able to send more numerous and frequent groups of immigrants to Palestine than the kabbalists had been able to organize in the past" (idem, *Jewish History: Recent Generations* (in Hebrew), vol. 1, Book 4 (Merhavia, 1962), 127).

4 On the studies by M. Eliav and A. Morgenstern see J. Barnai, "Trends in the Study of the Jewish Community in Palestine in the Middle Ages and the Early Modern Era" (in Hebrew), *Cathedra* 42 (1987): 94-97, 111, 115, 117-19.

5 A. Morgenstern, *Messianism and the Settlement of Palestine* (in Hebrew) (Jerusalem, 1985).

6 An especially typical example is A. Horowitz, ed., *Mosad ha-yesod* (Jerusalem, 1958). See ibid., 53-118, and cf. Y. Kaniel, *Continuity and Change* (in Hebrew) (Jerusalem, 1984), 27-28.

7 For a more detailed bibliography, consult Y. Ben-Arieh, *Jerusalem in the Nineteenth Century: Emergence of the New City* (Jerusalem and New York), 468-88.

8 Ibid., 177.

9 Ibid., 121.

10 S. Baron, "History of the Jerusalem *Yishuv*" (in Hebrew), in *Sefer Klausner* (Tel Aviv, 1937), 304-305; I. Bartal, "The Jews of Eastern Europe and Palestine, the *Aliyot* and the Structure of the Ashkenazi *Yishuv*" (in Hebrew), *Cathedra* 16 (1980): 11; idem, "Moses Montefiore and Palestine" (in Hebrew), *Cathedra* 33 (1985): 158.

11 S. Halevi "'Manifesto' against the Establishment of the Lemel School" (in Hebrew), *Cathedra* 5 (1978): 203.

12 I. Bartal, "Petah Tikva - Between Ideological Roots and Circumstances of the Times" (in Hebrew), *Cathedra* 9 (1979): 60-61; Y. Kaniel, "The Controversy Between Petah Tikva and Rishon Lezion as to Which was Settled First, and its Significance" (in Hebrew), *Cathedra* 9 (1979): 46-52; idem, "The Palestine Settlement Enterprise and the Founders of *Petah Tikva*" (in Hebrew), *Cathedra* 16 (1980): 154-60.

13 Josef Rivlin was a central figure in the founding of the *Vaad kol ha-kollelim*, the superordinate organization of *kollelim* that formed the basis of the Ashkenazi social establishment in the late nineteenth century.

14 A. R. Malachi, "Jerusalem in 1876" (in Hebrew), in *Chapters in Old Yishuv History* (in Hebrew) (Tel Aviv, 1971), 145.

15 To elucidate the difference between the traditional connection to Palestine and the roots of modern nationalism, and to present them as two disparate phenomena that merged only at a relatively late stage in the history of the Jewish national movement, see S. Ettinger and I. Bartal, "The First *Aliyah*: Ideological Roots and Practical Accomplishments" (in Hebrew), *Cathedra* 2 (1982): 197-227.

16 This matter recurs consistently in the dialogue conducted between the Eastern European *maskilim* and the ruling authorities on the "reform" of traditional society. In their memoranda and correspondence, *maskilim* such as Yosef Perl, Yitzhak Ber Levinsohn, and Avraham Mapu reiterated the claim that the *Hasidim* were harming the state in various ways and that they were the true political enemy. The authorities generally responded to this allegation by saying that the *Hasidim* constituted a majority of the Jews and that a respected component of Jewish society, one that was

not politically hostile, should not be agitated. See for example, the introduction by A. Rubinstein, in Yosef Perl's *The Essence of the Hasidic Cult* (in Hebrew) (Jerusalem, 1977), 11-14; and B. Dinur, ed., *Correspondence of Abraham Mapu* (in Hebrew) (Jerusalem, 1970), 284-88.

17 The Jewish community in the city (and also one of the *kehalim*) is referred to in various languages during different periods and in different regions of Europe during the late Middle Ages by names derived from the Latin corporate term *"universitas."* Thus we encounter *università* in seventeenth-century Italy and *Universitas Judaeorum Poloniae* (*"klal yehudei malkhut polin"*) in eighteenth-century Poland.

18 "From the Soil the Truth Will Emerge" (in Hebrew), in A. L. Frumkin and E. Rivlin, *The History of the Jerusalem Sages* (in Hebrew), vol. 3 (Jerusalem, 1929), 131.

19 Concerning the activities of the *Perushim* immigrant community in this direction, consult source material in A. Morgenstern, *Emissaries of Jerusalem: The History of the Rozenthal Family, 1816-1839* (in Hebrew) (Jerusalem, 1987), 50-63, 106-108; idem, "The *Perushim*, the London Missionary Society, and the Establishment of the British Consulate in Jerusalem" (in Hebrew), *Shalem* 5 (1987): 120.

20 J. Katz, "Zionism and Jewish Identity" (in Hebrew), in J. Katz, *Jewish Nationalism: Essays and Studies* (in Hebrew) (Jerusalem, 1979), 75.

21 A. Druyanov and S. Laskov, eds., *Writings on the History of Hibbat Zion and the Settlement of Palestine* (in Hebrew), vol. 1 (1870-1882). (Tel Aviv, 1982), 52.

22 Ibid., 91.

23 It should be noted here that the role of the rabbi in the *kehillot* of Palestine in the early New *Yishuv*, as viewed by researchers, departed from the rabbi's historical standing in the traditional *kehillah*. In premodern *kehillot*, the rabbi did not play such a decisive role in the religious life of the town, since the threat of modernity did not yet exist. Moreover, the rabbi was a salaried employee of the *kehillah* and, in fact, often had no hand in the decisions of the *kahal*. It was this very upturn in the prominence of the rabbi that attested to the transition from a corporation to a society requiring the reconstitution of its functions and authority. Compare, for example, the discussion of the rabbi's authority in Y. Kaniel, "Religion and '*Kehillah*' in the Worldview of the First and Second *Aliya* (1882-1914)" (in Hebrew), *Shalem* 5 (1987): 191-93.

24 Druyanov and Laskov, *Writings on the History of Hibbat Zion*, 95.

25 For a classic example of an Eastern European Orthodox periodical, see E. Etkes, *Rabbi Yisrael Salanter and the Beginnings of the Musar Movement* (in Hebrew) (Jerusalem, 1983), 276-85.

26 Regarding the attributes of Orthodoxy in general, see: M. S.

Samet, "Orthodox Jewry in the Modern Era" (in Hebrew), *Mahalakhim* 1 (1969): 29-40; idem, "Ortodoksiya" [Orthodoxy], in *Hebrew Encyclopaedia*, vol. 32 (Jerusalem, 1981), s.v. "Shinui ve-masoret" [Change and Tradition], 193-200.

27 *Bylaws of Meah Shearim* (in Hebrew) (Jerusalem, 1889).

28 In this regard, cf. I. Gliss: "The Meah Shearim bylaws may serve as an example of a lawbook for any community of Torah-observant Jews that wishes to arrange their affairs in all areas, particularly relations with their neighbors, in accordance with the Torah and the Laws of Israel, as interpreted and elucidated in the *Shulhan Arukh* and other rabbinic decisors." This is therefore a clearly Orthodox presentation of a new phenomenon in the history of community statutes. See I. Gliss, *Jerusalem Neighborhoods* (in Hebrew) (Jerusalem, 1962), 58-59.

29 A. Fuerst, *New Jerusalem* (in Hebrew) (Jerusalem, 1946), 63-64.

30 M. Friedman, "On the Structure of Community Leadership and the Rabbinate in the Ashkenazi Old *Yishuv* in the Late Ottoman Period" (in Hebrew), in *Chapters in the History of the Jewish Community in Jerusalem* (in Hebrew) (Jerusalem, 1973), 273-88.

31 These are discussed in detail in H. Herzog, "The Sociological Sense of the Concepts 'Old *Yishuv*' and 'New *Yishuv*'" (in Hebrew), *Cathedra* 32 (1984): 99-108.

32 S. Shamir, "When Did the Modern Era in Jewish History Begin?" (in Hebrew), *Cathedra* 40 (1986): 138-58.

Esther Benbassa
Centre de Recherche sur la Civilisation de l'Europe Moderne
C. N. R. S. / Université de Paris, Sorbonne

Zionism and the Politics of Coalitions in the Ottoman Jewish Communities in the Early Twentieth Century

In the second half of the nineteenth century, new partners in leadership appeared in the Jewish Ottoman communities. Zionism was one of these new partners.

The Palestine issue was incontestably the principal reason for the official entry of Zionism into the Turkish Jewish community beginning in 1908 (which is not to say that there had been no prior contact with Jewish nationalism by the Ottoman Jews). Neither in Turkey nor in other large Jewish centers, however, was the function of Zionism within the community always directly linked to this issue. In the case of the Turkish Jewish community, it would be more accurate to speak of Zionisms, in the plural, and to make a particular distinction between currents brought in from the outside and local nationalist variants.[1] Zionism or nationalism, according to the conjuncture, was the new political partner from Europe. Its goal was to prepare the way for negotiations over Palestine with the Ottoman authorities. To achieve this aim, it relied on support from the community, from both within the institutional structure and among the various strata of local Jewish society. Places on the political scene had already been marked out by other, previously established, interest groups, such as the Alliance Israélite Universelle (hereafter, the Alliance).[2]

Communal institutions were administered by an autocratic system which depended in part on a *hahambaşı* (holding the title of Chief Rabbi) or on a *kaymakam* (*locum tenens* of the Chief Rabbi), and in part on an oligarchy of

---

This article was translated from the French by Barbara Pieroni.

dilettante community leaders. The positioning of forces along the peripheries of the communal institutions was a common practice in the nineteenth century. This practice fostered the absorption and control of groups of malcontents or of those whose aspirations simply could not be met within the existing institutional structure. In this way the peripheral force would ready its troops for the exercise of power and, in so doing, become structured, or re-structured, as a political force. Both the Alliance and the Zionists, groups from abroad, followed this "political tradition" in their own way.

There was nothing original about this political tradition. It constituted an option for survival (or for biding time) for a group excluded from power or for an oppositional force in an oligarchic system. The interest lies in the refinements brought to this strategy by the concerned parties and in the evolution of the relation between each of these parties and the center—namely with the central forces holding power within the community.

THE ALLIANCE MOVES TO THE CENTER

From the beginning the Alliance functioned both as an alternative power and as a locus of alternative power by taking over certain prerogatives of the community's institutions, the administration of education for example, without cutting itself off definitively from the communal authorities.

The classic stakes of political struggle in the community again came into play with the arrival of the Alliance as a foreign partner and the position it began to occupy in communal life, in spite of its definition as a philanthropic organization. In the nineteenth century this struggle primarily involved the confrontation between the laity and the clergy, although there was also internal friction within each of these groups. The Alliance acted within the community through the intermediary of members of the local elite who, although this was the most natural locus for the practice of their power, had not been successful in operating within the institutional establishment. Some members of the local leadership who held positions of authority in the community were, in fact, unable to exercise the privileges of their position.

The absence of democracy in the communal institutions, which was further reinforced in the last decades of the nineteenth century by the authoritarian regime of Abdulhamid II (1876-1909), and the concentration of power in the hands of a political clique which took place during this period, led to the further limitation of an already restricted mobility. The field of political action for the Jew, as a *dhimmi*, was restricted to the community arena. This limitation rendered the struggle for power all the more fierce and explains, perhaps, the intensity of conflict, sometimes disproportionate to the issues at stake, of the political debates within the community. Accession to a position of responsibility within communal institutions represented the pinnacle of social and economic ascent. Community leaders, those anxious to set innovative projects in motion as well as those motivated simply by the desire for power, did not hesitate to turn to those alternative forces which might, in the long run, help them reach their goal.

The Alliance was one such potential force. A new force whose base was abroad it was less vulnerable than others. The Alliance, however, precisely because it was a philanthropic society, lacked both the perspectives and the dynamics of a political party. Its troops reached power solely as the result of socio-economic conditions. The Alliance did not practice mass politics. The active participation of the population in the political life of the community had already been limited by the *hahamhane nizamnamesi* (Organic Statute)[3] and suffrage based on property qualifications.[4] Moreover, no communal elections had been held in Istanbul since 1865.[5] In fact, the first universal suffrage elections (women excepted) were not held there until 1910-1911. It was rather through the intermediary of local leaders supportive of its work and through the intermediary of its trusted Haim Nahum, the elected *kaymakam*,[6] that the Alliance began to assert itself into strategic positions. This was due especially to the support which Haim Nahum was given by the new regime coming out of the "Young Turk" revolution (23-24 July 1908).[7]

ZIONISTS AND THEIR OPPOSITION PARTY STRATEGY

The official Zionism which began in 1908 to function locally in the guise of a banking company, the Anglo Levantine Banking Company, was wholly the movement of a political organization. Here lies the critical difference betwen the Alliance and the Zionists. The Zionist "party", as a party, had a political program which was adapted to current conditions, both outside of and within the community. Certainly the community was second among the political priorities of the Zionists. Nevertheless, the community served as a point of departure for negotiations with the government. Distinctions should be made between local projects according to their direction by the Zionist Organization abroad, by leaders sent to the community, and by Zionists recruited locally.

In any case, Zionism was faced with making a place for itself on the political scene of the community alongside other special interest groups. In particular, Zionism had to confront the political center, now occupied by the "Alliancists" (friends of the Alliance) who were opposed to Zionism. In order to do this, Zionism had not only to employ the time-honored strategies of the local community, but also to innovate. The Zionists had little hope of recruiting among the local notables who had been won over by the Alliance even if, for a time, they did continue working in this direction. Only those milieux into which the Alliance had not gained entry—and the groups cut off from the center—remained open to them.

Although it had been assumed that the majority of those who would go through the educational system would espouse the ideology of the Alliance, this ideology had not had a great impact on the general population. Thus, the public represented a potential source of real support in the conquest of communal institutions, when the right moment arrived. As for those groups which had been excluded from the center of the political scene, they hoped only to reach it. Zionism, by defining itself from the outset as an opposition party, was bound to attract those excluded from and discontented with the community regime in place. These groups were capable in turn, with the help of the populace, of pushing the Zionists into a position of power.

While the Alliance recruited those excluded from the center on an individual basis, Zionism, as an opposition party, had the privilege of negotiating with political interest groups or "ethnic" groups, and of contracting coalitions. This policy of consolidation was part of the Zionists' local strategy and there was no lack of prospective partners falling into this category. Zionists did not accord equal importance to all of the peripheral interest groups. The former status of their relations with the group, the reasons for the coalition, the potential of the ally, and the particular conjuncture constituted the decisive parameters.

The Zionists also tried to associate themselves with groups still in power who had been weakened by the success of the "progressives" and who thereby found themselves on the periphery of the inner circle of power. The rabbis and a certain conservative core still holding communal authority fell into this category. They represented an easy group of supporters to attract and a valuable one, for they could potentially play a role both as an opposition force and as a new power base.

FIRST OFFENSIVES AS A UNITED FRONT

The Zionists had begun to use the tactic of a united front against the Chief Rabbinate in Istanbul, seat of the central authority of Ottoman Judaism, from the moment the "Alliancist" camp reached power. This tactic had been employed both in the capital and in the provinces. The first objective was to prevent the reinforcement of power of the "Alliancists" and, in so doing, to keep the right-hand man of the local "Alliancists", Haim Nahum, from obtaining the post of *hahambaşı* in the upcoming elections. The second objective was to undermine any initiatives emanating from the center which were destined for the communities in the provinces, in order to impede any centralization of power which might endanger the small clusters of power formed by the different communities dispersed throughout the Empire. These clusters of power represented the available political loci within which peripheral forces could take action.

Immediately following the election of Haim Nahum to the position of *kaymakam*, divisions in the community worsened over a series of issues which had already been debated before the election. The toughest opposition came from those who had just been removed from power,[8] identified as "conservatives" by the new leaders, and who attempted to further destabilize the precarious communal regime which had been set in place with great difficulty.[9] Although they were not openly active in Istanbul at this time, the Zionists were in a good position to observe the maneuverings of the opponents to the new team. They did not fail to take advantage of this situation on their own turf. Later, when they were in a position to mobilize locally recruited forces, they went into action in the capital itself.

In the first months following the "Young Turk" revolution, the dynamic of change, which also affected a portion of the Jewish population, had worked in favor of the "Alliancist" group and of Nahum, both perceived as "progressives" even though their communal projects were not diametrically opposed to the policies of those whom they had just dethroned. The people thus found themselves animated by an enthusiasm brought by the moment which was favorable to those who were seen as new leaders (who seemed right for the new situation). These new men hadn't been tainted by the "court" intrigues of fallen communal leaders, who had been associated with the overturned Hamidian regime.[10] Some of the "progressives" were even personally linked to the new Ottoman regime, which furthered their merit in the eyes of the Jewish population. In truth, the people did not play a decisive role in the "Alliancists'" rise to power; they approved this rise after the fact in a wave of enthusiasm rather than through deliberate choice.

The nature and the meaning of the coalitions contracted outside of the capital between the Zionists and diverse interest groups against the Chief Rabbinate are well-illustrated by the two episodes analyzed below. Both incidents are representative of the conjunctural strategies employed and of the political climate of the moment. It should be added that the dispute between the Alliance and the Zionists was not a new one (it went back as far as their struggles in Bulgaria at the end of the nineteenth century, for example). Their dispute, in fact, had simply become aggravated the emergence of new stakes in the political arena.

THE PANIGEL AFFAIR

The unrest which characterized the aftermath of the "Young Turk" revolution spread progressively to the Ottoman provinces and their Jewish communities. The "progressives" who had come from the ranks of the "Alliancists" began to demonstrate their desire to take hold of the reins of power in their respective communities. Here too, a distinction must be made between the program of the Alliance in Paris and that of local recruits. The latter went far beyond the prudent recommendations of the conservative Paris headquarters. Furthermore, the Alliance in Paris was distant from the local centers of power and the passion which this power aroused in the local communal leaders.

The communities of Damascus, Saida and Jerusalem raised the issue of the dismissal of their Chief Rabbi. In Jerusalem this was simply a case of reopening an affair which had been provisionally settled, after many vicissitudes, with the invalidation of the election of Jacob Meir in 1907.[11] In the same year, Eliahu Panigel had been appointed *kaymakam*. The irregularity of the appointment and the role which former leaders of the community in Istanbul had played in this affair could serve as a pretext for the "progressives" to demand the dismissal of Panigel, all the more so because Panigel had not carried out the election of a titular *hahambaşı* as was stipulated by the *hahamhane nizamnamesi*.

Against the "progressives" or "Alliancists", Panigel was supported by the conservative forces still in power. The *Hilfsverein der Deutschen Juden*[12] (hereafter the *Hilfsverein*), a rival of the Alliance, had also joined forces with Panigel. The Zionists acted in concert with the conservative groups, including the Orthodox.[13] In this case, of course, the Zionists sided with those who still held power in the Jerusalem Rabbinate or who were associated with it. We must not lose sight of the fact, however, that "conservatives" had lost their supremacy in the capital. While Jerusalem occupied an important place in the Zionist program, the primary objective, in this instance, was the struggle against the Chief Rabbinate in Istanbul. While the latter could not name the different Chief Rabbis of the provinces, the *hahambaşı* and his entourage carried considerable weight in the elections and in their official ratification by the Ottoman authorities. It was feared that they could name someone close to them and, in that way, control the Jerusalem Rabbinate.

The "progressives" demanded the dismissal of Panigel. The director of the Alliance Trades School in Jerusalem, Abraham Antébi, worked actively in this direction despite the fact that the Alliance had firmly committed him to neutrality.[14] The lack of fervor on the part of the Alliance in its support of the Jerusalem "progressives" was due, in part, to the fear of attracting the wrath of Germany's Orthodox groups and of the Zionists, as had happened during the Meir-Elyashar affair in 1906-1907. The Alliance had demonstrated a similar attitude in regard to the "progressives" and Haim Nahum following the "Young Turk" revolution, even though it had until then given full support to its *protégé*.[15] In the final analysis, the Alliance was undoubtedly less progressive than were its local adherents. The latter rallied under the flag of the Alliance, in spite of the Alliance itself, for lack of an alternative.

In this affair, Antébi defied repeated remonstrances and pressured Isaac Fernandez, president of the Regional Committee of the Alliance in Istanbul, to intervene through Nahum.[16] Once the issue of Jerusalem had been resolved, Antébi planned to tackle the reorganization of the community of Jaffa.

The adversaries of the Alliance criticized the organization for infiltrating Jewish philanthropic works, for taking over, along with Nahum, the Chief Rabbinates of the Empire, for attempting to curry the exclusive favor of the "Young Turks" and for refusing all association with the *Hilfsverein* and the Zionists. In a word, the Alliance was accused of trying to establish a monopoly of power for itself.[17] The interim governor of Jerusalem also supported the "Alliancist" group and was leaning toward the dismissal of Panigel. Even though they did not act in concert and did not adopt the same line of action, all of these partners were identified with the Alliance and so formed a clearly delimited group which had to be fought.

Exterior factors also contributed to the sharpening of divisions. Thus, the intervention of the German ambassador further complicated the affair.[18] For the "Alliancists" there was no question that the Zionists, the Orthodox, Germany and the *Hilfsverein* were working hand in hand.[19] This is what led directly to the "Germano-Zionism" charge so often evoked by Antébi, the Alliance, the "Alliancists" and even the *Quai d'Orsay* in Paris.

In reality, the fact that the Zionists and the *Hilfsverein*—outsiders in a sense—became allies with the "conservative" "insiders" during the Panigel affair, can only be explained by tactical motivations. Both groups opposed the influence of the Alliance and France, which could only increase with the definitive election of Haim Nahum.[20] This is how a united front against the Chief Rabbinate in the capital was formed.

THE FRANKFURT LETTERS

In the affair of the Frankfurt letters, the Zionists again took action outside of the capital, but this time they also sought the intervention of partners within the city. Although the "conservatives" had lost their advantage in Istanbul, given the institutional structures they had not been completely ousted from positions in communal administration during the authoritarian takeover of some of these positions. The conservative laity had certainly been forced to yield their positions to the "Alliancists". The rabbis, however, the majority of whom remained tied to the former leaders, still retained a voice within the power structure. The members of the *meclis-i ruhani* (religious council)[21] in the capital also held seats in the *meclis-i umumi* (general council).[22] In this capacity they were to intervene in the designation of the future *hahambaşı* of the Empire.

These clerical members of the *meclis-i umumi* had received registered letters from Frankfurt, signed by a number of rabbis officiating in different European cities.[23] "The signatories requested them, in the name of the *Torah*, of *Judaic interests* and of *Palestine* to vote without partiality to either the man or the great and powerful Society."[24] The "society" in question was none other than the Alliance. Haim Nahum, the man most implicated by these missives, attributed them to the workings of the Orthodox, the *Hilfsverein* and the Zionists, who were accusing him of being in the service of the so-called "society."[25] The "progressives" developed the same analysis.

One might think that the analysis of the "Alliancist" camp was the result of a subjective bias. This was not the case since the Zionists, on the local level, were not at all hiding their intentions. The Salonican Zionist press explained that if the Alliance was working for Nahum, there was no reason that others could not fight in favor of their own candidates.[26] In fact, the adversaries of the Alliance proposed the candidacy of the Chief Rabbi of Egypt, R. Shimeon, of Orthodox tendency. Indeed, for the Zionists, Nahum was under the thumb of the Alliance which was credited (wrongly) with having a great influence on the "Young Turk" government, an influence which had allowed it to place its men in the key positions within Ottoman Jewry after the revolution.[27] German Jewry was no less fearful of the nomination of Nahum to the post of *hahambaşı* as this nomination might lead to an increase in French influence in the East.[28] The intervention on the part of the *Hilfsverein* with the German Foreign Ministry had not remained without effect. The Minister was notified at the German embassy in Istanbul that the naming of Nahum to the post of *hahambaşı* was not desirable since the candidate was a francophile and openly supported the "Young Turks".[29]

Once again, as in the Panigel affair, the Orthodox, the Zionists, and the *Hilfsverein* found themselves united with the blessing of Germany. Later, in the capital, this association, with slight variations, was to reoccur with the participation of new interest groups such as the Ashkenazim or the *B'nai B'rith* (locally called the *Béné Bérit*).[30]

ZIONISTS AND RABBIS: THE *HISTADRUT HA-RABANIM*

Zionists also contracted alliances with conservatives, including the rabbis, not only in Istanbul, but also in Salonica.[31] As was the case with the mobilization of the rabbis against Haim Nahum and the oligarchy in Istanbul, the role played by the Zionists in Salonica is incontestable. The very initiator of the mobilization of the rabbis against Haim Nahum and the oligarchy in Istanbul was David Markus,[32] a representative of the *Hilfsverein*, and a rabbi of the Ashkenazic community known for his favorable position towards the Zionists.

When the *meclis-i umumi* was dissolved in 1910, opening the way for new elections, Nahum did not ask its clerical members to resign as he did the lay members. Although the *hahamhane nizamnamesi* stipulated that the clerical members were to be elected by the lay members,[33] there was no indication that they were to be elected members for life; only the seven rabbis who comprised the *meclis-i ruhani* held that privilege.[34] Nahum, however, extended this privilege of permanent membership to all the clerical members of the *meclis-i umumi*, thus taking advantage of the habitual imprecision of the *nizamname*. This concession was intended to avoid arousing any discontent among the rabbis, longtime opponents of the "progressives", which, if expressed, might be taken up by the Zionists in order to bring that part of the population still attached to tradition to rise against a visibly weakened Chief Rabbinate.

After the elections, the Zionist press began to evoke and to support the awakening of the orthodox religious movement.[35] Among the plans discussed there figured the creation of a *beit ha-midrash* (House of Study) and a *Histadrut ha-rabanim* (Union of Rabbis).[36] The desired goal, presented as the result of a decision coming from the clergy themselves, was to have the rabbis now play an active role.[37] The reality looked somewhat different. Actually, this *Histadrut ha-rabanim* was to bring together the twenty clerical members of the *meclis-i umumi*.[38]

The grouping of all the clergy under one banner would have led to a sort of collective dialogue about attitudes to adopt within the *meclis-i umumi*.[39] The rabbis in question potentially constituted a strong opposition force (if only by their number, one quarter of the *meclis-i umumi*) which diverse opinion groups would have an interest in winning over.

In spite of the efforts deployed by Nahum and the "Alliancists" to assure that the elections to the *meclis-i umumi* went according to their wishes so that their sympathizers would form the majority,[40] there were Zionist infiltrations which were inevitable given the context of the moment. As for the clergy, they had no reason to support the group in power.[41] Indeed, at the meeting of the new *meclis-i umumi*, at which gathered the eighteen clerical and forty-four lay members[42] (of the eighty required), Nissim Russo, a local Zionist militant, was elected to the *meclis-i cismani* with fifty-one votes,[43] that is 82.25% of the total suffrage. Abraham Farhi, a member of the "progressive camp" and close collaborator of Nahum, had been president of the *meclis-i cismani* formed in the wake of the "Young Turk" revolution and was president of the retiring *meclis*. He received only 46.77% of the vote (that is 29 votes).[44] This difference, between the results obtained by a recent adherent to Zionism and a local leader long known for his communal activities, was a reflection of the political choices of the new *meclis-i umumi*. Furthermore, Russo was not the only member of the *meclis-i cismani* who was favorable to Zionism. Haim Reisner, the president of the Ashkenazi community, was also elected. It is possible that the new *meclis-i umumi* simply wished to promote new, more effective people into positions of executive power. Nonetheless, the fact that all but two of the clerical members of the *meclis-i umumi* were present, while nearly a quarter of the lay members were absent, must not be overlooked. Even though it is difficult to evaluate the exact role played by the clerical members in this election, their concern for a massive representation remains evident.

From that moment on the Zionists, who called for the democratization of communal institutions, allied themselves with the conservatives. These same conservatives, however, heads of communal institutions under the rabbinate of Moshe Halevi, Nahum's predecessor, had not particulary distinguished themselves by their application of democratic methods. This was an alliance developed in response to the particular conditions of the time and one which lent itself to the accelerated infiltration of the Zionists into communal institutions. It should be added that the *Hilfsverein* was included in this coalition, for the strongest proponent of the reorganization of the clergy, D. Markus, had close ties with this organization.

The attempt at a reorganization of the clerical milieux was to provoke a crisis whose first destabilizing effects became manifest with the strike of the rabbis. This strike was accompanied by the closing of the rabbinical tribunals and the interruption of the rabbis' activities in communal worship.[45] Partisans of the Chief Rabbi sought to dissolve the *Histadrut* under the pretext of certain stipulations of the *hahamhane nizamnamesi*.[46] One year later, during the conflict over the agreement signed with the Ashkenazim, the clergy would pronounce itself unanimously against Nahum and his friends and, in so doing, played into the hands of the Zionists.[47] Following this, the movement became so marginalized that no more was heard about it.

THE ASHKENAZI PARAMETER: A SPRINGBOARD TO POWER

From the end of the nineteenth century, the disagreement between the Sephardi and the Ashkenazi communities in Istanbul was regularly revived. This conflict was not unique to the capital, for one finds it also in Jerusalem.[48] In Istanbul, an agreement had been passed between the two groups in 1890. This agreement established the rights and the duties of the Ashkenazi community without distinction between nationalities (there were, in fact, several Ashkenazi communities).[49] This did not succeed, however, in ironing out the difficulties between them which resurfaced on several occasions.

Toward schism

Under the rabbinate of Haim Nahum, the conflict was exacerbated by the divergence in views between the *hahambaşı* (a Sepharadi) and both the president and the *baş haham* (Principal Rabbi) of the Ashkenazim, known for their Zionist sympathies. Although they had been reconciled by the 1890 Agreement, the argument which opposed the Ottoman Ashkenazi communities (*Aschkenasische Kultusgemeinde*) and the foreign or Austro-Hungarian Ashkenazi communities (*Oesterreichisch-ungarisch-israelitische Kultusgemeinde*), relative to the sharing of revenues of the tax on meat which they received from the Chief Rabbinate,[50] resurfaced in 1910 and distrupted the fragile *status quo* which had governed relations between the Sephardi and Ashkenazi communities. The most alarmist among them even predicted a schism, basing their prediction on certain endeavors undertaken by the Ashkenazi community toward becoming a religious group separate from the Chief Rabbinate, following the example of the Karaites and the *Francos*.[51] In this period of communal tension, when any issue was potentially a volatile one, this disagreement was not long in turning into a polemic.[52] The direction which this affair was to take was indicated by the apparent support which the Ashkenazi community leaders were receiving from the Zionists. Another indication could be seen in the intervention of the *Osmanischer Lloyd*, a paper associated with the German embassy in Istanbul, which published articles by the Ashkenazim aimed at, and considered insulting by, Nahum and the Chief Rabbinate.[53] This scission could but open a new field of action for the Zionists. The nationalist Ottoman paper financed by the Zionists, *Le Jeune Turc*, supported the claims of the Ashkenazim, or more accurately, of the Ashkenazi leaders.[54] At a higher level, pressure to move in this direction had also been placed on the Ottoman authorities. When the bill on military service was submitted to the Military Commission of the Chamber, there had been a discussion of Jews, Karaites and Ashkenazim.[55] But the schism was not complete.

The 1912 Agreement

The issue was invoked again on the occasion of the signing of an agreement between the *meclis-i cismani* (of Zionist tendencies) and the Ashkenazi community. The agreement was signed without the knowledge of the *hahambaşı* on 26 January 1912.[56] This event provoked a new crisis which concluded with the resignation of Haim Nahum[57] and which paralyzed communal institutions for a period of six months.

A comparison of the agreement which had already been signed with the Ashkenazim in 1890 and the one signed in 1912 does not yield many striking differences. On a certain number of points, however, the latter agreement represented a considerable setback in many of the gains made in 1890.

The reaction of Nahum to the signing of this agreement was out of proportion. His reaction appears almost surprising if we keep in mind the composition of the *meclis-i cismani* which signed the agreement and the political convictions of some of the Ashkenazi officials. The "progressives" were no longer the only ones running the community, as had been the case from the time of the "Young Turk" revolution until the election of the new *meclis-i cismani* in April of 1911. The tense relations between Nahum and this *meclis* leads one to think that the crisis concerned more a question of priniciple[58] than the signing of the agreement itself or the content of this agreement. This event potentially presented the occasion for the dissolution of this *meclis*, or at least for the undermining of its authority through the annulment of the agreement. Considering the fragility of his own power and of the communal institutions, Nahum could ill afford to allow the *meclis-i cismani* to freely exercise its supremacy. Refusing to share power with the Zionists, he either had to leave or to oust them.

In the episode of the 1912 Agreement, there had been a testing of power. This was only the beginning. With their appropriation of new loci of power and by attracting new partners who were still outside the power structure, the Zionists threatened to quickly gain the upper hand. It is in this context that the aggravation of the conflict and the determination on the part of Nahum and his friends not to go along with the 1912 Agreement can be understood. This event demonstrated the exceptional nature of a situation where the *meclis-i cismani* and the *hahambaşı* were no longer on the same side. Such a situation was unmanageable in an autocratic system with an imprecise "constitution," especially when that constitution had rarely been enforced. Hence the period of politics among friends came to an end.

THE WAR OF ATTRITION

Haim Nahum opted to resign, convinced that the government would refuse to accept it. As he had anticipated, the Minister of Justice and Religion, followed by the Council of Ministers, refused to accept his resignation, and also disapproved of the conduct of the *meclis-i cismani*.[59]

However, even as the government proclaimed its rejection of the resignation, the *meclis-i cismani* continued to consider it valid.[60] Normal functioning of communal institutions remained suspended. Thus the *meclis* acted against the decision of the government, which further complicated the situation.

After many vicissitudes, in March 1912, the *meclis-i umumi* was convoked to make a resolution. The debate was stormy, at times violent.[61] Of the sixty-five members present, two abstained and thirty-three voted in favor of maintaining the Agreement, results which represented both a censure of Nahum and the support for the accused *meclis-i cismani*. A solution to the conflict had not been the main preoccupation of the voters; instead, they were more concerned with evaluating the respective strengths of the different interest groups.

The evolution of the situation attested to the fact that the strategy of the "Alliancist-Nahumist" group, especially that of their leader, was not working. Nahum had sinned by lack of maturity[62], but his friends had been unable to adapt themselves to new conditions, unable to pass from dilettantism to the stage of politicking which the Zionists had adopted.

As a final recourse, Nahum asked the government's aid in invalidating the vote.[63] By legitimizing the annulment of the 1912 Agreement, the Ottoman authorities would indirectly strengthen his power. The outcome of the vote had proven that Nahum could no longer count on the *meclis-i umumi*. The Zionists, their sympathizers, as well as the clergy, by tightening their ranks had gained the advantage. On the other hand, Nahum seemed to have maintained solid support in the government.

The opinion of the State Council was long in coming. Tired of fighting, the *meclis-i cismani* had submitted its resignation.[64] The latter had counted on the degeneration of the situation to save its position. The State Council finally decided in favor of the *hahambaşı*.[65]

Nahum had managed to get out of a situation manifestly unfavorable to him by assuring himself of a personal victory with the help of the government. The latter was clearly indispensable to the consolidation of his power which was being seriously threatened by the Zionists.[66] Even the official medium of the Zionist workers in Palestine, *Ha-Poel Ha-Zair* (Journal of the Second *Aliyah*), recognized this.[67] The new *meclis-i cismani* had lost all of its Zionist character and its new president was described as "a fervent admirer of the civilizing work of the Alliance."[68]

The argument over the Agreement of 1912 was also settled; it was to be considered null and void.[69] The Ashkenazim did not definitively renounce its claims, but Nahum was once again the master of the situation.

CONTINUITY IN COALITIONS

The collaboration between the Zionists and the Ashkenazim was to continue after World War I. They appeared as partners in the new developments which were to take place both in the community and in local Zionism. The Ashkenazim's claims were met in the proposed regulation elaborated by the Jewish National Council, a kind of unitary communal structure set in place after the Allied occupation of Istanbul in November 1918 to compensate for the absence of Haim Nahum. At issue was the internal autonomy of the Ashkenazi community and its proportional representation in communal government.[70] The Zionists had been the artisans of the institution of a Jewish National Council, a development closer in nature to a *coup d'état*. Zionist allies such as the *B'nai B'rith*, the *Makabi* (Society of Nationalist Gymnastics) and the *Hilfsverein*, through the intermediary of its local representative Israel Auerbach (appointed Secretary General of the Council), shared seats on the Council. The Zionist camp thus bore witness to the fidelity in its coaltions.

The spirit of the times favoring union, the two Ashkenazi communities, the Ottoman and the foreign, merged on 1 January 1919,[71] and formed a Provisional Executive Committee of Ashkenazi Jews.[72] The president of this committee just happened to be the Zionist, D. Markus,[73] who was equally involved in the affairs of the *Histadrut ha-rabanim* and of the 1912 Agreement, and who was also linked to the *B'nai B'rith*. The manifesto[74] published in Yiddish and French on this occasion expressed an unreserved support for the Jewish cause in Palestine as well as for full support of the Jewish National Council. The newly established organization wished to remain resolutely autonomous. In any case, it was in the interest of the Zionists, amid the struggles over the Ashkenazi issue which had continued since 1910, that the Ashkenazi community free itself of Sephardi guardianship. In this way the Ashkenazi community would be able to choose an autonomous Chief Rabbi within its own denomination. Such a choice would in turn contribute to the weakening of Haim Nahum's function and to the diversification of the loci of decision making. This fusion of the two Ashkenazi communities and the affirmation of Ashkenazi autonomy which followed, were the products of a skillful maneuver made in preparation for the return of the *hahambaşı*, who had been sent on assignment by the Ottoman authorities at the end of 1918.

In the program for the *Organizational Statutes of the Turkish Jewish Communities*, which was elaborated by the Zionists after the definitive resignation of Nahum in 1920, the Ashkenazi community, thereafter termed as the *Aschkenazim Kultusgemeinde für Konstantinopel und Umgegend* (Community of Ashkenazim of Constantinople and its Environs), benefitted from a series of privileges, among them interior autonomy within the framework of the larger Sephardi community, all recorded in writing in the appendeces.[75]

The coaltion between the Zionists and the post-war Ashkenazim was not a fortuitous one. On the one hand, after the Russian Revolution of October 1917 and the pogroms which followed it, Istanbul served as a refuge for thousands of Russian Jews. The latter had already been in contact with Jewish nationalist movements, as well as with revolutionary trends, in their country of origin. Thus, they were open to the Zionist movement. In addition, during the same period, the Zionists developed a new line aimed at both the Russian Jews and the Sephardi populations which had been left battered by the war. This had socialist overtones and invoked the theme of class struggle. The time had come to take advantage of the overwhelming pro-Zionist movement which had spread throughout the capital and in the provinces. Communal institutions still remained in the hands of the "Nahumists" who feigned siding with Zionism in order to tap into the "undecided" vote.

From that time on, the local Zionists represented a real force, as opposed to the official Zionism (represented by the World Zionist Organization) which was all but absent in the capital, inasmuch as it no longer had need of the Ottomans in order to settle the question of Palestine. The coalition with the Ashkenazim continued to function as it had in the past; divisions would only have weakened the movement. Furthermore, considering the respected role which the Ashkenazim occupied in the local Zionist leadership, to alienate the Ashkenazi community would have been a serious blunder. This alliance was indispensable to the local Zionists (mostly Sephardim) who were anxious to take over communal institutions. Moreover, there was some discussion of Jews of foreign origin participating in community elections.[76] Refugees from Eastern Europe, all Ashkenazim, fell into this category. In fact, the Ashkenazim represented a potential electorate. The Zionists, by allying themselves with them, foresaw the possibility, with the aid of their increasingly numerous Sephardi supporters, of occupying the majority of seats in the future *meclis-i umumi* and of defeating Haim Nahum and those associated with him.

The coalition between the Zionists and the Ashkenazim as an "ethnic" group fell into the larger framework of a regrouping which could schematically be termed "German"—even if the customary denouncement of a Germano-Zionist plot was not always well-founded. The origin of the majority of the Zionist leaders, the geographical implantation of the Zionist Organization, as well as the language spoken within the Organization and by the most active elements in the movement pointed in this direction.[77] It goes without saying that conditions in the Empire fostered this association, in reaction to the "French" camp which was little attracted to Zionism. The *Hilfsverein* was a German Jewish organization.[78] The *B'nai B'rith* lodges were composed of Jews who had German roots. The first *Makabi* Society of Istanbul had been founded by young German Jews, and it was I. Auerbach, German Zionist leader and representative of the *Hilfsverein* in the capital, who had directed it after the "Young Turk" revolution.[79] The Zionist leaders sent to Istanbul by the Zionist Organization were, if not all Germans, at least all Ashkenazim (except for the last, Israel Caleb).[80] The Zionists widely publicized, in cities like Istanbul and Salonica, the work of the *Hilfsverein*, the rival of the Alliance.[81] The support accorded this Organization by the Ashkenazi population, especially in Istanbul, due in part to the fact that the language of instruction in the schools was German, must also be taken into account. Thus, although it had first been only the result of circumstance and conditions, the alliance within the German camp eventually became a natural one.

TOWARD A POLITICIZED JEWISH PUBLIC LIFE

The conjunctural coalitions established by the Zionists in Istanbul and in the provinces did not all demonstrate consistency. One need only consider the relations between the Zionists and the *Hilfsverein*. In Istanbul and in Salonica, they were maintained alive within the framework of the struggle against the Alliance. In Palestine they were tending toward decline. This disintegration in the Zionist/*Hilfsverein* relations in Palestine began in 1913 with the *Tekhnion* affair (the Institute of Technology in Haifa) which arose over the choice of language to be used in teaching in this establishment.

In Istanbul the maintenance of this relationship was a strategic necessity. There was no avenue for the Zionists to change camps, for the other camp was that of the "Alliancist" Chief Rabbinate. The clear dichotomy between the two blocks did not prevent defections within the group in power. At least, this is how the vicissitudes experienced by the communal institutions in 1911-1912 may be explained. Furthermore, after the war, there was an increase in the lack of firmness shown by the group in power which had been observed before the war.

One of the major differences between the Zionists and the "Alliancists" is explained by the type of support from which each group benefitted from the exterior and from within.

For its part, the Alliance refused to provide the aid necessary to combat Zionism locally and to keep from losing ground.[82] The most it offered was its moral support to Haim Nahum, who was trying desperately to organize his troops against the Zionists. The Alliance, distant, paralyzed by the Zionist specter, and the secretary of the Alliance, rigid, ill-versed in the affairs of the Ottoman community and incompetent in political policy, offered little help to the *hahambaşı*. At best Jacques Bigart, left behind by new developments, took recourse in the outdated method of the *bahşiş* and proposed to Haim Nahum that he bribe the members of the Ottoman parliament to provoke an anti-Zionist debate in the Chamber or, further, that he use his influence in high places to put an end to the Zionist landslide.[83]

The Zionists, on the other hand, put the complete arsenal of a modern political party into place in order to achieve their objectives. The essential elements of this arsenal included representatives of the Zionist Organization, seasoned political leaders, a press system,[84] diversified partnerships,[85] local militantism, and the reinforcement from the Organization itself. To this was added a political program. The status and structures of the Alliance itself prevented the elaboration or diffusion of such a political strategy and program.

It is true that each of the two groups had its own ideology. Zionism, after the Hamburg Congress of 1909, had provisionally shifted its policy on Palestine and had subscribed to the principle of the integrity of the Ottoman Empire. It had also developed a progressive local political program. The Alliance had only its ideology to diffuse, and this ideology did not prove itself to be adaptable to local context, in spite of the success of its schools. In the beginning the Zionist ideology had been no better adapted to the local communal context, but it was later modified and shaped to meet the current and local conditions.

It would be erroneous to think that the Zionist party was united at a local level. In spite of divisions, however, it manifested a unity of action, at least *vis-à-vis* the exterior.

In order to reach their objectives, the Zionists developed a populist discourse, a discourse heard but rarely before that time, and especially not from the local leaders who had always kept their distance from the people, and had been used to adopting a paternalistic attitude, and maintaining a benefactor/debtor relation with those out of power. The Zionists succeeded in presenting in clear terms the problem of the lack of democracy in Jewish institutional life and especially in putting the oligarchic regime into question. Progressively they exploited the antagonism among the classes in their discourse. They revelled in opposing the oligarchy, the rich, and their assistants, and encouraged the lower middle class and the poor to struggle. They planned to chase these "oppressors" from positions of power in the community, replacing them with Zionists who were close to the people and to the people's concerns. This discourse, related through channels which were open to the people, was equal to the task of seducing them. The Zionists went to the people and, by according a calculated importance to them, were able to render them responsible. In so doing, they transformed the people into an additional source of power favorable to the Zionists. In addition, through their support of the Zionists, the middle classes were given some opportunity for representation in the positions of leadership held by the upper bourgeoisie.

The strategy of an opposition party formed against the Chief Rabbinate and the Alliance functioned by focusing in particular on Haim Nahum. In effect, the Zionists had openly declared war on the Alliance in the capital and in the provinces. Certainly the struggle was the most violent in Istanbul.[86] The position occupied by the *hahambaşı* within the "Alliancist" group explains, in part, the intensity of the struggle waged against him. But this explanation is perhaps not sufficient.

Nahum did not possess the means to form his troops into a party. His entourage was composed of ineffective businessmen who busied themselves with communal affairs during the little free time which they had available. They were not equipped to confront the Zionists. The period of local dignitaries had given way to the politicization of the local arena, with new stakes and an unprecedented pluralism. The strategies which had been employed in the past by the "progressive" communal leaders against the clergy and the "conservatives" were no longer effective. The Zionists had allied themselves with the clergy but, according to their program, they had taken a more democratic and a more innovative position in comparison to the leadership in place. Between their discourse and reality, there was certainly a real gap.

The Alliance did not actively support its local leaders, nor did it concretely support Nahum. During this period, moral support was no longer sufficient. For their part, the local leaders were no longer prepared to make either financial or personal sacrifices to oppose Zionism. They proceeded to undertake certain moves toward reorganization, especially in 1919, when they realized that even Nahum was going to definitively abandon the struggle.[87] Both the Alliance and the local leaders counted on Nahum to redeem the situation. He was the guarantor of their interests and of communal order. Nahum was, in fact, alone. The coalitions which he had tried to form, for example with the *B'nai B'rith* at the time of its implantation in Istanbul, did not produce the expected results. The *B'nai B'rith* allied itself with Zionism. A newspaper such as *El Tiempo*, faithful as it was to the *hahambaşı* and to the Alliance, was not enough to confront Zionism, even if it performed this task with relative success. The power of the *hahambaşı* was thus propped up by the authority of the government. The "Young Turk" leaders, in turn, did not hesitate to support Nahum, guarantor of order in the Jewish community.

The "Young Turk" regime, however, was characterized by great instability. The repercussions of this instability extended to the authority of Nahum who, gradually, had lost the popular support of his early days. Had the government been strong, he too would have been stronger. Alone and therefore vulnerable, but also relatively well-fixed in a high position and considered capable of influencing government policies with regard to Zionism, Nahum became a favorite target of Zionist party attacks. Once again, the Zionists exaggerated what they saw as the supernatural powers of Haim Nahum.

The fierceness of the attack against the *hahambaşı* was deplored, even at the level of the World Zionist Organization.[88] Nor did the European Powers fail to oppose Nahum, as a function of their designs on Palestine.[89] This tendency was strengthened after the war, with the Allied occupation of the capital. The local Zionists and the British united in stirring up propaganda campaigns hostile to the *hahambaşı*.[90] The latter was supported by France, whose local action was no match to that of the opposing group. The intensity of this meddling increased due to issues at stake locally.[91]

The strategies elaborated by those Zionists who had been delegated by the World Zionist Organization were soon taken up by the local Zionists, who tended to be nationalists. Since before the war, it had been difficult to separate the contributions of the two groups. After the war, the local Zionists took the upper hand, but the interferences between the two components, nationalism and local Zionism, did not really cease. In any case, it was the local Zionists who benefitted concretely from Zionist policy, for they began to climb sporadically to strategic points in the community. By 1920, they won the communal elections by universal suffrage. A certain opportunism on the part of those locals, relatively numerous, who fulfilled their own ambitions in this way, with no adhesion to the Zionist ideology, cannot be excluded. Once in power, they acted no differently than those who they replaced.

In the final analysis, the Zionists' policies only furthered the disorganization of the already sufficiently rattled communal leadership. Their program was not executed, for in the local context it was rather utopian. More time was needed to plan a new organization of the community. In 1923, the advent of the Republic was to drive all forms of nationalism and all impulses toward reform underground.

The fact remains that the Zionist opposition party strategy politicized communal life—both within the institutions of the community and among the people—by introducing new factors and issues. This strategy demonstrated that alternative means of communal administration existed, if only in theory. Certainly we can not limit Zionism in this local context to this single aspect of its action. Nevertheless, in this case, it took precedence over the others. Zionism brought a new dimension of Westernization to Ottoman Judaism and, in so doing, brought a new dimension of modernization: a politicized Jewish public sphere.

Abbreviations

AAA	Auswärtiges Amt Akten (Bonn)
AAIU	Archives de l'Alliance Israélite Universelle (Paris)
AU	*L'Aurore* (Istanbul)
CAHJP	Central Archives for the History of the Jewish People (Jerusalem)
CZA	Central Zionist Archives (Jerusalem)
EA	*El Avenir* (Salonica)
EJ	*El Judio* (Istanbul)
ET	*El Tiempo* (Istanbul)
HH	*Ha-Herut* (Jerusalem)
HM	*Ha-Mevaser* (Istanbul)
JC	*Jewish Chronicle* (London)
LO	*Lloyd Ottoman* (Istanbul)
MAE	Archives du Ministère des Affaires Etrangères (Paris)
MO	*Le Moniteur Oriental* (Istanbul)
PRO	Public Records Office (London)
ST	*Stamboul* (Istanbul)
UI	*Univers Israélite* (Paris)

NOTES

1 See Esther Benbassa, "Le Sionisme dans l'Empire ottoman à l'aube du 20e siècle," *Vingtième Siècle*, no. 24 (October-December 1989): 69-80.

2 The Alliance was an organization founded in Paris in 1860 for the emancipation of the Jews and their "moral and material restoration." Between 1862 and 1914, this organization instituted, in the Mediterranean Basin, a considerable educational system (for boys and girls) which included trade schools and agricultural schools. On the Alliance in Turkey, see Aron Rodrigue, *French Jews, Turkish Jews: The Alliance Israélite Universelle and the Politics of Jewish Schooling in Turkey, 1860-1925* (Bloomington, Ind., 1990).

3 For the original text of the *hahamhane nizamnamesi*, see *La konstitusion para la nasion israelita de Turkia* [Constitution of the Israelite Nation of Turkey] (s.l.: Estamparia del Jurnal Israelit, 5625 [1865]).

4 In principle, only those who paid the *kizba* (community tax, *petcha* in Salonica) participated in community elections. See the review of communal elections in ET, 21 October 1910.

5 Date of the first elections conforming to the stipulations of the *nizamname* promulgated during the same period. Careful study of the functioning of "democracy" in community life, at least in Istanbul, reveals that the principle of elections was not always observed.

6 On Haim Nahum and the beginning of Zionism in Turkey, see Esther Benbassa, "Haim Nahum Effendi, dernier Grand Rabbin de l'Empire ottoman (1908-1920). Son rôle politique et diplomatique," 2 vols. (Thèse de doctorat d'état ès lettres, Université de Paris III, 1987); idem, *Un Grand Rabbin sépharde en politique* (Paris, 1990).

7 The current state of our research does not allow us to evaluate accurately the role played by the "Young Turks" in the nomination of Haim Nahum. It is known, however, that during his stay in Paris toward the end of the nineteenth century, Nahum frequented certain of the "Young Turks" in exile who subsequently came to power. These personal relations could only have been favorable to his nomination. Jacob M. Landau is stronger in his affirmation of the role played by the new leaders in this nomination. See Jacob M. Landau, "The 'Young Turks' and Zionism: Some Comments," in *Studies in Honor of Raphael Patai*, ed. Victor D. Sanua (Rutherford, N.J., 1983), 203.

8 AAIU, Turkey XXX. E., Haim Nahum to Paris, 8 October 1908; ET, 14, 16 and 28 October 1908.

9 See the succession of strikes by Jewish butchers. One of the most considerable community revenues was the meat tax, the *gabela*. By refusing

to pay this tax to the Chief Rabbinate, the butchers were trying to paralyze the administration: ET, 9 and 11 September 1908; ET, 5 and 11 November 1908; AAIU, Turkey II. C. 8, Haim Nahum to Paris, 15 September 1908; JC, 2 October 1908; *El Burlon*, 21 January 1909.

10   The supporters of Haim Nahum had succeeded in gathering a crowd of 15,000 in a popular section of Hasköy (a quarter on the Golden Horn) in October 1908: ET, 21 October 1908; AAIU, Turkey XXX. E., Haim Nahum to Paris, 24 December 1908. We must determine how much truth there is in these figures, exaggerated at will by pro-Nahumist propaganda. During this period, large press organizations such as *El Tiempo* supported the "Alliancists," while others like *El Telegrafo*, linked to the former community regime, fearing for their future (especially their financial future) preferred to keep quiet. It was some time later that the Zionists created their own opposition press.

11   On the rabbinical question in Jerusalem, see among others: Rachel Sharaby, "The Grand Rabbinate of Jerusalem, Conflicts and Personalities, 1906-1914" (in Hebrew), *Cathedra* 37 (1985): 95-121. The Porte had vetoed the nomination of Jacob Meir (under the influence of the Chief Rabbinate in Istanbul), on the pretext of his ties with foreign societies, one of which was the Alliance.

12   The *Hilfsverein der Deutschen Juden* was a German Jewish organization founded in 1901 for the improvement of the social and political conditions of the Jews of Eastern Europe and the East, which developed a small educational system in the Ottoman Empire.

13   AAIU, Turkey XXX. E., Haim Nahum to Paris, 7 December 1908.

14   AAIU, Secretarial Register 218, 26 August 1908; 30 September 1908; 23 October 1908.

15   On this subject see Esther Benbassa, "L'Alliance Israélite Universelle et l'élection de Haim Nahum au Grand Rabbinat de l'Empire ottoman (1908-1909)," in World Union of Jewish Studies, *Proceedings of the Ninth World Congress of Jewish Studies*, Division B (Jerusalem, 1986), 3:84-85.

16   AAIU, Israël I. G. 2, A. Antébi to I. Fernandez, 2 September 1908.

17   AAIU, Israël I. G. 2, A. Antébi to Paris, 18 October 1908.

18   ET, 19 November 1908; AAIU, Turkey XXX. E., Haim Nahum to Paris, 7 December 1908.

19   AAIU, Turkey XXX. E., Haim Nahum to Paris, 7 December 1908; AAIU, Secretarial Register 219, Jacques Bigart to Haim Nahum, 11 December 1908.

20   AAIU, Turkey XXX. E., Haim Nahum to Paris, 15 January 1909.

21   It was composed of seven members.

22   It was composed of sixty lay members and twenty clerical members. There was also the *meclis-i cismani* (lay council), composed of nine

members, which represented the executive authority and which had been quickly taken over by the "Alliancists."

23 AAIU, Turkey XXX. E., Haim Nahum to Paris, 24 December 1908; ET, 1 January 1909; UI (18), 16 January 1909: 568-69; JC, 22 January 1909.

24 AAIU, Turkey XXX. E., Haim Nahum to Paris, 24 December 1908. Underlined in the text: "bli nesiat kapayim la-ish o la-hevra ha-gedola ve-ha-kabirat koah."

25 AAIU, Turkey XXX. E., Haim Nahum to Paris, 15 January 1909.

26 EA, 12 January 1909.

27 *Ha-Yehudi*, 8 October 1908; *Der Israelit*, 17 September 1908; cited by Lucien Lazare, "L'Alliance Israélite Universelle en Palestine à l'epoque de la révolution des 'Jeunes Turcs' et sa mission en Orient du 29 octobre 1908 au 19 janvier 1909," *Revue des Etudes Juives* 138 (1979): 329-30.

28 Isaiah [Yesayahu] Friedman, "The *Hilfsverein*, the German Foreign Affairs Minister and the Polemic with the Zionists, 1908-1911" (in Hebrew), *Cathedra* 20 (Tamuz 5741 [July 1981]): 103.

29 Friedman, "The *Hilfsverein*," 101.

30 The *B'nai B'rith* is a Jewish organization structured on the model of the Masonic Order in lodges and chapters, founded in the United States by German Jews in 1843.

31 AAIU, France IV. D. 16, Minister of Foreign Affairs, Office of Political and Commercial Affairs to N. Leven, 14 December 1910, report of M. Choublier, marked "confidential".

32 HM, Passover 5671 (13-20 April 1911).

33 *Konstitusion*, Art. 16, p. 8.

34 *Konstitusion*, Art. 20, p. 11.

35 ET, 17 April 1911.

36 HM, 5 Sivan 5671 (1 June 1911).

37 ET, 17 April 1911 (information drawn from *Die Welt*, official medium of the World Zionist Organization, and from the *Jewish Chronicle*).

38 HM, 5 Sivan 5671 (1 June 1911).

39 ET, 17 April 1911.

40 On this subject, see Benbassa, "Haim Nahum," 1:361-81.

41 EJ, 20 March 1912.

42 ET, 3 April 1911.

43 HM, 7 April 1911.

44 HM, 7 April 1911.

45 ET, 22 May 1911.

46 On this subject, see in particular *Konstitusion* Art. 9, p. 6. On the vicissitudes of this affair, see ET, 22 and 26 May 1911.

47 EJ, 20 March 1912.

48 On this subject, see Mordechai Eliav, *Intercommunal Relations within the Yishuv at the End of the Ottman Period* (Jerusalem, n.d. [brochure]); idem, *Palestine and the Yishuv in the 19th Century, 1777-1917* (in Hebrew) (Jerusalem, 1978), 156-61.

49 For the text of the Agreement see ET, 30 June 1890. It was reproduced in AU, 17 March 1912.

50 AU, 24 June 1910; AU, 6 January 1911; ET, 26 December 1910.

51 ET, 26 December 1910. The question of the *Francos* (Jews of foreign nationality, in particular of Italian origin) is different from that of the Karaites whose multi-secular schism went beyond the limits of the Ottoman communities. The administrative separation of the *Francos* in Istanbul from the Sephardi community goes back to 1862. See *Archives de la communauté italienne* (Istanbul), letter (in Italian) from the Legation of the Kingdom of Italy to the foreign Israelite community of Spanish and Portuguese rites in Constantinople, signed by M. Cerruti, 2 May 1862.

52 ET, 6 January 1911; 1 June 1911; 5 June 1911; 9 August 1911.

53 ET, 6 January 1911.

54 ET, 26 December 1910. The article in question was apparently published on 25 December 1910. This issue could not be located in the existing collections of this paper.

55 ET, 26 December 1910.

56 For the text of this Agreement, see MO, 1 February 1912; AU, 17 March 1912 (in Judeo-Spanish and in French).

57 ET, 31 January 1912; ST, 1 February 1912; MO, 1 February 1912; EA, 2 February 1912; LO, 3 February 1912; JC, 9 February 1912; EJ, 20 March 1912.

58 On this question of principle, see MO, 1 February 1912. Having been informed of his resignation, the Secretary of the Alliance in Paris responded: "There must be motives, motives which the public is not in a position to appreciate behind this serious decision of Mr. Nahum, motives which must not be inspired solely by the resolutions of the Consistory [*meclis-i cismani*]." See AAIU, School Register 232, Jacques Bigart to A. Benveniste, 7 February 1912.

59 ST, 2 February 1912; EA, 9 February 1912; MO, 6 February 1912; MO, 19 February 1912; ET, 19 February 1912; JC, 23 February 1912.

60 ET, 5 February 1912, minutes of the meeting of the *meclis-i cismani* of 5 February 1912, in which it was decided that the *hahambaşı* was to be considered as having resigned by one vote less than an unanimous margin; ET, 12 February 1912; EA, 16 February 1912; AAIU, Turkey XLI. E., A. Benveniste to the President, 27 February 1912.

61 ET, 15 March 1912.

62 AAIU, Turkey XLI. E., A. Benveniste to the President, 28 March 1912.

63 EA, 25 March 1912; ET, 8 May 1912.

64 AAIU, Turkey XLI. E., A. Benveniste to the President, 4 June 1912.

65 ET, 7 June 1912, taken from the newspaper, *Le Jeune Turc.*

66 CZA Z3/44, from I. Auerbach to the *EAC (Engeres Aktions-Comitee)*, 25 March 1912; AAIU, Turkey XLI. E., A. Benveniste to J. Bigart, 23 July 1912.

67 *Ha-Poel Ha-Zair*, 12 July 1912.

68 AAIU, Turkey XLI. E., A. Benveniste to J. Bigart, 23 July 1912.

69 CAHJP, HMB/819 (microfilm), letter signed by L. Schoenmann and H. Reisner, 21 July 1912; ET, 31 July 1912. It would be appropriate to add that the Agreement was not put into practice, contrary to what A. Galanté seems to suggest in his *Histoire des Juifs d'Istanbul* (Istanbul, 1942), 2:209.

70 For the projected regulations, see: PRO, 371/4171/47289, R. Webb to the Foreign Office, received 26 March 1919.

7 ET, 25 February 1919; AAIU, Turkey XLI. E., A. Benveniste to J. Bigart, 28 February 1919. See also in the same bundle: *Appel/Oyfruf* (in French and Yiddish).

72 AAIU, Turkey XLI. E., *Appel.*

73 For the regular correspondence between D. Markus and the Zionist Organization, see CZA, Z3/44. An entire series of letters attesting to the relations between this militant and Zionism is to be found in this bundle.

74 AAIU, Turkey XLI. E., *Appel.*

75 See AAIU, Turkey XLI. E., received 17 February 1911.

76 In the most recent prior elections of 1910-1911, only Jews who were Ottoman subjects had participated: Gran Rabinato de Turkia, *Las eleksiones para el meclis umumi* [The Elections for the *Meclis-i Umumi*] (Istanbul, 5671 [1910]), 4. The *Commission de contrôle électoral*, established to define the methods of the vote in 1920, stipulated that any Jew twenty years or older, without restriction of nationality, was eligible to vote. For the complete text of the plan dated 26 January 1920, see ET, 30 January 1920.

77 CZA, Z2/11, V. Jacobson to David Wolffsohn, 14 December 1911.

78 Jacques Bigart, secretary of the Alliance, fearing, among other things, that the lodges in the East were serving German interests, had tried in 1911 to persuade Haim Nahum to forbid their establishment in Istanbul and in other Eastern centers. See AAIU, Secretarial Register 225, J. Bigart to Haim Nahum, 14 February 1911.

79 David Ramon, *The Makabi in the Balkans* (in Hebrew) (Tel-Aviv, 1945), 95-96.

80 He was a Bulgarian of Sephardi origins. His nomination was not ratified by the British until 1919. See PRO, 371/4176/56952, H. Weizmann to the Foreign Office, 10 April 1919.

81 HM, 15 Heshvan 5671 (17 November 1911). The Zionists also exploited the tension between the Alliance and its German committee which developed over the rapprochement between the latter and the *Hilfsverein*.

82 AAIU, Turkey XXX. E., Haim Nahum to Jacques Bigart, 19 December 1910; AAIU, Turkey I. G. 1. E., J. Loria to Paris, 16 November 1910; J. Bigart to J. Loria, 22 November 1910; E. Nathan to Paris, 21 March 1912; J. Bigart to E. Nathan, [28] March 1912, rough-draft of letter no. 1917.

83 AAIU, Turkey XXX. E., Jacques Bigart to Haim Nahum, 26 November 1909; 22 November 1910.

84 For the press, see Esther Benbassa, "Presse d'Istanbul et de Salonique au service du Sionisme (1908-1914). Les motifs d'une allégance," *Revue historique* 276 (October-December 1986): 337-65.

85 See Esther Benbassa, "Associational Strategies in Ottoman Jewish Society in the Nineteenth and Twentieth Centuries," in Avigdor Levi ed., *The Jews in the Ottoman Empire* (forthcoming).

86 See the correspondence between David Wolffsohn and Narcisse Leven: CZA, Z2/32, D. Wolffsohn to N. Leven, 21 February 1911; J. Bigart and N. Leven to D. Wolffsohn, 3 March 1911; D. Wolffsohn to N. Leven, 10 April 1911. The originals of these letters are in German; these are English translations. The original of the last letter is dated 9 April 1911.

87 AAIU, Turkey I. G. 1, A. Benveniste to Paris, 13 April 1919.

88 CZA, Z2/9, D. Wolffsohn to V. Jacobson, 20 June 1910; V. Jacobson to D. Wolffsohn, 23 June 1910; CZA, Z4/888, M. Dizengoff to M. Ussischkine, T. Zlatopolski, and I. A. Naiditch, 26 August 1919.

89 See for example the ambiguous relations of Germany in this regard: AAA, Türkei 195, K.178268-178271, R. von Kuhlmann to B. Hollweg, 15 February 1917; AAIU, Turkey XXX. E., Haim Nahum to Jacques Bigart, 27 April 1919.

90 PRO, 371/4167/59630, A. Calthorpe to the Foreign Office, 15 April 1919; 371/4168/68621, A. Calthorpe to the Foreign Office, 16 April 1919; 371/4168/68621, rough-draft of response to the letter of 16 April 1919, carries the signatures of O. A. Scott, G. Kidston, M. D. Peterson.

91 MAE, Levant 1918-1929, Sub-series Turkey, vol. 112, A. Defrance to S. Pichon, 31 July 1919; 16 August 1919.

Riva Kastoryano
*Centre d'Etudes et de Recherches Internationales,
C. N. R. S., Paris*

From *Millet* to Community: The Jews of Istanbul

Historical and sociological research on the Jews of France situates their emancipation within the context of the universalist ideology created by the Revolution. The passage from the Old Regime to the Republic is treated as the beginning of a process of assimilation considered as an indicator of the access to modernity.

A study of the integration of the Jews of Turkey in the modern period could lead to parallel interpretations. The passage from the Ottoman Empire to the secular Turkish Republic, from a pluralistic Empire to a nation state modeled on the French Jacobin state, led to a change in the juridical status of religious minorities. In the Ottoman Empire each religious community—the Greek, the Armenian, and the Jewish—defined as a *Millet*,[1] enjoyed relative autonomy in the organization of their internal affairs in return for the payment of a poll tax (*cizye*). The process of modernization, namely of westernization, undertaken by the Empire throughout the nineteenth century included in its aims political centralization, secularization, and nationalism.[2] This led to a serious erosion of the juridical status of the *Millets* in 1856, accompanied by the granting of equal rights for all Ottoman subjects, Muslims and non-Muslims. The same principles were adopted by the Turkish Republic established in 1923. Muslims and non-Muslims were, from then on in principle legally equal as Turkish citizens.

Modernization signifies social mobility as well as geographic mobility, and is accompanied by a redefinition of values, of relations with the environment, and social integration. The *Millets* of the Ottoman Empire, together with the central power and the activist urban elite, opted for the West as the central model of reference in the access to modernity. International commerce and the development of networks of commercial relations contributed to the opening of Greek and Armenian communities towards Europe. As for the Jews, even though they were urbanized but on the whole, underdeveloped economically, their entry to modernity was effectuated through the action of intellectuals influenced by the Jewish Enlightenment of Europe as well as the general process of modernization underway within the Empire. The initiative of these intellectuals and of like-minded notables helped the establishment of the Alliance Israélite Universelle and its schools, whose mission was to inculcate Western values to a "backward" community and to ensure its "regeneration" by education.[3] This enterprise was designed to achieve for the Jews of the East the same emancipation which had been won by the Jews of France. The path of education thus led to an opening towards Western and universalist values, and to social mobility for the members of the community. Education, then, would facilitate the community's integration into the larger society.[4] Within the same perspective, the politics of cultural and linguistic homogeneity adopted by the nationalist Republic was accompanied by a strict control of communal institutions and education. However, the efforts of the centralized and (from 1928 onwards) secular nation state did not lead to the assimilation of religious minorities in modern Turkey. Even though Republican logic implied the integration of non-Muslims into the dominant society, the logic of the group limited such integration to a particular social mobility and to the growth of social and economic relations with the larger society.

The study of the Jews of Istanbul over three generations and of their integration into contemporary Turkey demonstrates that even though the *Millet* system no longer exists juridically, the social organization of the Jews of Istanbul shows a distinct continuity as a *Millet* in their sociological self-definition as well as in their perception of the social and political environment. The passage from the pluralistic Empire to a Turkish nation state, far from leading to the assimilation of its minorities, has paradoxically led instead to the relative closure of the Jewish community. Internal as well as external factors explain this well-demarcated communal identity.

In this first phase of my research, I have studied the criteria of the cohesion of the group. How have the different moral and religious values, those borrowed from Western societies and from Turkish society which delineate the boundaries of its identity, been re-elaborated to assure both an internal adjustment of the group and its integration into Turkish society?

THE SOCIAL ORGANIZATION OF THE JEWS OF ISTANBUL

The great majority of the Jews of Turkey are Sephardi, the descendants of the Jews who found refuge in the Ottoman Empire after their expulsion from Spain in 1492. The language that they speak is called "the Jewish language" by the elder members of the community; today it is increasingly referred to by scholars as Judeo-Spanish. According to many sources, the massive wave of immigration from the Iberian Peninsula eventually swamped the local Byzantine Jews and led to their assimilation into the Sephardi majority; the linguistic homogeneity of the community certainly suggests this. A small minority of the Jews of Turkey are of Ashkenazi origin. Most of the latter arrived in Turkey during the nineteenth century, or during the middle of the twentieth century when they fled the Nazi occupation of Europe; they number approximately 1,000 to 1,500 today. Yiddish, their communal language, has practically disappeared; however, they do not speak Judeo-Spanish. There is also a small community of Arab Jews, who originate from southeastern Turkey along the Syrian border (primarily from Aleppo) and speak mostly Arabic, and also a small community of Georgian Jews. To these should be added a Karaite community whose members are not clearly defined as Jews, both within their own self perception or by outsiders, and also do not form a part of the institutional structures of the community.

The total number of the Jews of Turkey is estimated to be between eighteen and twenty thousand. According to unofficial sources, there are only three families left in Edirne, about 2,000 individuals in Izmir, and several families in Ankara. By contrast, in the middle of the nineteenth century there were 150,000 Jews in the Ottoman Empire. At the beginning of the Republic, there were 81,454, of which 47,035 lived in Istanbul[5] which had a total population of 373,124.[6] The evaluation of the population numbers for today are very approximate as the official census no longer has a classification under the rubric of "religious community" or "linguistic community" as was the custom until the national census of 1960[7] (see Article 12 of the Constitution). Since then, the internal censuses of the community remain the only reliable sources. Only the Chief Rabbinate, based in Istanbul, registers individuals as they participate in religious practices, such as births, marriages, and deaths. Also, different communal institutions keep track of contributions to charitable organizations and of the communal tax (*kizba*).

These population statistics are closely linked to historical events and developments that affected neighboring countries and certain provinces. For example, the Turco-Russian War of 1878 led to the immigration of many Bulgarian Jews to Turkey, and many Jews of Edirne migrated to Istanbul during and after the Balkan Wars of 1912-1913. Many disasters and catastrophes, such as fires in the traditional quarters of provincial cities, also pushed many families to immigrate to Istanbul.

The deterioration of relations between the central power and the religious minorities, most notably the Greeks and the Armenians, and the beginning of compulsory military service for all Ottoman citizens irrespective of religious origin also affected the Jews, with many choosing to leave Turkey. Economic factors played an important role too, and from the beginning of the twentieth century onwards, mass emigration movements developed, with the most important countries of destination being France (for those who spoke French), and Latin America, whose language— Spanish—was familiar to the Jews of Turkey. There are no statistics on these departures, but interviews with families residing in Istanbul reveal that one or several members of the family or their descendants are to be found in these countries. But the most important wave of emigration, which considerably diminished the number of Jews in Turkey, followed the foundation of the State of Israel and the migrations which took place in the years 1948-1960.[8] Many Jews left the small provincial cities, with isolated families leaving for Istanbul, the metropolis and the commercial capital of modern Turkey which still retains elements of a certain cosmopolitanism, and where they felt more secure thanks to the presence of their co-religionists.

FROM LOCAL COMMUNITIES TO THE COMMUNITY

In Istanbul, the division of the city into distinct communes made each district (*mahalle*) an autonomous local community, represented by a religious leader.[9] The quarters best known for their large Jewish concentration are Balat and Hasköy, on the two sides of the Golden Horn, and Ortaköy, Kuzguncuk, and Kadıköy, on both sides of the Bosporus, and Galata-Péra located in the European part of the city.[10] These areas also attracted other families from different provinces after their migration from the interior of Turkey. There were also many cases of internal migrations from within the same cities which gave rise to new local communities in Istanbul. For example, after the antisemitic disturbances in Thrace in 1934, Jewish families from Edirne established

From Millet to Community: The Jews of Istanbul / 257

themselves in Sirkeci (the quarter near the railway station in the European coast of the city) and founded a community with its own synagogue.

The Jewish migratory movements were not limited to migrations towards the West or towards Istanbul. Massive geographic mobility within the same city also led to the dissolution of local communities. In our own day, traditional quarters such as Balat, Hasköy, and Kuzguncuk have nothing left but a synagogue to attest to a Jewish presence and to serve as a referent for the "community of origin." However, in Balat one can still find some shops whose Jewish owners live in the "modern" sections of the city, as well as several poor families who are assisted by communal charitable institutions.[11] The historic importance of the Jewish presence in these areas of Istanbul is demonstrated by the existence of a home for the elderly in Hasköy and a Jewish hospital in Balat.

Several motivating factors appear in the recollections of interviewees which account for the departures from the traditional quarters. Fire was one of the many objective reasons for moving away:

> I was born in Dağhamam, [and] my father, my grandfather, my mother, the entire family was born there. When I was nine months old, there was a great fire [in 1920]. One speaks in Jewish history of the great fire of Dağhamam.[12] We are very proud to be from Kadıköy. After the fire, my father was obliged to go and live for a short period in Kuzguncuk (the nearest Jewish quarter) . . . [because of] financial problems; we left after six months for Ortaköy (on the other side Bosporus). My father bought a house there. The families which had left Dağhamam before us had already formed a community there. Hence I lived in Ortaköy until I was seven or eight years old.

Not only could a fire cause the total disappearance of the Jews from a quarter, a fire in an individual house, that is to say a personal catastrophe, could also be a reason to change residence:

> I was three years old when our house in Kuzguncuk burned down and my father bought another house in Haydarpaşa. It was like that during this period, the Jews advanced[13] from quarter to quarter; from Kuzguncuk to Kadıköy and then to Moda, etc.

These departures, sometimes justified by the parents' choice of school for their children, nevertheless expressed a rupture with the traditional way of life:

> My father saw the future, [and] he wanted to send me to the French school. It was difficult to go each day from Ortaköy to Saint-Benoît. Thus, we left for Kuledibi [the area of the base of the tower of Galata] in 1928, when I was eight years old.[14]

Beyond such circumstantial rationalizations, moving reflected an aspiration for upward social mobility and for modernity. The choice of Galata as sign of social ascent was linked to the very special place occupied by this quarter in the history of Istanbul. Galata was the most European part of the city and was largely inhabited by foreigners and a westernized elite. It was a symbol of elegance and refinement: "I never went to the great street of Péra without my gaiters and my cane" said one interviewee. Galata was the center of international commerce, and all the foreign banks were located there. The path of modernization, opening towards other worlds hence led the Jews to Galata.

Professional activities were often both the cause and the effect of this opening. Of course, the departure from the traditional quarters could be a result of social ascent, but it also provided economic and social opportunities which benefitted many people:

> I was born in Balat, and we had always lived in Balat. But all the great firms were in Istanbul, for example the Fratelli Hayim firm or other printing houses were in Péra. Therefore we moved to Şişhane [Galata] in 1927-1928; I was sixteen years old, [and] I was working in this printing company.

As for travelling tradesmen who had a specifically Jewish clientele, such as fishmongers,[15] the departure from Balat or Hasköy had become imperative:

> I began to sell fish in the 1940s; at first started at Kuledibi. During this period we moved from Hasköy to Galata. The Jews used to live in the small houses around the Italian synagogue. There were no Şişli, Gayrettepe, [or] Etiler at that time.[16] The wealthiest lived around the sixth district [north of Galata]. We moved to Şişhane because all the Jews were moving there, just as if they were going to Israel. Once in Şişhane, we were all finished with Balat and Hasköy.

Thus, families followed the general pattern of migration if they did not want to feel excluded, and especially if they did not want to be classified in a less desirable status group within the internal hierarchy of the community.[17]

The marriage registers since 1901, which are in the archives of the Chief Rabbinate of Istanbul, show the quarters, the profession of the father of both husband and wife, the date of the marriage, and the amount of the dowry that the family of the bride paid to the groom. Apart from the dowry, which usually was registered as a fictitious sum to prevent communal taxation on the declared amount, all other data which show the changes in professions and in areas of residence confirm the above testimonies. Departures from Şişhane and Kuledibi (south of Galata) by those who had been there for a while began in 1930-1940 towards the north, to Péra and Taksim.

The aspiration to "modernity," which in this case manifested itself by economic and urban integration, explains this movement towards the "top."[18] In other words, just as traditional communal life was reconstituted in the quarter, the proof of upward social mobility manifested itself through the departure from the "ghettoized" areas. As for those who came to these areas a little later, they remained until the 1960s.

The geographic mobility of the Jews in the city continues, and the migratory "flux" orients itself towards the new residential quarters of the city. As a result, as new areas are built, the migratory movement follows. The classic trajectory since the 1920s has been the passage from Galata to Taksim, from Taksim to Şişli and Nişantaş, quarters of the westernized Muslim elite where Salonican Jews as well as *dönmes* have lived since the beginning of the century.[19] The latter areas became fashionable for a great majority of Jews in the 1950s. For the last dozen years, the movement has been towards the Bosporus. The choice of quarters is of course made within the limits of financial possibilities, but even more as a function of networks established during previous moves and social aspirations.

Sociological studies on ethnic groups show that the realization of upward social mobility usually leads to the dissolution of the group. *A priori*, the historical evolution of different local Jewish communities could confirm this hypothesis. But at the moment, it appears that for the community of Istanbul the criteria for upward social mobility have in fact maintained the boundaries of the group. Indeed, new regroupings which are the result of "fashions" in the community, underscore the pursuit of upward social mobility already underway without, however, implying a rupture with the communal mode of existence.

INSTITUTIONS

The community is represented formally by the Chief Rabbinate, located in Istanbul. The Chief Rabbi, the official representative of the group, is elected by the members of the community and is authorized by the Council of Ministers. The decision of the council is published in the official journal. A religious and a lay council are constituted under the direction of the Chief Rabbi. The religious council is composed of four rabbis who guide religious life, i.e., circumcisions, *bar mitzvas*, marriages and burials, divorces etc., in short all activities linked to religious practice and run according to religious law.

As for the lay council, it has a hierarchial structure and is composed of 35-40 people—including the president and vice president. Many factors play a role in the selection of the members of this council. The most important qualifications concern the level of instruction and profession; the vast majority of its members are in the liberal professions, most notably the law. This implies a certain degree of integration into Turkish society, and the existence of networks of relations outside of the community. But, in a closed community where the social status of the individual is not based solely upon professional status, the trajectories of families are as important as individual professional success. Consequently, the network of intra-communal relations have as much weight as the links with outside society. Another criterion of selection is the political socialization of the individual, i.e., his participation in communal activities, institutions and associations, youth clubs, etc. Participation in such activities demonstrates a prospective member's familiarity with the working of the communal bodies as well as his level of interest in the community.

The lay council defends the interests of the community. Its task is to ensure the functioning of its institutions (welfare organizations, hospitals, and schools), and to oversee the preservation of its heritage. The lay council informs and advises the Chief Rabbi who is recognized as the only intermediary with the state. In the language of the Jews of Turkey, the term "community" has taken on an institutional meaning (as the translation of *cemaat*) and refers solely to the Chief Rabbinate, the central body which represents the interests of the collectivity.

As for other institutions—synagogues, schools, hospitals, youth and sports clubs, and welfare agencies—all are run in accordance with the *Vakıf* law passed in 1935.[20] These are non-profit; their revenues are derived from contributions from members of the community. The *Vakıfs* are autonomous in their administration, in their internal direction and in their decisions concerning the functioning of the institutions. They contribute 5 percent of their revenue to the *Vakıf* organization which depends directly upon the state. Since 1960, these *Vakıfs* are limited as far as their expenses are concerned when these are connected with the renovation of religious sites (especially the synagogues) or with new acquisitions (the purchase of land, the construction of a communal school, etc.).

There are actually twenty-six synagogues in Istanbul attached to nine *Vakıfs*, and two synagogues attached to the Chief Rabbinate. The synagogues, together with the associations known as "welfare organizations," the youth clubs and the schools, are located in the traditional Jewish quarters mentioned above (see the appendix).

The location of institutions followed the movement of individuals. The strength of the Jewish concentration in the quarter of Galata led to the creation of the synagogue *Neve Şalom*, the most important synagogue of today, located at the base of the Galata tower. The synagogue of Şişli is also the product of the departures from the strongly Jewish quarters mentioned above and the settlement of Jewish families in this district between 1950 and 1960. This same period which saw the beginning of great economic growth in Turkey also witnessed the great social advancement of the Jews and of the Turkish population as a whole, thanks to the process of industrialization and rapid urbanization. At the same time that internal migration was taking place in the city, some families sought to catch up with the others in the process of modernization by vacationing in places such as along the coasts of the Marmara Sea, the Asiatic coast of the Bosporus and/or the Princes Islands. Around this movement grew small synagogues in Caddebostan (on the Asiatic coast of the Bosporus), Büyük Ada and Burgaz (islands in the Marmara Sea which have a large concentration of Jewish families in the summer). Geographic mobility also led to the closing of several synagogues because of a lack of attendants (see the appendix).

This being said, movement within the city since the 1960s has not given rise to the creation of new synagogues. Nevertheless, the lay council of the Chief Rabbinate has petitioned the public authorities for permission to restore the old ones. This is the case of the Zülfaris synagogue located in Galata and closed to the public since 1950. The building is in the process of being transformed into a museum to celebrate the 500th anniversary of the arrival of the Jews from Spain in Turkey (1992). Other such initiatives have come from individuals who are attached to their local communities of origin and are personally interested or active in restoration projects such as that of the synagogue of Kuzguncuk. Others are attempting to preserve some of the oldest sites of worship in Istanbul at Balat. Those originating from the Balat quarter have thus mobilized themselves to assure a regular *minyan* in the oldest synagogue of Istanbul, that of Balat, in order to prevent its closing.

THE DEFINITION OF THE BOUNDARIES OF THE GROUP

The diminishing of the size of the Jewish population of Turkey throughout the twentieth century has led to a continuous restructuring and redefinition of its boundaries.[21] The dissolution of local communities has given rise to the emergence of one single community. The latter is defined above all by the transparency in the social relations between its members. In other words, everyone knows everything about everyone else, their past as well as their present. Conversations revolve around the inhabited quarter, the economic status of the individual and its evolution in the context of rupture and/or continuity across the generations, his or her local education as well the chosen language of communication. The control of social success more than religious conduct leads to a quasi-homogeneity of the group which, while functioning as a distinct entity separate from the society as a whole, also undergoes the same changes.

The cohesion of the group is assured by a combination of solidarity and rivalry. The adherence to communal institutions and activities for their survival are founded on the sentiment of solidarity within the well-defined community. The welfare commissions serve to integrate those who would otherwise be left behind because of their social or personal status (orphans, the old, the unmarried or the handicapped).

Solidarity also appears within the professional sphere where the older members of the community introduce the younger members to a variety of jobs and help them to find a place in the job market by either lending them money or giving them work. The narratives on the professional trajectories of men, especially of "self-made men," underscore the importance of these networks of solidarity:

> I started to work at my uncle's place; he had a factory manufacturing cotton boxes and asked me to help him and today I continue the business.

Or:

> I knew something about the tannery business, I had worked for a long time with a shoemaker. One day a distant relative on my father's side asked me for help when he was starting his business and I became his partner.

This solidarity is, in fact, the expression of a trust which "can exist only among ourselves." This explains the preference for Jewish accountants and Jewish directors in businesses owned by Jews. Such reciprocal trust not only permits the advancement of the employer's business, but also assures the individual promotion of the employee, thanks to his "references" within the community and the new relations he establishes in the workplace. The system of group solidarity continues even in our own day when the level of education of the young, who are just beginning to enter the work force, is far superior to that of the preceding generations.

The solidarity is consolidated by an internal rivalry within the group. This rivalry is founded on the criteria of upward social mobility, on the degree of modernization, and hence on the degree of integration of the members into the society. Indeed, the community prevents the exclusion of individuals by redefining its boundaries through the inclusion of new social values due to a great opening in the residential, professional, economic, social, cultural, and linguistic spheres.

By closing in on itself, the group creates a classification and an internal hierarchy which, in their own turn, assure its cohesion. For example, the period of departure from the traditional quarters becomes a criterion for internal hierarchy as much as the "community of origin" because of its representation in the collective imagination. Economic success, the level of education, the languages spoken and even the accents, the degree of integration within Turkish society, and the network of social relations with the world outside all lead to a social classification. The networks within the group are demonstrated by social contacts and even by membership in communal institutions, which themselves are classified according to their "modernity" and the social status of their successive leaders. Of course, the order given to these criteria varies from one generation to the next according to the evolution of Turkish society. This has manifested itself in the transition from French to English as the modern and useful foreign language, by the importance given to higher education and, increasingly, to professions associated with university training rather than to a continuation of the father's profession; in short, this is indeed modernization defined as a "transition from an attributed status to an attained status."[22]

Marriages follow the same model of modernization. Even though "arranged" marriages continue to exist, endogamy according to the place of origin (in terms of the internal classification) has disappeared. Spatial proximity and the frequenting of the same places (schools, clubs in the vacation spots, etc.) favor meetings outside the group of reference. Moreover, marriage according to the latter criterion no longer makes any sense for those born in the 1960s or 1970s, the period which saw their parents' social mobility. Nevertheless, social ascent and a greater openness to the outside society, achieved in large part by the schools, inevitably increases the number of marriages between Jews and Muslims. Such marriages are difficult to calculate statistically, but this theme recurs in all the sermons of the Chief Rabbi in order to attract attention to the menace of assimilation. It is thus incumbent upon the communal institutions and their activities to become more open to the outside world in order to prevent the "exit" of the young.

The permanent search for social control, which is confirmed by the continuing spatial proximity of individuals in the city by voluntary regroupings, and by the adoption of new, redefined values within the closed circle, underscore once again the communal structure of the group. This is institutionalized by the weekly newspaper Şalom. Founded in 1947 and discontinued in 1983, the newspaper began to be republished by a group of young volunteers a few years later, and today is the only public voice of the community. The newspaper reflects the sensibilities of the latter, the themes selected, and the languages used, confirm the boundaries of the group as well as the desire to transmit its identity. Apart from information concerning world Jewry, the articles in Şalom deal with the history of the Jews of Turkey (an increasingly frequent topic because of the approaching 500th anniversary); with their social success and their integration into the societies in which they live, whether in Turkey or abroad; with community news, such as births, *bar mitzvas*, marriages, and deaths; and with religious information in Judeo-Spanish (descriptions of prayers, or explanation of holidays). Thus, the newspaper defines and redefines the increasingly flexible and expanding frontiers of the Jews of Turkey and, at the same time, reconfirms their ties to world Jewry. By including news about individuals who are far away and by reestablishing networks which have disappeared over time, the newspaper creates for the majority an identification with and a sense of belonging to a specific collectivity, as well as acting as an international referent.

Thus, the internal and external dynamics of the group underscores an economic and social integration into society while affirming the will to maintain its communal structure and to assure the perpetuation of its identity. Here lies a contradiction characteristic of all groups in minority situations: integration into the surrounding society—a sign of modernization—and at the same time the desire to affirm its own identity and define its boundaries.

RELIGION: BASIC IDENTITY?

The analysis of the communal structure and the redefinition of its boundaries based on external elements neglects the identity of the group which forms the origins of its structuring. This identity is founded on a common religion, a common past, common experiences, a long-term commonality of linguistic and culinary references, and a demarcated place in society which pushes individuals to constitute a group. But like all communities, the Jewish community of Istanbul constructs and reconstructs its identity as a function of both external elements and the dynamics of internal factors. Linguistic assimilation, the process of secularization, and a greater opening towards the surrounding society seems to have emptied the community of its religious content. In fact, religious practice is also subject to an internal classification in terms of social ascension and access to modernity.

The *Millet* system gave a juridical definition to a religious community. Today, the community has the sociological definition of an ethnic group where religion, the basis of identity, inputs in terms of tradition and culture. It presents itself as "a social fact" rather than as a system of belief. In the process of modernization, the Jewish community has undergone the same path of secularization as urban Turkey. The religiosity of the generation of the turn of the century has been replaced by a decrease in collective religious practices, and submission to religious law appears as a "delay" in the process of "development." For the "modernized," Kemalist Republican generation, religious practices assumed a "symbolic" aspect and were defined as traditional and cultural rather than as religious. The will to perpetuate Jewish identity and to transmit it to future generations was limited to the observation of the principal holidays: *Rosh Hashana* (the Jewish New Year), *Yom Kippur* (the Day of Atonement) when one reserved a place in the synagogue nearest to one's residence, and *Pessah* (Passover). Secularization has reduced these practices to an individual and familial level, that is to say, to the realm of the private. The ceremonies of *bar mitzva* and religious marriages, both individual and collective social events, are submitted to the social control of the members of the community. They become criteria of "social judgment," but also of the attachment to tradition and to the person's Jewish identity. The celebrations are, of course, demonstrations of social status but also serve as proof of non-assimilation, of the maintenance of traditions, and act as the symbol of the closed nature of the group.

The observance of the religious rituals is also under the control of communal institutions, particularly the Chief Rabbinate. For the last few years, the latter has imposed the respect of religious dietary law, such as the insistence on kosher meat and the prohibition of shell fish in the menu of receptions given on these occasions. This strictness on the part of the Chief Rabbinate appears as a defensive attitude of the community *vis-à-vis* the evolution of Turkish society where for the last dozen years, Islam has become a means of political mobilization.[23] Just as secularization emptied the community of its religious content, the rise of Islam in Turkey has led the members of the community to affirm, above all, a religious identity. Daily religious practices are increasingly reintroduced into families, especially among the young. Thus, the increase of the religious affirmation of Islam in the public sphere of modern Turkey has led to the increasing importance of religious practices within the Jewish community itself, even though they continue to be maintained strictly in the private sphere.

ATTRIBUTED IDENTITY

Not only does the environment and social movement influence communal attitudes, but the politics of the state also has a direct effect on the affirmation of identity. For example, the education laws which have introduced compulsory courses on the *Koran* for all children (Muslim as well as non-Muslim) in secular schools since the beginning of the 1980s, has led parents (especially of the younger generation) to attempt to give their children an affirmation of their own religious identity, the Jewish identity, which is more convincing in practice than a secular discourse based on tradition and an indifferent attitude towards religion. This is largely a reaction to a political stance of the state which touches the core of the group's identity and the principles of secularism which the Jews have opted for in their process of integration into society, even if this form of secularization had a particular logic in the Turkish context.

Following the abolition of the Caliphate in 1924, the religious minorities of Turkey renounced their rights of protection stipulated by the Treaty of Lausanne.[24] According to this treaty signed in 1923, the minorities had won the right to speak their communal language even in the public sphere, for example, in religious tribunals if necessary, and to maintain and perpetuate religious institutions. The renunciation of these laws by the minorities themselves after the adoption of the Swiss Civil Code as the law of the land in 1926, implied their will to "assimilate" by giving up their particularity in the public realm.[25] However, it is more than likely that this was a projection of the wish of the state for a linguistically and culturally homogeneous new Turkey.

Nevertheless, censuses indicate the presence of "religious" and "linguistic" communities until 1960. In actuality, the distinction between Muslim and non-Muslims survived. This was particularly explicit in the application of the wealth tax in 1942.[26] The public authorities proceeded with a two-fold classification: Muslims and non-Muslims. Two other categories were added: *dönmes* and foreigners.[27] This famous tax was justified by the state as a way to restructure the Turkish economy during wartime—which had affected it indirectly—and was based on an unequal treatment of its citizens. The non-Muslim citizens were taxed 10 times more than Muslim citizens with the same income. The claim was that the wealth of the non-Muslims had increased because of profiteering during the war, while the Muslim Turks were preoccupied with military service.[28] The non-payment of the total requested sum (which was often the case since it far surpassed the real fortune of individuals) resulted in deportation to work camps in Aşkale, in eastern Turkey. The tax was abolished after one year.

The constitution of 1961, as if it wanted to erase this lapse, declared once more the equality of all citizens without distinction before the law.[29] This did not, however, remove the compulsory declaration of religion on the identity card of all Turkish citizens. In popular belief and language, being Turkish is synonymous with being Muslim. The definition of the Turk is thus intimately linked to the self-conception of the Turkish nation state. The Turkish nation, like the German nation, is an ethnic entity, where the nation and the people (*Volk*) are one and the same. The non-Muslims are defined as minorities (as in *azınlık* or *ekaliyet*) in the Turkish Republic.

These terms are not without controversy. In our own day when the Kurdish population of Turkey is asserting its own ethnic identity as a minority, the public authorities are attempting to redefine the very concept of minority itself. The majority discourse of the politicians insists upon the definition of a minority that was used in the Lausanne Treaty, that is, a *religious* minority.[30]

Riots against religious minorities are as explicit in their intentions as the practices of the state. The riots against the Jews in Thrace in 1934, led to massive emigration towards Istanbul. The mass riot against the Greek minority in September 1955 led to fear and the turning inwards of the Jews as well as of the Greeks, often neighbors within certain quarters of the city. In addition, public opinion which always uses the same categories, such as Muslim *vs.* non-Muslim, made no distinction between Greeks, Armenians or Jews. As a result, all minorities find themselves in the same situation, even if the distinctions between communities persist, sometimes rife with friction, a fact which further enforces the identity of each group.

FORMATION OF AN INTEREST GROUP

The minority identity attributed to its historical and political definition is also reinforced by the environment. This leads to an ambiguity, not necessarily in the self-definition of the group, but in its public behavior. The motto of the Jews of Turkey has been for a long time, "in order to live happily let us live hidden," expressing their low profile in the public domain. This attitude explains the absence of mobilization among the Jews of Turkey. A small fraction of the community, activist and militant thanks to its links with the West, was involved with the Zionist movement at the turn of the century.[31] But, their activities remained rather limited in the eyes of public authorities. This attitude also explains the silence of the Jews during the Second World War, or even during the implementation of discriminatory measures.

Today the maintenance of a low profile is considered by the younger generation to be a habit of the old. An improved economic, social, cultural, and linguistic integration into Turkish society as equal citizens has led to a change in thinking. The discourse of the members of the community underscores the fact that:

> The image of the Jew has changed, he is no longer the fearful Jew (*korkak yahudi*). The Jew is more self-confident today, on an international level because of the post-war period and creation of the State of Israel, and on a national level because of his economic weight in modern Turkey.

If the image of the Jew has effectively changed in Turkish society, this is partially due to a greater opening towards the outside by individuals who have contributed to the economic development of Turkey, and who act in the interest of the nation, thereby transcending their group and community interests.

> By leaving the closed Jewish community, and by mingling with a "societal community" we have obtained positive results. We have created situations which have led to sympathy and to respect for us. We have for example created schools and villages, we have given important donations. Our initiatives to demonstrate coexistence with Turkish society have increased the acceptance of our community.

These are individual acts. The citizen acts before everything else as a member of a national community to which he or she belongs and with which he or she identifies. The expected results are, however, collective: to make oneself accepted, to move away from popular stereotypes, because "the acceptance of self comes through the acceptance of the community of belonging." This proof of loyalty to the nation state and the collective conscience of the group has led the Turkish governments to project onto this population an emphasis of its links to international Jewry, and hence, of its assumed ability to influence international public opinion. In this perspective, the Turkish government solicits the presence of influential Turkish Jews within the different commissions representing Turkey in Brussels and

From Millet to Community: The Jews of Istanbul / 269

Washington. The explicit aim is to counteract actions against Turkey undertaken by the Greeks and Armenians, members of the former *Millet* system of the Ottoman Empire, migrants constituting pressure groups and influential lobbies in their countries of settlement such as the United States or Europe. The implicit aim is to influence the foreign policy of Europe and of the United States regarding Turkey.[32]

> The Turkish government asked me for a representation abroad as a Jew. I go there as a representative of Turkey and not as a Jew, as a Turkish business man. Today, Turkey is like other countries, the mentalities have changed. Just as one is before everything else an American and then a Jew, [and] one is first French and then a Jew, we are Turks before anything else. But of course, I have a special relationship with a French Jew or an English Jew whom I meet during conferences. A better dialogue is created between us. The government asks us to have a role in European and American lobbies, of course, we do our best to obtain positive results. "It is our duty to help the country." [In English during the interview.] You are a Jew but you work for the good of your country.

The ultimate action to influence international public opinion is the preparation for the celebration of the 500th anniversary of the arrival of the Jews from the Iberian Peninsula in Turkey. Special commissions have been created for this in different European countries and in the United States. The extent of the events prepared in this respect demonstrate the public gratitude of the Jewish community to Turkey: the Turkish historical heritage has permitted the *Millet* to perpetuate and maintain its identity; its positive political action during World War II distinguished Turkey from European countries and its neighbors regarding their attitudes *vis-à-vis* the Jews. Moreover, Turkey is the first country whose population is 99 percent Muslim to maintain diplomatic relations with Israel. At any rate, an international political action on the part of Turkish Jews for their country can only help in the maintenance of good relations between Israel and Turkey, which would further strengthen the minority's sense of security.

The public expression of gratitude on a global scale inserts the community into the political sphere. It is incumbant upon the Chief Rabbinate, the only official institution recognized by the state, to assure such a representative function. The increased role played by individual Jews in the international arena in favor of Turkey has recently led (in 1989 to be precise) to a change in the structure of the lay council. The latter is now divided into a commission of councillors (the honorary council) named by the Chief Rabbi and an executive commission. The commission of councillors has subcommittees to supervise the diverse areas of action. The commission of foreign relations, as the name indicates, occupies itself with international affairs, and the juridical commission deals with internal affairs. As for the executive commission, its members are also a part of the honorary council, but their activities generally concern daily affairs: the functioning of institutions, help for people in material difficulty (poverty, illness, solitude), etc. Thus, representation in the international domain has led to a restructuring of internal relations within the community.

The new division of labor within the secular council of the Chief Rabbinate is thus the result of political roles attributed to individuals *qua* individuals. The collective responsibility for such a function has included them in the principal institutions, reinforcing their status and increasing their fame within the group as well as with the outside. Also, the new division of labor implies an increased number of people in the lay council which also is a direct result of the growing public activism among Jews of Turkey. The action of influential notables—"the ambassadors of the Jews of Turkey"—is buttressed by young people active in different communal agencies. Their passage into the central institution is considered as a promotion. But objectively, the new activism is a response to the needs of the administration of the community. In fact, the number of institutions has remained unchanged since 1960, while the Jewish population has diminished. The will to maintain these communal bodies, to diversify their activities in order to attract the young and to assure their identification with them, the duty to respond to the needs of the disadvantaged members of the community in economic difficulty, all encourage a greater number of people to invest their time and energy on a voluntary basis in communal affairs.

The new division of labor renders the communal activities more efficacious. It permits each community to make explicit the collective interest when this interest relates to identity: to assure its perpetuation through the generations. The political function of individuals responsible to both the Turkish state and the Jewish community brings a favorable response on the part of the government, now more attentive to the interests of the latter. Concretely, this is manifested on many levels. First of all, attention is given to immediate needs such as, for example, the request by a delegation of the lay council for the exemption of non-Muslim children from the compulsory courses on the *Koran* in the secular elementary schools. This request, made in collaboration with other religious minorities, was taken into consideration by the public authorities, and the government's favorable response was made officially public in August 1990.

The construction of a new Jewish school is very much a part of the general aim to defend the community's interest and to preserve its identity. With its appeal to the Jewish bourgeoisie of Istanbul, the school is intended to replace the old communal one which had lost favor and did not fit the needs of either the parents or the children:

> We aim to create a communal school more adapted to the image of the Jew in Turkish society. We want all families to identify with the school and send their children to it. The ultimate goal is to help young people meet each other and to facilitate their marriage, because nothing replaces the friendships created at the school.

Discussions about the school have led the secular council to request the public authorities to elaborate on or update the 1965 law of the *Vakıf*, i.e., to remove the restrictions related to the restoration of religious institutions and the acquisition of new property, and to prevent the destruction of old cemeteries, etc.; in short, to preserve the institutional heritage, to assure its survival within the community, and to maintain the security of the latter within Turkish society.

* *

*

The Jews of Istanbul constitute a quasi-homogenous community in terms of social class, interest, and attitudes. The diminished number of its members has led to a transparency in its social relations. Its cohesion is assured by a readjustment of its traditional values, but also of its economic and social mores. Behind the shifting boundaries of the group, the "individual becomes the collectivity"; individual actions have a collective consequence in terms of their own representation within both the interior of the group as well as within the larger society. The individual member is judged in the group by his or her economic and social role in society, and he or she is judged by society as a result of his or her belonging to a community.

The values which maintain the community as a separate entity are, however, reactualized thanks to the relations with the surrounding society. In effect, the community's internal classification criteria are intimately related to the evolution of Turkey. The nationalism which was at the origin of the creation of the Turkish Republic was accompanied by political and economic modernization. The Turkish nation state, inspired by the Jacobin model of the centralized state, defined its values in the image of Western societies: a greater openness, the social mobility of individuals, and the political participation of its citizens. The 1950s witnessed the birth of a middle class and of an industrial bourgeoisie which slowly replaced the old military bureaucracy in the public sphere.[33] Implicated in this process of modernization and social integration, the Jews followed the evolution of the larger society, as is shown by their greater social mobility in the 1950s and 1960s and their increasing openness *vis-à-vis* the larger society.

The integration of the Jews in Turkish society is the result of the "nationalization" of its minorities.[34] Nevertheless, this integration has certain limits as to the level of the identification of the group with the society on the one hand, and its acceptance in the public sphere as a religious "minority" on the other. Already at the end of the last century, the internalization of Western values dispensed by the schools of the Alliance, became the norm for the community, and led its members away from an identification with even the new, secular Turkey. Today, the Turkish Jews identify on the whole with a social class which has followed the same process of modernization. This class is the national bourgeoisie which uses the West as the model for its cultural, economic, and political aspirations. The industrial elite and its counter-parts among the members of the Jewish community have the same political weight in so far as both represent the interests of the country in the international arena; both negotiate the fate of Turkey in its relations with the Western powers.

On the national level, the political integration of the Jews is limited to certain areas. The lack of liberalism in the emancipation process of the Jews has distanced them from traditional religious institutions without integrating them into Turkish national institutions.[35] Today, their economic position and their networks place them in prestigious positions in national economic organizations, such as the Foundation for Economic Development, or give them important status within the ranks of the employers' unions. Furthermore, an intellectual opening towards the outside and the diplomas of higher education lead some slowly to occupy positions as professors at universities. But the political role attributed to the individual, a member both of the national and the Jewish community, is exclusively situated in the international arena, which stresses for him or her the sense of belonging to international Jewry, in direct continuity with the time when the Ottoman Jewish *Millet* was seen as forming a part of the larger Jewish people.

Thus, the individual integration encouraged by the State is taken over by the State, and transformed into an issue of collective gratitude. "It is a double game [in English in the interview]." Indeed, the formation of an interest group at the request of the State has given a cautious group, whose entry into political life was timid, the opportunity to express its presence as a Jewish community in Turkey and to collectively defend its interests, thereby reinforcing its existence as a distinct community.

Appendix I.

THE SYNAGOGUES
(Synagogues connected with the *Vakıfs* and the Chief Rabbinate)

1. *Vakıf* of Neve Şalom:
    the synagogue of Neve Şalom
       of Şişli
       of Zülfaris (closed)
       of Heybeli Ada (Bet Yaakov)
       of Burgaz
       of Unkapanı (closed)
       of the *Frankos* (Galata)

2. Ashkenazi Synagogue of Yüksek Kaldırım

3. Synagogues of Balat (where 16-18 families reside):
    Ahrida
    Yambol
    Istipol (closed)
    Kasturia (closed)
    Tçhana (closed)
    Selaniko (closed)
    Oratory of the hospital of Balat

4. Synagogues of Hasköy:
    Mallem
    Karaite synagogue Bnei Mikra
    Oratory of the home for the elderly

5. Synagogue of Ortaköy:
    Etz Ha-Hayim

6. Synagogues of Kuzguncuk (where 15 families reside):
    Bet Yaakov (also called Etz Ha-Hayim and Kal de Abaşo)
    Verane or Kal de Ariva

7. Synagogues of the Asian Side:
   Hemdat Israel
   Cadde Bostan

8. Synagogue of Büyük Ada:
   Hesed le-Avraam

9. Synagogues of Istanbul:
   Sirkeci
   Mahmut Paşa Çorapçı Han

Synagogues connected to the Chief Rabbinate:
   Synagogue of Bakırköy
   Synagogue of Yeniköy

THE SCHOOLS

The Jewish secondary school of Beyoğlu (*Bene Berit*)
Primary school, first *Karma*
Primary school, second *Karma* (closed for 15 years)

CHARITABLE SOCIETIES

Association for the Relief of Poor Students (*Mishne Tora*)
Commission of the *Vakıf* of Neve Şalom: Association for the Relief of the Sick (formerly called the Tuberculosis), with a branch called *Matan Be-Seter*.
Association for Relief and Care (*Sadaka Umarpe*)
Association for Relief for the Elderly (*Asile de Viellards - Moshav Zekinim*)
Association for the Relief of Orphans and the Poor
Association for the Renovation and the Continuation of the Synagogues
Commission of the *Vakıf* of the Ashkenazi Synagogue of Yüksek Kaldırım Süt Damlası (Goutte de lait)
Vakıf of the Hospital of Balat Or Ha-Hayim
Association for Assistance at the Jewish Secondary School of Beyoğlu
Association for Assistance at the Jewish Primary School (First *Karma*)

LOAN BANKS

Küçük İstikrazat Sandığı (Bankalar vakfı) (Bank for small loans)

CULTURAL ASSOCIATIONS AND SPORTS CLUBS

Yıldırım Youth Sports Club and Cultural Association
The Friendship Association (Dostluk)
The Friendship Association (Arkadaşlık)
Association of Art and Culture
The Fraternal Association (closed)
Cultural Association of Göztepe (residential quarter on the Asiatic coast)

NOTES

1 This term has been put into question by B. Braude and B. Lewis regarding the social and political reality it represents and its reflection on the organization and administration of the minorities in the Ottoman Empire. See Benjamin Braude and Bernard Lewis, eds., *Christians and Jews in the Ottoman Empire*, 2 vols. (New York, 1982), especially Benjamin Braude, "Foundation Myths of the *Millet* System," in *Christians and Jews in the Ottoman Empire*, 1:69-88. According to the author, the use of this term dates back to the nineteenth century and was projected into the past to define the status of minorities in the Ottoman Empire.

2 Bernard Lewis, *The Emergence of Modern Turkey* (London, 1961).

3 Aron Rodrigue, *De l'instruction à émancipation. Les enseignants de l'Alliance israélite universelle et les Juifs d'Orient 1860-1939* (Paris, 1989). See Esther Benbassa, "Processus de modernisation en terre sépharde," in *La société juive à travers les âges*, S. Trigano, ed. (forthcoming).

4 Rodrigue, *De l'instruction*; idem, *French Jews, Turkish Jews: The Alliance Israélite Universelle and the Politics of Jewish Schooling in Turkey, 1860-1925* (Bloomington, Ind., 1990).

5 Official census of 1927, taken from the entry for "Turkey," in *Encyclopaedia Judaica* (New York, 1971).

6 According to the police census of 1922. See Z. Toprak, "La population d'Istanbul dans les premières années de la République," in *Travaux et recherches en Turquie* (Leuven, 1982).

7 According to the general census of the city of Istanbul, there were 47,173 Jews in a total population of 741,148 in 1935. See *Office*

Central de Statistiques, Recensement général de la population en octobre 1935, Province d'Istanbul (October 1936). In 1945, the number of Jews in Istanbul increased to 49,552 in a total population of 972,773. See *Recensement général de la population en octobre 1945*, Province d'Istanbul (Ankara, 1949). According to the national census of 1960, the last one which mentioned the number of religious and linguistic minorities, there were 35,485 Jews in Istanbul's total population of 1,882,092. See *Census of Population, 23 October 1960, Population of Turkey.*

8 Cf. Walter F. Weiker, *The Unseen Israelis. The Jews from Turkey in Israel* (London, 1987), 22, Table 2.

9 Bernard Lewis, *Jews of Islam* (Princeton, N.J., 1984), 126.

10 For more details see A. Galanté, *Histoire des Juifs d'Istanbul*, 2 vols. (Istanbul, 1941-42), 1:chapter 2.

11 M. C. Bornes-Varol, "Balat, vielle communauté juive d'Istanbul," *Revue des Etudes Juives* 147 (July-December 1988): 495-504.

12 Indeed, police statistics state that there were only three Jews in Kadıköy. See Toprak, "La population d'Istanbul."

By constrast, the statistics of the number of students in the schools of the Alliance Israélite Universelle show that the school in Dağhamam was empty in the 1890s (the last registration date of 1881 shows a total of 246 students); Rodrigue, *French Jews, Turkish Jews*, 91. However, it could be that the families that remained there did not send their children to the Alliance school because it began to be considered as a communal school, and their social position required that they send their children to foreign schools instead.

13 *İlerlemek*, a word with a double meaning in Turkish, signifying at the same time a geographic move to the north of the city and social ascent.

14 After the Alliance schools closed in 1925, Jewish families had to choose between schools administered by Christian clergy or the *Bene Berit lycée* where instruction was conducted partially in Hebrew and also in French and in Turkish.

15 According to the archives of the Alliance Israélite Universelle, peddlers, water-bearers, and shoe-shiners were common professions among the Jews at the beginning of the century; cf. Paul Dumont, "Une source pour l'étude des communautés juives de Turquie. Les archives de l'Alliance Israélite Universelle," *Journal Asiatique* 267 (1979): 101-35.

16 New residential quarters which attracted the majority of the Jews after the 1960s.

17 See R. K. Merton, "Reference Group Theory and Social Mobility," in *Class, Status and Power*, eds. R. Bendix and S. M. Lipset (New York, 1953), 510-16.

18 Turkish play on words which expresses both an upward mobility and the northern part of the city.

19 The disciples of Shabbetai Zevi. The *Dönme*, also commonly referred to as the Salonicans, constituted an intellectual and urbane elite quite active in the "Young Turk" movement and in the birth of the Turkish Republic. See Gershom Scholem, *Sabbatai Sebi* (Princeton, N.J., 1973)

20 Fuad Köprülü, "L'institution de *Vakouf*. Sa nature juridique et son évolution historique," *Vakıflar Dergisi* 2 (1942): 3-49.

21 F. Barth, ed., *Ethnic Groups and Boundaries. The Social Organization of Culture Difference* (Boston, 1969). In the introduction, the author conceptualizes the flexibility of the frontiers of a group's identity (pp. 1-39).

22 See the introduction in R. E. Ward and D. A. Rustow, eds., *Political Modernization in Japan and Turkey* (Princeton, N.J., 1968).

23 N. Göle, "Ingénieurs musulmans et étudiantes voilées en Turquie. Entre le totalitarisme et l'individualisme," in *Intellectuels et militants de l'Islam contemporain*, G. Kepel and Y. Richard, eds. (Paris, 1990), 167-93.

24 See the Treaty of Lausanne, art. 38-44 in *Lozan Barış Konferansı; Tutanaklar, Belgeler*, vol. 1, section 2, trad. S. L. Meray (Ankara, 1970). 61-63.

25 See also Aron Rodrigue, "From *Millet* to Minority: Turkish Jewry in the Nineteenth and Twentieth Centuries" (Paper delivered at the Fondation Nationale des Sciences Politiques, March 1989).

26 F. Ökte, *Varlık Vergisi Faciası* (Istanbul, 1951). See also E. C. Clark, "The Turkish *Varlık Vergisi* Reconsidered," *Middle Eastern Studies* 8 (May 1972): 205-17. Çağlar Keyder, *State and Class in Turkey: A Study in Capitalist Development* (London, 1987), 113.

27 Ökte, *Varlık Vergisi Faciası*, 48.

28 Ibid.

29 Art. 12 of the Constitution of 9 July 1961. According to this clause every individual, regardless of language, race, sex, beliefs, or religion, is equal before the law.

30 B. Ecevit in a statement in the newspaper *Cumhuriyet* in August 1988 asserts that the Kurds do not constitute a minority in Turkey since they participate in the public sphere and can be civil servants (by implication, as opposed to non-Muslims who are indeed not in public life).

31 Esther Benbassa, *Un Grand Rabbin sépharde en politique* (Paris, 1990).

32 For this see E. M. Uslaner, "One Nation, Many Voices: Interest Groups in Foreign Policy Making," in *Interest Groups in Politics*, A. J. Cigler and B. A. Loomis, eds. (Washington, D.C., 1986), 236-58.

33 Keyder, *State and Class in Turkey*.

34 Rodrigue, "From *Millet* to Minority."

35 Rodrigue, *ibid*.